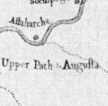

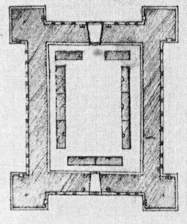

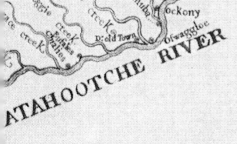

AKEN IN THE NATION

57 WILLIAM BONAR

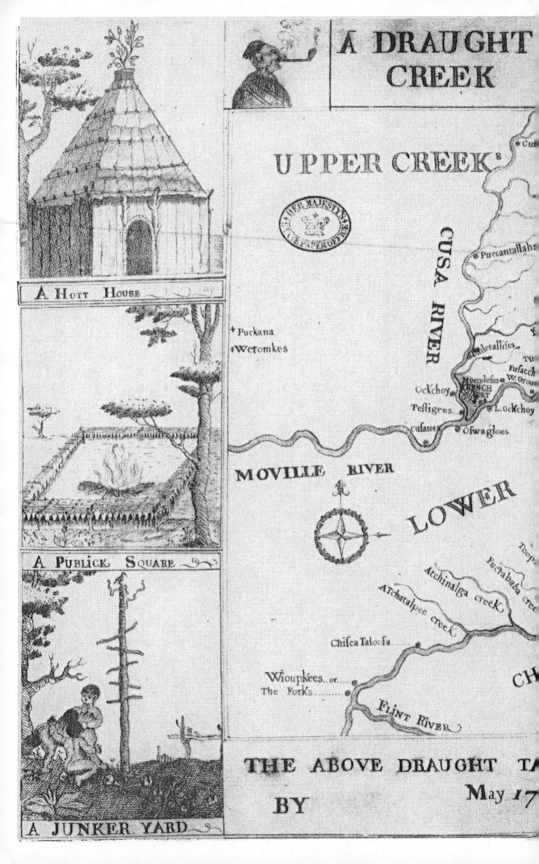

A DRAUGHT ... CREEK

UPPER CREEK

HER MAJESTY'S ... BETTER OFFICE

CUSA RIVER

• Cus...
• Puccantallahe...

• Puckana
• Wetomkes

...tallifes
Tus...
...fucch...
W. Or...

FRENCH
FORT
Ockchoy
• L. Ockchoy
Tefligees
...fatee
• Ofwagloes

MOVILLE RIVER

LOWER

Toop...
Fuchabala cre...
Atchinalga creek

Atchatalpee creek

Chifca Taloofa ......

CH...

Wioupkees.. or.....
The Forks.........

FLINT RIVER

A HOTT HOUSE

A PUBLICK SQUARE

A JUNKER YARD

THE ABOVE DRAUGHT TA...

BY ... May 17...

Kathryn E. Holland Braund

Deerskins & Duffels

The Creek Indian Trade
with Anglo-America,
1685–1815

University of Nebraska Press
Lincoln & London

In Memory
J. Leitch Wright, Jr.

The paper in this book meets the minimum require-
ments of American National Standard for Information
Sciences – Permanence of Paper for Printed Library
Materials, ANSI Z39.48-1984.

First Bison Books Edition: 1996

Frontispiece: A Draught of the Creek Nation, made in
1757 by William Bonar. Reproduced with the permission of the Controller of Her Majesty's Stationery Office, courtesy of the British Public Record Office,
CO700/Carolina 21.

Library of Congress Cataloging in Publication Data
Braund, Kathryn E. Holland, 1955-
Deerskins and duffels: the Creek Indian trade with
Anglo-America, 1685-1815 / by Kathryn
E. Holland Braund.
p. cm. – (Indians of the Southeast)
Includes bibliographical references and index.
ISBN 0-8032-1226-7 (alk. paper: cl)
ISBN 0-8032-6126-8 (pa.)
1. Creek Indians – Commerce. 2. Creek Indians –
Economic conditions. 3. Creek Indians – History –
18th century. 4. South Carolina – Commerce – Great
Britain. 5. Great Britain – Commerce – South
Carolina. I. Title. II. Series.
E99.C9B73 1993 381'.45675 – dc20
92-26355 CIP

Contents

Illustrations and Maps

Series Editors' Introduction

In 1784, Alexander McGillivray, the Great Beloved Man of the Creeks, wrote that "Indians will attach themselves to and Serve them best who Supply their Necessities." McGillivray's opinion was shared by everyone, Indian and white, who was involved in the complex business of politics and diplomacy in the eighteenth-century Southeast. Native leaders exchanged gifts to ritually cement agreements, and Europeans were expected to do the same. But on a grander scale, Indians and Europeans traded their products in marketplaces and trading posts planted throughout the region. The ritual significance of gift exchange remained, but the desire for profits and goods soon began to dominate the trade.

Europeans and Indians both prospered as they adapted to the styles and interests, as well as the valuables, of the other. Captives for the slave markets and deerskins for English tanners purchased tools, utensils, weapons, and clothing. Creek men and women valued these goods and incorporated them into their daily lives. As these products of English industry became ever more commonplace, they ceased to be luxuries and instead became "Necessities." Necessity, along with the pernicious qualities of rum, changed the trade in ways both subtle and profound. Never a simple economic affair, trade became political and jeopardized the autonomy of the Creek Nation. The challenge for McGillivray and other Creek leaders was to figure out a way to guarantee the flow of goods at the lowest political cost.

Scholars have long known what McGillivray knew, that trade defined peace, bound peoples together, and provided the foundation for political relationships. Through economic dependence, trade also threatened the political autonomy of Native American nations. It is surprising, therefore, that we have no systematic, comprehensive analysis of the trading system. With this study, Kathryn Braund has begun to fill that gap. The Creeks were major participants in the eighteenth-century trade with the English of South Carolina and Georgia. Drawing on a rich body of documents, Braund has described the traders as well as the trade and has explained the politics as well as the economics of the business. With a perspective both English and Creek, she has woven a story that, we believe, makes a significant contribution to our understanding of Creek history. We welcome this volume to the Indians of the Southeast Series.

THEDA PERDUE   MICHAEL D. GREEN

Preface

Of all the southeastern Indian tribes, none were more eager for trade or more adept at securing it than the Creek, or Muscogulge, Indians. For the Creeks, the maintenance of a steady trading relationship with a European power was essential to their survival as a people. Guns were necessary for defense, woolen and cotton textiles offered improvements over traditional attire, and metal tools were prerequisite for more efficient labor. Geography placed the Creeks in the midst of the three-cornered struggle for empire among Spain, France, and Great Britain. At one time or another, all three of the great powers courted the Creeks. As it turned out, the Creeks courted only those who offered a plentiful trade.

It was the Anglo-American colonists, first in South Carolina and later in Georgia, who cultivated Creek friendship and captivated Creek consumers. The Philadelphia naturalist William Bartram, who toured the Creek country during the 1770s, recorded that the establishment of a peaceful trade alliance with the British colonies was regarded by the Creeks "as one of the most glorious events in the annals of their nation."[1] By the late eighteenth century, Creek town life, government, and economy had been irreparably changed by the Indians' participation in the trade. It is these changes in Creek life—social, political, and economic—that this study will detail. At the same time, certain features of Creek society proved remarkably resistant to change, and these too will be examined.

Trade is a mutual affair. The deerskin trade, so very important to Creek history during the eighteenth century, should also be considered in light of its importance to the history of several British colonies, notably South Carolina, Georgia, and East and West Florida. Frontier entrepreneurs combined the trade with speculation in land and cattle raising. The economic importance of these interrelated activities underwrote the success of all four colonies. At the individual level, a substantial part of the backcountry population depended on the deerskin trade for a livelihood. Charleston, the early South's greatest commercial city, owed much of its success to its position as wholesaler for the Indian trade.

The trade and the regulation of the traders were viewed by many British administrators as a vital tool for the management of Indian relations. For frontier farmers, the trade and peaceful relations with their Indian neighbors were a life-and-death concern. With the retrocession of the Floridas to Spain in 1783, that nation too found the deerskin trade an indispensable aid to its foreign policy, as did the new American nation. Thus, this study will also attempt to detail the white end of the trade: as an adjunct of foreign policy and as an economic force in southeastern history.

My interest in the Creek Indians started at Auburn University, Alabama, which sits in the heart of the land once claimed by the Muscogulges. There, Frank L. Owsley, Jr.'s excellent lectures on the early South provided my first glimpse at the exciting world of the southeastern frontier. As I began my studies in earnest, I was amazed at what appeared to be three different kinds of literature on the eighteenth-century Southeast. There were the histories of colonial South Carolina, Georgia, West Florida, and East Florida. Such works, even the best ones, seemed populated by cardboard Indians, if indeed the Indians were mentioned at all. There were also Indian histories, such as David H. Corkran's outstanding works on the Creeks and Cherokees, which detailed white-Indian relations during the colonial era. Corkran's groundbreaking studies told the story from the Indian point of view, with heavy emphasis on foreign relations. Then there were the works by John R. Swanton and others that concentrated on ethnology but hardly mentioned important historical details and trends. Even taken together, these studies, at least for me, presented a disjointed picture. The Creek side of the story remained obscure.

After reading Verner W. Crane's classic work *The Southern Frontier, 1670–1732* (1929), I became fascinated with the deerskin trade and began my writing career detailing the attempts by colonial and imperial governments to police the commerce. It was Robin F. A. Fabel who pointed me to the eighteenth-century British manuscripts that detail so much eighteenth-century Creek history. His expert counsel during the early years of my graduate studies propelled me further into the dark recesses of dusty library corridors stocked with microfilm readers. It was he who introduced me to the exciting world of folio numbers.

Later, I stumbled across an article on ethnohistory and began to rework my early study into a history of the Creeks and their trading economy. I went to Tallahassee with my ideas and found a friend in J. Leitch Wright, Jr. Though he did not see the final result of my efforts to transform my essays on Anglo-Indian relations into "real" Creek history, his enthusiasm for the idea has continued to be an example and inspiration. Richard A. Bartlett stood by me, and my manuscript, in those last lonely and frantic months before the Florida State University promoted me from student to scholar. I will always treasure my memories of his steady nerve, cheerful nature, and attention to detail. Later, Mike Green's patient readings of my manuscript and his supportive, solid advice helped me organize my thoughts into what I hope is a decent study of the eighteenth-century Creek deerskin trade. Theda Perdue, Greg Waselkov, and Robin Fabel also gave me many good suggestions, and I appreciate their valuable assistance and support through the years. I would also like to thank the others who read my manuscript and thoughtfully recorded their suggestions as to how it might be improved, particularly J. Anthony Paredes, who read the earliest drafts of this work, and Peter H. Wood, who read the last. My debt to the vast body of historical literature is great, and the foundations laid by others have made my work easier. Any errors or omissions in this manuscript, either factual or interpretative, are completely my own.

A number of librarians and manuscript curators have been especially helpful during the preparation of this work. A host of librarians at Auburn's Draughn Library made every aspect of my work easier. I particularly wish to thank the folks in "MADD" and the Alabama Collection for their cheerfulness and competent handling of my every request. Appreciation for much helpful manuscript material is also extended to the William L. Clements Library, Ann Arbor, Michigan; the South Caroliniana Library, Columbia, South Carolina; the American Philosophical Society Library, Philadelphia, Pennsylvania; the British Public Record Office; and the Georgia Historical Society, Savannah. Alasdair McKerrell secured valuable photocopies from the PRO for me, and I will always be grateful for his kind assistance. I would also like to thank Fordham University Library, Frick Art Reference Library, the British Public Record Office, and the Royal Library of Denmark, Copenhagen, for their permission to use the illustrations for this volume. I also thank Christopher Peters for helping me prepare the preliminary maps.

I would especially like to thank Kyle, my husband, friend, proofreader, and sounding board. He has stood by me, encouraged my efforts, helped me in every way he could, and tolerated my history habit with grace and good humor. His support, both financial and spiritual, has been instrumental in the completion of this study. I hope it will, in some small way, vindicate his confidence in my ability.

PART ONE

Partners in Trade

CHAPTER I

The Eighteenth-Century Muscogulges

Them hey were the Muskogees or Muscogulges: the word *Muskogee,* or *Muscogee,* signifying land that is wet or prone to flooding; *ulge* designating a nation or people.[1] But the Carolinians called them *Creeks,* and the name stuck. Their territory extended from the Atlantic seacoast westward to the Tombigbee River of present-day Alabama and stretched southward from the Savannah River, which divided Creek and Cherokee lands, into Florida. Between the Savannah and the Tombigbee lay three major river systems that dominated Creek geography: the Oconee-Ocmulgee-Altamaha; the Chattahoochee-Flint-Apalachicola; and the Coosa-Tallapoosa-Alabama. The town, *talwa* in Muskogee, was the basis of Creek political and social life. Muscogulge towns, ensconced in the center of the Indians' extensive territory on the piedmont plateau, were flanked by the fall line and were situated along the large rivers and creeks flowing from the heart of their country to the sea. Viewing a map, one is stunned by the logic, real or accidental, that foisted the name *Creeks* on these people.

There are many theories as to why the Muscogulges came to be known as Creeks. The veteran Indian trader and historian James Adair wrote, "It is called the Creek country, on account of the great number of Creeks, or small bays, rivulets and swamps, it abounds with."[2] Alexander McGillivray, the best-educated eighteenth-century Creek, made the same claim some years later, as did Benjamin Hawkins.[3] William Bartram reported that the English traders called the Indians "Cricks" because the traders "observed that in their conversation, when they had occasion to mention the name of the Indian nation, if any of the Indians were present, they discovered evident signs of disgust, as supposing the traders were plotting some mischief against their nation, etc., so that they gave them this nickname, *Cricks.*"[4]

3

The generally accepted view on the matter, promulgated by the historian Verner Crane, relates that the Chattahoochee River Muskogees had kinspeople living along Ochese Creek, a branch of the Ocmulgee River. Ochese Creek was a main line of defense for the Carolina colony and the first stopover between the Savannah and Chattahoochee rivers. For the South Carolinians, the Indians living along Ochese Creek, and their western relatives, were of supreme importance. After their first contact with the "Ochese Creek Indians," South Carolinians soon began referring to them as the "Creek Indians" or "Creeks," a convenient appellation that was later applied to all Muscogulge tribes.[5]

It is no wonder that the English, for whatever reason, devised a general designation for the Muscogulges, for the Indians were actually a confederation or alliance of friendly towns or tribes. The majority of the towns were Muskogean-speaking, and their oral history points to an early migration from the West. Muskogean-speaking immigrants began drifting into the Southeast during the late Mississippian period, perhaps around A.D. 1200, incorporating native populations into their ranks.[6] By some method these diverse tribes formally agreed to live in peace. Evidence of just how and when the amalgamation occurred does not survive. It is likely that the early peoples who came to the piedmont simply found nonaggression pacts preferable to warfare and channeled aggression into athletic competition between towns. Indeed, ball play, "the little brother to war," was an important aspect of Creek political and social life.[7] Through time, the alliances of peace and friendship were strengthened and came to include shared beliefs, shared rituals, and kinship.

Muscogulges were on hand to greet Hernando de Soto, who in 1540 brought disease, depopulation, and displacement to the Creek country. As their numbers diminished, the political, social, and economic features of precontact societies were lost or abandoned. The survivors regrouped, salvaging and reorganizing those cultural components deemed essential by the remnant populations.[8] One recent study argues that during the last third of the seventeenth century, the incursions of Europeans and the beginning of the Indian slave trade resulted in "vast population movements and forced the birth of the Creek Confederacy, a political expedient of unarmed refugee groups banding together for survival."[9] But many of the ties predated the European intrusion. And Muscogulges, from the beginning, were beneficiaries, not victims, of European trade.[10] It is true that during the seventeenth century, the Muscogulges welcomed many harassed peoples into their territory. The result, as William Bartram observed, was a confederacy that consisted "of many tribes, or remnants of conquered nations, united."[11] Bartram traveled through the Creek towns and estimated that the confederacy was two-thirds Muskogee and one-third Stinkard, the common term used for non-Muskogean speakers. In the early part of the nineteenth century, Albert Gallatin wrote that seven-eighths of the confederacy spoke Muskogean. Gallatin, an expert on American Indian languages, enumerated five languages within the Creek Confederacy: Muskogee, Hitchiti, Uchee, Natchez, and Alabama.[12] The important point is that the newcomers joined an established network of allied towns that predated large-scale white-Indian interaction.

By the end of the seventeenth century, when the Spanish, French, and English invaded this territory in earnest, whatever else these Indians were—Kolomoke, Tuskegee, or Okchai—they were part of a larger whole: the Creek Confederacy. Later, still other tribes arrived who, according to James Adair, "usually conversed with each other in their own different dialects, though they understood the Muskohge language; but being naturalized, they were bound to observe the laws and customs of the main original body."[13]

Among these "reduced, broken tribes, who have helped to multiply the Muskohge to a dangerous degree" were the Alabama speakers who became an important part of the confederacy and rose to prominence during the French period, from 1714 to 1763. Most of the Alabama towns were situated along the conflux of the Tallapoosa and Coosa rivers, and many were actually peopled by remnants of other smaller tribes from the lower reaches of the Alabama River, tribes that had been decimated by earlier slaving raids and epidemic disease. Adair stated that within six miles of Fort Toulouse, there were seven distinct "nations."[14] From the north came Tuskegee speakers. Hitchiti peoples drifted northward from the Gulf Coast.[15] In the 1680s, groups of Apalachee Indians, whose villages were in northern Florida, left their homeland to escape Spanish oppression. Others fled their homeland in the wake of English-Creek invasion and conquest in the early eighteenth century and settled among the earlier migrants, who were scattered throughout the Creek towns on the Chattahoochee and Flint rivers.[16] Tuckabatchee, one of the most important of the Creek towns in the late eighteenth and early nineteenth centuries, is linked to Shawnee refugees who entered the region sometime after 1675 after successful Iroquois expansion into their homeland.[17]

The Muscogulges, though of different tribes and speaking different languages or dialects, had become a nation by the time Europeans discovered them. They shared a common culture and history, were linked by a network of related clans, and claimed and defended certain lands as their own. Headmen from the various towns frequently met to discuss matters of mutual concern. The towns on the piedmont possessed a distinctive world view and usually followed the same foreign policy. The tribes were more like each other than they were different, and they were distinct from their neighbors: the Cherokees, Choctaws, and Chickasaws.[18]

By the end of the eighteenth century, the confederacy encompassed, among others, Chickasaws, Shawnees, Natchez, Yuchis, and Yamasees. On occasion, the Creeks extended invitations to other tribal groups to join the confederacy. During the Anglo-Cherokee War, some beleaguered Lower Cherokee towns received invitations to relocate within the confines of Creek territory. The Cherokees refused.[19] But many others were eager to join the powerful Creeks and sent delegates to various Creek towns to ask if they could join the confederacy and live in peace. The Creeks were almost always receptive, as in 1772, when a Chickasaw delegation formally petitioned the council of Abicouchees for permission to settle among the Upper Creek towns. The headman at Abicouchee told them they were welcome, on the condition they acknowledge Creek jurisdiction and abide by the decisions of the united Creek councils. The Abicouchees were most likely a group of re-settled Chickasaws themselves, since Bartram noted that they spoke a dialect of Chickasaw.[20] Another well-known Chickasaw band lived at the Breed Camp. According to British Superintendent of Indian Affairs John Stuart, "These are despised by their brave Countrymen who remain at home, as Dastards, who basely deserted their Country; & abandoned the sacred Deposite of their Ancestor's bones, which they had in their Charge."[21] Regardless of the feelings of their Chickasaw countrymen, the inhabitants of the Breed Camp regarded themselves as Muscogulge. When the Europeans eventually lumped all the disparate tribes of the piedmont together, they did so with good reason.

The confederacy was divided into two geopolitical divisions, called the Upper and Lower towns by Europeans. Although this division predated the establishment of trading relations with Britain's Atlantic colonies, the designation owes its origin to the relative position of the two main trade paths that linked the Creeks with South Carolina: the Upper and Lower trade paths. The Upper Towns lay along the Tallapoosa-Coosa-Alabama river system and comprised the Alabama, the Tallapoose (or Okfuskee), and the Abeika (or Coosa) tribes, of which the latter two were true Muskogean-speakers. Among the more important Upper Towns were Muccolossus, Tuckabatchee, Little Tallassee, Okfuskee, and Okchai.

The Lower Towns were scattered along the banks of the Chattahoochee, Flint, and at times, Ocmulgee rivers. Coweta and Cussita were the most prominent Lower Towns. Apalachicola, though in decline by the eighteenth century, predated Muskogee occupation of the region and held a respected place in the confederacy.[22] Most of the Lower Towns were peopled by Cowetas, who like the Tallapooses and Abeikas were Muskogean-speakers. There were also many non-Muskogee Lower Towns which were governed by Cowetas.[23] By the mid-eighteenth century, certain groups who would later acquire a separate identity as Seminoles could be found around San Marcos de Apalache (St. Mark's), near the confluence of the Wakulla and St. Mark's rivers, and along the St. John's River (Alachua) in Florida. These nascent Seminoles were still under Lower Creek jurisdiction during the eighteenth century and were considered a part of that nation.[24]

The Upper-Lower dichotomy was extremely important, for distance and relative location gave Upper Creeks and Lower Creeks a slightly different view of the outside world. Though they acknowledged their kinship and unity, the Upper and Lower towns held separate councils, claimed separate territories, and very often pursued different foreign policies. It is this division into Upper and Lower nations that gives the term *Creek Confederacy* real meaning.

In addition to the geographic and tribal division of the towns into Upper and Lower Creeks, all Creek towns were classified as either red or white towns. Among all the southeastern Indians, the color white symbolized peace and purity; red—the color of blood—represented war. White towns were associated with peace and treaty making, whereas red towns were associated with warfare. Though much concerning these designations remains a mystery, they clearly had ceremonial, historical, and administrative significance and point to the complex nature of Muscogulge political organization. During the historic period, this division most often asserted itself in ball play, for only teams from opposite moieties, or "fires," could play each other. A town that lost repeatedly to its rival was forced to change its affiliation. Such literal changes of color, reminiscent of modern sports fans who "jump on the bandwagon," render it difficult to make broad generalizations about this aspect of Creek political organization.[25] Although such diversity and division might be confusing to others, the Creeks knew who and what they were. First, they were citizens of their town and tribe, from either an Upper or a Lower Town, and last, but of equal importance, they were part of a larger body called "Creek" by the European outsiders.

Muscogulge population declined dramatically in the sixteenth century due to Spanish incursions, and later Creeks would acknowledge that they were "the remains of a Great Nation."[26] During the next two centuries, the Creeks escaped large-scale devastation from European diseases, especially smallpox, as well as warfare. Although there were sporadic outbreaks of various diseases, these were neither widespread nor unduly damaging to the population at large.[27] Overall, Creek population in the eighteenth century stabilized and began to increase erratically, with the incorporation of new members and natural increases tending to offset the exodus of future Seminoles into Florida and losses due to endemic warfare with the Choctaws.

Information on Creek population in the late eighteenth and early nineteenth centuries is extrapolated from the number of gunmen, a name given to Creek warriors. Generally, the British, and later the Americans, multiplied the number of gunmen by a factor of three ($3:1$) to estimate the total population. James Wright, the governor of Georgia from 1762 until the Revolution, recorded in 1773 that the number of women and children could be calculated at a ratio of two or three per gunman.[28] In 1790, the American agent Major Caleb Swan reported that the "useless old men, the women and children may be reckoned as three times the number of gun-men."[29] However, there are known omissions and inaccuracies in much of the extant data, and there is good reason to believe that many observers seriously underestimated the number of noncombatants. For one thing, Europeans seldom ventured into family compounds and other areas where women, children, and the elderly spent much of their time. Residence patterns based on the extended matrilineal family amplified the befuddlement. Most important, gunmen suffered higher mortality rates than other segments of the population. In the 1760s, James Adair noted that "in every Indian country, there are a great many old women on the frontiers, perhaps ten times the number of men of the same age and place."[30] Based on anecdotal evidence regarding the size of family groupings and known inconsistencies in the record, the number of gunmen should instead be multiplied by a factor of four ($4:1$) or even five ($5:1$) to obtain a more accurate representation of the population. To further complicate the issue, by the end of the eighteenth century, the term *gunman* was extended to include "boys of fifteen, who are hunters." In earlier counts, only grown men (warriors) were included.[31]

Estimates of Creek population in the late eighteenth and early nineteenth centuries ranged from 2,000 to 6,000 gunmen. The reliability of such data varies depending on the source. South Carolina enumerated 2,619 gunmen and a total population of 8,777 Creeks in 1715. A French report of a few years later put the number of gunmen at 2,500.[32] In 1764, John Stuart, who served as British Superintendent of Indian Affairs from 1762 until 1779, reported the Creek population at 18,000, based on 3,600 gunmen, and a ratio of five noncombatants per warrior.[33] In 1773, Governor Wright, whose estimates were derived from the careful and experienced observations of traders, reported that there were 4,000 Creek gunmen. Using Wright's factor of three, one arrives at 12,000 Creeks. Using the higher factor of five, one estimates the population at 20,000 individuals at the start of the American Revolution, a figure that is probably more accurate.[34]

The Creeks' traditional neighbors were not so numerous by the late eighteenth century. Although many scholars assert that the Choctaw tribe was the largest in the southeast before the American Revolution, most estimates of Choctaw population are based on inflated French figures. By 1773, after widespread contact between the Choctaw and the English, James Wright placed their military strength at 2,500 gunmen. He believed the total Choctaw population for the same period was no more than 7,500. But using a larger ratio of women and children to warriors, it may have reached 12,500. There were between 9,000 and 15,000 Cherokees, whereas the Chickasaws numbered only 1,350 to 2,250.[35] Georgia's white and black population grew slowly from 1733 until 1763. After that time, population rose rapidly, from a total of about 10,000 in 1760 to 33,000 by 1773. The populations of Pensacola and St. Augustine were trifling by comparison.[36]

By the end of the eighteenth century, American estimates placed Creek military strength between 5,000 and 6,000 warriors, and it is evident that Creek population continued to increase during the early nineteenth century. In 1790, Major Swan noted the number of Creeks at 25,000 to 26,000. Unfortunately for the Creeks, the population of their American neighbors expanded at a much faster rate.[37]

Physically, the Creeks were "a hardy well made Set of people." From an early age, they anointed their bodies with bear grease and various herbs that accentuated their "dunn copper tint." Men plucked facial hair and also managed to acquire high foreheads by adroit removal of some hair from the crown: "what hair remains they plait or braid behind wearing a variety of things mixt with it, such as Strings, Shells, and feathers; some wear pieces of Metal and Shells to their Ears, which are almost always cut or Slit in uncom-

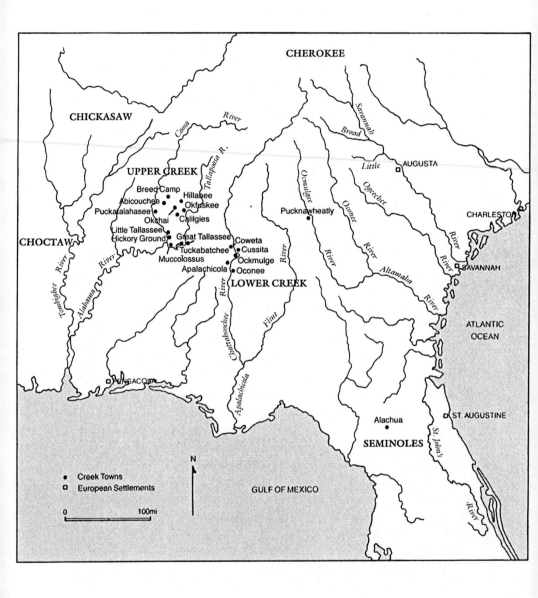

CHEROKEE

CHICKASAW

Coosa River

Broad

Savannah River

UPPER CREEK

Tallapoosa R.

Little

AUGUSTA

Breed Camp
Abicouchee
Puckatalahasee
Okchai
Little Tallassee
Hickory Ground
Hillabee
Okfuskee
Calilgies
Great Tallassee
Tuckabatchee
Muccolossus
Apalachicola

Pucknawheatly

Ocmulgee

Oconee

Ogeechee

River

River

CHARLESTON

Coweta
Cussita
Ockmulge
Oconee

LOWER CREEK

Altamaha River

SAVANNAH

CHOCTAW

Tombigbee River

Alabama River

Chattahoochee River

Flint

River

ATLANTIC
OCEAN

PENSACOLA

Apalachicola

Alachua

St. John's

ST. AUGUSTINE

N

• Creek Towns
▫ European Settlements

SEMINOLES

GULF OF MEXICO

0   100mi

River

1. The Creek Country

mon Shapes, others have rings in the gristle of the Nose, and others large broad Bracelets round their Arms and Wrists."[38] European men frequently commented on the beauty of Creek women as well as their petite stature.[39] Personal adornment with feathers, beads, paints, earbobs, and gorgets of silver or copper was the rule. Leading men and others sported indigo-colored tattoos depicting natural objects such as the sun and moon, animals, hunting and battle scenes, and "beautiful fanciful scrolls" that adorned "the breast, trunk, muscular or fleshy part of the arms and thighs, and sometimes almost every part of the surface of the body."[40] Nudity was the norm for children during the warmer months, and sultry summers also meant very little covering for adults. Bearskins and buffalo robes provided winter warmth.[41]

Kinship was matrilineal, meaning that an individual took his or her family descent through the mother's line. Therefore, a child belonged to the clan of the mother, not the father. Those who claimed a common (and known) ancestress constituted a matrilineage, which was the most important family unit in Creek society. The extended matrilineal household was large and usually included a variety of age groups, including a mature woman and her husband, their unmarried children, married daughters and sons-in-law, grandchildren, and elderly male relatives and other dependents. Caleb Swan was impressed by such family compounds: "These houses stand in clusters of four, five, six, seven and eight together, irregularly distributed up and down the banks of rivers or small streams; each cluster of houses contains a clan, or family of relations, who eat and live in common."[42]

Clans were composed of matrilineages that possessed a common, though distant and usually mythical, ancestor. Clans were represented by animals, such as Bear, Eagle, Wolf, and Tyger (panther). One of the most powerful clans was associated with a natural phenomenon, the Wind. Only four clan names are mentioned in colonial records—Wind, Tyger, Bear, and Eagle—although numerous other clans appear frequently in later records.[43] George Stiggins, a mixed-blood who composed a history of the Creek tribes in the early nineteenth century, contended that there were "nine clans or families Viz the Wind the Bear the Panther the Bird the Polecat the fox the Potato the Red Paint and the isfanna which is composed of many small ones—of all the clans the most numerous & previledged is is [sic] the wind family."[44] Members of every clan lived in each village of the confederacy, and custom dictated that a fellow clansman was welcome in the household of his relatives, even if he was personally unknown to his host.[45]

Just as Creek towns were divided into red and white divisions, clans within each Creek town were deemed to be either white, the *Hathagålgi*, "those who stick together," or the *Tcilokogålgi*, "people of a different speech." The designation of a particular clan as either white or *Tciloki* varied from town to town. This dual division of clans had tremendous political significance. For example, the mico from a white town almost always hailed from a white clan, and generally speaking, a town's war leaders were chosen from among the red clans. Members of red clans held the micoship in red towns but usually were not eligible to direct certain civil ceremonies. This division was also important in ball play and provided an easy way to devise the rosters for intratown ball practice as Creek sportsmen prepared for the real thing against other towns.[46]

The clan organization was "the strongest link" in Creek social and political organization. Stiggins asserted that "by their observance of it they are so united that there is no part of the nation detached from the other But are all linked harmonised and consolidated as one large connected family for by their family prescribed rules there is no part of the nation but a man can find his clansmen or their connection."[47] Clan law guided the course of an individual's life, providing an elaborate set of social rules and etiquette. A clan was legally bound to seek retribution for any crime against one of its members or to pay for any wrongdoing committed by a fellow clansman. Thus, the clan, following established rules for reprisal and retribution of crimes, was the cornerstone of Creek justice, in effect becoming a posse as need dictated. War and hunting parties were composed of men from the same clan. Clan elders saw to the distribution of communal cropland, arranged and approved marriages, and were responsible for training young men who would be eligible for holding offices to which the clan was entitled. A man always had an abiding interest in his own offspring but was bound by tradition and clan law to help supervise the upbringing and education of his sisters' male children, who were of his own clan.[48]

A young woman was allowed to express her personal preference for prospective mates, but clan elders had to approve her choice. Since Creeks always married people outside their own clans, a man's clan affiliation was always different from that of his wife and children. It was not uncommon for clan elders to arrange a suitable marriage for a girl at an early age. But even then, a young woman could not be forced to take a husband against her will. The young man, or his female relatives, presented a marriage proposal to the elder women of his intended bride's matrilineage. Once a woman and her clan accepted a proposal of marriage, the man had to prove that he was a good provider in order to consummate the marriage. In precontact society, this meant very little other than providing meat and deerskins for the woman and her children. With the advent of a trading economy, it also came to mean the acquisition of European cloth and other goods. According to Benjamin Hawkins, the bridegroom was obliged to secure

> a blanket, and such other articles of clothing as he is able to do, and sends them by the women [of his clan] to the females of the family [clan] of the bride. If they accept of them the match is made and the man may then go to her house as soon as he chooses. And when he has built a house, made his crop and gathered it in, then made his hunt and brought home the meat and put all this in possession of his wife, the ceremony ends. They are married, or as they express it, the woman is bound.[49]

After marriage, the husband took up residence in his wife's town, or in the section of his own town where his wife's clan resided, for a woman always lived near the other women of her lineage. A Creek woman's husband built her dwelling and storage buildings and prepared the cornfields belonging to her matrilineage, but the land and improvements remained the property of her family. By helping prepare and plant the fields belonging to his wife's clan, a man made his spouse subject to the very strict laws of adultery. This is particularly appropriate, for cornfields often provided a handy rendezvous for those involved in illicit relationships.[50]

Though divorce was acceptable, it was not common after the birth of children. This was no doubt due to the fact that the father was still responsible for the maintenance of the young children and their mother until she married again. Polygamy was also allowed in Creek society. By the eighteenth century, when husbands' responsibilities had come to include procuring trade goods for their wives and children, relatively few men took more than one wife, since only the best hunters could manage the burden of providing for more than one wife and set of children. White traders, with a ready access to goods, found it easier to outfit multiple wives. Furthermore, before a man could take a second wife, he had to obtain his first wife's consent.[51] This was often difficult, and some men resorted to "a great deal of force and craft" to secure permission. Additional wives were usually sisters or other close relatives of the primary wife, and jealous women could insist the new bride take up residence in her household and then assign her "all the drudgery of the place as a waiting maid."[52]

When her husband died, a woman was forced to endure a grueling four-year widowhood unless she was released from mourning by her husband's clan. During this period, she was not allowed to comb her hair, wash, or wear ornaments of any kind. Inventive widows devised all manner of stratagems to escape this protracted bereavement. In 1772, one desperate widow convinced the people of Tuckabatchee that her dead husband came "to her sometimes in the night" and lurked about the town square. After enduring several days of fasting and sitting up all night in order to secure his appearance before the assembled townspeople, Tuckabatchians correctly concluded it was a hoax designed to thwart widowhood requirements. More commonly, a woman simply seduced her deceased husband's brother or other near relation and persuaded him to marry her, thereby releasing her from a widow's onerous obligation. This was relatively easy to do, for a man did not require his first wife's permission to marry his brother's widow. If a daring widow eloped with a man who was not from the same clan as her dead husband, she was liable to be treated as an adulteress unless she and her new husband could elude her first husband's clan until the Busk, the Creeks' annual harvest celebration. In contrast, a widower was forced to mourn his loss for only four months.[53]

Creek men and women followed very gender-specific work patterns. Hunting and warfare defined manhood for Creek males, but there were also a number of other important activities they undertook, including the construction of private habitations and public buildings and the production of canoes, tools, musical instruments, equipment for ball play, and ceremonial implements. Men were the leaders, not only in government of their towns but also of their clans. Women raised food and families. Creek women cultivated and cared for the communal cornfields and private vegetable plots, gathered wild food and herbs, and were responsible for the manufacture of clothing and household items such as baskets and pottery.[54]

The subsistence economy of Muscogulge men and women followed a seasonal cycle, but their disparate employments meant that men and women spent much of their time apart. The ethnologist John R. Swanton quoted one of his best Creek informants, who noted, "In ancient times men and women were almost like two distinct peoples."[55] While women were primarily occupied in their homes and fields, men tended to spend most of their time in the town square and other public places. An American army officer reported, "Every family has two huts or cabins; one is the man's, and the other belongs to his wife, where she stays and does her work, seldom or ever coming into the man's house, unless to bring him victuals, or on other errands."[56]

Concepts of purity were paramount in Creek ceremonialism and everyday life. Purity—the absence of pollution—was achieved by the separation of opposites, including men and women.[57] Thus, at certain times, men and women were completely separated from each other. This was especially true during a woman's menstrual cycle: "They oblige their women in their *lunar retreats,* to build small huts, at as considerable a distance from their dwelling-houses, as they imagine may be out of the enemies reach; where, during the space of that period, they are obliged to stay at the risque of their lives. Should they be known to violate that ancient law, they must answer for every misfortune that befalls any of the people."[58] Childbearing meant further separation. The anthropologist Charles Hudson has noted, "As with the women, the men were ritually isolated when they were most completely men."[59] Accordingly, men abstained from contact with their wives both before and after warfare and during certain ceremonial events, ball play, and ritual purification before hunting.[60] Although the lives of Creek men and women were strictly regulated by social customs and taboos, they were nonetheless intricately linked by affection and economic cooperation.[61]

The Creek town, or *talwa,* was the heart of Creek social, political, and economic life. A *talwa* represented not simply the town itself but the tribe of people who inhabited it. In the historic period, there were about sixty major towns. Creek town and village sites were remarkably stable during the late seventeenth and the eighteenth centuries. James Adair stated that towns and villages were "very commodiously and pleasantly situated, on large, beautiful creeks, or rivers, where the lands are fertile, the water clear and well tasted, and the air extremely pure."[62] Creek townships presented some variety in design, but there were certain common features. At the center of a town, and usually at the highest point within its limits, were the public areas including the square ground, a winter council house variously called a hot house or rotunda, and a ball field, known as a chunkey yard.

The public square was the ceremonial and governmental center of the town. In 1772, David Taitt, a member of the British Southern Indian Department, visited Tuckabatchee. His description of that town's square is one of the clearest available. According to Taitt, the square was "formed by four houses about forty feet in length and ten wide, open in front and divided into three different cabins each. The seats are made of canes split and worked together, raised about three feet off the ground and half the width of the house, the back half being raised above the other about one foot."[63] These houses, sometimes called cabins or beds, were plastered over with either red or white clay and covered with extravagant sketches and paintings. William Bartram spotted "all kinds of animals, sometimes plants, flowers, trees, etc., . . . figures of mankind in various attitudes, some very ludicrous and even obscene; even the *privates* of men are sometimes represented, but never an instance of indelicacy in a female figure." Bartram's sensibilities were further excited by paintings of men with animal heads and other "monstrous" figures composed of heads, trunks, and "members" from a variety of species. He concluded, "They are the wretched remains of something of greater use and consequence amongst their ancestors." However, it is more likely that these figures symbolized the totems of various clans, perhaps indicating seating order.[64]

Creek men gathered each morning in the public square to discuss town concerns, smoke tobacco, and partake cassina, a tea made from the leaves of yaupon holly (*Ilex vomitoria* Ait.). European visitors dubbed the potion "black drink" because of its color. But symbolically, cassina was a "white" drink, imbibed only in the spirit of peace and friendship. On certain occasions, cassina was vomited by the Indians as a means of purification before serious discussions.[65] All public ceremonies were held at the square ground, and foreign visitors were formally received there as well. Certain towns, with more prestige and thus larger squares, hosted meetings of headmen and head warriors from several towns when the need arose.

During winter or inclement weather, government and ceremonial functions moved to a heated council house, or rotunda. This winter council house was generally round, up to thirty feet in diameter, and had a sloped, pointed roof supported by stout poles. Seats lined the walls. The building had only one entrance, and the smoke from a single ceremonial fire escaped through a vent in the center of the roof. In most cases, the hot house was situated at the northwest corner of the square, with the door facing southeast. Taitt described the hot house at Tuckabatchee as

a square building about 30 feet diameter rounded a little at the corners; the walls are about four feet high; from these walls the roof rises about twelve feet terminating in a point at top; the door is the only opening in this house for they have no window nor funnel for the smoke to go out at; there is a small entry about ten feet long built at the outside of the door and turned a little round the side of the house to keep out the cold and prevent the wind blowing the fire about the house; they make a circle of pitch pine split small, or in lieu of the pitch pine they use small dry canes, leaving a small space of the circle open where the fire is lighted, still keeping some person employed to add pitch pine or canes to one part of the circle while the fire consumes the other.[66]

The seating arrangement in the various public areas was determined by clan, age, rank, and other considerations. Women and children were not allowed within the bounds of the square and the hot house at certain times.[67]

The chunkey yard was also an integral part of a Creek town. The yard itself was continually swept clean and often was surrounded by banks of earth from the repeated sweeping. Chunkey was the most popular game of all the southeastern Indian tribes. Players rolled a stone disk and then attempted to estimate where the stone would stop rolling. The object was to see who could land their stick or spear closest to the place the chunkey stone stopped. Other games that required more space were played on specially cleared lands near the town if the chunkey yard could not accommodate them. Whereas chunkey was played by men from the same town, another game, known to us simply as the ball game, was played between teams from different Creek towns. In this game, teams maneuvered a small ball of stuffed deerskin the length of the field by any means at their disposal, including using specially designed ball sticks, carrying it in their mouths, and passing it to team members. A team scored when the ball was advanced between the goals: two upright poles located at both ends of the field. Some fields were over one hundred yards in length. Creek ball play was arduous and required rigorous physical training. Serious injuries and deaths were not uncommon during the fierce competition. Victory was a cause for intense celebration, and during the historic period, townspeople gambled heavily on the outcome—bets being waged with goods of European origin. The chunkey yard was also the setting for various ceremonies and dances. During war, captured enemy warriors were often tied to two posts, each about twelve feet high, located at the end of the yard. Here, they were tortured and burned at the stake to atone for the deaths of Creek warriors.[68]

These public areas were enveloped by an orderly arrangement of private dwellings. Extended matrilineal families lived together, and family size determined the number of buildings and the extent of the compound. Usually, such complexes consisted of several buildings, each with a designated use, such as living quarters or storage. The complexes of related extended matrilineal families were grouped together, forming clan neighborhoods. During the eighteenth century, an English trader's residence and store became an integral part of a Muscogulge town.

Each town or village was surrounded with the community's cornfields and hunting ranges. As a town's population expanded and placed a strain on existing fields, new satellite settlements were established within the town's jurisdiction. The inhabitants of these satellite hamlets were still considered citizens of the "old" or "mother town" and returned there for ceremonial occasions. A town's population varied depending on whether or not these outsettlements were included in the census. Okfuskee, once the largest of the Upper Creek towns, reported a population of three hundred gunmen at mid-century but contained only thirty gunmen by the early 1770s. Likewise, the population of the Great Tallassee had dropped from one hundred gunmen to thirty by the same period. The rest of the inhabitants had established two new settlements. Some of these detached villages were very small, whereas others eclipsed the mother town in size and political importance. In some cases, the old towns were completely abandoned.[69]

A good harvest was a reason for thanksgiving, for the Creeks, like all other southeastern Indians, were horticulturalists and depended on the bounty of their fields for the main part of their diet. The Creek people were more than adequate farmers. Men prepared the fields and helped plant the crop. Women and children tended the corn, and both men and women participated in the harvest. Famine was rare.[70] Each woman also cultivated a small garden plot for the use of her immediate family. In addition to corn, Creek farmers planted beans, peas, gourds, and pumpkins. Beans and corn were usually planted in common fields: the corn stalks serving as natural support poles for the beans, and the nitrogen-fixing beans providing fertilizer for the fields. It has been postulated that one acre of the highly fertile riverine soil in the Creek country, interplanted with a mix of corn, beans, and squash, was adequate to provide a year's supply of food for one person.[71] Strawberries, plums, and a variety of wild nuts, berries, and roots complemented the vegetable diet. By the eighteenth century, peaches, oranges, apples, watermelons, and sweet potatoes transplanted by Europeans added further variety. William Bartram even spied rice being cultivated in one Lower Creek town. Lower Creeks, especially those near the coast and in Florida, also tended fig trees.

Meat, supplied by hunters, consisted of deer, bear, turkey, and a rare

buffalo, as well as rabbits, squirrel, and other small game. The many rivers
and ponds of the piedmont provided a variety of fishes, including trout and
bream. The fall line location of many Creek villages facilitated the fish harvest. Coweta and Cussita sat on opposite sides of the shoals along the fall line
of the Chattahoochee River. At the termination of the steep falls, Creeks
used scoop nets to gather "hickory shad, rock, trout, perch, catfish, and
suckers" from two channels formed by the rocky shoals. During periods of
high water, when the shoals were flooded in the spring and summer, the nets
were abandoned for hooks.[72] In the more southern Creek villages, alligators
were plentiful. By the middle of the eighteenth century, hogs and cattle
began to assume an important place in the Creek diet. Chickens, introduced
by English traders, provided eggs and meat.

Creek women were inventive cooks, and no European visitor ever failed
to mention the variety and flavor of Creek cuisine. Creek women preserved
fruits, vegetables, and meat by drying them. Bear fat was a prized seasoning.
Both the oil and the "milk" extracted from hickory nuts pleased European as
well as Creek palates. Meat and fish was boiled, roasted, or smoked. Vegetable and meat stews were standard Creek fare. The most important of all
Creek corn foods was hominy, and from it, they made a variety of dishes,
including *sofkee*, a corn gruel or stew usually flavored with venison.[73]

A council composed of civil and war leaders administered town affairs.
The town's chief executive official was the mico, sometimes translated as
"king" by Europeans. George Stiggins asserted that the Creek towns were
"under the moral guardianship of their *mic cul ga* which term is the plural of
mic co a term of gradation more applicable to the office of overseer or guard-
ian in my conception than that of a King."[74] It was the mico's responsibility
to direct the regular daily meetings of the town's council, receive visitors,
and serve as the town's spokesman in diplomatic matters. The mico's position gave him little material advantage over his people, and he dressed, lived,
hunted, and worked the same as everyone else in the town. The South
Carolina agent Thomas Nairne visited the Upper Towns in 1708 and reported:

> All the Governing which the Town allows the Chief is first howing his
> field of corn, giving him the first Dear and Bare that is taken at every
> generall hunt, fat or lean he must take it as it comes, for these honest
> men don't pretend that their subjects should contribute too much, to
> maintain a needless grandure. They are content to share with their

people in assisting and setting them a good Example the better and more patiently to endure the necessary toils of life.[75]

By the middle of the eighteenth century, a few headmen had been able to use their relationship with the traders or the British to enhance their material position. But more often than not, leadership led to poverty as time spent governing meant time away from the hunt.[76] The mico did control the distribution of the corn and goods from the public granary, but these he used to entertain visitors or support those in need and not to augment his wealth or support his family. In some towns, there were several lesser chiefs who also held the title of mico. In such cases, the "supreme" mico was designated by the name of the town.

Various offices were linked to specific clans in each town, and clan prerogative was paramount in filling any vacancies. Thus, it was usually a man's nephew (his sister's son) or other close relation, and not his biological son, who inherited his position. The relationship between clans and certain offices varied from town to town. Thus, at Okchai, the mico was always from the Bear clan, whereas at Tuckabatchee, members of the Eagle clan named the mico from among their ranks. At Coweta, the Wind clan held the highest position in town government.[77]

The manner in which a clan divined its choice for mico is not adequately recorded, but clearly the one chosen represented the most able from a prominent matrilineage within the clan. Once inducted, a mico held his position for life "or during good behavior."[78] Benjamin Hawkins noted the hereditary nature of the micoship: "On his death, if his nephews are fit for the office, one of them takes his place as his successor; if they are unfit, one is chosen from the next of kin, the descent is always in the female line." In the event of "age, infirmity, or multiplicity of cares," the mico could select an assistant from among his kinsmen.[79] Europeans occasionally thought that sons succeeded their fathers, as at Coweta, where the mico Malatchi is usually taken to be the "son" of the Emperor Brims. But in that most Muskogee of towns, matrilineal descent was also the norm. A careful reading of the evidence clearly demonstrates that Malatchi and Brims were "of the same blood," meaning of the same clan.[80] Although heredity was exceedingly important, war honors and service to the community also provided for advancement in the relatively fluid world of eighteenth-century Creek politics. Age and experience were highly regarded. Ability counted above all: "If one is not equal to his office, they elect another."[81]

The mico, usually called the headman by Europeans, was advised by a number of lesser chiefs and councillors. Among the most important was the *henihalgi,* dubbed the "Second Man" by Europeans. The Second Man received "all orders from the mouth of Chief" and carried them "about to the people."[82] He was the true town administrator and saw to the erection and maintenance of public areas and buildings, directed the building of new houses, and oversaw work in the communal fields. He also supervised the preparation and serving of cassina. During the historic period, a number of these men attained prominence as diplomats, the most notable being the Second Man of Little Tallassee during the 1760s and 1770s.[83]

The town's most respected councillors were the Beloved Men, a title bestowed on individuals of outstanding merit from various ranks, particularly famous warriors. Beloved Men were widely regarded for their wisdom and experience. However, by the end of the eighteenth century, the best-known Creek Beloved Man, Alexander McGillivray, was young. Although his clan lineage was undoubtedly important, his education, intelligence, and knowledge of Anglo-American society certainly played a major role in his rise to power. Spiritual leaders, known as priests or conjurers, directed ceremonials and mediated between the spiritual and material world. Sometimes called Firemakers, they were charged with the solemn responsibility of lighting the new fire during the annual Busk.[84]

The town's leading warrior, the Tustunnuggee (Tastanage) Thlucco, or Great Warrior, earned his position due to prowess in battle. He was selected by the mico and council from among the town's most distinguished warriors. If he possessed powerful oratory and popularity in addition to bravery and skill in battle, he could become more important than the mico, especially during times of war. Even in peacetime, the Great Warrior was a powerful force in Creek political life, since he controlled the fealty of the young warriors of the town.[85]

The aged and the young were accorded other roles in Creek political life. Even if an individual did not possess a title or hold a high rank in government, he was valued and respected. All citizens owned the land equally, and the hunting territory was community property.[86] Although clan law dictated certain codes of conduct that had to be followed, Muscogulges were in no way subject to the rigid social classes known in Europe at the time. Indeed, the Creek people experienced a freedom unknown in most parts of the world.

One historian has aptly observed that Creek government "was a bit loose."[87] Creek towns were fiercely independent. The advancement of European settlement and heightened contact through trade forced the development of cooperative maneuvers, and as a result, Creek town autonomy suffered as coalition and collective negotiation became a necessity. Town headmen and councils possessed no coercive authority, no "supreme uncontrollable power, [with] an absolute authority to decide and determine," which, from a British perspective, was essential for good government.[88] But the Creek people valued democracy above efficiency. Creek leaders relied on prestige, gained from birth or noble feats, and on oratory to persuade and cajole their fellows. It was a rare and notable occasion when a headman could not find someone in his village to disagree with him. The result of such independent thinking was neither anarchy nor inaction. For on most domestic issues, there was little disagreement (so far as history has recorded). It was foreign policy, especially after the arrival of Europeans, that raised the specter of dissent and disagreement. Most towns never held a single viewpoint toward the proper diplomatic course. The result was the rough equivalent of a party system, with popular headmen raising support from certain segments of the population of their own towns and regions. When they acquired a sizable following, they became a force to be reckoned with. During the seventeenth and eighteenth centuries, such men were relentlessly courted by European nations, and the attention augmented their authority. Creek townspeople espoused a variety of attitudes and frequently supported different, sometimes even conflicting, policies. It confused and irritated Europeans, but the Creeks enjoyed the talk and the debating.

The result of these different opinions, after 1670, was watchful neutrality as factions tended to offset the actions of each other. These shifting "alliances" kept French, Spanish, and British policymakers on their guard. Two hundred years later, the Creeks' action looks like a policy, but it was simply the result of government by coalition and faction. The Creeks did not plan to play the Europeans off against each other, but it did work out that way, at least until 1763.[89]

The role of women in the Creek decision-making process was completely ignored by European observers and is thus excluded from the written record. Even though William Bartram related that he "neither knew nor heard of any instances of the females bearing rule, or presiding either in council or the field," there is mention of the Beloved Woman of Coweta in the historic record, and it is likely that most other Creek towns appointed Beloved Women.[90] Although the function and role of Beloved Women will never be completely understood, we do know some important facts concerning these women. They were from among the most prestigious families, most likely the sisters or other near relations of micos. Beloved Women dispatched and received messages from important women from other tribes, as in 1775, when a Cherokee Beloved Women included a message for the Beloved Woman of Coweta in a peace talk. The Beloved Woman of Coweta was allowed to speak before the town council.[91] There were other "official" positions for women in Creek society, though their titles and responsibilities have been lost to history. "Women of Note" usually accompanied Creek diplomats when they met with Europeans. In recognition of their status, these women often received presents from the British.[92] Some women accompanied Creek war parties, but their status and functions remain fuzzy.[93] In the eighteenth century, many Creek women married deerskin traders. Acting as interpreters and serving as advisors to both their husbands and their clans allowed these women to expand their influence and doubtless provided the ambitious many opportunities to gain status in their own right as cultural intermediaries.

Even if they did not occupy official roles in government, enough hints remain to show that women were a potent political force, especially in matters of war and peace and clan retribution. Through ridicule, pleading, and their own brand of oratory, they too could persuade. Their greatest impact was on their immediate clan members as they lobbied uncles, brothers, and sons. But husbands were also well informed of their views. By demanding satisfaction for a relative killed by an enemy, they could effectively stir up a war party. Women determined the fate of war captives, who were sometimes enslaved, sometimes adopted into a clan, and on occasion tortured to death by Creek women seeking retaliation for their own dead. On the other hand, women could also cool war fever in the name of preserving the lives of their sons, brothers, and husbands.[94]

The Creek country possessed all the things that man has eternally sought to avoid: death, disease, crime, and famine. But these were only occasional reminders of mortality, and for most of their lives, eighteenth-century Creeks could, with good reason, celebrate, dance, and enjoy themselves. Even war was usually a source of celebration by the eighteenth century. Creek men found advancement through warfare, which normally consisted of small forays against weaker opponents. After 1540, Creeks suffered little from the attacks of their enemies. When they were not employed at politics, horticulture, hunting, or war, most Creek males could be found at the edge of the square ground playing or watching a ball game, gambling on its outcome, gossiping, and after European settlement, drinking rum—in short, having a good time. Women too played games. Indeed, aside from any political implications the outcome might have, ball play was one of the Creeks' highest amusements.[95]

Creek life was filled with ceremony and celebration. The return of hunters might mean a village-wide dance and feast of bear ribs barbecued with honey. William Bartram, invited to one such revelry, enjoyed the festive atmosphere as the inhabitants of Little Talahasochte discussed "cheerfull subjects . . . [such as] hunting adventure, jokeing, News of love, intreagues &c., The Youth & Young fellows dancing singing & wrestling about the Fire."[96] For the Creeks, hospitality and generosity to guests, white or red, was itself a cause for rejoicing. Exuberant youth might need no reason at all for a night of singing and dancing round the village fire, and they had a host of dances for any occasion that might require one.[97] The dances were accompanied by chanting and singing as well as music from such instruments as the drum, rattles, and a flute made from the tibia of a deer's leg.[98] But dancing was more than a pleasant pastime: the women at Calilgies in the Upper Creek nation danced a ritual dance with warriors in the hot house the night before a war party set out against the Choctaws in 1772. And women in other towns danced the same dance at an accelerated tempo as warfare became commonplace in the seventeenth and eighteenth centuries.[99]

The most important of all Creek ceremonial occasions was the Busk or the Green Corn Dance, held in late July or about the beginning of August in celebration of the harvest. The Busk marked the beginning of a new year of plenty and was greeted with days of fasting, dancing, cleaning and cleansing rituals, and the forgiveness of all crimes except murder. Part of the new harvest was sacrificed, new fires were made, and a period of religious introspection was followed by celebration.[100]

The Creeks were devout people, espousing belief in a Great Creator or Supreme Being who was the giver of life. The Muscogulge deity was omniscient, and a leading chief conceded in 1767, "God is the father & Creator of us all Red as well as White people."[101] By appealing to the spirits of the universe, such as the sun, the moon, or other nature spirits, Creek religious leaders sought to provide rain, a good harvest, or protection for warriors on the warpath. Whites might consider such rituals superstition, but the Creeks believed and continued their traditional ways long after Christians invaded their country.[102]

The Creek domain was a land of contrasts. The confederacy itself was an anomaly of unity and division. The same people who regarded their children with tenderness flayed captured enemies alive. They enslaved others and sold them to the white men who came to their country, making a mockery of the freedom and independence they valued so highly. But the most notable contrast came after the establishment of commercial relations with European settlers. "A plentyfull Trade from all parts of the world" brought an exotic array of material goods to improve and complicate native life.[103] The Creeks did not abandon their past, but the trade—and the alliances it represented—brought subtle changes and introduced new elements into the Muscogulge world. By the eighteenth century, cloth and metal tools had become essentials. Guns, bought with deerskins, made the Muscogulges the preeminent power in the Southeast. But Creek power rested solely on the technology of outsiders. Power and dependence proved to be the greatest contrast of all. The deerskin trade—more than ancient traditions, lifeways, and alliances—became the dominant force in Creek destiny.

CHAPTER 2

Trade:
"The Original Great Tye"

John Stuart, who supervised British Indian policy in the South from 1761 until his death in 1779, consistently affirmed that trade was the basis of white-Indian relations. In a 1764 report to the Board of Trade, he eloquently stated:

> The Original great tye between the Indians and Europeans was Mutual conveniency. This alone could at first have induced the Indians to receive white people differing so much from themselves into their country. Before they were acquainted with Europeans they supplyed their few wants with great labor for want of Instruments. Love of ease is natural & they envied the facility with which they saw Europeans Satisfy much greater wants. An ax, a knife, a Gun, were then deemed inestimable acquisitions, and they could not too much caress or admire people, who contributed to their ease & happiness by Furnishing them with such instruments.[1]

Stuart was correct. The exchange of native produce for European manufactures was the fulcrum on which Indian relations turned. Trade and alliance went hand in hand, and the Muscogulges were never able to escape the diplomatic implications of their economic ties. Native customs and attitudes toward both trade goods and trading partners worked to shape the commercial relations they established with outsiders, and Europeans were forced to respect—and often adopt—the diplomatic customs and domestic traditions of their Indian trade partners. More than other European intruders, the British were able to successfully meet Creek needs on Creek terms.

Europeans did not have to explain commerce to the Indians. Long before Europeans disrupted the pace of native life, a brisk trade was being conducted among the aboriginal inhabitants of the Southeast. The vast network of well-traveled trading paths that linked Indian villages across the eastern part of North America extended from the Gulf Coast through the Appalachian Mountains and the Tennessee River and on into the Great Lakes region. Salt, conch shells, feathers, flint, pigments, skins, furs, cassina, silver, galena, copper, clay pipes, and figurines were among the more common aboriginal trade goods. Evidence suggests that large Mississippian complexes, such as Moundville and Etowah, served as staging areas for collection and export of local produce and as redistribution centers for imported goods. One of the major precontact trading routes appears to have passed through Tuckabatchee, one of the most important Muscogulge towns.[2] De Soto saw baskets of pearls, copper-tipped weapons, and storehouses of deerskins at Cofitachique, believed to have been located near present Camden, South Carolina. That populous town was the center of an extensive trade between the Atlantic Coast and the piedmont.[3] The aboriginal exchange network was so widespread that a special trade language developed to expedite negotiations between the various tribes in the Southeast. The Mobilian trade language, a mixture of Creek, Choctaw, Alabama, and other Muskogean languages, is the best known. One scholar has noted that Muskogee (Creek) also served as a lingua franca among the various ethnic groups of the southeastern piedmont. Thus, the intriguing possibility exists that aboriginal trade ties actually brought the tribes of the Creek Confederacy together.[4]

Aboriginal exchange networks represented more than mere economic ties, for Indians traded only with friends and allies. Formal negotiations inevitably included an exchange of gifts. These diplomatic gift exchanges symbolized the ritual joining of the two parties and were an affirmation of faith in the continuance of the relationship. Trade, the exchange of one commodity for another, was entirely another matter, aimed at the redistribution of scarce resources among various peoples. But trade was possible only after the proper ceremonials, which included the exchange of presents and an affirmation of alliance. Archaeological evidence indicates that certain goods, such as precious metals and pearls, may have been reserved for use solely by chieftains and other high-ranking officials, and many items had ideological and ritual significance. Others, such as salt, yaupon, medicinal herbs, furs, processed leather, quality flint, and quartzite, were widely used by all the peoples of the aboriginal Southeast.

In many instances, early trade contacts between Indians and Europeans were undertaken for the same reasons that Indians traded among themselves. Thus, many highly prized European trade goods, such as glass beads, mirrrors, and certain metals, were valued because they were similar to native materials and had religious and ritual significance.[5] But the Muscogulges, like other tribal groups, were quick to see that many European manufactures had more than ceremonial significance. With De Soto, they got their first prolonged glimpse of the European weaponry. De Soto's guns made a lasting impression on the natives, and when Tristan de Luna arrived on the Gulf Coast in 1559 to colonize, the Creeks quickly put him and his guns to work chastising their enemies. De Luna's colony failed, but the Muscogulge regard for European weapons reached new heights. Spain established St. Augustine in 1565, but the Spaniards were more interested in protecting their treasure fleets and converting the coastal tribes than establishing any serious trade with the interior. Nonetheless, Spanish colonists and officials did engage in a limited—and often indirect—trade with interior tribes, including the Muscogulges. Most of the trade was conducted by individuals and soldiers in Pensacola and at scattered Spanish settlements and mission sites. The trade consisted mainly of deerskins and foodstuffs in exchange for brass ornaments, glass beads, iron tools, rum, and cloth. Guns were in short supply, primarily because of restrictions placed on their distribution by Spanish authorities. Even so, some Spanish arms did find their way into Creek hands. Spain's Apalachee allies served as the middlemen in this trade until government prohibitions wrecked the commerce.[6]

With the establishment of the English colony of Virginia in the early seventeenth century, Muscogulges received a hard lesson about the necessity for firearms when their Westo enemies to the north acquired guns. They sought relief from this imbalance, and soon after settlers landed at Charleston, Muscogulge diplomats appeared asking for a trade and help against their gun-toting enemies. The Carolina colony obliged, but the small, irregular commerce merely whetted Creek appetites. Creek-Carolina prosperity was firmly cemented in 1685, when Henry Woodward and 250 men arrived at Coweta, the preeminent Muscogulge town, located on the Chattahoochee River. Creeks ogled and eagerly fondled the brightly colored cloth, the tinkling bells, the shiny beads, the iron knives, and the lean muskets of the English. Bundles of deerskins were quickly prepared, and Coweta's leading man ordered his townspeople to erect a trading stockade.[7] Representatives from the Tallapoose towns arrived to confer with Woodward, and all Creeks solemnly declared themselves to be allies and friends of the English at Charleston. Woodward is the first trader known to have reached the Creek country, but others soon followed.[8] Woodward's packtrain was the beginning of the most powerful factor in Muscogulge life for the remainder of the colonial period: the trade of flintlock muskets, metal tools, and European textiles for Indian deerskins and other produce, including captive enemies. Carolina reaped huge benefits as hides and furs from interior tribes soon became the colony's major export.[9] Between 1699 and 1705, Carolina shipped an average of over forty-five thousand deerskins annually to London. And between 1705 and 1715, the trade in deerskins was the most valuable business endeavor in the colony.[10]

The Spanish, anxious over the proximity of the English to their missions in north Florida, immediately sought to end the budding relationship and demanded that the English traders withdraw from the Muscogulge villages. When the English refused, Spain attempted to punish the Creeks. Lieutenant Antonio Matheo, the commander of Apalachee, moved northward with a force of 250 soldiers. The Spaniards burned Coweta and Cussita and other leading Lower Towns. The Creeks hid the Carolina traders and gathered more deerskins.[11] Despite Spanish attempts to wreck the Creek-Anglo trading alliance, Woodward returned to Charleston with a train of 150 Indians carrying loads of deerskins.[12] To reduce the time and trouble of carrying loads all the way from the Chattahoochee, some Creeks soon moved their villages eastward, to the Ochese Creek branch of the Ocmulgee River, to be nearer their trade partners. Even the threat of Spanish arms could not deter the commerce, and as the Creeks acquired their own weapons, Spanish opposition was quieted.

In the early years, trade caravans such as Woodward's were rare, and much of the trade was conducted at Carolina plantations or in Charleston when Indian delegations arrived laden with deerskins to trade for cloth and guns.[13] Nearly a century after Woodward's trek, the roving naturalist William Bartram was introduced to a grizzled old Creek at Muccolossus who recounted with pride the glory of his youth. Bartram stated, "He said, that when he was a young man they had no iron hatchets, pots, hoes, knives, razors nor guns, that they then made use of their own stone axes, clay pots, flint knives, bows and arrows; and that he was the first man who brought the white people's goods into his town, which he did on his back from Charleston, five hundred miles on foot, for they had no horses then amongst them."[14] Soon, however, itinerant traders began to appear more and more frequently, locking the Creeks into a steady—and tempestuous—relationship with the British colonies. Ancient Indian footpaths were transformed into the most extensive system of trading paths found in English North America. Within a few years of Woodward's appearance at Coweta, duffel blankets, iron hoes, and flintlock muskets had become essential to the Muscogulges. John Stuart was not the only Briton—or Creek—to note, "A modern Indian cannot subsist without Europeans; And would handle a Flint Ax or any other rude utinsil used by his ancestors very awkwardly; So that what was only Conveniency at first is now become Necessity and the Original tye Strengthned."[15]

The Creek-Anglo alliance, from the beginning, was based on respect for Creek sensibilities. And the relationship, at least in Creek eyes, was a relationship between equals. Even though the British traders brought powerful and exotic goods, the Muscogulges treated the traders as they might have any other tribe who came into their territory and asked for permission to settle among them. The strangers who arrived at Charleston were accorded the status of allies: Friends and Brothers. A white path linked the Creek towns and Carolina, now acknowledged to be "of one fire." Formal exchanges between Creek towns and the Carolinians were marked by all the pageantry and symbolism of Creek diplomacy. Carolinians, and the Georgians and Floridians who followed them, became regulars at Creek square grounds, smoking the calumet, drinking black drink, and patiently enduring the measured formality of the Creek town meeting. British agents became adept at reading and sending encoded messages via beaded belts. For the English, dances and speeches, giving and receiving names and titles, and exchanging presents all became the price of doing business. For the Creeks, it proved that their allies not only valued their friendship and culture but also respected their strength.

Though the Creeks, out of courtesy, paid the English the compliment of regarding them as "Elder Brothers," it was still the English who were forced to learn the melodious Muskogee tongue, for few Creeks expressed any willingness to adopt the harsh and strident tones of their new friends. And when powerful micos and great warriors from the Creek towns traveled to Charleston, Savannah, and other British towns, they carried their world view with them. Governors and Indian agents, like the traders who mingled with the Creeks on a daily basis, always sought to impress the Muscogulges with grand buildings and large cannons. But the Creeks were seldom impressed with such things. Instead, to please their partners, British governors and admirals, agents and council members, one after the other, decade after decade, smoked the calumet, awarded presents, bestowed honorific titles, and spoke of the white path that linked the English and Creek towns.

Though deerskins were always the staple of the Creek-Carolina exchange, Carolina planters needed horses and slaves and paid well for them. Horses from Spanish Florida, especially around Apalachee, made their way to Carolina via Creek hands. Some horses were obtained in trade with the Spanish, but most were stolen. Creek enemies, particularly the Choctaws and the depopulated remnant tribes along the Gulf Coast, became prime candidates for enslavement and sale to Carolina.[16]

For the Creeks, the sale of captive enemies represented a new dimension in the treatment of non-Creeks. Enemy warriors were usually killed outright; the majority of captives were women and children. Under Creek custom, these individuals did not belong to a Creek clan and thus had no rights within Creek society. Before the establishment of markets for such slaves, war captives had faced either a grueling ordeal of death by torture or life as a slave among the Creeks. Before, Creek slaves might have hoped for return to their own people or eventual adoption by a Creek clan with all the rights of a full member of Creek society; now they became marketable trade items. There is no doubt that the emergence of markets for Indian slave labor hastened the death and destruction of countless individuals and tribes in the American South. History has condemned Europeans for their role in the establishment and encouragement of the Indian slave trade. But the Creeks were guilty too. Far from being hapless cogs in the British wheel of expansion and exploitation, the Creeks embraced the role that opportunity thrust before them. The aggressive pursuit and sale of non-Muscogulges presented a striking contrast to the Creek embrace of Anglo-Americans, who quickly forged ties of alliance and commerce, and kinship, with the Creeks.[17]

Meanwhile, the French arrived on the Gulf Coast, and with the establishment of Mobile and New Orleans, an intense rivalry among the three European powers for control of the interior and its people began. The French and Spanish who visited the town squares of the Muscogulges were accorded the same hospitality that was meted out to the English. Unfortunately, from the Creek perspective, more often than not the French and Spanish came empty-handed. Creek headmen always listened intently to their coaxing speeches, but the heavy blankets, broad metal hoes, and well-made guns that the English had left behind served as silent reminders of the Muscogulges' commitment to Carolina.

The arrival of the French was a godsend for the Choctaws, who slowly began acquiring French guns, thereby making themselves less inviting targets for Creek slavers. Smaller tribes along the Gulf Coast also sought French aid against the Creek menace, and in 1701, the Tohomés and Mobilians asked for, and received, French support. Undaunted, Muscogulge warriors took to stalking the Spanish mission Indians around Apalachee more intensely. Creek relations with the Apalachees and their Spanish overlords had been strained since the Spanish invasion of the Lower Creek country in 1685. In the following years, the Apalachees acted as middlemen for Spanish trade goods going into the Creek towns. When the Spanish supply of goods dwindled, Lower Creeks and Apalachees rounded up Spanish horses to take to Carolina to exchange for English goods. The Apalachee-Creek relationship was not an easy one, and the two groups sparred sporadically. In 1702, Creek gunmen, reacting to market demands, raided the missions, burning villages and taking slaves and horses for sale in Carolina. Apalachees, armed with bows and arrows, retaliated, marching northward toward the Lower Creek Towns. But the Carolina traders armed and organized Creek warriors to meet the threat. The Creeks routed the unwary enemy. Six hundred Apalachees were killed or taken prisoner.[18]

With the outbreak of Queen Anne's War in 1702, slave raiding took on an added fervor. Creeks, tied to the English by common enemies and a need for guns, joined them in the struggle against Spain and France. French-armed Choctaws hounded Upper Creek villagers, and Creeks retaliated in kind. In 1704, Creek warriors joined Colonel James Moore of South Carolina and participated in a series of destructive assaults against the Spanish missions among the Apalachees, reducing them to "old fields."[19] Moore and the Creeks destroyed over two dozen mission villages plus scores of smaller Indian settlements and Spanish ranches. Approximately 4,000 Apalachee Indians were killed, enslaved, or forced to relocate along the South Carolina frontier. Surely Moore and his men must have exchanged wry smiles as they marched their war booty toward Charleston along the major Creek trade artery.[20] With the destruction of the Apalachees, the South Carolinians had defused the Spanish threat, acquired a considerable number of Indian slaves, and created an Indian buffer between themselves and other hostile groups. At the end of Queen Anne's War, England—and her Creek allies—stood victorious.

Meanwhile, the Creeks had to search harder for victims. Overwhelmed by bellicose Creek slavers, surviving Timucua and Tocobaga Indians fled southward, leaving much of the Florida peninsula uninhabited.[21] By 1708, the South Carolina Indian agent and explorer Thomas Nairne reported that Creek slavers were "obliged to goe down as farr on the point of Florida as the firm land will permitt. They have drove the Floridians to the Islands of the Cape, have brought in and sold many Hundreds of them, and Dayly now Continue that Trade so that in some few years they'le Reduce these Barbarians to a farr less number."[22] The Creeks prospered and, with their superior technology and success, acquired a new haughtiness and feeling of invincibility. Chickasaw Indians, allied to the Carolinians and usually friendly with the Creeks, participated in these slaving raids, particularly concentrating on their bitter enemies the Choctaws.

There were excellent reasons for hunting enemies. In 1700, Charles Levasseur, a Frenchman, reported that the English were among the Upper Creek villages exchanging a variety of goods for deerskins and buffalo hides. "But the greatest traffic between the English and the savages is the trade of slaves which the nations take from their neighbors whom they war with continuously, such that the men take the women and children away and sell them to the English, each person being traded for a gun."[23] Thomas Nairne, perhaps the most knowledgeable Indian countryman of his day, reported that slaves were more valuable: "A lucky hitt at that besides the Honor procures them a whole Estate at once, one slave brings a Gun, ammunition, horse, hatchet, and a suit of Cloathes, which would not be procured with much tedious toil a hunting."[24]

Moreover, as the enemy was reduced and driven away, vacant land was claimed by the raiders. Thus, Creeks acquired not only trade goods, slaves, and battle honors but new hunting lands as well. By the eighteenth century, Apalachee had become a Creek province, as had the lower reaches of the Alabama River, stripped of its original inhabitants by European disease and Creek slave raiders.[25] The British, who acquired the Floridas in 1763, were told from the beginning that the Apalachee "old fields" were Creek lands, by right of conquest. John Stuart explained to his superiors: "They Joined with the Carolina Colonists, conquered and extirpated the Apalachee Indians; and demolished the Spanish Forts and Settlements in that Country. By their perpetual incursions they reduced the formerly numerous aborigines to so inconsiderable an handfull; that being unable to make a longer stand, they removed with the remains of the Yamasies to the Island of Cuba about the time of the Last declaration of War with Spain."[26]

As the hostilities cooled following Queen Anne's War, the French continued to support Choctaw ambitions with trade, but they also sought to mend relations with the Creeks. By 1712, the French and Upper Creeks had come to terms, both sides relishing the prospect of trade more than continued warfare. Until their ouster from North America in 1763, the French continued to pose a threat to total English dominance of the Creek trade. They had more success among the Alabamas, who were far from Carolina and only a canoe ride away from Mobile. Most Abeikas, Tallapooses, and Lower Creeks found a trade with Carolina more convenient.

Despite the success of the English peddlers, there were problems with the trade alliance. Overzealous Creek consumers and underhanded Carolina traders combined to create havoc in the exchange system. Avarice is as old as trade itself, and both the Creeks and the Carolinians were guilty. Creeks, eager to possess the material goods of the Europeans, especially their guns and cloth, quickly found themselves mired in debts they could never hope to repay. Even though inflated prices and faulty weights had contributed greatly to the problem, unprincipled traders seized goods and even relatives of the heaviest debtors in an attempt to make the most of their investment. Traders bullied and beat those unable to satisfy their debts and merely enraged and insulted the rest. Creek-Anglo relations were strained indeed.

The Creeks were not alone in their distress. The Yamasee Indians were distant relatives of the Muskogees and had originally claimed territory near St. Augustine. At Carolina's urging, they had moved to nearby Savannah River locations to facilitate trade.[27] Expanding Carolina settlements, the decimation of coastal deer herds, and the loss of the slave trade combined to force them deeper and deeper into debt. The Yamasees were even harder hit by seizures of relatives for the Charleston slave market and other trade abuses. Their resentments nurtured by the French, Creek warriors joined with the Yamasees in 1715 to attempt a reform of English trade practices. When Carolina learned of the forthcoming rebellion, the frontier stalwart Thomas Nairne was sent to the Yamasee town of Pocotaligo with assurances that Carolina would secure redress for all legitimate grievances. Nairne was slowly roasted by the Yamasees, and a general massacre of most English traders throughout the backcountry quickly followed. The Chickasaws, whose very survival depended on English arms, protected their traders. The Cherokees quietly mulled over their options and, in the end, killed the Creek emissaries sent to woo them and joined the Carolinians. But virtually every other backcountry tribe with any connection to Carolina joined the revolt. There seems to be justice in the fact that among the early belligerents were some of the Apalachee Indians, who had been resettled along the colony's borders. As the trade rebellion continued, Charleston narrowly escaped destruction.[28]

Like the Carolinians, the Creeks suffered from the war. In need of arms and surrounded by hostile Europeans as well as enemy Indian nations, they soon made it known that peace was possible. Thus, in 1716, South Carolina sent Theophilus Hastings and John Musgrove as emissaries to the Creek towns. Hastings delivered presents and ironed out a peace settlement with leading Creeks. Musgrove arranged for the marriage of his mixed-blood son, Johnny, to Coosaponokeesa, the niece of the most powerful Creek headman, Brims of Coweta.

The Yamasee War officially ended in late 1717, when Lower Creek headmen journeyed to Charleston and negotiated a new trade treaty for all the Creek towns. In addition to establishing rates for trade goods, the treaty included a clause that guaranteed Creeks a supply of ammunition against any enemy tribe not at peace with the English. In return, the Creeks promised to mind their manners, protect the traders and their property, and punish those guilty of crimes against the English. Thus, the Carolina-Creek trade reopened but this time under the close supervision of the colonial establishment, which sought to prevent abuses and thereby spare the colony another devastating Indian war. The war virtually ended the trade in Indian slaves. Meanwhile, disenchanted Creeks had moved back to their old town sites on the Chattahoochee.[29]

With the Yamasee middlemen dispersed and many Creeks unwilling to travel to Carolina to barter deerskins, the trade moved in new directions. The huge capital required to obtain trade goods from Europe and to collect, store, and ship large numbers of deerskins and furs meant that professional merchants now assumed the direction of the trade. A new kind of commerce emerged from the chaos, and the professional traders, backed by seaboard merchants, took control of the trade away from the planters and the part-timers.[30] Savannah Town, located at the fall line on the Carolina side of the Savannah River (across from modern Augusta, Georgia), became the frontier entrepôt of the new trading system. Fort Moore, erected soon after the close of the Yamasee War, was established to protect and police the traders and their warehouses.[31]

Eager to reestablish their business, Carolina traders headed for the Creek towns. There they discovered the French had made some inroads in the commerce, but by parceling out goods at extremely low prices and pointing out the deficiencies of French merchandise, they soon recovered their customers.[32] The trade quickly recovered. In 1721, the trade reverted to private control, due largely to the influence of members of Charleston's mercantile community, whose profits had suffered from the meddling of politicians.[33]

Disillusioned with the English, the Alabamas invited the French to establish a fortified trading post, Fort Toulouse or the Alabama Fort, in the heart of their territory, at the confluence of the Coosa and Tallapoosa rivers.[34] It took time for the English trade to recover, and the French made small strides in acquiring a portion of the Muscogulge market. Hindered by poor supply lines, the absence of credit, and a penchant for patronizing Creek enemies, France failed to establish a viable economic link with the confederacy. A quarter-century after the establishment of Fort Toulouse, Sieur Hazeur, its commander, bemoaned the variety and popularity of the English goods and was reduced to furtively gathering samples of English ribbon to send home as examples of the types the Creeks preferred. According to Hazeur, the English not only pandered to Creek taste in goods and established credit accounts but also sold their goods "at a better price by more than half than our traders." Hazeur likewise noted that English traders were quick to insinuate themselves into Creek town life, making marriage "alliances" with the leading families and embracing Indian life. "It may even be said," the commander reported, "that the English have a patience that will stand every test, since it has often happened that when traders have been mistreated and even knocked on the head by Indians, there has not been a question at all of vengeance or of satisfaction."[35]

Suave diplomacy, free gun-repair services, and excellent brandy did win Creek friends, however, and the French managed to compete for a meager portion of the Upper Creek market until 1763. Judging by the amount of goods sold at the fort in 1744, the scholar Gregory Waselkov has postulated that the French could have obtained up to 7,500 deerskins (approximately 15,000 pounds) from the Creeks that year. In contrast, Carolina shipped 130,884 pounds of deerskins in 1743–44 and 305,717 pounds in 1744–45. Although records are not precise on the origin of the deerskins, the Creeks would have produced a significant number.[36] The French fort was especially valued as a source of powder and lead, which were doled out parsimoniously by the English, especially during periods of tension between Creeks and the British colonies.[37] This advantage was offset by the fact that the French had relatively few guns to distribute, and frequently these were damaged in transit. The situation, according to one French report, led the

Indians to believe that the French were "entirely poor" and unable to man-ufacture goods as well as the English did.[38] Other items were almost always in short supply, and the French soldiers at the garrison were often obliged to obtain cloth and other goods suitable for presents to the Indians by swap-ping their powder and heavy lead shot for English textiles. Likewise, the fort was heavily dependent on neighboring hunters for its supply of fresh meat.[39]

The Franco-Creek alliance, from start to finish, was more political than economic and served mainly to irritate the English. By dispensing large presents of trade goods, making grand promises, and repeatedly pointing out the dangers of British encirclement, the French did manage to build a limited—and influential—support base among the Upper Creeks. Those Creeks irritated at villainous English trade practices swelled the ranks of the statesmen, and as a result, the Creeks somehow managed to maintain a precarious neutrality when the colonial powers went to war. Carolina's trad-ers loudly decried the "Priest, Popery, and Brandy" of the French and consis-tently called for military action against Fort Toulouse and other French outposts.[40] Though poor, France's friends were loyal, and the lowly post was never besieged by pro-English forces. And even the most Anglophile Creek was forced to acknowledge that the French establishment provided a useful service by forcing the English to be more solicitous of Creek sov-ereignty. In South Carolina, and later Georgia, there were frequent mur-murs about the necessity of building an English post to counter French machinations, provide protection for traders, and keep the Creeks in line. After much arm-twisting, the Upper Creeks reluctantly consented to an English fort. An insignificant effort was made at Okfuskee, but the "fort" was never more than a heavily guarded trading post. Animosity between South Carolina and upstart Georgia soon lead to the abandonment of the "fort" and the idea.[41]

French administrators at Toulouse and Mobile constantly urged that more and better trade goods be made available for the Creeks. They believed that if the French could deliver sufficient goods, the Creeks would drive the English from their towns. Louisiana Governor Vaudreuil was convinced that the English traders were

restless and quarrelsome spirits who cause division everywhere and who the Indians tolerate only because they bring them goods and supply them abundantly with them. If the French could do the same thing, they would without contradiction be preferred. They are more to the liking of the Indians and are perfectly in sympathy with them, so the Indians, even those of the English, every day tell our traders that if they were in a position to supply them with the things that they need, they would never permit the English to come upon their land.[42]

Perhaps Vaudreuil was right. The most influential British trader among the Upper Creeks, Lachlan McGillivray, told colonial officials the same thing in 1758, and John Stuart repeated the assertion of his superiors in London in 1764.[43] But it made little difference. In the end, economic realities triumphed, even among Francophile Muscogulges. When eleven British traders were murdered by dissidents in 1760, the majority of the Creek headmen moved quickly to reassure Georgia that it was a "misunderstanding." They begged the surviving traders to return to their stores. As one Creek diplomat explained, the Indians "must soon be a wretched people" should they be forced to depend on Toulouse for supplies.[44] It is instructive that when France and England went to war against each other, as frequently happened in the eighteenth century, the English traders were allowed to move their storehouses into the center of Muscogulge towns for protection against possible assault by the French or their Indian allies.[45]

France's ouster from North America in 1763 following Britain's resounding victories during the Seven Years' War had few repercussions on the Creek exchange economy. Nor did Spain's withdrawal from the region at the close of the war have any impact on the Creeks. For though the Creeks had lived in relative peace with the French since 1715, Creek-Spanish relations had remained uneasy. Spain, unlike France and Britain, sought to convert and missionize the native peoples they encountered in the South. The Creeks, unwilling to conform to Spanish ideals, remained distant, often attacking the missions or the villages of Spanish Indians. The famed Spanish horses and cattle of peninsular Florida were often the targets of Creek raiders. St. Augustine was viewed more often as a military objective than a market, and Creeks usually visited that town in the company of an army of Georgians. Over the years, a handful of Creeks did seek links with Spanish authorities. During times of peace, Creeks visited Spanish Pensacola and other Spanish settlements in Florida to receive presents. The Spanish seldom had goods to trade, however. Some Creeks even made the journey to Havana and returned home with presents. A limited trade with Cuban fishing boats along the Gulf of Mexico continued well into the 1760s. But steady trade between the two peoples was virtually nonexistent, and the Spanish were never contenders—either economically or politically—for a Creek alliance.[46]

The Creeks' "true magnetic predilection for the British" was no mystery.[47] Greater variety, better quality, cheaper prices, and easy credit terms won the grudging loyalty of Creek consumers. In addition, Anglo-America could provide a dependable supply of goods, something the French had great difficulty doing during the eighteenth century when the British navy controlled the trading lanes to America.[48] British traders, with their shrewd business sense, inborn aplomb, and lusty familiarity, quickly wormed their way into the marrow of Creek life. It was almost always a British trader who sat in a Creek square ground, hoisted black drink with relish, and toasted his eager customers. As that intrepid chronicler Thomas Nairne observed in 1708, "They Effect them most who sell best cheap."[49]

CHAPTER 3

Merchants to the
Muscogulges

From the end of the Yamasee War until the American Revolution, the Creek Indians enjoyed virtually unbroken trade ties with the British colonies. These ties bound the Creeks to Anglo-America as firmly, to use a Creek image, as a vine winds its tendrils around a tree. Whereas the economic tie indicated a larger alliance between peoples, at the most basic level the link was intimate and personal, between hunter and trader, mico and merchant. Indeed, deerskin traders served as the most direct link between the Muscogulges and the British colonies and served not only as suppliers but also as representatives of their society and government. Before 1763, gentlemen's agreements and the French threat combined to limit the trade to a relatively small group of daring and industrious men. Through trial and error, these men transformed the deerskin trade from the province of peddlers to an avocation for the ambitious. After 1763, the most successful expanded their operations into Britain's new Florida colonies. The merchants to the Muscogulges not only exerted a profound influence on native society but shaped the economy and politics of Britain's southern colonies as well.

The best-known early Indian trading merchant was Samuel Eveleigh, a native of Bristol, England. Eveleigh served on Carolina's Indian Board from 1712 until the Yamasee War, when new regulations took effect that prohibited those engaged in the Indian trade from sitting on the board. Nonetheless, Eveleigh maintained a powerful presence in the direction of South Carolina's trade policy. Of more importance, he was among the first to employ credit in the Indian trade. Eveleigh's influence extended deep into the frontier, and he established a number of frontier outlets that outfitted traders and served as collection points for hides garnered in the trade.[1]

Among the more colorful—and most unusual—of the trading stores supplied by Eveleigh was one established in 1732 by Johnny Musgrove and his Creek wife Coosaponokeesa at Yamacraw Bluff on the Savannah River, later the site of Savannah, Georgia.[2] Coosaponokeesa, better known in English records as Mary, had been taken from Coweta by her white father when she was seven years old and sent to Pon Pon, South Carolina, where she was "baptised, Educated and bred up in the Principles of Christianity."[3] She and Musgrove had married shortly after the ratification of the Creek-Carolina peace treaty following the Yamasee War and established a trading store in South Carolina.[4] In 1732, at the invitation of local Indians, the Musgroves relocated to Yamacraw Bluff. Mary claimed they took in twelve thousand pounds of deerskins annually over the next few years, which amounted to one-sixth of Charleston's total deerskin exports.[5]

In January 1733, General James Oglethorpe and his Georgia colonists arrived at Yamacraw Bluff, and Mary quickly assumed the role of interpreter and Indian advisor. Samuel Eveleigh, who supplied their store and purchased their deerskins, had recommended the pair to Oglethorpe. Eveleigh opened a line of credit for the general and his band of colony builders, and in return, he expected favors from Oglethorpe and the Georgia Trustees. His aim was to secure a monopoly of the Indian trade through Georgia, and he offered to finance a fort to guard the new settlements—and his proposed trading establishment. Eveleigh even had a location in mind: a parcel just across the Savannah River from Fort Moore, the Carolina fort erected after the Yamasee War to protect Savannah Town.[6]

Oglethorpe had other plans. With the help of the Musgroves, Georgia quickly obtained a land cession and negotiated a trade treaty with the Creeks.[7] Eveleigh was completely bypassed when, in 1735, Oglethorpe reached an agreement with a number of Indian traders and ordered a town to be built at the fall line of the Savannah River. The new town was dubbed Augusta in honor of the Princess of Wales, and according to one eighteenth-century traveler, the site was "perhaps the most delightful and eligible of any in Georgia for a city."[8] Below the falls, the river ran just over two hundred miles in a gentle, meandering course from Augusta to the sea at Savannah and was ideal for transportation of goods to and from the Indian country. Oglethorpe's site selection was no coincidence. It was the spot coveted by Eveleigh, and traders from South Carolina had already established warehouses across the river at Savannah Town, now often called New Windsor, the village settlement around Carolina's Fort Moore.[9]

The general's offer to award land to those who moved their stores to his town paid off, and soon stores and "victualling houses" were under construction.[10] Augusta's superior location at the head of the major trading path to the southern Indian nations made the general's offer doubly attractive. Locating on the Georgia side of the river saved the trouble and expense of transporting goods back and forth across the Savannah River on the journey from storehouse to Indian nation. There were additional incentives: many of the new settlers were Carolina debtors who found it better to relocate across the river in Georgia than to risk arrest in Carolina.[11] Newcomers to Georgia quickly noted that the land around Augusta was fertile and that slaves could be used to increase one's productivity without interference from higher-ups in Savannah, who frowned on slavery and rum.[12]

More than one of Augusta's early storekeepers complained that the isolation of the settlement contributed to disorderly conduct and fierce competition. Kennedy O'Brien, one of the town's first inhabitants, was also among the first to bemoan the "Ill Regulation of the Indian Trade."[13] John Miller, another of the original Augusta storekeepers, likewise complained of storekeepers who built stores miles from Augusta on Indian land along the trading path. Indian traders could be supplied there without traveling all the way to Augusta, "thereby defrauding their former Creditors."[14] James Frazer, the owner of a trading boat, eventually became conservator of the peace at Augusta and was the most successful of the original Augusta traders. After his retirement, his son-in-law, Edward Barnard, continued his business.[15] These men were joined by swarms of others. One official report claimed that six hundred traders descended on Augusta in the spring of 1740. Others maintained those numbers were exaggerated, but there were at least thirty permanent storekeepers in the settlement, each of whom would have fitted out numerous traders.[16]

By 1741, Augusta was, according to one rosy report, thriving "prodigiously."[17] The rough little village was declared "the most flourishing town in the Province."[18] Augusta's success was largely related to the growing popularity of tanned deerskin for clothing and other uses. Between 1710 and 1714, a vicious plague infected European cattle herds. Roughly one-half of France's cattle succumbed during the epidemic, and the contagion spread throughout the continent. The plague reappeared periodically over the next several decades, particularly in 1750, with dire consequences. As a result, England banned the importation of cattle and cattle hides from Europe, thereby causing serious shortages in the English leather-working industry and increasing the demand for American deer hides.[19] Moreover,

Augusta's founding coincided with a period of rapid commercial expansion within the British empire, which continued until the American Revolution. Available credit, better shipping, expanding markets for deerskins, and better communications provided the true impetus for Augusta's economic success.[20] Augusta quickly became the heart of a vast trading system that stretched from the manufacturing and commercial centers of the British Isles to Charleston, South Carolina, and, via Augusta, to Coweta, Okfuskee, and beyond.

Despite Augusta's success, Savannah was unable to capture Charleston's role as commercial capital for the southern colonies. There were a number of good reasons for this. Charleston's merchant community was well established, and newcomers to Savannah found it difficult to compete with Charleston's capital, credit lines, and foreign trade connections. Savannah also lacked adequate storage and shipping facilities until the early 1750s. Deerskins remained Georgia's only viable export to Great Britain until the 1760s. The lack of other cargoes suitable for ballast hampered regular shipments of skins from Savannah. Moreover, the personal contact and ties between Charleston merchants and leading Augusta storekeepers tended to make Charleston the logical destination for Augusta's produce.[21] It was not until the 1760s that Savannah emerged as a leading port.

Mary Musgrove, together with Jacob Matthews and Thomas Bosomworth, her second and third husbands respectively, continued in the deerskin trade, as well as participating in other economic ventures. They remained at Yamacraw Bluff and, as a result, lost out to the more enterprising traders who settled at Augusta and sponsored trading expeditions into the Creek towns. Though she maintained a powerful influence on Oglethorpe and the Indian trade, she was never able to overtake the success of the Augusta traders.[22]

Augusta's burgeoning merchant community still faced tough competition from well-established business across the river in South Carolina, especially George and Samuel Eveleigh's New Windsor store, operated by an astute young businessman and trader named Martin Campbell.[23] Archibald McGillivray and Company provided further impediments to those just beginning in the trade. Archibald McGillivray's firm was the largest trading company of the day. McGillivray had entered the southern Indian trade at an early date and conducted business with every southern Indian nation. By 1741, McGillivray had taken a number of other traders into his company as partners, but he remained "sole manager and director" of the firm. McGillivray's partners were George Cussings, Jeremiah Knott, William Sludders, Alexander Wood, and Patrick Brown.[24]

Both Archibald McGillivray and Alexander Wood retired from the trade in 1744, and Patrick Brown established himself as the new director of the company. He reorganized it under the name Patrick Brown and Company and moved the company's headquarters across the river to Augusta. The same year, Martin Campbell left his position as storekeeper for the Eveleighs and established his own warehouse in Augusta. The arrivals of Brown and Campbell marked a turn in Augusta's fortunes, and from 1744 on, Augusta was the leading frontier outpost for the southern Indian trade. Augusta's success was firmly tied to the success of the companies of Patrick Brown and Martin Campbell, for the two firms and their successors dominated the southern Indian trade until the American Revolution.[25]

Patrick Brown and Company continued in business throughout the 1740s, and many other traders and storekeepers moved their operations to Augusta. By the end of the decade, Patrick Brown had joined forces with men from two other companies, "for the more effectual carrying on the Trade." In the absence of firm documentary evidence, the composition of this famous company must be deduced from clues scattered throughout the official records of the colonies of Georgia and South Carolina. It appears that most of the seven original partners had been traders with the old Archibald McGillivray and Company.[26] The most notable of Brown's new partners was John Rae, and the new firm was known as Brown, Rae, and Company. Informally, it was commonly referred to as the Augusta Company or, more notoriously, the Company of Seven. Brown, Rae, and Company dominated the southern deerskin trade and drove most of its competitors out of business. Brown himself was licensed to trade with the Creek towns of Calilgies, Hillabee, Muccolossus, and the Fish Ponds. Like Brown, John Rae was an Irish immigrant; he had been in Georgia since about 1734. Rae was the proprietor of a trading boat, and he transported the skins collected by the company to Charleston on his boat. He also had connections to the Chickasaw Breed Camp in the Upper Creek Towns and the license for the Lower Town of Coweta. Rae also traded in the Chickasaw Nation. Two of the firm's other partners, Isaac Barksdale and George Galphin, were associates of Rae's and had been members of his old firm, Rae and Barksdale. Isaac Barksdale was licensed to trade at several Upper Towns, notably Okfuskee. George Galphin managed the lucrative and prestigious Coweta store. William Sludders, Brown's associate from Archibald McGillivray and Company, also joined the new firm. Sludders held a trading license for the powerful Upper Town of Okchai and was a confidant of the Gun Merchant of Okchai. When Sludders died in 1753, the company temporarily lost the Okchai trade, "to the Great Detriment and Loss" of the partners. Lachlan McGillivray, a kinsman of Archibald's, was another partner. Before joining Brown, Rae, and Company, Sludders and Lachlan McGillivray had done business together as Sludders, McGillivray, and Company.[27] Daniel Clark, who had been associated with Lachlan McGillivray in the firm of Clark and McGillivray, also joined the new company. Lachlan McGillivray held the license for the Upper Towns of Puckatalahasee, Weoka, Wetumpka Old Town, and Little Tallassee, but he was largely based out of Little Tallassee. Clark operated stores in Coosa and other Abeika villages along the Coosa River.[28] By the time Patrick Brown died in 1755, his company, according to credible accounts, handled 75 percent of the Creek and Chickasaw trade.[29]

In addition to the seven original partners, most of the other Creek and Chickasaw traders of note were associated with Brown, Rae, and Company in one way or another. Thomas Deval, who had worked closely with Sludders, Lachlan McGillivray, and Clark, was the trader at Puckatalahasee, the westernmost town of the Creeks. Deval is perhaps best known for providing the anglicized name of one of the leading chiefs of the Upper Creeks, Deval's (or Duvall's) Landlord, who was the headman of Puckatalahasee. Lachlan McGillivray actually held the licence for that town, and Deval disappears from the record in the early 1750s. Other well-known traders with ties to the company were James Germany, William Struthers, Timothy Barnard, John Ross, and James McQueen. Struthers was the nephew of William Sludders.[30] Dugald Campbell, who had been the clerk for Rae and Barksdale, joined the new company in the same capacity. In 1765, Campbell parlayed his knowledge of the Indian trade into a position with the British Indian Department in 1765 as "Storekeeper of Indian presents and provisions" at Mobile.[31] A close associate of Brown, Rae, and Company was John Pettigrew (Pettycrew). In addition to keeping a store, he was a trader to the Chickasaw Nation and had large stocks of horses. He was a member of Courtonne, Pettycrew, and Company.[32]

The firm's most famous members, George Galphin and Lachlan McGillivray, were among the most influential traders to the Creek Nation, and their careers were remarkably parallel. Lachlan McGillivray of Dunmaglass, Scotland, arrived in Georgia in 1736 as an indentured servant. It was not until the 1740s that McGillivray entered the Indian trade, and it is likely that he was employed by Archibald McGillivray's firm.[33] According to one early, though unauthenticated account, young McGillivray journeyed into the Indian country with a group of fellow Scots. He was rewarded for his service with a pocketknife, which he promptly traded to the Indians for deerskins, and "the proceeds of this adventure laid the foundations of a large fortune."[34] By 1741, McGillivray was already respected as a Creek interpreter, and in 1744, South Carolina entrusted him with the sole responsibility of negotiating peace and establishing trade with the Choctaw Indians. McGillivray's Choctaw venture was a dismal failure, but by that time he had established himself as one of the leading traders to the Upper Creek Nation. When he married Sehoy Marchand, a woman of the prestigious Wind clan reputed to be the mixed-blood daughter of a French officer at Fort Toulouse, his ascendancy in the Upper Nation was assured. McGillivray's influence in the Upper Towns was enormous, and from his base at Little Tallassee or the Hickory Ground, he provided information to both South Carolina and Georgia concerning Indian matters. His information on French activities at nearby Fort Toulouse was especially valuable before 1763.[35]

George Galphin was McGillivray's counterpart in the Lower Towns. Galphin left Ireland in 1737, abandoning his wife of little over a year. Like McGillivray, he must have entered the Indian trade almost immediately on his arrival in South Carolina. Galphin ensconced himself at Coweta, the most prominent town in the Lower Nation, and married Metawney, the daughter of the headman of Coweta. The union produced three children and financial success for Galphin, who became the principal trader to the Lower Creeks and usually wielded more influence in the nation than colonial governors or Indian superintendents.[36]

The success of Brown, Rae, and Company was due to the diverse skills of the partners. Brown and Barksdale largely functioned as retail merchants, ordering goods from wholesale merchants in Charleston and keeping records of goods sold, skins purchased, and other matters. They also worked as traders. Brown sometimes found it necessary to chase debtors as well.[37] Rae, with his slaves and those he employed, transported the skins to Charleston. In Charleston, the company usually found ready markets for the skins, often selling on consignment to various merchants, notably Samuel Eveleigh.[38] Sludders, Galphin, Clark, and McGillivray were the chief traders and oversaw the company's affairs in the Indian nations. The company outfitted numerous other traders, each of whom had his own base in the Creek country.

Much of the company's early success was due to the fact that "two or three of them [partners] were always in the Nation to make the most of their affairs."[39] The exact terms of employment are not clear, but generally an individual trader was advanced goods on credit by the company. After the trading season, he was expected to settle up with the company storekeeper in Augusta. The company also hired wage employees. Although it is hard to ascertain whether or not the company itself owned slaves, the individual partners certainly did. These slaves not only worked in the vegetable patches but also performed a myriad of chores associated with the trade, both in Augusta and in the Indian nations.[40] The traders and others in the partners' employ required constant supervision.

Those outside the company accused members of Brown, Rae, and Company of conspiring to form a monopoly to control all the Creek trade. Thomas Bosomworth, Mary Musgrove's third husband and business partner, had a keen interest in Creek affairs and resented the influence of the company. While serving as an agent for South Carolina to the Creek nation, he wrote of the partners:

> [They] seem to look upon the whole Trade of the Creek Nation as their undoubted Right and whatever Part they are deprived of they are apt to imagine an Encrochment upon their Property, and that in all Matters regarding the said Nation, their Advice and Opinions ought to be decesive. . . . the greatest part of the Traders in that Nation are under their Influences and Authority and obliged implicitly to obey the Dictates of their Masters.[41]

Bosomworth was not the only one who complained. When Galphin appeared before the Georgia council in September 1750 asking that he and Pettigrew be appointed constables in the Creek Nation, the board turned them down because they were members of the "monopolizing company at Augusta."[42]

The charge leveled against Brown, Rae, and Company hint of ruthless competition and less-than-exemplary business practices. Brown, Rae, and Company raised the ire of fellow storekeepers by sending goods directly into the nation to resupply certain traders. Those thus supplied returned their deerskins to Brown, Rae, and Company. This arrangement allowed debtors to other storekeepers to avoid their creditors (and jail) and continue trading. The company also piqued Savannah's small merchant community, since it consistently conducted its business through Charleston.[43] Continued complaints from competitors led the president and assistants of Georgia to recommend that no licenses be granted in 1752 "to those of this Company, or any who recide and have Stores at Augusta, and keep Servants to carry on their Trade in the Nation."[44]

Brown, Rae, and Company, denying the "Envious & Malicious" reports, asserted, "We . . . have risqued our all in the Colony, & have been no Small Benefactors to it, for we must say (& without Vanity) that our House is the best Acquainted with Indian Affairs of any in this Colony, & that it is us who by our Endeavours, have in a great Measure kept the Indians on good Terms with this Colony as well as Carolina."

In addition to listing their services to the colonies, the partners raised the specter of "an Inundation of Raw Unexperienced people among the Indians." The partners added, "[These people] would effect many other Traders as well as ourselves [and] would soon raise such a Combustion as would not easily be allayed, & ought therefore by all means to be prevented." Their arguments, as well as their promise to divert their shipping through Savannah "as this colony begins to flourish," apparently swayed the Trustees, for there is no record that any member of the company was ever denied a license.[45] Nonetheless, complaints were continually lodged against them for having "not only a General Store at Augusta, but . . . likewise Each of them Licenses for different Towns in the Indian Nation." Some felt the solution should be to deprive storekeepers of trading licenses, since this put "two different Branches of the Trade in one Person."[46] But no such prohibitions were ever applied.

Patrick Brown died in July 1755. The other members gradually broke away and joined new ventures, though they continued to have business relations with one another. Most of the firms that dominated the trade in the 1750s and 1760s included members of the old Brown, Rae, and Company. By 1764, John Rae, George Galphin, and Lachlan McGillivray were the only surviving members of Brown, Rae, and Company. George Galphin set up a store at Silver Bluff, which he had purchased in the 1740s. Galphin also established other trading posts in the Creek country, and by the time of the American Revolution, he had captured the lion's share of the Creek trade. Lachlan McGillivray continued his Upper Creek connection. Although they continued to obtain licenses in their own names after the Seven Years' War, the surviving members of the old firm seldom undertook the "Fatigue of going into the Nation themselves."[47] Instead, they hired substitutes for whom they posted bond.

Brown, Rae, and Company did not hamper the success of Macartan and Campbell Company, operated by Martin Campbell and his brother-in-law, Francis Macartan. The two firms were not rivals in the traditional sense, for Martin Campbell hired out boats on more than one occasion from John Rae, and the Augusta storekeepers often purchased goods from one another. It appears that the two firms had friendly relations and cooperated more than they competed. Macartan and Campbell had important links to the Upper Creek Towns and the Chickasaw Nation and did relatively little business with the Lower Creeks. In addition, Macartan and Campbell acted as exporters; the firm was the sixth-largest exporter of deerskins out of Charleston between 1743 and 1763. To the lasting confusion of historians, Campbell's son, Macartan Campbell, carried on the family business under the name Macartan, Campbell and Son from 1764 until the American Revolution.[48] There were many other merchants and trading companies that operated out of Augusta, including Robert Crooke, Alexander Mackintosh, and James Jackson, of Crooke, Macintosh and Jackson, another important supplier for the Creek towns.[49]

Although there is no doubt that larger trading companies conspired to monopolize the trade, leading Creek headmen supported the restriction of the trade to a few men who were personally known and acceptable to their people. Though the deerskin trade was ostensibly an economic enterprise, it represented much more than that to the Muscogulges. As an outward manifestation of the larger alliance between two cultures, merchants and traders represented Anglo-America. The presence of competing traders hawking their wares and hustling for customers was at once unsettling and abhorrent to the Muscogulges—even if the result meant better exchange rates. Via patient negotiation with leading Anglo-Americans, Creeks defined the terms on which they wished to trade. And even though the routines established and the prices fixed may have been unfairly profitable for the powerful few who came to control the trade, Muscogulge headmen, and their people, appreciated the order and reliability the system offered. As the Earl of Egmont recorded in his journal in 1734 after negotiations with the Creek trade delegation that visited England, "They desired there might be but one English dealer to every town, and he to be lycensed, that they might know who to complain of, and be Sure of redress if ill used, for multitude of Traders only bred confusion and misunderstanding." The delegation made the journey to England some years before the establishment of large Creek trading concerns. No doubt the delegation had adopted its position after persuasion by Oglethorpe and others. Still, the Muscogulges accepted the idea completely and repeated it frequently in the years that followed.[50]

These storekeepers and traders not only controlled the backcountry economy but also contributed mightily to the growth of Georgia. During Georgia's first two decades, the prohibitions against slavery and importation of rum hampered the development of plantation agriculture and the establishment of a trade in foodstuffs with the West Indies, making the deerskin trade one of the few sources of income for the enterprising Georgian. As it had been in South Carolina, the fur trade was Georgia's first business. Following the transfer of the colony to royal control, agriculture became more important, but until the American Revolution, the Indian trade continued to play a dominant role in Georgia's economic prosperity.[51] Likewise, the tax revenues from the deerskin trade provided needed income for the young colonial government. In addition to financing the port at Savannah, the duty on deerskins was used to pay for the fort and battery on Cockspur Island.[52]

Through Georgia's land-grant provisions, virtually every major trader managed to accumulate land. The acquisition of slaves made it possible to receive further land grants. Storekeepers and traders thus acquired thousands of acres and became planters as well as Indian traders. Many purchased land as well and acquired sizable holdings in both South Carolina and Georgia. Lachlan McGillivray, for example, acquired title to 11,190 acres before 1776.[53] The land was put to a variety of uses, including the production of rice, indigo, corn, and naval stores. The acreage itself often proved a worthwhile investment, since land speculation was as popular as any other economic activity on the Georgia frontier.[54]

Like all other southerners who could afford them, the traders and merchants owned slaves and cattle. In addition to working in the Indian nations, the slaves performed agricultural labor, tended large herds of cattle, and operated gristmills for their owners. In many ways, the production of barreled beef (and pork) was an adjunct to the Indian trade. Cattle were tended and processed for the market by slaves and fetched a handsome price on the West Indian market. Slaves also harvested timber and oversaw backcountry sawmills. Rum, easy to dilute and even easier to sell to Indians, was an excellent way to attract deerskins. In fact, the exchange of lumber, particularly staves and shingles, and foodstuffs for West Indian rum constituted an important trade "triangle" in the years before the American Revolution.

After the transfer of Florida to British control in 1763, new outlets for Georgia beef appeared. George Galphin quickly sought Creek permission to drive herds of beef cattle to West Florida, hoping to profit from the extreme shortage of meat in that province. Galphin's cattle drive, though it may have been profitable in the short run, earned him the stricture of the Upper Creek headmen. The Creeks disliked cattle and repeatedly complained of traders who kept herds in the nation. Creek resistance deprived Georgians, even those with influence in the Indian country, of an opportunity to profit from the West Florida market. East Florida was more accessible, but St. Augustine provided only a limited demand for beef.[55]

In 1765, John Rae, George Galphin, and Lachlan McGillivray jointly petitioned the Georgia assembly for fifty thousand acres for a township to be settled by Irish immigrants. Once the land was granted by the Georgia assembly, the men actively promoted the settlement and advertised for immigrants. The settlement, Queensborough, was located on the Georgia frontier, adjoining Creek lands. The three promoters publicly promised to help the immigrants establish themselves and to provide cattle, tools, and even board and employment to the newcomers until they were self-supporting. They hoped that the Queensborough township would stimulate the back-country economy, thereby benefiting Augusta and its citizens. The scheme held out the promise of profit, for new settlers would eventually buy horses, cattle, and slaves, in addition to all manner of consumer goods, from Augusta's storekeepers.[56] At least one of the Queensborough settlers, John Brown, also found employment in the Indian trade. A native of Scotland, Brown arrived in Georgia in 1764. He obtained two hundred acres in Queensborough and built up herds of cattle, hogs, and horses. He supported his plantation with the profits he made fashioning tin kettles, bells, and other items for sale to the Indians.[57]

Rae, Galphin, and McGillivray were not driven by economic motives alone. One is struck by the sincerity of John Rae's assertion: "I will do everything in my power to assist them; for nothing will give me more satisfaction than to be the means of bringing my friends to this country of Freedom."[58] Trouble between the Creeks and the Irishmen hampered the full development of the scheme, as did royal disfavor and the outbreak of war. But there is no doubt that the Augusta traders provided considerable impetus for the growth of Georgia. Detractors claimed that the township was designed to serve as a buffer between lands already owned by Galphin, Rae, and McGillivray and the Creeks. But it is preposterous to suppose that Georgia's leading Indian merchants needed protection from their customers. In fact, they stood to lose the most if the Creeks and their new neighbors did not get along.[59]

The Augusta storekeepers and traders served Georgia in other ways as well. John Rae, George Galphin, Francis Macartan, and many others held a variety of civil offices, including justice of the peace, tax assessor, tax collector, surveyor of roads, and delegate to the Georgia assembly.[60] On numerous occasions, traders acted in both official and unofficial capacities as interpreters and diplomats, supplying intelligence and serving as a vital link between the two very different worlds. Of course, such service was not without reward. Serving as a messenger for a governor enhanced the prestige and authority of the trader in Creek eyes, for the Creeks entrusted only their most well-respected speakers with such duties. In the wake of tensions between Georgia and the Creeks at the height of the Seven Years' War, Lachlan McGillivray used his influence in the Upper Towns to restore relations with the Creeks at his own expense. The grateful Georgia assembly, recognizing the value of his actions, publicly thanked the trader for his services to the colony. During the same period, Coweta's firm pro-English bias owed much to the influence of Georgia Galphin, who would not enter the town and conduct business when the French flag flew from the town's council house.[61]

In addition to their economic and civic contributions to the colony, many of the storekeepers were interested in the cultural and spiritual life of the backcountry. At the height of the licensing controversy in 1751, the new minister at Augusta, Jonathan Copp, related that the citizens of Augusta were "much given to Strife amoung themselves." He added, [But] "in Justice to a certain Company of Seven vizt Brown, Rae, & Merchants in copartnership who are ye chief Promoters of ye Trade, . . . They have Contributed more toward the Building the Church and ye in'ted Parsonage House than all the Rest of ye Inhabitants of this Town."[62] In addition, the company pledged to pay half of the parson's annual salary, a feat that no doubt did much to earn Copp's unrestrained loyalty.

It was undoubtedly John Rae who spearheaded the company's support of the church. By all accounts, Rae was a fair and devout man. When he was indicted for the manslaughter of an Augusta woman in 1771, his friends did not falter but leaped to his defense with proof of his "unblemished Character" and quickly petitioned for royal mercy. Their pleas did not go unheeded.[63] Respected businessmen, in addition to supporting the local church, also needed a place to detain rambunctious employees and others who ignored the law or avoided paying their debts. Accordingly, it was Lachlan McGillivray who presented a bill to the General Assembly of Georgia calling for the erection of a jail at Augusta.[64]

Running a successful trading establishment required literary and mathematical skills, and most of the established traders possessed a rudimentary education. Many traders, if their Creek wives would allow it, also sent their children to Charleston or Savannah for a "proper" education.[65] Daniel Clark left money not only to the church but also to the Charleston library.[66] George Galphin and Lachlan McGillivray encouraged the Chickasaw trader James Adair to write a book about the southern Indians and supplied Adair with much of his information. Adair dedicated his work to them and in its preface thanked them for their patronage. The book, one of the most important sources on southern Indians, testifies to the intelligence and literary skills of at least one trader. Judging by the few remaining letters of Galphin and others, it is clear that Adair's ability was not an anomaly.[67]

George Galphin and a host of other merchants, notably William Spalding of East Florida, also supported one of the most important scientific expeditions of the eighteenth century: William Bartram's tour of the southeastern colonies and the Indian country during the early 1770s. George Galphin entertained William Bartram at Silver Bluff and provided the naturalist with letters of recommendation and credit, good at his numerous stores in the Creek country. Galphin's traders and packhorsemen guided the botanist and helped lug his bulky boxes of botanical specimens through Florida and the Creek country. Drawing on his own observations and on conversations with Galphin and other deerskin merchants and traders, Bartram penned the most memorable firsthand account of the eighteenth-century South, detailing its flora, fauna, and native inhabitants in *Travels through North and South Carolina, Georgia, East and West Florida*.[68]

The real key to success in the Indian trade was credit. Although many Charleston merchants owned their own warehouses, ships, and slaves, they depended on their London or Bristol connections for the financial backing and credit necessary for the collection, shipping, and distribution of both deerskins and trade goods. In many cases, financial backing came from English leather sellers or brokers who purchased the deerskins and then resold them to manufacturers. One eighteenth-century business analyst noted, "It is a very genteel business, but their returns being large and slow, (they buying all their undressed deer-skins with ready money, and giving large credit) it requires a very large capital to carry it on."[69] In London, the leather sellers had incorporated by the early 1770s.[70]

Where there is credit, there is debt. Despite the seeming success of many leading traders, the Indian trade was not always a profitable business, especially after 1763. Stiff competition and treaty agreements fixed the prices for trade goods, heavy losses from various causes were common, and the inability of the Indians to pay their debts forced many traders into financial difficulty. To profit and prosper, merchants and traders found it necessary to commit fully to the trade—it was not a one-season adventure but a long-term business venture.

The best-known London firm with Augusta ties was that of William Greenwood and William Higginson. Greenwood and Higginson advanced credit to George Galphin and a host of other Augusta traders. And on more than one occasion, they were forced to institute legal proceedings to recover long-overdue debts. The most famous cases involved the heirs of George Galphin, who finally settled with the firm in the 1790s.[71] But numerous other Augusta traders also found themselves in serious debt to Greenwood and Higginson. In 1781, Thomas Netherclift declared he did not have the resources necessary to repay the claims against his company by Greenwood and Higginson. He submitted a proposal to them for the discharge of his company's debts and tersely offered "to devote the remainder of [his] life, if it should be required, toward discharging to the last farthing the debts of G & H."[72] The English firm of Logan, Guerin, and Vanderhorst was also a major supplier for the southern Indian trade.[73]

The most interesting way in which the established traders attempted to extricate themselves from their heavy debts to British trading concerns was the transfer of land, known as the New Purchase, from the debtor Indians to the traders in 1773. The cession, consisting of over two million acres, was actually made to Georgia, and commissioners were appointed to sell the land. All proceeds from land sales were to be applied to retiring the debts of the Cherokees and Creeks to their traders. James Wright, Georgia's governor, was so taken with the scheme that he went to London to present the case for allowing the transaction. The cession, in addition to increasing Georgia's size, seemed guaranteed to attract new settlers and stimulate the colony's economy.[74] In fact, the land was to be sold for less than five shillings per acre, which was considerably lower than its true value, for the express purpose of attracting settlers.[75] George Galphin was able to present proof of Creek indebtedness to his establishment worth 9,791 pounds, 15 shillings, and 5 pence. Galphin was not alone; claims were presented by every Georgia Indian trader.[76] In the end, Augusta storekeepers and Charleston export merchants simply passed their claims along to London merchants, who found themselves holding vouchers entitling them to proceeds from the sale of Creek land. Greenwood and Higginson alone held one-half the claims.[77]

Shortly after the New Purchase, Galphin retired and turned control of his trading establishment over to his nephew David Holmes, to his sons, George, John, and Thomas, and to an old acquaintance, John Parkinson. He pledged his own good name as security for the new firm, Galphin, Holmes, and Company, and wrote to Greenwood and Higginson in London, "No people in these parts ever went into trade upon a better footing—they buy off no old debts, they will have nothing to pay me for, but what good[s] will be left upon hand after the trade is fitted out." Further, Galphin "let them have the use of the House, Stores and plantation," where he "carried on the trade, clear of rent." The new company's assets, by Galphin's reckoning, stood at £10,000. Galphin, determined to be a country gentleman, hoped to devote the remainder of his life to the management of his plantations, cattle herds, and sawmills.[78] He later reminisced, "When I sol^d of all my Consern in trade I thought to be Easey the remainder of my Live."[79] Unfortunately for Galphin, the American Revolution interfered, and he was never able to collect the money due him by Georgia. Nor were the times kind to Galphin, Holmes, and Company. The general decline in the market for deerskins in the mid-1770s coupled with the beginning of the American Revolution to ruin the firm. In 1791, Galphin's estate was sued for £13,566 by Greenwood and Higginson. Galphin's heirs were forced to sell what property they had managed to retain through the war years in an attempt to settle their account.[80]

Lachlan McGillivray also retired from the trade in the years just preceding the American Revolution. In 1781, he made plans to return to Scotland. McGillivray later stated that the management of his plantations was too much for him, due to his age and his "infirmities," and that he wished to "extricate himself from the distress and perplexity he had laboured under in Consequence of the Troubles." He therefore turned the management of his lands over to his cousin and heir, John McGillivray, in return for an annual annuity of £500. The McGillivrays' loyalty to the British government ultimately cost them their lands, slaves, and honored position in Georgia politics.[81]

With the retirement of the old-line Augusta storekeepers, new names appeared on trader ledgers. Notable were James Jackson and Edward Barnard.[82] John Gordon, who at various times operated from Frederica, Georgia, and Savannah, by 1759 ran a thriving business in Charleston and was one of the major exporters of deerskins from that city. A heavy investor in East Florida, he was a friend of Governor James Grant's and supplied many of the Creek traders of the period. His main London contact was Greenwood and Higginson.[83]

As a result of its overwhelming victory in the Seven Years' War, Britain obtained all French and Spanish territory east of the Mississippi River, except the city of New Orleans. The transfer of East and West Florida to Great Britain in 1763 had tremendous implications for British-Creek relations and presented new opportunities for those wishing to open trading establishments. James Spalding and his business associates were the most successful of the new traders who attempted to gain a share of the Creek trade after 1763. Spalding, who was born in Scotland in 1734, arrived in Georgia in 1756. From his base at Frederica, St. Simon's Island, Georgia, he established a number of stores in Georgia and British East Florida. His two most famous warehouses, Spalding's Upper Store, on the east bank of the St. John's River, and Spalding's Lower Store, near present-day Stokes Landing, served as supply depots for a number of smaller trading posts that his traders opened in East Florida. Spalding's major partners were Donald McKay and Roger Kelsall. Donald McKay died in 1768, and the firm continued under the name Spalding and Kelsall. Spalding and Kelsall purchased many of their trade goods through John Gordon of Charleston and the Savannah merchant Basil Cowper. Like many of their fellow traders at Augusta, both Spalding and Kelsall, as well as Gordon and Cowper, remained loyal to the king and migrated to the Bahamas after the American Revolution.[84]

The best known of all the Creek trading firms, Panton, Leslie, and Company, simply took over the Spalding and Kelsall establishment. William Panton and John Forbes, two of the original partners in the new company, had had business contacts with Spalding and his partners before 1776 through Gordon's Charleston firm. Panton had been Gordon's clerk from 1765 to 1772, and Forbes was Gordon's nephew. Charles McLatchy, who operated Spalding and Kelsall's stores, was also one of the original partners of Panton, Leslie, and Company.[85]

James Spalding and his partners were not the only ones to seek their fortunes in the Floridas. The prominent Charleston merchant John Gordon used his influence with East Florida Governor James Grant and Indian Superintendent John Stuart to help establish Galphin's traders at Picolata and San Marcos de Apalache (St. Mark's) after 1768, when the military posts were abandoned. Galphin's men were supplied from Gordon's warehouse.[86] More than a few established Georgia and South Carolina traders opened branch offices in West Florida. Among these was Lachlan McGillivray, who in 1763 sent his cousin, John McGillivray, to Mobile to enlarge the McGillivray trading network. John established West Florida trade connections with the Creeks, Chickasaws, and Choctaws and ultimately controlled all his uncle's other business as well.[87] Other successful new operations were headed by Daniel Clark, Peter Swanson, James McIntosh, William Struthers, and John Miller. At one time or another, most of these men were involved in partnerships or cooperative ventures. John Miller, one of the most successful, became a partner of John McGillivray's, and like many traders before him, he managed to build up large assets in land and slaves. He too became involved in colonial politics and held a variety of public offices, including justice of the peace. He also served in the assembly.[88] John Fitzpatrick, whose trading house was located at Manchac, was another West Florida success. Fitzpatrick's business was mainly with the Choctaw traders, including the Mobile export and trading companies of John McGillivray, William Struthers, William Swanson, and John Miller. Of these, McGillivray, Struthers, and Miller were also involved in the Creek trade.[89]

Boosters of Mobile and Pensacola especially hoped to open new trade contacts with the Creeks and their western neighbors, the Choctaws. Many traders were successful in opening a trade route from Mobile to the Choctaw nations, thus circumventing Creek control over their enemy's trade.[90] Pensacola, which bordered Creek territory, seemed destined to rival Augusta as a trade entrepôt. A "very good road from the Upper Creek Nation" to the tiny village seemed to augur sure success.[91] But the majority of the Creek trade continued in the same channels after 1763. The Upper Creeks at first welcomed a trade from Pensacola as a way to receive lower-priced goods. But when the anticipated price changes did not occur, most Creeks found it more convenient to continue associating with their old traders from Augusta. The Creeks aptly observed, "When a path is new made it does not at once become a great path."[92]

Though West Florida attracted its share of merchants and factors for British firms, Charleston and late-blooming Savannah merchants held the upper hand. Establishing vast trading networks simply took time. From the beginning, West Florida trading houses experienced the normal start-up delays. In addition, they were hampered by erratic supplies of trade goods from their London factors. As it turned out, their major import was rum, and that commodity proved their most valuable trade asset, much to the distress of leading Creek headmen and the British Indian Department. By the time the new business networks stabilized, however, an embargo of the

Creek trade in 1774, followed by the American Revolution, had ruined most of the West Florida firms.[93] The swarms of novice traders who left West Florida for the Creek country with rum-laden packhorses did little to change the course of the commerce, and until the American Revolution, traditional Creek trade channels remained virtually intact.

Mobile firms were able to take over the formerly French-dominated Choctaw trade. Some Creek traders also dealt with trading houses there. Many of those skins found their way via Mobile to New Orleans, where prices paid for deerskins equaled those of Charleston. From there, the deerskins were sent to France, where a revival in leather manufacturing was under way. At other times, hides were shipped directly from Mobile to London. Even so, as late as 1774, caravans of packhorses were guided from Mobile and Pensacola through the Creek Nation along the Creek trading path to Augusta.[94]

Like the Augusta traders, the merchants in the two Florida colonies played an important role in the development of the local economy. In fact, deerskin accounted for 88 percent of the total produce exported from the two Floridas in the years before the revolutionary war.[95] The Indian trade served as a stepping-stone to other endeavors, primarily plantation agriculture, lumbering, and cattle raising. By the time Panton, Leslie, and Company had taken over the Creek trade in the years after the American Revolution, the deerskin trade was in decline. Then, more than ever before, the trade served as a diplomatic tool and bolstered peaceable Indian relations. Panton, Leslie, and Company was perhaps the most diversified of all the Indian trading firms, carrying on an extensive trade in foodstuffs, salt, and naval stores. The Indian trade also served as a convenient cloak for the smuggling operations "necessitated" by the Spanish government's tight regulation of commerce.[96]

For the English-speaking merchants and traders, the deerskin trade was first and foremost a business endeavor. It formed the heart of the backcountry economy and brought prosperity to many involved in it. Traders also contributed to their colonies in noneconomic ways, as diplomats, advisors, and local community boosters. Though their contribution to the establishment and growth of Georgia, Carolina, and the Floridas was important, the greatest legacy of the Muscogulge merchants and traders was their impact on Creek society. Their guns, cloth, rum, and mixed-blood progeny changed the course of Creek history.

PART TWO
Hunting and Trading

CHAPTER 4

The Creeks as Producers
for a
Trade Economy

The Creek-Anglo deerskin-trading alliance rested on the simple exchange of goods. The raw materials of the Creek country—offered for barter—brought a wealth of manufactured goods into Muscogulge towns. The foundation of the largest economic concern in the colonial South was laid on the labors of Indian hunters, who by traditional methods produced one of the most valuable southern exports during the colonial era. Like other Native Americans involved in the fur and hide trade, the Creeks became, as the anthropologist Harold Hickerson so artfully phrased it, "a kind of vast forest proletariat."[1]

The Creeks embraced the opportunities afforded them by geography and good fortune and became commercial hunters—producers for the world market economy. Their primary target was the white-tailed deer, *itchu* to the Muscogulges. They also pursued beaver, bear, raccoon, and other fur-bearing animals. With minimal adjustments, the Creeks continued their customary way of life and were enriched by their access to "a plentyfull Trade."[2] And when hunting alone failed to satisfy their needs for British goods, Muscogulges discovered other ways to participate in the developing trade economy of the southern backcountry.

It is impossible to tell how the Muscogulges viewed this economic transformation, for they left no record of their feelings. But their actions indicate a relatively rapid and easy shift to new economic pursuits. Diseases introduced by early explorers and travelers had destroyed much of the South's human population in the sixteenth and early seventeenth centuries. As the region's population of humans dropped, that of the white-tailed deer and other game animals rose.[3] The Muscogulges viewed the herds as one of their most valuable resources, and they did not hesitate to exploit the animals.[4]

Commercial hunting did not interfere with the established rhythm of their subsistence economy. Spring and summer were reserved for planting and harvest. Traditionally, fall and winter had been the time to stalk the white-tail. As commercial hunters, the Creeks continued these patterns.[5] The lower temperatures of late autumn meant thicker coats and fatter and better meat, since fall acorns and berries provided abundant deer feed. There was also less likelihood of meat spoilage in colder months. And as the heavy vegetation of the southern forests shriveled under frost, travel became easier. Early winter was also the rutting season, a time when bucks became aggressive and abandoned the deep cover of the forest in their search for mates.[6] Does followed the bucks, and all ages and sexes became easier prey. A modern hunters' handbook provides an accurate description of the deer's condition by declaring that the rutting season "reduces otherwise super-wary, super-clever bucks to blathering idiots."[7] Autumn also became the time for trade.

According to John Stuart, the Creeks possessed "the most extensive hunting-ground of any nation to the southward."[8] Large ranges were necessary, for one deer requires approximately one hundred acres for sustenance.[9] Muscogulge hunters could travel freely anywhere under Creek jurisdiction in search of game. Still, it seems that most hunters tended to range in fairly well-defined areas over which their town or tribe had some claim through long occupation, assimilation, or conquest.[10] Hunters from Coweta and neighboring towns tended to stalk game to the east and north, where Creek lands adjoined Cherokee and Georgia lands, and especially along the Oconee and Ogeechee rivers. According to Alexander McGillivray, this area was among the most valuable Creek hunting grounds and produced over three thousand deerskins annually.[11] Hunters from the southernmost Lower Creek Towns moved south and west into the Florida peninsula. The Tallapooses and Abeikas ranged in what is today northern Alabama and central Tennessee, even crossing into non-Creek territory beyond the Tennessee River. Alabama tribesmen pressed westward toward the Tombigbee River, which was the boundary with Choctaw lands, and southward along the Alabama River and toward Pensacola in their search for deer.[12] The fertile forests along the Tensaw and Escambia rivers were highly prized hunting grounds for all Creeks.[13] Creek hunters from Chehaw and Tallassee ventured into the Okefenokee Swamp in search of deer, bear, and alligator.[14] The Latchoways and other East Florida villagers hunted all along the Florida peninsula, even as far south as the cape.[15] During the long winter hunting season, Creek hunting parties could be found from Tampa Bay to the Cumberland River valley, and they trekked as far west as the Trinity River in Texas.[16]

Even though the reason for the pursuit of deer changed, the Creek hunt retained much of its tradition. Through ancient rituals, solemn ceremonies, and elaborate hunting dances, hunters sought assistance from higher powers and protection from the dangers of the chase.[17] In slow, measured cadence, deer slayers sang out to elusive prey, exhorting the deer to "Awake, arise, stand up!" and surrender to their fate.[18] Before setting out, hunters underwent ritual purification by steaming themselves. Creek conjurers assiduously prepared medicines to attract deer. Hunters rubbed some of these preparations on their skin; other medicines were ingested before leaving camp. These rites undoubtedly had the practical effect of ridding hunters of their human odor. Guns were bathed with special elixirs as well. If these medicines proved successful, a hunter rewarded his conjurer with a deerskin.[19]

Creek hunters also carried charms to attract deer. Some hunters were partial to the "physic-nut," a yellow fruit about the size of an olive. The Indians told William Bartram that the fruit had "the power of charming or drawing that creature to them; from whence, with the traders, it . . . obtained the name of the physic-nut, which means, with them, charming, conjuring, or fascinating."[20] Physic-nuts were transported, along with other paraphernalia, in a buckskin or otter-skin pouch, which might also contain the foot of a small deer, sewed securely in the corner, to lure deer and other game.[21] Creeks also valued special crystals or crystal-like objects of vegetable origin, called *sapiyá*. The crystals were carried, along with red pigment, in a deerskin pouch. Opening the pouch, the hunter allowed the sun's rays to fall across the crystal, which caused it to "dance" in the pigment. The ritual supposedly drew deer to the hunter.[22] Other exotic charms included colored horns taken from a horned snake that lived in deep water. Having obtained the horn, the hunter then needed only to sing in order to tantalize the *itchu*.[23]

Creeks hunted the fur-bearing animals of the Southeast for purely economic motives.[24] Even so, Creek hunters maintained a special relationship with the animals they pursued. Tradition required that slain animals be treated with respect and honor. Failure to follow tribal mores could mean disease or even death for the careless. For example, hunters were proscribed from taking the skins of sick animals. In 1766, a contagious distemper spread through the southeastern backcountry. Indian hunters found deer "lying dead, some in a helpless condition, and others fierce and mad." Fearing pollution from the prostrate beasts, most Creeks avoided contact with the afflicted animals they happened upon. Despite the warnings of a village conjurer, one hunter collected the skins from dead animals anyway. When the hunter later stepped on a cane and injured his foot, knowing Creeks understood the cause of his misfortune.[25] With the passage of time, however, there was a tendency, especially among the young, to abandon many of the old rituals and taboos.[26]

The first buck killed each season was sacrificed as a religious offering, and hunters awarded the choicest parts of the meat to the fire. The trader James Adair noted:

> They commonly pull their new-killed venison (before they dress it) several times through the smoke and flame of the fire, both by the way of a sacrifice, and to consume the blood, life, or animal spirits of the beast. . . . And they sacrifice in the woods, the milt, or a large fat piece of the first buck they kill, both in their summer and winter hunt; and frequently the whole carcass. This they offer up, either as a thanksgiving for the recovery of health, and for their former success in hunting; or that the divine care and goodness may be still continued to them.

They occasionally prepared the venison in their villages. Adair wrote, "They dip their middle finger in the broth, and sprinkle it over the domestic tombs of their dead, to keep them out of the power of evil spirits."[27] Doubtless, there were scores of other rites undertaken by devout Muscogulges. Most of these, and their meaning, have been lost through time.

Before they acquired guns, Creeks hunted with bows and arrows. Often, Creek men disguised themselves with deerskin and cautiously approached browsing deer from downwind. The Frenchman Jean Bossu observed Alabama hunters in 1759: "They take with them into the woods a dried head of the male of the species. They cover their backs with a deer skin and put an arm through the neck of the dried head, into which they have put little wooden hoops for their hands to grip."[28] Thus disguised, the stealthy hunter knelt, raised the stuffed head, shook nearby branches, stamped the ground with his foot, and imitated the buck's mating call. The dominant resident buck moved in quickly to investigate the shenanigans. The ruse allowed a hunter to get close enough to deliver a powerful, and deadly, blow. Even after acquiring guns, Creek hunters continued to use this technique to their advantage. Experts reportedly harvested up to four hundred deer in one winter using this ancient trick.[29] The less fortunate might find themselves the recipient of unwelcome attention from an angry—or amorous—buck.

Wise to the ways of deer, Creeks created clearings around oak and chestnut trees by periodic burning of ground cover. Droves of deer gathered at these clearings in the fall to browse on acorns, woody twigs, berries and fruits of all kinds, and evergreens such as cedar. On his trip through the Alachua Savannah in north peninsular Florida, William Bartram happened upon an area that had recently been burned by the local Seminoles and noted that the savannah was, as the hunters intended, lush with new growth.[30] This very effective habitat management not only attracted deer and gave hunters clear shots at their prey but also made it possible for deer herds to expand by increasing their food supply. It seems logical that hunters established numerous zones of suitable habitat throughout their ranges, to which they returned year after year.[31]

The Muscogulges practiced "wildlife management" for other species as well. Bear were a highly valued game animal but were relatively rare. Thus, each Creek town maintained "a beloved bear ground" of preferred bear habitat composed of canebrakes and hardwood forests that included oak, hickory, and persimmon. Settlements and hunting were restricted in these areas, and bear could be taken only at certain times of the year.[32]

Before the advent of commercial hunting, gangs of hunters used fire to stampede deer into open areas or ravines, where bowmen had clear shots.[33] Creeks continued to use fire drives after they acquired guns.[34] In 1708, Thomas Nairne participated in many fire drives and stated, "Of all hunting deversions, I took most pleasure in firing rings for in that we never missed 7 or 10 Dear." His description is lengthy and instructive:

Three or 4 hours after the ring is fired, of 4 or 5 miles circumferance, the hunters post themselves within as nigh the flame and smoak as they can endure. The fire on each side burns in toward the center and thither the Dear gather from all parts to avoid it, but striving to shun a Death which they might often Escape, by a violent spring, they fall into a Certain one from the Bullets of the hunters who drawing nigher together, as the circle grows less, find an easy pray of the impounded dear, tho seldom kill all for some who find a place wher the Flame is less Violent, Jump out. This sport is the more certain the longer the grownd has been unburned. If it has not for 2 or 3 years there are so many dry leaves grass and Trash, that few Creatures within escape, and the men are forced to go out betimes at some slack place to the lee-ward.[35]

As deer numbers fell and their population density dropped during the eighteenth century, fire drives became far less effective, and their use declined.

White hunters in South Carolina and Georgia stalked deer "in the nighttime, by carrying of lighted torches through the woods." On seeing the fire, deer froze, their gleaming eyes making them easy targets for the night hunter. Although many whites frowned on this practice as being unsportsmanlike, Creek hunters did not eschew this method in their search for whitetails. Night hunting was eventually banned by the legislative assemblies of Georgia and South Carolina, primarily because cows and horses fell victim to night hunters as frequently as did deer. In the nineteenth century, the Muscogulges themselves passed a law concerning the practice. Reflecting the relative importance of hunting to stock raising, the Creek edicts exempted hunters from paying reparations to owners of stock if the hunter killed stock accidentally while setting the woods on fire or while hunting at night.[36]

Guns facilitated the harvest of deer from Creek territories and changed the nature of the hunt. Deception and stealth were still important, but a steady hand and plenty of powder and shot became essential. The most successful hunters were those whose careful and patient observation of deer and their habitat instructed them on the times and places where deer were likely to be. Then, as now, it was essential to know the lay of the land and to understand the regular habits of the deer in a particular area. This meant that hunters usually returned year after year to the same hunting ranges.[37]

Guns were often temperamental, and Indian men, excellent craftsmen well schooled in the art of constructing bows and arrows, quickly learned to repair their new weaponry. According to James Adair: "They can fresh stock their guns, only with a small hatchet and a knife, and streighten the barrels, so as to shoot with proper direction. They likewise alter, and fix all the springs of the lock, with others of the sort they may have out of use; but such a job costs the red artist about two months work."[38]

Temporary dwellings were established at semipermanent hunting camps throughout Creek hunting ranges. These shelters were constructed of stout poles and covered with pine bark and animal skins. An early Georgia settler, Philip Georg Friedrich Von Reck, wrote, "When they camp during travelling or on a hunt, they peel a pine tree and make a hut of bark or else skins and a few poles."³⁹ Some towns erected corncribs in remote areas of their hunting grounds and kept these stocked during the winter for the convenience of hunters.⁴⁰ Hunters traveled to their favorite hunting ground and shelter on horseback but left their horses at camp to stalk deer on foot. James Adair admired Indian stamina: "Their manner of rambling through the woods to kill deer, is a very laborious exercise, as they frequently walk twenty-five or thirty miles through rough and smooth grounds, and fasting, before they return back to camp, loaded."⁴¹

Creek men usually hunted with other men from their own clans. When they hunted in groups, the person who spotted an animal first and wounded it was entitled to the skin, whereas the meat was divided according to prior agreement, based largely on family size and need.⁴² Unless there was danger from enemy war parties, women, with children in tow, usually accompanied their husbands on most hunting expeditions. By the middle of the eighteenth century, it seems that the nuclear family—a hunter, his wife, and children—had become the single most important economic unit in the new Creek hunting economy. Such hunting parties traveled far and wide, usually on horseback. Lieutenant Thomas Campbell, who visited the Upper Creek Towns in 1765, reported that hunters took "horses sufficient with them to carry their provisions, blankets, and wives."⁴³ William Bartram met a Creek hunter, his wife, and children returning to their village from such a hunt. The group was "well mounted on fine horses, with a number of pack-horses" and "loaded with barbecued meat, hides and honey."⁴⁴ And in the early months of 1774, the lieutenant governor of Florida noted, "Several hunting parties with their women and children are among the plantations and not far from St. Augustine."⁴⁵

The need to acquire large numbers of deerskins meant that hunters and their families spent more and more time away from their villages.⁴⁶ The hunt began in October, and Creeks scoured the forest through the hard winter months, usually returning to their villages at the end of February.⁴⁷ By the late eighteenth century, towns were virtually deserted during the hunting season. Left behind were the aged, infirm, unmarried women, and widows and their children. The length of the hunt depended on the success the hunters enjoyed. Lieutenant Thomas Campbell had to wait five months for the hunters to return before he could complete his mission to the Upper Creeks in 1765.⁴⁸

Women performed numerous duties associated with the winter hunt. Before Creeks acquired horses, women carried most of the baggage and household goods, including dried corn and other foodstuffs. At the hunting camps, the hunters' wives were responsible for cooking and for gathering firewood and water. They foraged for hickory nuts and other forest produce while the men were away. When not so employed, women passed the time fashioning mats and baskets and looking after their children.[49] Creek hunters skinned the deer they killed, but their wives butchered the carcasses, smoked the meat, and processed the deerskins for home consumption and trade. Since men hunted in the lands traditionally tended by their clans, hunting temporarily disrupted the pattern of matrilocal residence and accentuated the influence of a woman's husband on her children.[50] For women, this meant more work, since they could no longer count on the assistance of members of their extended matrilineal household in completing routine chores.

Processing deerskins involved a number of time-consuming and tedious steps. After carefully scraping the fat and tissue from the deerskin, the women stretched the skins on frames and dried them in the sun. After drying, the skins were soaked. Then the hair was meticulously scraped from the hide, which was then soaked in a solution of water and deer brains. The skins were then pounded in order to soften them. After the skins had been stretched and dried once more, they were placed over a shallow fire pit and smoked. The skins were also dyed with vegetable pigments and by using different types of wood during the smoking process. The result was a soft and supple leather that women fashioned into leggings, breechcloths, skirts, and a variety of other useful articles. Most deerskins destined for the market were not subjected to such elaborate preparations but were half-dressed, which implied that they had been cleaned and scraped to remove both flesh and hair and had undergone preliminary smoking. Much of this work was done in the hunting camp and was later completed in the towns. Skins dressed by the Indians were more valuable than raw skins, reflecting the women's additional labor and a superior product. It was important that a skin be properly dressed by the Indian women. Poorly processed skins decayed quickly in warm weather, producing foul odors and attracting numerous vermin, especially worms and maggots, which quickly consumed the skins.[51] Unmarried young men and others with undressed skins often struck deals with unlicensed traders, but they received fewer goods, and their skins were most frequently traded for rum.[52]

By the 1760s, according to leading Augusta merchants, the Creeks refused to dress their skins and demanded that the traders take undressed hides at the same rate as dressed skins. Many traders were afraid if they did not take "raw" skins on Creek terms, their customers would go elsewhere, which was often the case. By this time, European leather dressers also began demanding unprocessed skins, and this proved a mixed blessing for the Creeks. Though they thought they were getting a better deal, usually they were not, for undressed skins were bought by the item rather than per pound. Although undressed deerskins did require less preparation, they were not worth as much in relation to trade goods. In effect, this resulted in a hidden rise in prices. Even so, it is apparent that the Creeks, specifically Creek women, perceived that it was to their advantage to trade undressed, rather than dressed, hides.[53]

The emphasis on commercial hunting rapidly depleted deer herds near Creek settlements. As deer numbers declined and Creek hunters had to travel farther from home to kill them, Creek negotiators attempted to have the value of their leather increase proportionally. Unfortunately, this logical application of the law of supply and demand did not work. For though the local supply was scarce, the overall production of leather remained high and exceeded the actual demands of the European leather market.

The smoked meat procured as an adjunct to the hunt was essential to Creek subsistence during the winter. Smoked and dried venison served as the main source of animal protein in the Creek diet throughout the year. On returning to their village, hunters were expected to distribute some of their meat to the elderly and those unable to hunt for themselves, as well as the able-bodied who had remained in the village to protect it from enemies and the conjurers who had provided the medicines that attracted the deer.[54] Young hunters, eager for rum, stripped the deer of their hides and shamelessly left the meat to rot.[55]

Deerskin traders did not have to urge Creeks to hunt—their goods were incentive enough. Unrecorded and thus unknown are the hunters' attitudes regarding the number of deer that it was necessary or desirable to kill. Before the development of a trading economy, Creeks hunted until their needs for meat and skins were satisfied.[56] Presumably, Creeks conducted their commercial hunts until they believed they had acquired enough hides to satisfy their needs, or at least satisfy their account with the village trader. It is impossible to know what other factors might have limited or encouraged their levels of productivity.

Scholars have estimated that the average Indian hunter killed about 20 to 30 deer annually, a figure that seems unduly low given the time and effort

Creek men devoted to hunting. Contemporary evidence suggests much higher yields. A 1741 report estimated that every Indian hunter harvested about 300 pounds of deerskins per year.[57] In the 1770s, William Bartram met a white man in West Florida who reportedly killed more than 300 deer per year.[58] It seems clear that, on average, Creek hunters harvested large numbers of deer, for both home consumption and trade. The lack of hard data on their productivity means that estimates must be based on surviving tax and custom records. Given such factors as the variable weight of deerskins and the incomplete and sometimes conflicting information, only a crude estimate is possible.

In 1764, John Stuart reported that the entire "Quantity of Deer skins Extracted Annually for all the Nations in this District does not exceed Eight Hundred Thousand pounds, half dressed."[59] The actual weight of the deerskins varied, depending on a number of factors including age and sex of the animal, the time of year it was slaughtered, and the animal's home range. The degree to which a skin was processed also affected its final weight. Generally, most southeastern deerskins weighed from 1 to 3 pounds when dressed, and a hide of 2 pounds is generally considered average. Taking a 2-pound deerskin as a benchmark, we find that Stuart's deerskins translate into approximately 400,000 animals, or perhaps up to twice that number, since many skins only weighed 1 pound. Stuart counted 13,941 gunmen, or hunters, in his department. Thus, according to Stuart's statistics, on average, a southeastern Indian hunter produced about 57 pounds of half-dressed skins per year (between 30 and 60 deer).

For many reasons, Creek productivity exceeded that of Stuart's "average" hunter. The Creeks were widely regarded as some of the best hunters in the Southeast, in large part due to their fine hunting ranges. Moreover, they were not troubled by the intense warfare that many other tribes faced, and they enjoyed opportunities to trade for most of the eighteenth century. In contrast, the Cherokees were repeatedly involved in wars with both the colonies and various northern tribes. According to John Stuart, the Cherokees lost one-third of their population to war and famine in the ten-year period from 1756 to 1766. And even though their trade prices were lower than the Creeks, Cherokee production, of necessity, dropped during that very troubled period. Given that the Chickasaw population was very small and that the Choctaws were not fully incorporated into the Anglo-American trading economy by 1764, the Creek percentage of the total southeastern yield was high. A very conservative estimate, derived from Stuart's figures, would place Creek production at an average of 100 pounds of deerskin per year per gunman for trade (about 50 deer per man, assuming each skin weighed 2 pounds). Doubtless those with more skill or luck would produce more, whereas others would do worse. If 4,000 Creek hunters each averaged 100 pounds of leather per year for trade, then the total estimated commercial harvest came to 400,000 pounds of leather or 200,000 deerskins, which is the total usually deduced from various export figures during the late eighteenth century. As the numbers indicate, Creek hunters and their wives were harvesting, at the very least, roughly one-half the deerskins traded in the Southeast during the late eighteenth century. In the 1760s, deerskins were valued at two shillings per pound. At that time, the Creek harvest was worth from six to ten pounds sterling per hunter and reached up to thirty-six thousand pounds sterling for the entire nation.[60]

But these very conservative figures of Creek productivity merely reflect available trade statistics. Significant numbers of deerskins were needed annually for home consumption as well. Leggings, moccasins, fringe, binding, women's garments, breechcloths or flaps, shot pouches, string for bows, game pieces, and household articles such as bedding required a tremendous number of hides.[61] There is no surviving evidence regarding the annual home consumption of deerskins; therefore, a crude estimate will have to suffice. Around 50 to 60 pounds of leather per nuclear family per year (25 to 30 deer) would seem the absolute minimum required to meet basic needs. When the needs of other dependents, such as the elderly, are considered, the annual household consumption probably totaled 100 pounds of leather per household or more.[62]

By taking the very conservative figure of 50 pounds of deerskin per hunter for home consumption and adding it to Stuart's figure for the total export of deerskins from the Southeast, we arrive at a total production of deerskins by all the southeastern Indians of 1.5 million pounds of leather annually.[63] Even this astounding figure does not take into account deerskins spoiled before shipment and other losses, deerskins shipped illegally, or increases in production after 1764. Given that the weight of deerskins varied between 1 and 2 pounds, this figure represents at least 1 million animals.[64]

Deer populations, though large, could not withstand the heavy harvest. In 1765, the Mortar of Okchai, a leading Upper Creek headman, noted with sadness, "Deer skins are become Scarce." He reported that the people from the Upper Towns "had formerly good Success in hunting" but were "now obliged to Cross the Cherokee [Tennessee] River for Game."[65] Hunters found it necessary to travel farther and stay in the field longer to maintain their productivity. White settlers stalked Creek deer as well, and by the middle of the eighteenth century, deer herds had completely disappeared from many areas. Areas of white settlement showed the greatest decline in wild game populations. Part of the problem also lay with the territorial nature of the white-tailed deer. If their food sources disappeared, as often happened when settlers moved in with their cattle and pigs, the deer would not move on to another range: they starved or were hunted out. The relatively long gestation period of deer and their low numbers of offspring (one or two fawns per season) were tremendous handicaps in the maintenance of population numbers when faced with serious predation and disappearance of habitat.[66] The buffalo were hunted out by the early decades of the eighteenth century, and the numbers of beaver, bear, bobcat, panther, and gray and red foxes declined dramatically in the years that followed.

In 1799, William Panton claimed that his company had never failed to export less than 124,000 deerskins (248,000 pounds of leather) annually since the end of the American Revolution in 1783.[67] Panton, Leslie, and Company traded with all the southeastern tribes; therefore, Panton's figures reflect not only Creek productivity but that of the other southeastern tribes as well. Although it is impossible to ascertain the correct percentage produced by the Creeks, it must have been considerable, perhaps between one-half and three-fourths of the company's total business. In 1803, the firm shipped only 79,500 deerskins (which weighed 203,200 pounds) from Pensacola, and these were primarily Creek deerskins. Panton, Leslie, and Company did not handle all the deerskins exported by the southern Indians, but they did handle the majority of the trade. Panton's greatest competitor, the government's Creek factory, which was established after 1796, handled only 50,000 pounds (25,000 skins) per year.[68] And a limited number were still shipped through Georgia. The surviving records, though sketchy, do indicate a slow decline in Creek productivity, which in turn reflected the decreasing numbers of deer. It is obvious that the productivity of Creek hunters dropped considerably with each passing year—perhaps by as much as 50 percent during the last quarter of the eighteenth century.[69] At the same time, Creek population was growing, which meant more hunters were producing fewer skins.[70]

Though commercial hunting and the production of merchantable deer hides remained the backbone of the Creek trade economy, Creeks found other ways to obtain European goods. With the decline of the southeastern deer herds, these activities became important adjuncts to the deerskin trade. In addition to procuring hides and furs for the trade, the Muscogulges offered a variety of goods and services to their Anglo-American allies and modified such traditional customs as gift giving to conform to the realities of the new trade economy.

Creeks engaged in ritual gift exchanges at diplomatic events, and they viewed such gifts as a prerequisite to Indian ceremony and tangible proof of friendship and alliance. The Creeks, who knew the value of their deerskins, regularly presented bundles of peltry to governors and other imperial officials.[71] The gift giving, in the eyes of the British at least, was one-sided. Gradually, the original concept of reciprocal gift exchange had become skewed, and by the late eighteenth century, the British were receiving only token presents of deerskins, turkey buzzard feathers, and calumets from the Creeks, whereas the Indians themselves were the recipients of goods worth thousands of pounds sterling, including arms, ammunition, blankets, clothing, and rum. The British resented it, but Creek headmen constantly reminded them that their king was rich and powerful and could afford to be generous to his poor Creek "Friends and Brothers."[72] Lieutenant Governor John Moultrie of East Florida sensed this and lamented to the Earl of Dartmouth that he had "always fed and clothed their people when they came to see [him] hungry and naked, which was not seldom, for this treatment they took so well that their visits [were] very frequent."[73] When they visited their "elder brothers" in Georgia and the Floridas, the Muscogulges, arguably the best hunters and horticulturalists of the southern backcountry, frequently arrived "hungry and naked" and eagerly pointed out the riches that their allies possessed and were, under Muscogulge tradition, bound to share.

A chief received the "presents" in the name of his town and then redistributed the rum and other goods, usually ammunition, to his warriors. Suits of clothes, guns, and other personal items he retained for his own use.[74] The presents served as a mark of friendship and proof that Britain could supply the Indians. As one scholar has aptly observed, the gifts served to "validate Great Britain's credentials as a patron and trading partner." Wily Creeks saw the gifts as a way to offset high prices, and they never let the British forget that ceremony required presents. Such insistence, at times, earned them a reputation as shameless beggars in British eyes.[75]

Carrying messages for governors, merchants, and the superintendent and his deputies also resulted in "presents" of trade goods. More than gifts, these "presents," as the British insisted on calling them, were wages for services

73

rendered. And the Creeks demanded high wages. In 1766, the charge for carrying a "talk" from the Upper Towns to West Florida was two kegs of rum, a gun, a blanket, boots, a shirt, a flap (breechcloth), and ammunition for each of three men: the equivalent of about eighty pounds of deerskin per man.[76] The British grumbled about the huge expense, but it was the only way to procure necessary services on many occasions. Serving as military auxiliaries was another popular way to earn goods from the British, particularly arms, ammunition, and rum. Such service also presented an opportunity to distinguish oneself in battle, capture booty, and thereby receive additional goods for captives or scalps.[77]

White colonists were filled with fears of Indian-black conspiracies against their settlements and actively discouraged Indian-black interaction. Since blacks often sought refuge from their white masters among the Indian tribes, colonial leaders devised a way to thwart Indian-black friendship as well as keep their captive labor force at work by hiring Indians to capture and return runaway slaves. Creek hunters were also excellent trackers, and throughout the eighteenth century, they served as slave catchers and traders. By the 1770s, every captured runaway was officially worth a gun and three blankets—the equivalent of approximately forty pounds of dressed deerskins. Indian slave catchers could—and often did—decide to sell their black captives on the open market to the highest bidder. This usually meant a Georgia escapee was sold in West Florida or even New Orleans. Though strictly illegal under British law, unscrupulous buyers nonetheless paid Creek slave catchers dearly for such merchandise.[78]

Creeks also participated in what the historian Daniel Usner has termed the frontier exchange economy.[79] In addition to venison, Muscogulges found ready markets for honey and beeswax, hickory nut oil, medicinal roots and herbs, and other produce in West Florida and Georgia. Creek baskets, pottery, finely dyed and decorated deerskins, and other articles were sought by white settlers, soldiers, and travelers.[80] Until 1763, locals offered vegetables, venison, and other wild game, as well as handicrafts, to the French at Fort Toulouse in return for trade goods.[81] After the establishment of British West Florida, one group of Alabama tribesmen received a contract (by treaty) to supply venison and wild fowl for Pensacola.[82] Later, Creeks bartered their produce, including cattle and other foodstuffs, at the factory stores established by the United States along the Creek-Georgia boundary.[83]

In the Creek towns, widows and other needy women received goods in exchange for supplying fresh vegetables, cooking, gathering nuts and berries, cleaning, and washing and mending clothing for traders.[84] If a trader was married, his wife performed these chores, but her family benefited from her alliance with the trader, usually by receiving presents or favorable trade rates. The proliferation of traders after 1763 proved a boon for the local economy. Creek producers exhibited a thorough understanding of the laws of supply and demand by raising the price for fresh vegetables. The "exorbitant" produce prices infuriated old-line traders, who were forced by market economics to go along with the increases.[85]

If traders raised their own vegetables, orphans, widows, and the aged were deprived of income, since traders no longer needed to buy food from them. Headmen refused to allow traders to use ploughs for this reason. With a plough, a trader or his servants and slaves could "easily raise more grain than all the old people of the town could do by using the hoe."[86] Grants of land to traders were kept intentionally small and were usually restricted to the amount of land a single man could clear by himself.[87] Providing for those who could not hunt troubled the Creeks, and this was one of the reasons they opposed the importation of slaves by traders before the American Revolution, since the traders used the slaves mainly to produce food.[88]

Creeks sometimes found customers for their produce among their aboriginal neighbors. Like the Creeks, Cherokee women placed a premium on their corn crop but were often cautious about selling their produce. Perhaps this was due to the fact that war and famine disrupted Cherokee production more often than it did Creek production. And at least on one occasion, in 1759 during the Anglo-Cherokee war, Lower Creeks traded nine ears of corn in return for a single used Cherokee stroud blanket. This was a tremendous bargain for the Creeks—the price of a new blanket was approximately eight dressed deerskins.[89] Creeks did not always sell their vegetables; they continued to distinguish between guests and customers. Envoys and others were still fed at the town's expense from the mico's granary.

The importation of cattle and other livestock into the Creek country by traders also created problems. Creek headmen not only complained about the livestock introduced into their midst by the traders but also refused to allow cattle to be driven through their territory. They had good reasons. The Indians justly feared that the free-ranging cattle would run through unfenced cornfields, destroying their harvest.[90] Cows also frightened deer and other game away from villages and competed with them for food. The availability of beef lowered the demand for venison and other wild game by traders and their employees. Conversely, in the absence of fresh beef, West Floridians turned to Indian hunters for their meat supply.[91]

A few headmen acquired cattle and some attempted to profit by selling their stock at Pensacola or St. Augustine. The best-known herdsman of the eighteenth century, Ahaye (Ahoya) of Alachua, was called the Cowkeeper. His contemporary, the Wolf of Muccolossus, also had a sizable herd of cattle.[92] But there were few Creek cow keepers. Large-scale stock raising simply could not coexist with deer hunting, and Muscogulge complaints concerning cattle spanned the colonial period.[93] Just as the Indians believed that deer and other game animals were responsible for a variety of afflictions, they blamed cattle for an outbreak of disease among humans in 1767. It "began with sharp pains in the head, at the lower part of each of the ears, and swelled the face and throat in a very extraordinary manner, and also the testicles." Those afflicted believed they had contracted the strange new disease from eating beef the traders had brought into their towns, since "their heads, necks, &c. magnified like the same parts of a sick bull." The coincidence undoubtedly hindered the shift from commercial hunting to stock raising among the Creeks.[94] But the American Revolution created lucrative markets for native beef in both East and West Florida, and the few Creek stockmen profited handily.

Although most Creeks disapproved of cattle, they welcomed horses into their country. *Echoclucco (ítchu láko),* which literally means big deer in the Muskogee language, had become an integral part of Creek life by the early part of the eighteenth century. Commenting on the prevalence of horses in the Indian nations, James Adair wrote, "But almost every one hath horses, from two to a dozen; which makes a considerable number, through their various nations." Women, in order to spare their tender vegetables and corn, tethered horses from planting through harvest.[95] Most of the horses raised in the Lower Creek and Seminole territories were descendants of Andalusian horses first brought to Florida by the Spanish. William Bartram, like scores of others, admired these sturdy ponies. "They are the most beautiful and sprightly species of that noble creature, perhaps any where to be seen; but are of a small breed, and as delicately formed as the American roe-buck." The horses of the Upper Creeks, widely known as Choctaw or Chickasaw horses, could reputedly trace their origin to the Spanish lands west of the Mississippi River. The Upper Creek horses were larger than those of the Lower Creeks and Seminoles, and Bartram noted that they were "perhaps not so lively and capricious."[96] Horses not only served as beasts of burden and provided transportation but also were a valuable trade commodity throughout the Southeast. Many headmen maintained stocks of horses and invented their own brands to distinguish their horses from those of others.

In addition to selling horses outright to obtain goods, on many occasions Creek stockmen retained title and collected fees for the use of their horses.[97]

Those who did not own horses soon learned how to acquire them. It took less time, conjuring, and effort to steal horses from white settlements than to stalk deer in the forest. Many Creek hunters, observing that the white people with their horses and cattle had usurped Indian hunting grounds, did not always view their actions as thievery. But there were acknowledged gangs of lawless Creek horse thieves. In 1769, one of the most notorious gangs pinched forty-seven fine horses from the Quaker community of Wrightsborough, Georgia. The Quakers formed a posse and paid a visit to the camp of the offending Creeks.[98] The leader of the Indian gang, an acknowledged murderer, "ordered the Indians to their guns, tomahawks and knives, [and] behaved in a most provoking manner, holding a tomahawk edgeways to a white man's face and threw out many threatenings which the white people forbore to resent, notwithstanding they were double the Indians number."[99] The Quakers, true to their principles, did not strike back and ultimately left it to colonial authorities to recover their horses. Other settlers, particularly the Irish at Queensborough, were not so pacific when their horses disappeared. And the thieves took Indian horses as well.[100] By the end of the eighteenth century, the capture and sale of stolen horses had become a thriving business all along the frontier. The horse thieves were not always men. In 1765, Emisteseguo of Little Tallassee recommended that women be given presents along with the men, since they often stole horses to trade for European goods.[101]

Unmarried women, or those whose husbands traded their skins for rum, occasionally used their feminine attraction to boost their earning capacity. William Bartram, respectable Quaker that he was, could not help himself from gawking at a "ludicrous bacchanalian" scene performed by a party of forty Seminole warriors bound for war against the Choctaws. The warriors, together with their traders and some women, consumed about twenty kegs of rum, roughly one hundred gallons. The men begged the women to drink with them. The sober Bartram watched in amusement as the women seemingly consented to the "frolick." They carefully pretended to drink but actually spat the rum into bottles they had hidden in their clothing. After the fun had ended, the women then sold their "recycled" rum to the merrymakers. Bartram wrote that the "dejected lifeless sots would pawn every thing they were in possession of, for a mouthful of spirits to settle their stomachs, as they termed it" when they began to sober up.[102]

Casual sexual liaison between Creek women and traders provided another avenue to obtain trade goods. The surveyor and historian Bernard Romans noted in the 1760s, "[Creek women] will never scruple to sell the use of their bodies when they can do it in private; a person who wishes to be accommodated here can generally be supplied for payment, and the savages think a young woman nothing the worse for making use of her body, as they term it."[103] Though single women were not rebuked for such encounters, the situation regarding married women was quite different.[104]

Opportunities to become a seller rather than a buyer resulted in the slow development of a new economic class among the Creeks. Before 1763, astute Creeks took advantage of trade-starved Choctaws. In 1757, a party of Choctaws attempted to trade with the French at Fort Toulouse. The French, who wanted to keep the Choctaws away from the English and avoid riling the Creeks, directed the Choctaws to native entrepreneurs. Accordingly, about fifty Choctaws turned their deerskins over to jubilant Creeks in exchange for worn blankets, flaps, shirts, and other goods. The Creeks then swapped the Choctaw peltry for new goods, at substantial advantage to themselves.[105]

It was a common and necessary precaution for traders to secure protection from the village chief, usually by marriage to a close female relative. For his protection and support, a headman received favorable rates and presents from the trader. Though few headmen participated directly in the trade, many other Creeks did. Bernard Romans noted, "There [are] few towns in this nation where there is not some savage residing, who either trades of his own stock, or is employed as a factor."[106] Unscrupulous whites found it advantageous to hire Indian factors, since they were exempt from British or colonial trade laws. A Creek factor could trade goods "in the woods" more easily and circumvent any limits on the sale of rum and ammunition or the extension of credit. Neatohowki, the Cowkeeper of Latchoway's nephew, operated a saloon near Spalding's licensed St. John's River store. He procured liquor from Spalding and returned the deerskins he obtained to the store. Still, Spalding could rightly claim that he did not traffic in liquor.[107]

Through marriage and apprenticeship, mixed-bloods swiftly climbed the economic and social ladders within Creek society. None illustrate this better than a young *mustee* Creek who was employed as a packhorseman for traders from Muccolossus. His mother had been a Choctaw slave among the Creeks and had been adopted by a Creek clan; thus he enjoyed full Creek citizenship. His father was of mixed Creek and white blood. This young *mustee,* whose name was not recorded, augmented his position in the trading economy by marrying one of the headman's daughters and thus becoming a brother-in-law of the town trader, who was married to another of the headman's daughters.[108]

A number of Creeks managed to become independent traders. One of the most successful Indian traders before the American Revolution was Bosten, or Boatswain, of Apalachicola, who acquired a sizable fortune through his trade with Georgia. Bosten delivered deerskins, furs, hides, tallow, oils, and honey via horse and boat to Frederica or Savannah. There, he purchased sugar, coffee, and "every other kind of goods suitable to the Indian markets." By the late colonial period, he owned fifteen slaves and had almost one hundred acres of land fenced and under cultivation. William Bartram visited his substantial establishment and left a careful record of the dwelling, cookhouse, and warehouse. Bosten left an indelible impression on the naturalist, who believed he had found positive proof that it was possible "for the Creeks to be brought over to our modes of civil society."[109] Bartram noted that Indian factors and traders had extensive dwelling compounds. He added, "Smaller or less wealthy families make one, two, or three houses serve all their purposes as well as they can."[110] This pattern of multiple household dwellings extended back to Mississippian times, but the Apalachicola trader had changed the function and the meaning of the Creek household. It was undergoing a subtle shift from the shelter of a matrilineage to a commercial establishment.

Bosten was certainly among the most successful Indian traders, but others acquired similar wealth and began to adopt the trappings of white society. After the revolutionary war, the number of Indians acting as agents for trading companies increased dramatically as seasoned traders retired, leaving Panton, Leslie, and Company little choice but to employ native agents, most of whom were the sons of white traders. By the end of the eighteenth century, Creek storekeepers were commonplace.

The Muscogulges were relatively successful in modifying traditional subsistence tasks to accommodate the demands of the new trade economy. Although the Creeks devised numerous products and services to barter for manufactured goods, procuring and processing large numbers of deerskins always remained at the heart of the Creek trade economy. But if the Muscogulges believed that they controlled their own economic destiny, they were mistaken. The decisions of foreign governments and the vagaries of European markets determined not only exchange rates but also the demand for Creek deerskins. And though life might appear little changed on the surface, in subtle—and important—ways, commercial hunting and other production activities worked slowly and surely to change native society in a manner the Creeks themselves could not have imagined and did not fully understand.

CHAPTER 5

Traders and
Trading

The southern Indian trade was a complex economic enterprise, and the primary aim of all Indian traders was to make a profit by procuring deerskins for British markets. The flow of goods to the Indian country and hides to overseas markets required a variety of skills, talents, and of course, capital. The years following the Yamasee War witnessed the development of fairly standard trading procedures by backcountry merchants and traders, methods that were designed to minimize difficulties and maximize profits from the deerskin trade. Colonial squabbling and jealousy inhibited the development of an organized bureaucracy designed to oversee the trade, and there were no imperial regulations until relatively late in the colonial period. What developed instead, through a scattering of rules and regulations, was a de facto system that was supported by the leading Indian merchants and traders. Traders were granted licenses by South Carolina, and later Georgia, to trade at specific Indian towns. In turn, they posted bond and agreed to abide by various regulations established by the colony of their legal residence. Traders' conduct was subjected to cursory review by officials from both colonies, but for the most part, traders were left alone to do business. After 1763, the removal of the French, a rising colonial population, and the overthrow of colonial regulations by the British government disrupted—but did not end—established trading procedures. The time-honored methods of trading conduct established in the years following the Yamasee War outlasted both the British occupation and the deerskin herds of the American Southeast.

In general, those involved in the trade fell into the following categories: wholesale merchant, retail storekeeper, resident trader, packhorseman, boatman, and wage and slave labor, both skilled and unskilled. In the eighteenth century, the term *merchant* generally implied an importer-exporter who sold goods at wholesale prices, and this definition applied to the large Charleston merchants who were involved in the southern Indian trade. The foreign export portion of the deerskin trade was largely handled by Charleston merchants who conducted business for themselves and also acted as factors for British firms, meaning that they conducted business for British firms for a percentage of the transaction. A number of Charleston merchants owned frontier retail stores during the late seventeenth and early eighteenth centuries. But the shortage of honest and competent employees and the near impossibility of collecting money from debtors tended to drive Charleston merchants out of the frontier outlet business. Instead, the retail business was soon taken over by prosperous traders or "victuallers" who had established credit with coastal merchant houses and acquired trusted employees who could act as their substitutes and storekeepers in the Indian towns.[1]

There was a discernible pattern of economic advance among those involved in the trade. In the beginning, a man started out as an assistant to a well-established trader. Many young boys entered the trade as packhorsemen. During this period of apprenticeship, the neophyte trader—known variously as a deputy or assistant trader, a hireling, or simply a servant—learned the language and customs of the Indians and the fine points of conducting successful trade relations. Within a few years, he could obtain enough capital to buy his own goods or at least build a sufficient reputation to obtain credit and thereby proceed as an independent trader. If he was honest, he might obtain a license from either South Carolina or Georgia, or both, and secure his position at specific Indian towns. In time, and with a little luck, he might obtain slaves and hire laborers to work for him.[2] The ultimate achievement was to obtain a partnership with a frontier merchant or storekeeper.

The most successful traders, without exception, shared three related characteristics: good business organization, good character, and good personal relations with their Creek customers. All the principal Creek traders were members of trading companies and were experienced professionals who had spent many years in the trade.[3] Joining into partnerships with other traders kept overhead low and reduced competition in the Indian country. The members of the leading firms knew each other well and frequently assisted one another along the trade paths and in the Indian villages.[4] Like other businesses in the eighteenth century, most trading partnerships were based on friendship, similar backgrounds and ethnic origins, and family connections.[5] Second, the leading traders were usually the ones who were the most honest, or perhaps the least dishonest, and who, by long association, managed to gain the trust and regard of their customers. It was not only luck but also character that separated those who flourished from those who failed. George Galphin, arguably the most successful colonial Creek trader, prospered because of the good name he held among the Creeks. He acquired their respect the proven way. "I allwise made it a rule to tell them the Truth, which is the reason they allways put so much Confidence in what I say."[6] Trust was essential. William Struthers received the highest compliment from the Creeks when, based on his long and fair dealings with them, they nominated him for a position in the British Indian Department.[7] Finally, the successful trader always operated a well-stocked store in a specific Indian town under the protection of the local headman.

When white traders first appeared among the Creeks, the village mico often cemented his friendship with the trader by arranging a marriage to his niece or other female relative. Virtually every Creek trader took an Indian wife and raised a mixed-blood family. The Creeks accepted these unions as visible testimony of a trade alliance.[8] There were advantages for those traders who took a Creek wife. At the most basic level, marriage to a Creek woman linked an outsider to a specific clan, which supported him, protected him, and also guaranteed a certain number of customers from the clan network. Marriage, for practical purposes, meant that the trader became an honorary member of his wife's clan.[9] The traders realized these advantages, embraced the opportunity, and alarmed the French by such antics as "marrying [the Indians'] daughters and drinking and eating with them very familiarly."[10] As Thomas Nairne noted at the beginning of the eighteenth century:

> It is the easiest thing in the world, for an English Traveller to procure kindred among the Indians, It's but taking a mistress of such a name [clan], and he has at once relations in each Village, from Charles Town to the Missisipi, and if in travelling he acquants them with what fameily he is incorporated into, those of that name [clan] treat, and wait on him as their kinsman. There are some of our Countryman of such prudence and forecast, that in case one family should fail them, take care to make themselves akin to severall.[11]

At a more intimate level, Creek women provided companionship, served as interpreters, and helped their husbands learn the language and customs of their people faster. Creek women facilitated debt collection, tanned undressed deerskins procured through the trade, kept their husbands informed of tribal temperament, and warned them when there was danger. One eighteenth-century observer recorded,

> Traders are fully sensible how greatly it is to their advantage to gain their [Creek women's] affections and friendship in matters of trade and commerce; and if their love and esteem for each other is sincere, and upon principles of reciprocity, there are but few instance of their neglecting or betraying the interests and views of their temporary husbands; they labour and watch constantly to promote their private interests, and detect and prevent any plots or evil designs which may threaten their persons, or operate against their trade or business.[12]

The wife of the Upper Creek trader Richard Bailey shared "in all the toils of her husband when there was a necessity for it. She attended the pack horses to market, swam rivers to facilitate the transportation of their goods," and was "careful of the interest of her family and resolute in support of it."[13] In addition, when their husbands were away from their stores, Creek wives and their male relatives protected the trading establishments and looked after the traders' interests. For in Creek eyes, the trader's store, stock, and homestead were actually the property of his wife and her children.[14]

By marriage to important women, traders gained intimacy with village headmen. It is not surprising that many powerful eighteenth-century headmen came to be known by such appellations as Duvall's Landlord or McBean's Friend. Yet though the leading Creeks "allied" to traders by marriage received some material benefit, the alliance also carried with it the burden of settling differences between the trader and fellow villagers and addressing all concerns relating to the trade—a tremendous responsibility. In addition, the established traders were often accused of being greedy and monopolizing the trade. Still, the Creeks preferred that the number of traders be limited. The countless Muscogulge "landlords" and "friends" could thus supervise these "foreigners" and make sure they behaved properly within the context of Creek society.

Women who married traders usually benefited from the relationship. The wives of traders were important sources of information and advice for village leaders. With their brothers, uncles, and sons, these women often made key decisions concerning foreign relations. Gaining access to, and in some cases control of, a trader's stock of trade goods augmented the natural authority and prestige these women already possessed in the Creek community. And there were material benefits. One Creek headman believed traders were forced to charge high prices for their goods in order to recover the losses they incurred by giving large quantities of trade goods to their wives and mistresses. Some women did not wait for presents from their husbands. William Bartram witnessed the distress of one love-sick deerskin trader whose wife had ruined him by freely distributing all his goods to her relatives.[15]

Traders who married Indian women and established households in the Indian country, according to James Adair, "possessed all the needful things to make a reasonable life easy."[16] The "firm streaked bacon" produced by hogs raised in the Indian towns was reputed to be better than that available to settlers along the coast. Cattle were prized for their milk production, in addition to beefsteak. Chickens and goats added to the din around a trader's establishment. Following their husbands' instruction, Creek women learned to churn butter and make cheese and to substitute pork and beef for venison and bear.[17] What comforts the Creek country lacked were imported, and traders included chocolate, coffee, and sugar in their packs, in addition to other things. Traders introduced apples, peaches, potatoes, and other crops to Creek horticulturalists. Those with a taste for sweets also brought recipes, and Indian women learned to turn out "puddings, pyes, pastries, fritters and many other articles of the like kind" for their husbands. Traders did indeed, as James Adair asserted, live "in the greatest plenty."[18]

The free-ranging pigs and cattle were irksome to Creeks, since the livestock often damaged crops. To avoid this, traders usually established their dwellings "at a very convenient distance" from the town they served.[19] The inhabitants of Tallassee, on receiving a request from a trader to establish a homestead, took him to the Coosa River, "marked the front on the river and permitted him to call all his that he could clear and cultivate."[20] Under Creek custom, the town retained actual ownership of the land, and any produce of the fields was considered the property of the trader's wife. Creek traders, however, showed a remarkable disinclination to accept the native view and persistently believed they owned property in the Indian country. The Creeks knew better and silently humored their thickheaded guests.

Traders' dwellings and stores differed little from those of their Creek neighbors, with the exception that the former were usually larger—and could be bolted up. James Adair related that like the Indians, traders usually built a dwelling house, corncribs, chicken houses, a winter hothouse, and a storehouse for their goods. Traders adhered to native custom and whitewashed their dwellings "either with decayed oyster-shells, coarse-chalk, or white marly clay." Adair mused that the establishments of the traders, with "their various buildings," were "like towers in cities, beyond the common size of those of the Indians."[21] At Muccolossus, the trading post, like the households of the Muscogulges, "formed a complete square . . . [of] four oblong buildings of equal dimensions, two opposite to each other, encompassing an area of about a quarter of an acre."[22]

A trader's life followed a seasonal rhythm, linked to the winter hunt. Traders purchased supplies and began making their way to their stores by late summer. Their stores were opened by autumn, in order to fit out the hunters. By early November, it was possible to have goods worth up to one thousand pounds sterling within the confines of a Muscogulge store. Traders generally left their establishments at least once a year to exchange their deerskins and other peltry for trade goods, check in with their employers or partners, and take care of personal business in their home colony. Generally, they left the Indian territory in early May for Augusta or, later, Pensacola. The departure of the traders from the Creek towns coincided with the planting season, which meant that the deerskins arrived in Charleston or Pensacola during the late spring and were shipped during the hottest season of the year, resulting in a high spoilage rate.[23]

Though they married Creek women, most traders knew little of Creek "domestic economy." Benjamin Hawkins questioned a number of longtime Creek traders concerning the habits and daily lives of the Indians when he first visited the Creek towns in 1796. Mr. Marshall, a trader with twelve years of experience and two Creek wives, explained his ignorance of Creek households by "saying that during the whole of his residence he had not entered 3 of the Indian houses, that whatever business he had with the men he went to their doors, mentioned it to them, said and did what was necessary and left them, or sat under their corn house."[24] David Hay, who had resided among the Creeks for five years by the time he made Hawkins's acquaintance, said he had never entered an Indian house until he did so in the company of the agent and "had had no intercourse with the women."[25] Since these men had not frequented the households of the natives, Hawkins thought it meant that the traders had "no social intercourse" with their customers.[26] Though this was doubtless true in some cases, traders were regularly welcomed in the village square and were present at all the ceremonial occasions in Creek life, including ball play, dances, and celebrations of all kinds, particularly those conducive to rum drinking.

Although never privy to all the inner workings of town government and family life, the local trader was still a valued member of the community. Those who established links with leading headmen functioned as ambassadors, messengers, translators, and spies for their own governments. Likewise, many served as advisors and spokesmen for the Creeks. Directly and indirectly, they were the middlemen between two cultures. The majority developed a healthy respect and admiration for the virtues of Indian society. James Adair, the only trader to describe the life of the trader, wrote that in "all the Indian countries," each person lived "at his own choice, not being forced in the least degree to any thing contrary to his own inclination."[27] And Adair fondly recalled the many "gay hours" of friendly discussion he and other traders had enjoyed with their Indian hosts over the relative merits of Indian and white customs. Adair was especially impressed by the "natural, pertinent, and humorous observations" made by Indians regarding white society.[28]

Traders and the micos who protected them often developed lasting friendships, and headmen were fiercely devoted to their traders. Personal loyalty was especially important in the cutthroat business of the deerskin trade. In 1735, the Georgia agent Patrick MacKay stormed through the Creek towns seizing goods and expelling traders who held no Georgia license. But when he put the Okfuskee trader William Edwards in irons and had him tied to the town's chunkey pole in order to whip him for alleged misconduct, the mico of the Okfuskees demanded that his trader be set free. About the same time, Captain Allick of Cussita interposed himself in the dispute and pitched the Georgians out of town for harassing his trader.[29] Doubtless John Spenser delivered many thanks as well as more tangible rewards to his landlord, the Wolf of the Muccolossus, who prevented a French-inspired Creek mob from looting the trader's store and killing Spenser.[30]

Once securely established, a resident trader addressed his overriding concern: to exchange his imported trade goods for Indian peltry. The furs of beaver, bear, fox, and raccoon were sought for the British market, but the standard medium of exchange between Creek and trader was the skin of the white-tailed deer. The volume and the importance of the trade in deerskins beg the question of exactly what use the British made of the skins. Leatherworking was one of the largest industries in England. By the end of the eighteenth century, London had become the center of the tanning and leather-dressing industry, and much of the leather produced in London and other ports found ready markets not only in Europe but in America as well.[31]

Malachy Postlethwayt, the author of *The Universal Dictionary of Trade and Commerce* (1774), asserted, "It may be affirmed, with great truth, that the skins of our production, and those imported from our NORTH AMERICAN COLONIES, when dressed in this kingdom, make the best leather in the world."[32] Buckskin, the term for deerskins that had been dehaired and processed into a workable product, had a suede finish and was light, porous, and very tough. It was especially suited for clothing, gloves, and footwear. The demand for deerskins hinged on men's fashions. Yellow buckskin breeches were becoming increasingly fashionable by the middle of the eighteenth century. At first, they were worn only by laborers, but comfort and utility made them popular with all classes, including gentlemen. Postlethwayt reported that they were "universally worn from the tradesmen to those of first rank in the kingdom."[33] And they were becoming increasingly popular abroad. Buckskin breeches, it seems, served as the eighteenth-century equivalent of modern denim jeans. In the early part of the century, one type of English-made headgear, the "South Carolina hat," was fashioned from deerskin. Some deerskin was made into clothing in the colonies as well.[34] French manufacturers found it more cost-effective to purchase undressed skins from English leather sellers than to buy English-made breeches because of the government drawback on undressed hides. These undressed deerskins were then dressed and made into breeches in France and exported to foreign markets. But Postlethwayt was convinced that breeches made in France were "inferior in many respects" to those manufactured in England.[35] Deerskins were also sought by glovers, harness makers, saddlers, and bookbinders.[36]

By the 1760s, Creek deerskins had earned a reputation for quality and were preferred by London merchants over those of the Cherokees, according to the Savannah merchant James Habersham.[37] Traders obtained a variety of deerskins through the trade, but in general the skins were classified as dressed, half-dressed, or undressed, depending on the degree of processing. Indian dressed skins, or simply dressed skins, were fully processed by the Indians. Half-dressed skins were stripped of both flesh and hair but received little additional processing. Undressed skins, known variously as raw or green skins, or "skins in the hair," had been minimally processed to remove the flesh and, as one name implies, still held the hair.[38]

Deerskins were also graded by weight. Deerskins from the ranges of the Upper Towns were about twice the size of those from the Florida peninsula, were heavier, and were of better quality. A dressed deerskin weighed from one to two pounds, a pound being eighteen ounces. The skin of a mature buck weighed about two pounds, whereas dressed skins from younger bucks and does weighed only one pound.[39] Raw skins, on average, weighed three pounds and were bought by tally, reflecting their lower value. Traders lopped the snouts, ears, horns, and hooves off deerskins, a tactic that offended Indian sensibilities in addition to reducing the weight of the skin. Nonetheless, traders claimed that good, well-dressed, and trimmed skins reduced the weight of carriage and better preserved the hides.[40]

A dressed skin that weighed one pound was called a *chalk*, and tallies were kept by the use of vertical and diagonal lines so that Creek customers could clearly see their credits and debits. Larger skins, depending on weight, were worth two or three chalks.[41] The weight, quality, and manner of processing complicated exchange practices. In 1718, the South Carolina Indian Commissioners included the following rather nebulous guidelines in their trading licenses: "receiving all light drest Deer Skins (under a Pound Weight, each) after the Rate of three Hides, for two Pounds of heavy Skins; all heavy raw Deer Skins (weighing two Pounds and upwards, each) equal to a Pound Weight of heavy drest; raw Deer Skins not weighing two Pounds nor under a Pound, each, equal to a light drest Skin."[42]

By the last quarter of the eighteenth century, the demand for dressed deerskins fell while the demand for raw skins rose due to the requirements of the European leather industry. This consequently changed the value of a chalk. According to William Panton: "If the skin is small it goes for one chalk, if middling for two, if Large for three, & over. Sometimes four or five chalks is allowed for a very large buckskin." Usually, however, deerskins were bought for only one or two chalks credit, the larger animals being rare.[43]

Exchange rates were widely discussed and established between the Creeks and their traders.[44] These price schedules were attached to Creek treaties with the colonies and were based on an exchange rate of pounds of dressed leather per trade good or, for some items, number of skins per trade good. Although treaties and other regulations stipulated the use of scales to weigh deerskins, Indians frequently questioned the reliability of scales—usually with good reason. In 1738, Tomochichi confided to Oglethorpe that traders from Carolina commonly used bad weights. He therefore requested that official brass weights and scaled measures specifically designed for the trade be lodged with each village headman. Still, many Creeks distrusted the unfamiliar scales, although the Gun Merchant of Okchai, one of the most powerful Upper Creeks before 1776, did not. In 1756, he received a steel-yard scale and lessons on its use from Governor Lyttelton of South Carolina. The Gun Merchant believed that if the headmen controlled the scales, it would be more difficult for the traders to defraud their people. But scales, especially accurate scales, were virtually nonexistent in the Creek country. Of necessity, Indians became adept at accurately estimating the weight of their deerskins, and both traders and Creeks usually judged weight by feel.[45]

Trade goods were parceled out in a variety of ways. Cloth was measured by the yard or was traded in precut pieces. Beads were sold by the strand, powder was measured in handfuls or pints, and balls of shot were counted individually. Vermilion was often measured by the amount that would cover the tip of a knife.[46] Rum was sold in quart bottles or in kegs of four gallons.[47]

Transportation of goods to and from the Indian country presented a number of problems for the trader. In the early years of the trade, before horses were common, it was not unusual for the Indians to carry their peltry on their backs to frontier settlements in order to trade. But the growth of trading companies with resident trader-storekeepers who supervised the transportation of goods on packhorses to and from the Indian towns eliminated the need for Indian porters, who were rarely used in the Creek trade after the Yamasee War. Still, it was possible, even as late as the 1740s, to see Indians returning home from the colonial conferences with their "presents" strapped on their back. On one of his journeys through Creek territory, James Adair met the Wolf King of the Muccolossus "harnessed like a jack-ass, with a saddle on his back, well girt over one shoulder, and across under the other." But such sights were rare, and most Creeks—and traders—traveled the trading path on horseback.[48]

The path that led from Augusta into the Creek country split into two main branches, known as the Upper Path and the Lower Path, but numerous side traces linked the two major arteries and meandered through every Creek town. The Creeks knew the route well and called it "the old white path."[49] The Upper Path passed through the Upper Creek Towns at Okfuskee and continued westward to the Chickasaw and Choctaw towns. One branch from the Upper Path led to the Cherokee villages. The Lower Path's primary destination was Coweta, in the Lower Towns. From Coweta, it continued on to the Upper Towns and eventually passed by Fort Toulouse. There it divided, with one artery heading northwest to the Chickasaw towns and the other heading west toward the Choctaw country.[50]

The route from Augusta to the Creek country was "a very bad stoney and

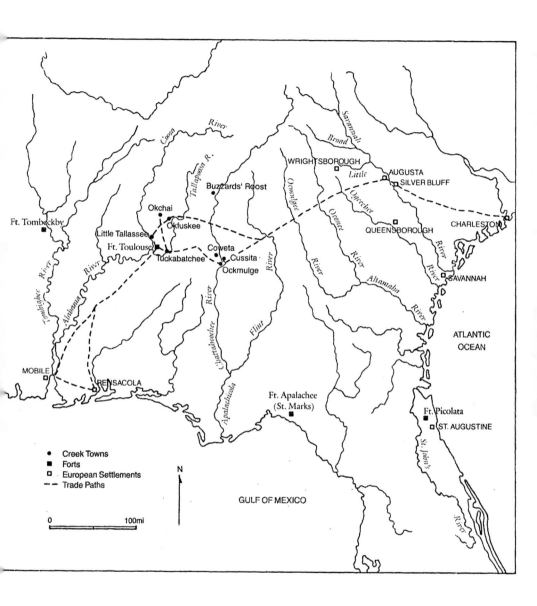

Ft. Tombeckby

Coosa River

Tallapoosa R.

Buzzards' Roost

Okchai

Okfuskee

Little Tallassee

Ft. Toulouse

Tuckabatchee

Coweta

Cussita

Ockmulge

WRIGHTSBOROUGH

Little

AUGUSTA

SILVER BLUFF

QUEENSBOROUGH

CHARLESTON

SAVANNAH

Savannah

Broad

Ogeechee

Oconee

Ogeechee

River

Tombigbee River

Alabama River

Chattahoochee River

Flint

Apalachicola

Altamaha River

ATLANTIC
OCEAN

MOBILE

PENSACOLA

Ft. Apalachee
(St. Marks)

Ft. Picolata

ST. AUGUSTINE

St. John's

•   Creek Towns
■   Forts
□   European Settlements
--   Trade Paths

N

GULF OF MEXICO

0   100mi

2. The Creek Country and Contiguous European Settlements, 1772

hilly Path," which made travel "tedious."[51] In 1767, Roderick McIntosh, who was visiting the Creek nation on official business for the superintendent of Indian affairs, took twenty days to travel from Augusta to Little Tallassee. Even though McIntosh was ill during the journey, the trip was not unusually long. It took James Oglethorpe twenty-seven days to travel from Charleston to the Alabama towns. A typical journey from Apalachicola, on the Chattahoochee River, to Augusta took David Taitt eight days in 1772.[52] On average, most traders expected to cover about 25 miles per day.[53] The path from Pensacola into the Creek country was narrow, and horses traveled single file. Lieutenant Thomas Campbell, who made an official journey to the Upper Creek Towns in 1764, spent eleven days traveling from Pensacola to Muccolossus, a distance of roughly 220 miles.[54]

The primary method of transportation was by horse, and caravans of traders with their packhorsemen to tend the animals were common along the trails leading in and out of the Creek country. One Georgia report in the early 1740s estimated that "above two thousand Horses" converged on Augusta in early spring, at the close of the hunting and trading season.[55] Caravans were usually composed of from sixty to one hundred horses, there being safety and efficiency in numbers. Galphin reportedly employed four hundred packhorses in his business.[56] A packhorseman's job was difficult and sometimes dangerous. But it was also profitable, and those involved in the trade could expect to earn from two to four times more than most other colonial laborers.[57]

In the 1840s, the historian Albert James Pickett interviewed a number of retired deerskin traders for his *History of Alabama*. Pickett's description is worth noting.

> The pack-horses used in this trade were generally small ones, raised in the nation, but were capable of sustaining heavy loads and of enduring great fatigue. A saddle of a peculiar shape was first placed upon the pony. The load consisted of three bundles, each weighing sixty pounds. Two of these bundles were suspended across the saddle, and came down by the sides of the pony, while the third was deposited on top of the saddle. The whole pack was covered with a skin to keep off the rain. Thus the pony sustained a load of one hundred and eighty pounds. Even liquids were conveyed in the same manner. Taffai [tafia], a mean rum, was carried on these horses in small kegs. Indeed, these hardy animals transported everything for sale; and even poultry

of all kinds was carried in cages made of reeds strapped upon their backs.[58]

William Bartram traveled the Creek path from West Florida to the Upper Creek Towns during the early 1770s in the company of a trade caravan. The thoughtful scholar found the journey unbearable.

> They seldom decamp until the sun is high and hot; each one having a whip made of the toughest cow-skin, they start at once, the horses having ranged themselves in regular Indian file, the veteran in the van, and the youngest in the rear; then the chief drives with the crack of his whip, and a whoop or shriek, which rings through the forests and plains, speaks in Indian, commanding them to proceed, which is re-peated by all the company, when we start at once, keeping up a brisk and constant trot, which is incessantly urged and continued as long as the miserable creatures are able to move forward; and then come to camp, though frequently in the middle of the afternoon, which is the pleasantest time of the day for travelling: and every horse has a bell on, which being stopped when we start in the morning with a twist of grass or leaves, soon shakes out, and they are never stopped again dur-ing the day. The constant ringing and clattering of the bells, smacking of the whips, whooping and too frequent cursing these miserable quadrupeds, cause an incessant uproar and confusion, inexpressibly disagreeable.[59]

When the caravan stopped for the day, the horses were unloaded and turned out to graze. A good part of the early morning was spent in rounding them up and reloading before the journey continued.[60]

The path was frequently interrupted by creeks and rivers. During the dry season, these were usually easy to ford. Larger rivers and streams were overlaid by "raccoon bridges," which were merely large trees felled across the banks. Horses were unloaded and swam across while the humans carried the baggage over on their backs. During periods of high water, these bridges were sometimes still effective, as David Taitt found in 1772 when the bridge he crossed was covered by three feet of water.[61] Swift-running creeks and larger rivers required more effort to cross. Thomas Nairne described the crude leather floats used by early traders: "They take a Bare skine, or large raw buck skine, without holes (or these sowed up,) this they lay up at the four corners and therein place anything of 50, 60 or 100 weight, their Gun fastned on Top of all, which they hold by the end, and therewith push the boat before them themselves swimming after. Thus they transport Powder Broad Cloth or any other goods without takeing the least wett." These floats could carry loads of up to one hundred pounds and were used to transport all manner of goods.[62] By the middle of the eighteenth century, traders hauled stout tanned-leather canoes. "At every River where they are to use it, they stretch it with stakes made on Purpose."[63] These ingeniously designed vessels were constructed from large pieces of tanned deerskin, "the sides over-lapped about three fingers breadth, and well sewed with three seams." According to James Adair's description, "Around the gunnels, which are made of sapplings, are strong loop-holes, for large deer-skin strings to hang down both the sides: with two of these, is securely tied to the stem and stern, a well-shaped sappling, for a keel, and in like manner the ribs." Adair reckoned that such a "leathern barge" was "fit to carry over ten horse loads at once, in the space of half an hour."[64] Like the simpler leather floats, the leather canoes were pushed, rather than paddled, by the traders.

For river travel, as opposed to transporting merchandise, Indians and traders used canoes hewn from oak logs. Benjamin Hawkins crossed the Ocmulgee River in a native boat in 1797. "Our canoe was a very bad one, scarcely fit to carry over two persons, made out of a decayed red oak, 10 feet long, and la[u]nched with the bark on." Such rude transports were preferred by Indians and traders alike due to the ease with which they could be concealed; when the canoe was overturned, it assumed the appearance of a decaying log.[65]

Those without boats were forced to construct a raft. During his journey, William Bartram received instruction on the fine points of river rafting, and the naturalist willingly collected dry canes, logs, and vines for the endeavor. He found the process "novel" and conceded that he "could not, until finished and put to practice, well comprehend how it could possibly answer the effect desired."[66]

> In the first place we laid, parallel to each other, dry, sound trunks of trees, about nine feet in length and eight or nine inches diameter; which binding fast together with grape vines and withs [withes], until we had formed this first floor, about twelve or fourteen feet in length, we then bound the dry canes in bundles, each near as thick as a mans' body, with which we formed the upper stratum, laying them close by the side of each other, and binding them fast: after this manner our

raft was constructed. Then having two strong grape vines, each long enough to cross the river, we fastened one to each end of the raft, which now being completed, and loading on as much as it would safely carry, the Indian took the end of one of the vines in his mouth, plunged into the river and swam over with it, and the vine fixed to the other end was committed to my charge, to steady the raft and haul it back again after being unloaded.

After ferrying all their baggage, the travelers swam the swollen river. Both the naturalist and his companion made it safely across, without the loss of baggage or life, as many others before and after them managed to do also.[67]

But such crossings were dangerous. Horses, exhausted by carrying packs, sometimes drowned while fighting swift currents, tangled vegetation, and debris-laden rivers. Bartram noted many alligators and snakes in the churning waters he faced. He preferred to swim the river with his breeches on, "for they contained matters of more value and consequence than all the rest of my property put together."[68] Some years later, Caleb Swan was overjoyed after his "uncommon and hazardous exertion" in crossing the flooded Altamaha River. Swan's companions killed a stray cow and "stretched her skin over hoops, in the shape of a bowl" to carry their baggage across the river. Four horses were drowned, but the Indians in his company frightened away the "voracious alligators" that inhabited the crossing by shouting a "general war-hoop."[69] The damage suffered by trade goods and deerskins during such crossings cut into profits and kept prices charged the Creeks higher than those for the Cherokees, whose villages were accessible by wide wagon roads. The absence of suitable invasion routes also meant that differences between the Creeks and the British colonists were settled by negotiation rather than force. Traders, aware of the hardships of the Creek path, consistently noted the difficulties an army would face attempting a march against the Creek towns.[70]

The caravans camped at established sites along the trading paths. Despite the toils of the trail, a trader's journey was not without some leisure. In addition to singing and dancing, boxing and storytelling were popular pastimes. Old Indian hands, when pressed by Pickett, fondly remembered their younger days. They noted that packhorsemen were exceedingly fond of tafia:

It cheered him in the forest and emboldened him in distress. With a bottle slung by his saddle he often indulged, while those before and behind him followed his custom. Those going to Pensacola and other places were frequently in want of the stimulant, and it was customary for the traders, whom they met coming from the market, to halt and treat and interchange jokes. The trader who suddenly rushed by a thirsty party was long remembered as a mean fellow.[71]

Deerskins and trade goods were carried in packs weighing from 150 to 180 pounds.[72] Once the skins had reached Augusta, they were unpacked and stored until transported to Charleston. At the storekeeper's warehouse, the skins received little additional processing other than trimming, but even this was not always done.[73] Slaves might occasionally "beat the skins" to ward off worm damage to poorly dressed skins, particularly during periods of warm weather.[74] The skins were then packed for the journey down the Savannah River and on to Charleston. The boats used in the trade, known as piraguas, were large flat-bottomed boats. By the early 1740s, there were five boats operating out of Augusta. Each made a minimum of "four or five" trips to Charleston annually. Postlethwayt reported that these trading boats could carry up to four and one-half tons, a figure confirmed by other sources.[75] One such boat owned by Macartan and Campbell was forty-two feet long and seven feet wide with a small stern cabin.[76] Piraguas required a steersman and from six to eight oarsmen, usually slaves. The trip to Charleston took only four or five days. The return trip upstream might take over two weeks of struggling with oars, paddles, or poles.[77] Even this part of the journey was not free of worry, as the Chickasaw trader John Highrider discovered in 1750 when Macartan and Campbell's boat was lost, with 2,100 pounds of his deerskins on board. As Highrider lamented to Governor James Glen of South Carolina, "[This] disappointed me of paying off a Debt I owed in Charles Town, and I am afraid that I would be put to trouble if I had gone there."[78]

At Charleston, the deerskins were turned over to export merchants who examined the pelts and repacked them for shipment overseas. Among the better-known merchants who handed deer hides were Samuel Eveleigh, Benjamin Stead, James Crokatt, John Gordon, and Henry Laurens. Deerskins were on the enumerated list and, by law, could be shipped only to England or a British colony. It was also necessary to pay an export tax on the skins.[79] The usual destination of Creek deerskins was London or Bristol.[80] The fate of deerskins taken to Pensacola was virtually the same, except for, usually, longer delays in West Florida before shipment to England.

The hogshead was the common packing crate for shipment overseas, but barrels, tierces, casks, and various other containers were sometimes used.[81] The capacity of a hogshead varied considerably. Postlethwayt, in his *Universal Dictionary of Trade and Commerce,* indicated that one hogshead would contain roughly 33 deerskins, a figure that is borne out by West Florida trade figures for 1766, when that colony exported 4,636 deerskins packed into 150 hogsheads.[82] But other records indicate a much larger container, and the standard capacity for a hogshead for most of the eighteenth century was 500 pounds.[83] On one occasion, the Savannah merchant Thomas Raspberry shipped one hogshead containing 330 "good, but small" deerskins, which weighed 474 pounds.[84] In 1772, the Charleston merchant Henry Laurens exported 20 hogsheads that contained 5,733 half-dressed deerskins weighing 10,935 pounds. This meant that Laurens's hogsheads contained approximately 287 skins apiece and must have weighed over 500 pounds each.[85] The design of the hogshead also varied. In the fall of 1771, Henry Laurens bemoaned extensive worm damage to one of his shipments of deerskins and laid the blame not only on the delay in shipment during the hot season but also on the "Openness of those new fashioned Hogsheads." He was sure there were no visible signs of worms when they were packed, and his frustration is evident from his declaration: "Please God I return to Carolina and transact any skin Business, I will go into the old Road of Packing with some Amendments."[86]

With each passing year, exports of deerskins increased. About 53,000 deerskins left Charleston annually from 1698 until 1715.[87] Export figures plunged in 1715 with the outbreak of the Yamasee War, and in 1716, only 4,702 deerskins left Charleston. During the war years, exports fell to 25,000 annually. By 1721, exports had recovered, and approximately 60,000 deerskins were shipped to overseas markets. Thereafter, export numbers climbed rapidly, especially as the development of specialized Indian trading companies out of Augusta forged links to Creek, Chickasaw, and Choctaw towns. One report stated that "about one hundred thousand Weight of Skins" were shipped from Augusta in 1741. In 1752, the Savannah merchant Joseph Habersham reported that 140,000 pounds of deerskins and 2,000 pounds of beaver pelts were sent down the Savannah River by Augusta merchants annually. Habersham noted in dismay that only about 5,000 pounds of these deerskins were sold in Savannah. The rest were sent via coastal vessels to Charleston and sold to merchants there or else shipped directly to England. During the same period, the French at Fort Toulouse obtained between 3,000 and 7,500 deerskins per year.[88] By 1758–59, over 355,000 pounds of deerskins, procured from various Indian tribes, left Charleston for Great Britain annually.[89] During the 1750s, Savannah emerged as a leading port, and until the outbreak of the American Revolution, exports from that city exceeded 200,000 yearly, peaking at 306,510 pounds of deerskins in 1768 and thereby matching Charleston in volume of deerskin exports.[90] In 1764, John Stuart asserted that the entire southeastern Indian trade had reached its limit with a total production of 800,000 pounds of deerskins per year.[91] After 1763, East and West Florida also exported deerskins. Exports from West Florida peaked in 1774, with just over 51,000 pounds of dressed deerskins and approximately 131,000 deerskins in the hair.[92] Incomplete customs records, smuggling operations, and the likelihood that customs receipts were fudged in order to avoid duties make it impossible to fully ascertain the total numbers of deer slaughtered for the trade.

In the years following the American Revolution, the trade slowly declined. After the revolution, Panton, Leslie, and Company handled the majority of the southeastern deerskin trade, which was shipped from Pensacola. In 1799, William Panton reported that his company's annual exports always exceeded 124,000 deerskins, or approximately 248,000 pounds of dressed hides per year.[93] The factory established by the new American government took in 25,000 hides, or 50,000 pounds of deerskins each year. Added to these were other outlets in Georgia and the Floridas. As these figures indicate, though the trade continued to be an important commercial activity, there was a clear decline in the numbers of deerskins by the end of the eighteenth century.[94]

Sir James Wright, the last colonial governor of Georgia, in the early 1760s gathered information on costs and profits in the deerskin trade. When he took into account shipping and insurance charges (+12.5%), profit added by importing merchants at Savannah (+15%), profits for the Augusta storekeepers (+20%), and the expenses the Indian traders incurred in actually getting the goods to the Indian towns and transacting business (+30%), goods that had cost £12,000 in London were sold to the Indians for £23,961. According to the figures Wright collected, these goods would have sold for £28,000 worth of deerskins, resulting in an 18 percent profit for the trader.[95] Wright gathered his figures from the traders themselves in order to determine proper government duties on the trade; thus there is every reason to believe that profits were even greater than the traders were willing to admit to a government official. John Pope, who toured the region in 1790, inquired into trade profits and concluded that William Panton, who held by that time an undisputed monopoly on the Creek trade, generally sold his wares at 500 percent of their prime cost.[96] These high returns had been true from the very beginning of the trade. As early as 1734, traders were obtaining blankets in Charleston for the equivalent of five pounds of deerskins. They sold the same blankets to the Indians for fifteen pounds of deerskins—roughly 300 percent of the cost.[97]

These markups and seemingly enormous profits caused concern to many, especially the Creeks. Yet there were many legitimate expenses involved in the trade. In 1787, William Panton found himself defending the current price schedule for the Creek Indians to the Spanish administration of Florida. He conceded that if one considered only the price traders paid for goods and what they received from the sale of deerskins, it would look as if they were making a 100 percent profit. Panton was quick to point out: "But in Truth this is not the Case. He is always obliged to give away some part to his headman of the rum for protection, the loss of horses, damage on the skins, expense of hirelings and other family expenditures added to bad debts which is as not possible to avow, leave the trader at the end of the year not much richer than when it began."[98]

Moreover, the quality of deerskins obtained through barter varied considerably. When a London merchant sent Henry Laurens an example of the fine quality of deerskins he wanted, Laurens found it necessary to educate his colleague on the realities of the deerskin trade.

> Unluckily our Deer in this part of the World are so far like the Men in your part that everyone has not so good a Coat as his Neighbour & we are forced to take them as they run without examination & if one was to wait until they could select ten Hogsheads of just such Skins as that it would take a great deal of time & require a very large purchase to cull out the quantity, indeed to be plain it is impracticable.[99]

When one added shipping, insurance, customs duties, and fluctuations in the price of skins on the European market, it is clear that profits were not as large as might be imagined. Nonetheless, there were profits to be made. Through the years, a steady trader, by sound management and huge markups, could make a comfortable living. Deerskin traders rarely became wealthy, but merchants and suppliers frequently did. Still, the key to a solid fortune was not so much the profits to be derived from the Indian trade but the accumulation of land and slaves through investments and colonial land grants.[100]

Though the price of deerskins varied from year to year, the rate of exchange between peltries and goods was about a pound of dressed deerskins for every six shillings current (South Carolina paper) money.[101] The southern Indians, in their attempts to obtain adequate supplies of European goods, ranged far and wide in search of deer. In addition to decimating herds throughout the Southeast, the overhunting flooded European peltry markets. As a result, from 1733 until 1769, there was a 27 percent decline in prices paid for deerskins. From 1769 until 1771, it appears that this downward pressure on prices was moderated by a shortage of cattle hides from Europe. Even so, throughout the eighteenth and into the nineteenth centuries, there was an overall decline in the price of deerskins on the world market.

On the other hand, the price of woolen fabrics and other trade goods rose. Also, in the two decades before the American Revolution, there was a tremendous increase in the number of traders working in the Indian territory. This heightened competition for customers resulted in lower prices for the Creeks but spelled disaster for their traders.[102] Put another way, traders found it necessary to pay more for cloth, guns, and other trade items as the price of deerskin fell on the world market. At the same time, they found that stiff competition made it necessary to sell the goods for fewer deerskins. With the passage of time, traders received less and less profit from the sale of the deerskins.

The economic difficulties engendered by the precipitous decline in the profits from the deerskin trade were compounded by the Proclamation of 1763. Among other things, the proclamation overturned colonial laws relating to the Indian trade by making it almost impossible for colonial governors to deny a license to anyone who could post a small bond. These licenses were "general," which gave the licensee the right to trade anywhere in the Indian country, and were not limited to a specific town. At a stroke, the old trading system, which had controlled competition by limiting the number and location of trading stores, was overturned. The proclamation required those with a license to obey any trade regulations established by the British government, but since there were none, chaos was the result.[103]

With the old restraints on competition removed, ambitious entrepreneurs, who knew little or nothing about Indians, found it easy to acquire a license, and hordes of inexperienced men headed west into Indian country. In addition to those attempting to earn an honest living by the Indian trade, there were scores of fortune seekers and adventurers among the newcomers. Not burdened by the overhead of established stores in the Indian towns and a ledger plagued by uncollected deerskins, these men carried plenty of rum and seemed privy to every dishonest business trick in existence. Most were, quite literally, on the lookout for a "quick buck." Established tradesmen and their Indian consumers found reasons aplenty to complain about the proliferation of unregulated traders in their midst. In his *History,* James Adair decried the abuses of these "corrupt and shamefully-indulged vagrant pedlars," noting that within a year of the issuance of general licenses, he lost "two and twenty hundred dollars-worth of goods at prime cost."[104]

In a memorial sent to John Stuart, a group of merchants and traders to the Creeks outlined the problem:

A number of new Traders have been sent into the Towns where there were already old ones, each of them carrying a quantity of goods equall to what they did, by which means the Indians [now have] a double supply in their towns other new traders finding no room in the Towns, have betaken themselves to the Woods and Settled themselves at Indians' Plantations in their Hunting Grounds, where they use every art to get the Skins from the Indian before he returns to his Town; if he passes there and comes home competition arises betwixt the old and New Traders for his custom; the latter has recourse to underselling and being many of them men of no Character or property, Stick at no arts to gain their point, and provided they can get Skins, will not consider what they cost thereby raising disgust & disatisfaction amongst the Indians, & occasioning them to desire further deductions, as imagining themselves hither to to [*sic*] have been imposed upon.[105]

The jostling for customers unsettled established trading relations and routines and irritated the Creeks as much as it did their regular traders. Though the Creeks enjoyed the rollback in prices, many angrily confronted their established town traders and demanded an explanation for the sudden shift in the exchange rates for common trading goods. Old-time traders were similarly enraged, for they had outfitted most of the hunters on credit at the beginning of the hunting season only to see their customers, on returning, take business elsewhere. Having obtained the deerskins, the newcomers set out for the market, leaving the old-timers to ponder how to pay their own debts and restock their stores. Creeks were further agitated when told by their old trader that their debts were still on his ledger and now due.

Faced with these conditions, even the most honorable merchants and traders cast about for ways to recoup their losses. Besides turning a blind eye to unethical practices of their own employees, they demanded that the trade be regulated, properly policed, and deposited in the hands of a respectable few in order to maximize profits and minimize tensions between the Creeks and the traders—thus, in the words of Stuart's memorialists, making it "worth the while of a man of probity and character to live amongst the Indians."[106] Thus, from 1763 until the end of British hegemony in the Southeast, the regulation of the deerskin trade was the dominant theme of Creek-Anglo relations and a major concern for colonial merchants, traders, imperial officials, and Creek consumers.

CHAPTER 6

"Runagadoes"
and the Regulation
of the Trade

Creek headmen, distressed by declining deer herds and their increasing dependence on European trade goods, asked Crown representatives at the Anglo-Creek Congress held in Pensacola in 1765 to force the traders to lower their prices. Governor George Johnstone explained to the assembled Creeks that traders must be allowed to profit; otherwise, they would be ruined and driven out of business. Johnstone smugly intoned, "I am well assured that if the Trade is Lowered, none but Vagabons & runagadoes will go to trade among you."[1] Johnstone was new to the region. The Creeks were not. They knew that prices were too high—and that their towns were already overrun by "Vagabons & runagadoes."

Though many frontier entrepreneurs were men of principle, the deerskin trade attracted more than its fair share of thoroughly disreputable characters. Many packhorsemen and other hired laborers were, according to one nineteenth-century Creek writer, a "debauched indolent dishonest set, without the fear of man or God and only afraid of labour."[2] Even the most highly regarded traders were frequently the target of criticism. A Carolina trader, incensed at the practices of the burgeoning Augusta Company, disdainfully reported in 1752 that the company was "a monstrous Sett of Rogues for the major Part of whom the Gallows groans."[3] Yet the faults and vices of the old-line traders paled when compared with the "Arab-like pedlars" who descended on the Indians after the opening of the trade under the Proclamation of 1763.[4] According to Superintendent Stuart, the backcountry was "infested with disorderly persons" with few scruples.[5] A report to the Board of Trade in 1764 stated that these traders were "not the honestest or Soberest People"—nothing less than understatement.[6] The same report acknowledged that traders and packhorsemen were "the very worst and most abandoned set of men."[7] Old-line traders themselves complained of the "bad morals and licentious manner" of the "new class" of traders.[8] One writer dismissed them as "monsters in human form, the very scum and out cast of the earth."[9] The veteran trader James Adair stated that most of the people who entered the trade after 1763 were "the dregs and off-scourings of our colonies." He added, "The greater part of them could notably distinguish themselves, among the most profligate by land or sea, no day of the week excepted, indeed the sabbath day is the worst."[10] David Taitt, the British agent to the Creek towns, noted that most of the traders, "excepting very few," were "deserters, horse thieves, half breeds and Negroes."[11] With the passage of time, the collective reputation of the trading class sank even lower. Caleb Swan declared in 1790 that the white inhabitants of the Creek country were "the most abandoned wretches that can be found, perhaps, on this side of Botany Bay." According to Swan, "There is scarcely a crime but some of them has been guilty of."[12]

From the very beginning of the Creek-Anglo trade, unscrupulous and raunchy scofflaws took advantage of Creek naïveté. The list of trade abuses was long and mean, and Creek consumers were sorely abused by many of the white people who came among them. There were two broad categories of trade abuses: unethical business practices and hooliganism in the Indian towns. In short, one might observe that those who ignored standards of decent conduct were involved in either cheating or beating the Indians.

Greed lay at the root of most trade evils. As Stuart noted, the traders "had no idea of adapting their manner of living to the profits of their trade but indulged themselves." He added, "And my lord, the coarse pleasures of an Indian trader are very expensive."[13] To maintain a steady profit margin, traders tried a variety of clever—and underhanded—techniques. By suspending the laws of physical science, traders found that an English pound weighed more in the interior than on the seacoast. According to many price schedules established for the trade, a pound of leather weighed eighteen ounces. But in some cases, it took up to one and one-half English pounds to make an Indian pound. Thus, according to testimony solicited by the Georgia Trustees from Johnny Musgrove, his Creek customers "were obliged to pay 160 of their pds. [for sixteen blankets] which makes 240 English pounds for what cost the Trader but 80 English pound."[14] Using false weights and measures and trading inferior goods were additional ways to increase one's profits. The Creeks, like all southeastern Indians, were quick to spot such scams and either avoided traders who used such methods or retaliated by stealing the trader's goods or deerskins or physically abusing him in some way. Spreading word of impending attack was a quick way to increase sales of guns and powder, and many Creeks stocked up at the first hint of menacing activity by Carolinians, Georgians, or Choctaws.[15]

But the most popular and effective way for a trader to boost his profit margin was to peddle rum, or tafia, as it was generally called. Old-line traders had always snuck rum into the Indian towns. Their customers—and their bank accounts—demanded it. Though Georgia banned the exportation of rum into the Indian country, South Carolina did not, and traders from both colonies carted kegs into the backcountry. The South Carolina agent Daniel Pepper, noting that many traders skirted Augusta with their rum ponies for fear of being caught by Georgia officials, dryly remarked, "Indeed they need not be afraid of the Magistrates of that Place seizing any unless they do it out of Spight, because they themselves do not furnish the Liquor, for I am credibly informed that a good many of the Traders, nay even Indians, are supplyed with that Article by the Storekeepers in Augusta and New Savannah."[16]

Though the Indian country was by no means "dry" before 1763, the prohibitions placed on the rum trade certainly kept the traffic under some restraint. With easier access to rum, the absence of the French "menace," and large numbers of traders competing in a limited market after 1763, the rum traffic exploded, and Creek towns reeked with the heady aroma of cheap West Indian tafia. By 1770, Charles Stuart, the deputy superintendent of Indian Affairs stationed at Mobile, believed that four-fifths of the purchases over the previous twelve-month period had been made with rum. "It is certain there is nothing the Indians like better, and nothing the traders had rather give."[17] In 1776, John Stuart reported that "for one skin taken in exchange for British manufacture," there were "five got in exchange" for rum.[18] For the Indians, rum was an expensive, and deadly, trade good.[19] The Creek love for spirits knew no bounds. Once inebriated, Indians were left to the mercy of their traders. And the more a hunter drank, the more he was willing to pay.[20]

From the traders' perspective, rum was cheap and always attracted plenty of customers. It was also easy to water the product down, thereby stretching inventory into even greater profit. The most common abuse, and the one that did the most harm to Creeks and established traders alike, was the practice of trading raw unprocessed skins for rum "in the woods." An itinerant peddler, possessing rum and little else, decoyed Indians returning from their hunts before they reached their camps or villages. It took little effort to persuade weary hunters to do business: "the enchanting force of liquors" did all the work.[21] The young were particularly vulnerable to this tactic. Some hunters, so seduced by rum, parted with all their skins and often even traded their guns for more of the trader's watered-down brew. Hunters who "drinked all their Skinns" earned only hangovers and were left impoverished, with ruined credit and no way to provide clothing for their families. This often led to "great Disturbances, quarrels and even Murders" once a hunter sobered up and realized his predicament.[22]

Such an occurrence also meant disaster for the well-established town trader who had advanced ammunition to the hunter on credit. Deprived of his repayment, the town's trader fell behind on payments to the Augusta storekeepers. In some Creek towns, three or four traders set up shop, where previously only one had been established. To entice hunters into their stores, traders offered "door prizes"—rum, of course. Prices of other goods were slashed and sometimes sold at cost. Inventive vendors offered a free keg of rum to any hunter who would open an account with them. Old-line traders had to do likewise or be driven out of business.[23]

Some employees of the more reputable traders were not adverse to freelance trading, and rum aided this endeavor. Francis Lewis, the regular trader at the Upper Creek Town of Tuckabatchee and an employee of George Galphin's, perfected a system of cheating not only the Indians but Galphin as well. The British agent David Taitt witnessed firsthand the inventive tactics of Lewis. "This man makes it a common practice to give rum to his wench for to purchase back the goods from the Indians which he has before sold or trusted them with, so that he is obliged to fit them out a second time on credit which greatly increases their debts to his employer but is a great profit to himself as the skins that he purchases with rum or goods bought with it he claims as his own." Lewis also made it a practice to greet returning hunting parties with rum before they could settle with the other trader at Tuckabatchee.[24] Like others who employed such methods, Lewis took the deerskins he procured in this fashion to Pensacola, which was also the source of his rum supply.[25]

When not cheating their customers, many traders busied themselves by insulting and abusing the Creeks in noneconomic ways. The manners of traders, when under the influence of rum, suffered a precipitous decline. Too much liquor made many traders "fitter for Bedlam or New Gate than to be trusted in an Indian Country." This was especially true of Charles Jordon. In 1752 he drank more rum than he ought to have, stripped naked, painted himself like an Indian warrior, and ran about Coweta with a gun threatening the stunned natives.[26]

Jordon was not the first. Decades earlier, when Augusta was a new town, Mr. Watson, a trader and partner of Johnny Musgrove's, "gave himself to drinking, and was so seldom Sober That it was hard to Guess if he was not Mad. He would be naked with the Indians, Drunk with them lye down with them, and sometimes pretended to Baptize them." When Skee, a Creek Indian, died of the flux after joining the trader in a month-long binge, Watson continually babbled about the man's death, much to the consternation of sober Augustans, who feared Creek reprisals for Skee's untimely end.[27] One trader, Thomas Ross, "suffered his Fear to get the better of his Reason . . . [and] turned perfectly lunatick and gave away all his Cloaths to Indians as he met them in the Path." The Handsome Fellow of the Okfuskees, on meeting the delirious trader, attempted to take charge of him, but Ross, believing that the headman wanted to kill him, fled into the woods.[28] At other times, traders—and government officials—were simply too drunk to perform their duties.[29] Perhaps rum explains the actions of John Adam Tapley, who shocked Coweta villagers when he was apprehended digging up graves in that town.[30]

Traders also incurred Creek displeasure by insulting leading men and showing scant respect for other townspeople. But the easiest way to gain the lasting enmity of a Creek warrior was to meddle with his wife. Traders, heedless of the danger involved, seduced married Creek women with trade goods and promises. Affairs between married women and traders not only made the wife liable to public beating and ear cropping but put the trader in jeopardy as well. Fights, assaults, and even murders sprang from such situations, and more than one trader lost his ears, as Creek custom dictated, for such impudent and immoral behavior. At a 1764 meeting, annoyed headmen noted that they did not care what single women did but warned traders to leave married women alone.[31] In their idle moments, traders hunted deer for themselves, set beaver traps, and tended the cattle they had imported into Creek towns, all of which violated the wishes of the Indians.[32]

Traders did not fare much better in their relationships with each other. They fought among themselves and spread rumors about their competition. Often a trader would ply his customers with tafia and then send them "to his neighbor to break his doors and plunder him."[33] Even the more respectable traders, such as Lachlan McGillivray, often left their establishments in the hands of ignorant and unprincipled underlings.[34] Nor were merchants and traders careful about checking into a servant's past, and criminals of all sorts found employment in the Indian trade.[35] Moreover, it was common practice for established traders to "entice away each other's servants, when on the point of carrying their peltry to market."[36]

The trade was not without perils, and more than one trader met an early death at the hands of angry Creeks. On May 16, 1760, eleven traders to several Abeika villages were killed in a general "massacre." The first trader murdered that day, John Ross of Sugatspoges, had made a will the year before in consideration of the dangers he was "daily exposed to."[37] Although political reasons have been assigned to the murders by one Creek historian, it is likely that the affair had a more personal beginning and developed from an argument, between one of Ross's black slaves and the son of the town's headman, over a woman.[38] Besides dangers, there were aggravations. In 1767, John Stuart chided Creek headmen for the ill treatment traders were subjected to, "Your people insult and Abuse our Traders on the path to your own Towns they Steal their Horses and Bells and Rob their Camps when they meet your people in the woods."[39] On other occasions, when traders were absent from stores or left them without proper supervision, it was not uncommon for Indians to empty a warehouse of its contents.[40] When one trader refused to lower his prices, local hunters broke into his store and "destroyed his household utensils such as pots, bowls etc. and spoiled all his victuals." Doubtless Creek transgressors had ample justification for such actions, but minor incidents escalated and often caused major diplomatic turmoil.[41]

The regulation of the trade, or more properly, the regulation and management of those trading with the Indians, was important, indeed essential, to colonial security. The first serious attempts to regulate the trade came in the wake of the Yamasee War. South Carolina instituted a state monopoly, but it lasted only a few years before pressure from Charleston merchants landed the trade back on its old footing.[42] By the time Georgia was established, Carolina had offered no real regulation of the trade but had attempted to use it, and the threat of its embargo, to control Creek foreign policy. In any case, laws regulating the trade were virtually impossible to enforce. When confronted by an agent of South Carolina in 1725, John Molton cogently expressed the sentiments of many Creek traders who came before and after him: "Dame you and the Governmt Both. The Worst that

1. A Creek man and woman. This sketch, by William Bonar, accompanies his "Draught of the Creek Nation." Note the duffel blanket worn by the woman and the gun carried by the traditionally dressed warrior. Reproduced with the permission of the Controller of Her Majesty's Stationery Office, courtesy of the British Public Record Office, C O700/Carolina 21.

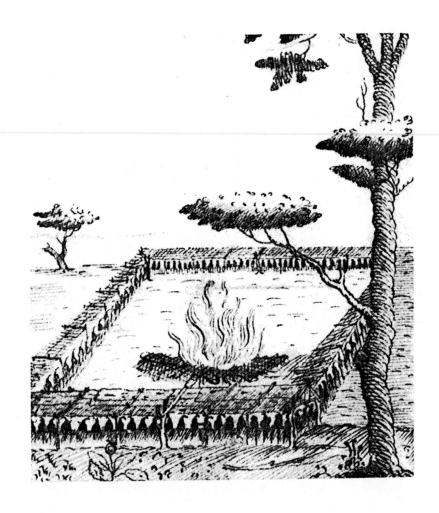

2. A Creek square ground, showing the covered pavilions
of the leading men. This sketch, by William Bonar, accompanies his
"Draught of the Creek Nation." Reproduced with the permission
of the Controller of Her Majesty's Stationery Office, courtesy
of the British Public Record Office, CO700/Carolina 21.

3. A Creek hothouse, or winter council house.
This sketch, by William Bonar, accompanies his "Draught of the
Creek Nation." Reproduced with the permission of the Controller
of Her Majesty's Stationery Office, courtesy of the British
Public Record Office, CO700/Carolina 21.

4. A chunkey pole. This sketch,
by William Bonar, accompanies his
"Draught of the Creek Nation."
Reproduced with the permission of
the Controller of Her Majesty's
Stationery Office, courtesy of the
British Public Record Office,
CO700/Carolina 21.

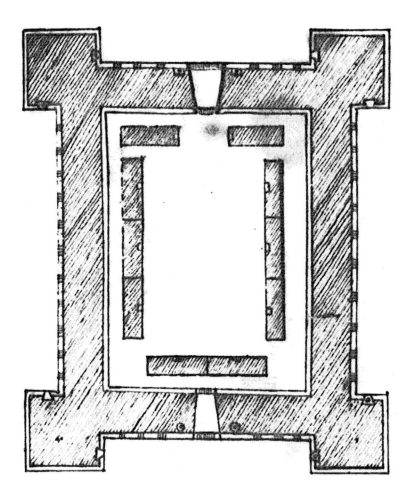

5. A diagram of Fort Toulouse. This sketch, by William Bonar,
accompanies his "Draught of the Creek Nation." Bonar, an agent for South
Carolina, assumed the disguise of a packhorseman to get close enough to spy
on the fort. Bonar reported that the fort defense was weak. Nonetheless, he was
captured by the French but was retaken by Creeks friendly to Britain when
the French attempted to transport him to Mobile. Reproduced with the
permission of the Controller of Her Majesty's Stationery Office, courtesy of the British Public Record Office, co700/Carolina 21.

6. Facing page, top: *An Indian Camp as They Make Them When They
Are Hunting,* by Philip Georg Friedrich von Reck. This is the only known
sketch of a Creek hunting site. Note the deerskins hung up to dry on the left
side of the shelter as well as the right rear. Also note the presence of women,
dogs, and European kettles. Courtesy of the Royal Library of Denmark,
Copenhagen, catalog signature Ny kgl. Saml. 565, 4°.

7. Facing page, bottom: *Indians Going A-hunting,* by Philip Georg
Friedrich von Reck. The figure on the left sports a traditional painted leather
blanket and carries a bow and arrow. The middle figure models the same
style, but in European materials. Note the duffel blanket and stroud leggings.
He also carries a gun and an imported kettle. The figure on the right is
wearing a leather jacket and leggings of uncommon design. Courtesy
of the Royal Library of Denmark, Copenhagen, catalog signature
Ny kgl. Saml. 565, 4°.

8. Above: *A Trading Boat Which Sails up to Savannah Town, 200 Miles
Higher Up Than Ebenezer.* From a drawing by Philip Georg Friedrich von
Reck. Reproduced with the permission of the Controller of Her Majesty's
Stationery Office, courtesy of the British Public Record Office,
CO5/638, p. 304.

9. Facing page, top: *The Georgia Indians in Their Natural Habit,* by Philip Georg Friedrich von Reck. The original sketch, in color, shows typical daily wear in the eighteenth century. The woman's skirt is of blue strouds, and her hair ribbons are red. The man's breechcloth is also of blue strouds. Courtesy of the Royal Library of Denmark, Copenhagen, catalog signature Ny kgl. Saml. 565, 4°.

10. Facing page, bottom: *The Indian King and Queen of Uchi, Senkaitschi,* by Philip Georg Friedrich von Reck. The original sketch, in color, shows that the woman is wearing a duffel blanket (white with red trim) and blue stroud skirt. The man wears a buffalo-skin robe, blue stroud leggings, and a breechcloth of red strouds. Courtesy of the Royal Library of Denmark, Copenhagen, catalog signature Ny kgl. Saml. 565, 4°.

11. Above: *A War Dance,* by Philip Georg Friedrich von Reck. Warriors, clad in stroud breechcloths, recount their heroic deeds. Note the guns in the pavilion. Courtesy of the Royal Library of Denmark, Copenhagen, catalog signature Ny kgl. Saml. 565, 4°.

12. A sketch of Hopthle Mico, a member of the Creek delegation to New York, by John Trumbull, 1790, detailing the typical dress of a leading Creek man in the late eighteenth century. Note the cloth turban, ornamental feathers, earbobs, trade-bead necklace, silver gorget, ruffled shirt, and great coat with metal buttons. He wears a medal awarded by the American government. Courtesy of the Charles Allen Munn Collection, Fordham University Library, Bronx, New York, and The Frick Art Reference Library.

Can be don[e] is to prevent my Comeing here Which is more than they Can doe for I Will Come."[43]

General James Oglethorpe was well aware of the economic and military importance of the deerskin trade, and he set about at once to secure its benefits for Georgia. In addition to establishing Augusta as a center for the trade, he spent considerable time cultivating the Creeks' friendship, even venturing into the piedmont to parley with leading Cowetas.[44] The result of Oglethorpe's determination to dominate relations with the southern tribes was a tense contest between Georgia and South Carolina for control of the Indian trade.

Both colonies passed laws intended to stop the more reprehensible trade practices. The most common feature of these regulations was the require-ment that traders post bond for their good behavior as well as that of their hirelings. Other usual requirements were that traders adhere to established price schedules, abide by strict limits in extending credit, use proper weights and measures, avoid the use of blacks and Indians as employees, purchase only properly prepared skins, and restrict their trade to a certain town or towns within the Indian nation.[45] Traders did post bonds and did reside in specific towns, but virtually every other regulation was ignored by the ma-jority of traders. It was almost impossible to catch and prosecute lawbreak-ers. This was especially true in the Creek Nation, where most licensed trad-ers were from the same company (Brown, Rae, and Company) and therefore unlikely to tattle on each other. Additional problems occurred due to the unwillingness of South Carolina and Georgia to cooperate on the matter of licensing. Thus, the trade and the traders, for all practical purposes, re-mained unregulated until the British government tried to establish cen-tralized control over Indian affairs in the mid-1750s in an effort to secure Indians to the British interest during the opening phase of the Seven Years' War.[46]

Well-informed people, both in the colonies and in Britain, had long noted the need for a system that would establish clear-cut authority over Indian affairs and end colonial squabbling. The earliest and most compre-hensive scheme was designed by Edmund Atkin in 1754 at the request of the Board of Trade. Not an original work, Atkin's plan pulled together current ideas on the management of Indian affairs. Atkin, a leading Charleston merchant, had served as a member of the South Carolina council for nearly twenty years. His knowledge of Indian affairs and his personal acquaintance with many of the leading Indian headmen added weight to his call for an ordered Indian system under royal control. Atkin, like many before him, suggested that all Indian tribes within British jurisdiction be divided into two districts, North and South, each headed by a superintendent. Atkin's scheme also contained recommendations on regulating the deerskin traffic.

Following the outbreak of war with France in 1754, Atkin's ideas gained new credence with the Board of Trade, and an Indian superintendency system was instituted. Edmund Atkin became the first superintendent of Indian Affairs in the Southern District in 1756, and he held the post until his death in 1761. Sir William Johnson was Atkin's northern counterpart. The appointment of the two superintendents during the early stages of the Seven Years' War marked a bold new departure for Indian relations in both the North and the South. The superintendents were to represent the empire's interest along the frontier and were specifically charged with securing the aid, or at least the neutrality, of the Indian tribes in the struggle against France. This, of course, meant a steady and well-regulated trade.[47] Atkin, however, was neither efficient nor effective as a superintendent. The fact that the Creeks were not hostile to Great Britain during the war years had little to do with his superintendency.

The real challenge for British imperial designs came after the establishment of peace in 1763. For as every imperialist knew, the true fruits of victory would come only if the southern colonies were allowed to prosper and grow in the absence of French machinations. Such prosperity was inexorably linked to the conduct of the surrounding Indians. Careful management was required. The man chosen to oversee Britain's postwar policy was John Stuart, who was well versed in Indian affairs. The Scottish-born Stuart had emigrated to South Carolina in 1748 and operated a mercantile establishment for a time. Stuart's business dealings were unsuccessful, and he held a variety of minor civil positions until his appointment as the second southern Superintendent of Indian Affairs in 1762.[48]

For Stuart, "Fixing the British Empire in the Hearts of the Indians, by Justice, and moderation" was the primary goal of his superintendency.[49] After the establishment of peace in 1763, Stuart conducted a number of congresses with various southern tribes. Every congress brought bitter complaints from leading Indians over nefarious trade practices and the steadily growing rum trade. Indians and colonials alike attributed the increasing frontier crime rate to the ill-regulated trade. According to Stuart, "The first and main step towards the right governing of Indians and bringing them under some police will be having Good men Traders in the different Nations subjected to good and wholesome regulations."[50] At a brief meeting following the Augusta Congress, Stuart and the governors of Georgia, South Carolina, North Carolina, and Virginia agreed, "There never was a time more seasonable for the establishing the Commerce with Indians upon a general safe equitable footing and which we are afraid will never be done by [the] respective Provinces."[51]

Yet Stuart was hobbled in his attempts to impose trade regulations by the Proclamation of October 7, 1763, which left the power to grant licenses with the various colonial governors. The proclamation neglected to set regulations for those licensed through its provisions. Aware of the proclamation's inadequacies, British policymakers began at once to devise guidelines for the Indian trade. Accordingly, in late 1764, Stuart received a copy of the "Plan for the Future Management of Indian Affairs," better known as the Plan of 1764.[52] The Plan of 1764 was supposed to be a policy paper and was directed to all those involved with the Indian nations. Stuart, and many others, were to comment on the merits and deficiencies of the plan before the Board of Trade made a final decision regarding its implementation.[53] Nonetheless, Stuart seized on the plan as a way to solve the problems in his district. The Plan of 1764 did not restrict the number of licenses granted but did provide new regulations for the management of the trade. It was to replace all colonial laws concerning the trade and reaffirmed the existing plan of superintendencies with two Indian districts. The superintendents were given complete authority to conduct affairs relating to the Indians; colonial governors and military personnel were forbidden to hold any meeting with the Indians or send messages to them without the approval of their respective superintendent and were to act in concert with him at any general congresses involving land purchases or other matters.

Superintendents were given the sole direction of the trade, but the prospective trader would still obtain his license from the governor or commander-in-chief of the colony where he resided. Licenses would be given only after bond had been posted, and they were to state the specific Indian town or tribe with which the licensee could trade, a welcome alternative to the general licenses under the Proclamation of 1763, which simply gave someone the legal authority to engage in commerce. Licenses were renewable annually, and traders were required to furnish the names of their servants and packhorsemen. The rum trade was strictly prohibited. Certain kinds of ammunition and rifle guns were disallowed. Strict limits were set for the extension of credit.

To help enforce these regulations, the superintendent was empowered to appoint deputies to reside in various colonies, as well as interpreters and blacksmiths to live in the Indian nations. Commissaries, to be stationed in the Indian towns, were responsible for enforcing imperial regulations and served as the superintendent's spokesmen among the Indians. Prices for goods were to be fixed by the commissaries; they would act as justices of the peace and were authorized to decide disputes between Indians and traders or between two traders.[54]

Stuart suggested that certain features of the plan be modified to conform with the needs of his department. He wanted to limit the number of traders to a ratio of 1 trader per 150 gunmen in order to reduce competition and rid the Indian nations of excess traders. He hoped that the superintendent would be given sole authority to grant licenses, thus facilitating the issuance of only a fixed number of licenses. Stuart was aware of the jealousies that might result from such a method of issuing licenses, and he proposed another method if his superiors found the first unacceptable. In his alternate method, a board, composed of council members from the southern provinces, would be established and would meet regularly with him to renew and award licenses along the lines he pointed out. Naturally, the superintendent had the authority to revoke licenses of traders who ignored regulations. West Florida Governor George Johnstone, who, like Stuart, was sensitive to the dangers of excessive competition, proposed that the number of traders be restricted to 1 trader per 300 gunmen. To determine the lucky few who would be duly licensed to conduct trade, Johnstone proposed a lottery.[55]

Stuart recommended that the tariff for trade goods be fixed at congresses between Indians and their licensed traders and not by the commissaries, as the plan indicated. Price-fixing would, Stuart thought, control competition among traders and establish rates of exchange that would be fair to the Indian and the trader alike. This alone, Stuart believed, would halt many reprehensible practices.[56]

The Plan of 1764 was never officially adopted. Even so, Stuart attempted to direct the Southern Department according to the principles of the plan, with his proposed modifications. He admitted later, the plan was "the light by which I have steered my course."[57] Indeed, for Stuart, the proper regulation of the trade, based on the Plan of 1764, was "a Necessary Step towards the proper Government of Indians."[58]

Stuart and Johnstone used the Plan of 1764 as a model for their conduct with the Creeks at the 1765 Congress of Pensacola, as well as with the

Chickasaws and Choctaws who met with Stuart and the West Floridians at Mobile the same year. They instituted nineteen trade regulations, based on the plan, which the West Florida traders agreed to obey. Price lists for trade merchandise were also established by the mutual consent of the traders and the headmen.[59] James Adair, one of those duly authorized to trade with the Chickasaws, declared the entire exercise "a shameful farce on œconomy and good order." For even though they swore to uphold the law and posted bonds, most of the West Florida traders "notoriously violated every essential part of their instructions." Rum flowed north from Mobile like a torrent. Exasperated Chickasaw headmen turned to Adair to relay their complaints to the authorities. But neither Adair's memorial nor the speeches of Chickasaw headmen could right the conduct of the traders, since West Florida had included no provisions for agents to police the Indian towns and apprehend those who violated the terms of the licenses.[60]

Nor did West Florida's new regulations solve the problems of the Creek trade. Most of the Creek traders were from Georgia and therefore were not covered by the law. Like the Choctaw and Chickasaw traders, the Creek traders from West Florida simply ignored the regulations. There was no talk of apprehending and prosecuting violators. By March 1767, John Stuart was openly calling for a meeting of Creeks and Cherokees and their traders to develop mutually agreeable trade regulations. Even when Stuart's superiors reproached him for his hasty implementation of the Plan of 1764 in West Florida, Stuart persevered and continued planning the Creek and Cherokee trade congresses.[61] He hoped that the results would persuade London to accept his ideas.[62] In the meantime, he asked the governors of South Carolina and Georgia to recall all general licenses.[63] In the future, Stuart wanted the prospective trader to be a person of "character and substance" who resided in the same colony from which the license was issued. Bonds were to be substantial. If the trader failed to obey the superintendent's regulations, the bond would be forfeited. In effect, such a step would return the trade to the old-line pre-proclamation traders, whose associated merchants and storekeepers would be willing to post bond for them.[64]

John Stuart's trade conference with the Creeks opened on May 5, 1767, at Augusta, with a gathering of the principal merchants involved in the Creek trade. He pointed out that he intended to institute temporary regulations to halt the "confusion" in the Indian territory caused by the lack of regulations and the unrestrained competition among traders from different provinces. He explained that the regulations would place traders and packhorsemen under his authority and make them liable to inspection by his commissaries. Concerning the price of goods sold to the Indians, Stuart noted that the Creeks had repeatedly insisted on an adjustment and that some compromise was necessary. Leaving the decision to the merchants, he asked that they "point out such articles, & reasonable abatement." He added, "I hope your Candour, love of order and Justice will induce you to comply with the desire of Government in this particular." The merchants complied. The prices set, generally from one to two pounds of leather cheaper than previously, were essentially the same as the prices proposed by the Creeks themselves at Pensacola in 1765. Some articles retained their former value, but the overall price reductions were substantial. In fact, the reductions largely represented the prices that many Creeks were already paying for goods; in early 1766, the trader William Struthers had reported that new traders had come into the nation selling their goods for generally a pound of leather less than the established prices.[65]

Self-preservation, not regard for their customers, motivated these individuals. Mostly veteran merchants, these men reported, "Tho' it may be imagined that nobody would go there . . . yet it is nevertheless true . . . [and] the number of adventurers are daily increasing, while the prospect of advantage becomes less and less." Unchecked competition and nefarious trade practices had driven most to the brink of financial ruin. Fully supportive of the superintendent, the merchants lowered their prices. Their real concern was to establish guaranteed market shares by limiting the number of traders through licenses that restricted traders to a single town or to a certain number of Indians.[66]

Tardy Creek negotiators delayed the beginning of the Creek conference, so Stuart traveled to Hard Labour to negotiate with the Cherokees and their traders. He then returned to Augusta to meet with the traders who resided in the Creek towns. He explained the earlier proceedings with the Augusta merchants and quickly obtained the traders' ratification of the new price schedule and a set of trade regulations. The superintendent also asked for their cooperation in bringing lawbreakers to justice. The following day, the Creeks joined their traders. In his opening address, Stuart announced that he had looked into the matter of high trade prices. He explained that the traders had voluntarily agreed to lower their prices. George Galphin then read the previously agreed-upon tariff, which the Indians accepted without any objection.[67]

The regulations that Stuart instituted were virtually identical to those he had established for West Florida traders in 1765. At last, Stuart thought, he had brought the Indian trade "under a Rational police."[68] Following the conference, Stuart asked the southern governors to insist that the traders post bond for their good behavior as well as that of their servants. In addition, he published notices declaring that all licenses not agreeable to the Proclamation of 1763 would be considered invalid after October 1, 1767.[69] This, of course, referred to the clause in the proclamation that made it mandatory for colonial traders to abide by regulations established by the British government. The governors of South Carolina and Georgia and the acting governor of West Florida, Lieutenant Governor Montfort Browne, promised their cooperation. Satisfied, Stuart forwarded copies of the traders' memorials and the journal of his two conferences to the Board of Trade, hoping that the documents would "justify" his conduct and persuade the board to adopt his ideas concerning the Plan of 1764.[70]

In early March 1768, the Board of Trade rejected the Plan of 1764. According to its report:

> [The plan] consists of such a Variety of establishments, and necessarily leads to such extensive operations, as to bring on an increasing expense, which, in point of Commerce, may exceed the Value of the object to which it applies, and being greater than the trade can bear, must if the present Plan should be permanent, either fall upon the Colonies, in which case it will be impracticable to settle the proportion each colony should bear, or become a Burthen upon this Country, which . . . would be both unreasonable and highly inconvenient.[71]

In addition, the board noted that such a system would be extremely difficult to enforce. Accordingly, control of the trade was returned to the colonies. The board noted the problems encountered by previous colonial attempts to regulate the trade and suggested that the individual colonies adopt Stuart's regulations.[72] Furthermore, faced with huge debts and irate colonists who resented taxation, the board severely cut Stuart's budget, forcing a reorganization of the southern Indian department.[73]

The full implementation of the Plan of 1764 would have generated a considerable expense. It is also true that the nature of the trade and the vast territory over which it extended would have made enforcement a challenge. Yet the plan was better than what had existed previously. The resident commissaries, more than mere symbols of the new order, did curb some of the most blatant violations. John R. Alden, the historian of Stuart's superintendency, has noted, "Whatever the merits of Stuart's plan for regulating the trade—and his plan was perhaps as good as experience could devise and the situation would permit—the superintendent never had an opportunity to give it a proper test."[74]

The colonial governors were quickly informed of the decision. Each one received extracts of John Stuart's 1767 regulations, and the Earl of Hillsborough, the secretary of state for the Southern Department, indicated that the king hoped they would be adopted by the colonies "as far as local circumstances, and peculiar situations will admit." Like before, all British subjects were to be given the freedom to engage in the Indian trade.[75] In mid-September, Stuart wrote to the governors informing them of the changes. The colonies were already aware of the new policies, however, and traders lost no time in taking the news into Creek towns.

Stuart was very disappointed by the Board of Trade's decision. He stated, "Had the Commissaries been supported properly they would most probably have succeeded in Introducing some order amongst a Set of Lawless People." He could see no advantage to colonial regulation of the trade. The major problem was the difficulty of obtaining cooperation among the several colonies. Stuart believed that even the best regulations would be worthless unless commissaries were appointed to inspect traders and see that the regulations were obeyed. It was the superintendent's conviction that the governors would "not Early agree amongst themselves about the appointment of such inspectors."[76]

With the abrogation of Stuart's regulations and the removal of his representatives in the Indian country, Creek towns "swarmed with lawless Vagabonds who [were] Subject to no Sort of Rule or Jurisdiction." The usual annoying trade practices accelerated.[77] The Creeks were powerless to do anything other than register their complaints to the governors, the superintendent, and his deputy. Stuart reported to London that the tribes "daily and loudly complained" about the trade.[78] The Indians, under the impression that new colonial regulations were to take effect in the near future, promised they would be patient until the laws were enacted and could be enforced. Stuart urged the colonies to give prompt attention to the Creek concerns and reminded the governors that some sort of enforcement agency would be necessary.[79]

West Florida, surrounded by Indian tribes and bordering Spanish Louisiana, was the first colony to adopt trade regulations. In May 1770, the newly organized legislature enacted a law that contained most of John Stuart's 1767 regulations.[80] Included were prohibitions against and restrictions on trading in the woods, selling rum to Indians, extending credit, and employing blacks and Indians. No commissaries were appointed. Nonetheless, the bill did include a clause that bound traders to obey commissaries in the event that any were appointed in the future. A penalty was instituted for noncompliance, and the law was to remain in effect for two years.[81] The province, pleading poverty, asked London to provide the necessary funds for the employment of commissaries. The Floridians noted that otherwise their rules would "remain ineffectual for want of means to put the law in execution."[82] The infant colony of West Florida stood alone in regard to a regulated trade.[83]

East Florida, which had few Indians and fewer traders, did not even have a legislature to enact such laws. In 1768, Governor Wright of Georgia had suggested a plan dividing the tribes among the colonies. He soon abandoned it when it became apparent that cooperation was unlikely. His colony eventually drafted a law for preventing trade abuses and controlling boundary violators, but the law was not acceptable to London. Thus, the West Florida law, which carried no enforcement agency, remained for a time the sole colonial attempt at securing order on the southeastern frontier.[84] The deputy superintendent of Indian Affairs, Charles Stuart, who resided in Mobile, reported to John Stuart that the West Florida trade regulations were useless.[85]

Passing a set of regulatory ordinances was relatively easy, but catching violators and successfully prosecuting them were difficult. The nature of the trade and the countryside hindered effective gathering of evidence against offenders. It was also hard to find witnesses who would testify, since they were often guilty of the same crimes and feared retaliation from those they testified against. Indian testimony was unacceptable under colonial law. Moreover, offenders were often tried by sympathetic juries. In addition, even with proof of guilt, one colony could not try traders who held a license from another colony.[86]

Charles Stuart's observations are telling:

Another great Obstacle to the proper Management of Indians is the difficulty in bringing Offenders to Justice for want of positive proof and so very nice are the Sentiments of our Lawyers, that nothing but what is agreeable to the very Letter of the Law, as it is practiced in England will take place without any allowance for Local Circumstances, and if I have influence Enough to have a malefactor brought down, there is no such thing as getting those who Brought him down paid for their Trouble, which make it difficult to apprehend them. . . . I really think that the most Effectual method of Ridding the Nations of such Evil Instruments would be, by putting them on board a King's Ship by pressing them, when they come down to renew their Licenses, & that the Information of a commissary who should be a justice of the Peace, with the Affidavit of one White Man, should be Sufficient Proof.[87]

The new governor of West Florida, Peter Chester, admitted that the West Florida trade regulations were ineffectual. He noted that traders committed offenses in the nations outside the jurisdiction of his province and that the courts would not even hear the cases against lawbreakers. Chester believed that if all the colonies would pass similar legislation, some of the more detestable practices might slacken. Since proof against traders was hard to obtain, he suggested that if Indians were allowed to act as witnesses, more convictions might be possible. He realized that any law was useless without enforcement and agreed with the superintendent that unless commissaries were appointed, there was no prospect for improvement.[88]

But colonial cooperation did not ensue. John Stuart had believed that the proper management of the deerskin trade would ensure Creek friendship and prevent bloodshed. The British government rejected this view and determined that the trade was more an economic activity than a diplomatic one. Policing the Indian trade would simply cost too much. Though Georgia adopted an Indian trade law just before the outbreak of the American Revolution, the war ended all hope of British regulation of the Indian trade. By the end of the war, new realities prevailed in the backcountry, making governmental regulation of the trade a moot point.

Meanwhile, Creeks and all other southern Indian tribes suffered from the unrestrained greed of "mercenary empirics" and from the disdain of self-serving bureaucrats.[89] Scurrilous freebooters, arrogant in the knowledge that they could not be stopped, undermined the authority of Muscogulge town councils, disrupted family life, and transformed young hunters into drunks and debtors. Creeks of all ages were affected by the lasting changes that crept into their lives because of the trade. As the abuses grew, tensions increased, and the Creeks themselves were forced to deal with the broader implications of their economic tie to Anglo-America.

PART THREE

The Trade and Its Impact on Native Life

CHAPTER 7

Consumerism and Its Consequences

The Creek people relentlessly pursued deer and developed a variety of ways to participate in the new market economy in order to obtain goods of European origin. In a word, they were consumers. William Bartram, one of the most astute visitors to the Creek country in the late eighteenth century, wrote of the Muscogulges, "[They] wage eternal war against deer and bear, to procure food and cloathing, and other necessaries and conveniences; which is indeed carried to an unreasonable and perhaps criminal excess, since the white people have dazzled their senses with foreign superfluities."[1] Bartram was careful to note both the extent to which Creek society had been transformed to meet the demands of the trading economy and the impact of imported goods on the Creek way of life. The European manufactures for which the Creeks labored so diligently were much more than mere "superfluities" or even "conveniences." Indeed, as Bartram noted, the Muscogulges viewed most trade goods as "necessaries," especially fire-arms; for without guns, they would have dwindled into obscurity. The cloth and tools—even the gaudy luxuries—represented a more advanced technology that offered real advantages and enriched Creek life. But there were also many hidden costs and burdens resulting from this new Muscogulge materialism.

The slate of goods available to the Muscogulges remained constant throughout the eighteenth century. Creek spokesmen were very specific about what they needed and wanted in exchange for their deerskins. Cloth, guns, and ammunition were priority items, but iron tools and manufactured ornaments were highly prized as well.[2] Most of the goods traded to the Creeks in exchange for their deerskins were produced in Britain, although some goods were procured elsewhere. The trade staples—guns, ammunition, and most of the cloth—were all of British manufacture.

The standard trade gun was a smooth-bore musket, which though it could and often did dispatch many Creek enemies, was more suited to hunting than to warfare.[3] The Indians preferred rifled guns that gave them the power to "kill point Blank at two hundred yards." But rifles made colonists nervous lest their potential enemies acquire "too much upon an Equallity." Rifles also produced larger holes in deerskins. As a result, traders were prohibited from peddling rifle-barreled guns.[4] By the middle of the eighteenth century, most Indian trade guns were produced in Birmingham, England, and were thus called Birmingham guns or, sometimes, Carolina muskets. They were ornately decorated to please Indian tastes, and usually the screw plates resembled dragons or sea serpents.[5] A trade gun was among the most expensive trade goods carried by the traders and throughout most of the eighteenth century could be obtained for sixteen pounds of Indian-dressed leather. A gun was essential for Creek hunting and warfare. Without one, it was almost impossible to secure enough deerskins with which to buy other goods. Gunflints, balls of shot, and powder were necessary accompaniments.[6]

Metal tools were popular goods. The new iron goods freed the Muscogulges from the necessity of fashioning cruder models from stone, eased Creek labor, and increased efficiency. Iron hoes, axes, knives, and hatchets came in a variety of sizes suited for various tasks. The metal knives and hatchets were also put to use against enemies. Stone tools were quickly abandoned for everyday chores, though stone axes still retained ceremonial importance. Likewise, iron scissors and imported needles were a tremendous improvement over sharp stone and bone and facilitated the construction of clothing from new textiles. Kettles were highly portable and well suited for use during the winter months.

The commerce could have been termed the cloth trade as easily as the deerskin trade, for fabrics of various weights, colors, and designs were the staples of the Muscogulges. Duffels, strouds, Limbourg, caddis, plains, garliz osnaburg, bengals, flannel, calico, and silk all had their place in the trader's pack. Duffels, a coarse woolen cloth originally produced near Antwerp, Belgium, was white, red, blue, or striped. Heavy duffel blankets and overcoats were prized as winter wear, and "blew Duffields for Match-coats" appears on virtually every list of trade goods compiled. Strouds, a cheaper cloth made from woolen rags, was specifically manufactured in Stroud, England, for sale to American Indians and was the most important all-season trade cloth. Strouds came in pieces about eighteen inches wide and was of two colors, bright scarlet or deep blue. Men's leggings, women's skirts, and men's breechcloths, commonly called flaps, were all produced from strouds, as were lightweight matchcoats. It took between one and one-half to two yards of duffels or strouds to make a matchcoat; one-quarter yard of strouds was sufficient for a flap. Limbourg, the French-made equivalent of strouds, was reputed to be of better quality than the English variety. Caddis, or caddice, was a worsted yarn or tape used for binding and for garters. Plains was a worsted fabric, whereas garliz, or garlits, was a linen cloth originally produced in Görlitz, Prussian Silesia. Osnaburg, or ozenbrig, was a coarse, lightweight linen produced in Osnabrück, Germany. Bengals were piece goods, of various fibers, exported from Bengal. Usually of raw silk or cotton, bengals, either striped or plain, were popular for use as shawls and turbans.[7] Traders even found a market for the "shavings, or shreds, of fine scarlet cloth" they found littering their packs. These were eagerly purchased by Indian women, who first boiled the fragments to extract the scarlet dye and then mixed the colored liquid with the juice of *Rubia peregrina* to produce brilliant scarlet dyes that transformed even the dullest linen and cotton goods offered by their traders.[8] Wool binding, gartering, and silk ribbon were also important items to Creek consumers.

Most trade cloth was either red (scarlet) or deep blue (indigo). Although these colors had certain symbolic significance in Creek cosmology, their increasing appearance on Creek clotheshorses had less to do with cosmic concerns than the dictates of native fashion and a love of vibrant colors. Vermilion, or mercury sulfide, a deep scarlet pigment, did have ritual significance: mixed with water or bear grease, it was used regularly by Creek warriors. A product of China, this improved war paint was shipped to England before being repackaged and sent to American Indians.[9]

Variety and abundance marked the barter in beads, and traders carried, among other types, seed beads, barleycorn beads, and enameled beads.[10] Venice and Amsterdam supplied most of these, which were strung into necklaces and also were used to decorate shot pouches, garters, sashes, belts, and other items of clothing. Adair affirmed that the tribes in the Southeast liked them "so much as to make them their current money in all payments."[11] Whatever the ceremonial or religious significance beads may have had, by the eighteenth century they had primarily become fashion accessories for most Muscogulges. However, beads did retain their primacy as a mode of communication. Wampum belts, adorned with European beads of varying sizes and colors, conveyed diplomatic messages among Indian tribes and between the colonies and their aboriginal neighbors. In this case, though the medium had changed, the colors of the beads retained their traditional intertribal significance. Red, black, or blue were the heralds of danger, death, or war—white symbolized peace.[12]

The new European textiles and decorations revolutionized Creek dress. Before the arrival of Europeans, Creeks had worn little clothing during the hot summer months. In winter, they wrapped themselves in tanned deerskins and furs. They decorated their bodies with tattoos, body paint, feathers, and earrings and gorgets of shell, coral, animal bones, and copper. Realizing at once the advantages of cotton, linen, and wool over their usual dressing, they mingled the new clothing materials with the old.[13] Flaps, as many have noted, faintly resembled the regalia worn by Scottish Highlanders. Where once leather had sufficed, now gaudy strouds "pass[ed] between their thighs, and both ends being taken up and drawn through a belt round their waist, the ends fall down, one before, and the other behind, not quite to the knee." The garment was "usually plaited and indented at the ends, and ornamented with beads, tinsel lace, &c." Mantles, made "of the finest cloth" the Indians were "able to purchase, always either of a scarlet or blue colour," were embellished with lace, fringe, silver or brass bells, and scarlet flamingo feathers. Traditional moccasins made from tanned deerskin remained popular but now were richly finished with trade beads. Cloth leggings, personalized with beadwork and tinkling bells, stretched from the ankle to the knee.[14]

Women's and children's styles were generally not as sophisticated as the men's. During the warm season, women wore only "a bit of coloured cloth tied round their waists," to the complete delight of the traders.[15] In cooler weather, they added "a little short waistcoat, usually made of calico, printed linen, or fine cloth, decorated with lace, beads, &c." Brooches, feathers, and "incredible quantities" of silk ribbons adorned their hair.[16] Red and yellow hair ribbons for women were especially popular.[17] Children generally remained naked until puberty. In winter, both women and children kept warm by donning European-made blankets.[18]

Creeks also adopted the clothing styles of the European newcomers. The acceptance of European styles was no doubt hastened by the British practice of awarding suits of clothes, minus trousers, to favored chiefs. Needles, thread, and cloth were also distributed as presents. With the establishment of Georgia, Scots proudly arrayed in tartans descended on the Southeast. The Indians admired their plaids, headdresses, and lack of trousers. Creek women who visited the white settlements or accompanied their husbands to diplomatic congresses were careful to note details of European fashion.[19] Using their new needles, thimbles, and scissors, Creek women became adept at fashioning the imported textiles into European-style clothing. Ready-to-wear shirts were extremely popular among Creek men and were available in both checked and white cloth, with and without ruffles. By the early nineteenth century, native dress had assumed a decidedly Scottish look.[20] Creeks adorned their costumes with shells and other traditional ornaments as well as trade beads, lace, fringe, embroidery, and other decorations.[21]

Belts and boots, hats and handkerchiefs, overcoats and petticoats were shipped thousands of miles to reach Creek buyers. Thimbles, copper tinklers, imported buttons, and bells were strung together to form necklaces and enliven Creek garments. Brass and copper wire were also used as decorative accents. Silver gorgets and arm and wrist plates added exotic glamour. Creek men swathed their heads with cloth and attached baubles to their turbans. Brass trade bells, ostrich feathers, and horn and ivory combs became hair ornaments. Silver earbobs and brooches completed the new Muscogulge fashion. Once costumed, Creeks gazed into imported mirrors and admired the result.[22]

But native material still retained importance, especially on ceremonial occasions. At a "dancing assembly," one visitor to the Creek Nation was astounded by the dress of the women dancers. They "dressed their legs in a kind of leather stockings, hung full of the hoofs of the roe deer in the form of bells." He counted 493 "claws" dangling from one dancer's stockings. In addition, the women wore earrings, bracelets, and other ornaments. When he considered that about sixty-two deer had been necessary to produce the "claws" adorning just one of the dancers, he determined that the costume was "an instance of luxury in dress scarcely to be paralleled by . . . European ladies."[23]

If guns were essential, metal tools and manufactured cloth necessary, and ribbons and other ornamental gewgaws luxury, then West Indian rum was the great evil of the trade. In the absence of any real social prohibition on drunkenness, Creeks found no reason to restrain themselves. Clear-headed Muscogulges correctly understood the inherent dangers of liquor but could do nothing to overturn its popularity or to prohibit the rum trade. Creeks did not drink alcohol in a ceremonial context. Indeed, the very nature of such Creek purification rituals as the expectoration of black drink, fasting, and sweating tended to sober anyone under the influence. Surviving evidence clearly indicates that Creeks drank large quantities of rum to enjoy themselves. While drunk, Creeks abandoned the tight restrictions placed on them by clan etiquette and acted as they pleased, ignoring social taboos. Men and women, freed from their inhibitions and social restraints by tafia, made merry in bawdy orgies lasting several days. Perhaps some sought refuge from the stress and strain of life, but most simply sought release and revelry. One East Floridian, Denys Rolle, was especially irked by the frequent frolics of drunken Seminoles who camped near his settlement on their journeys to and from St. Augustine. Their rowdy "Singing, Dancing, and Hallowing" disturbed his prayers and made his family ill at ease. Still, he could do nothing but row the drunks across the river and offer them coffee for the inevitable "Head-ach" that accompanied sunrise.[24] By the nineteenth century, Creeks had even invented a dance in which they behaved like drunks.[25]

Joy was fleeting. The Creek writer George Stiggins noted that the problem existed "from the national chiefs to the poorest dregs of the nation." He grimly described the unfortunate results of alcohol abuse:

> Chiefs common men and women will wallow in filth and mire so long as they can raise the means to purchase spirits to drink[.] during such time of frenzy they will fight each other indiscriminately frequently takeing each others lives, and when such fracus is over they attribute the whole scene to the spirts they have drank, very truly saying it was not them but the liquor what was in them that fought, well knowing and meaning their peaceable disposition toward each other when in their natural state of sobriety.[26]

Such observations were universal among those who wrote about the Indians. The Georgia surveyor William DeBrahm wrote of the Indians, "[They] love strong Liquors, especially Rum or Brandy, at all times, which they prefer to anything in the World, and this is the only Commodity, for which they exchange their Horses; but great Care must be taken that, after they have consumed the Liquor, they dont steal and carry off the Horse; this is the only Theft they are known to be guilty of, which besides the Crime of the Lie, Knavery and Drunkenness were not known to them, before the Europeans Arrival in America."[27] Those desperate for a drink sometimes even stripped the "wearing shirts" from their back to exchange for liquor.[28]

Upon sobering up, a Creek, if he remembered, regretted his actions, which included everything from breaking down the trader's door to murdering fellow merrymakers. Though there was debate, those guilty of indiscretions while under the influence were generally held accountable, even for accidentally killing others during drunken brawls. Nor were adulterers forgiven. And of course, more than one Creek quite literally lost his shirt, gun, or entire season's catch to the trader's keg.[29]

Price lists were established for all the aforementioned trade items and were set forth in treaties between the colonies and the Creeks. Though individuals might make better or worse deals on occasion, the official exchange rates remained fairly constant throughout the eighteenth century.[30] Creeks knew the established price schedules well, and traders found it hard to raise prices on cloth, blankets, or ammunition and arms, the staples of the Creek trade. But on other items, such as vermilion, knives, scissors, and earbobs, prices fluctuated depending on demand and availability, and Creek consumers often paid more than the official rates for scarce goods.[31]

The rate of exchange established for common goods differed slightly from colony to colony and varied over time. In 1765, the tariffs established in West Florida and Georgia were similar and reflect the standard rates of exchange that existed for the first two-thirds of the eighteenth century. Generally, for one pound of half-dressed leather, a Creek could buy twenty strands of common beads, forty bullets, one dozen pea buttons, a small knife, ten to twelve flints, one-half pint of gunpowder, about one yard of ribbon, one pair of scissors, or one ounce of vermilion. A duffel blanket, at eight pounds of leather, and trade guns, at sixteen pounds of leather or more, were among the most expensive goods. The price of rum was not fixed, but a bottle usually cost one pound of leather, whereas a keg required twenty-five pounds. Fabric prices ranged from one pound of leather for three or four yards of caddis to eight pounds of leather for two yards of heavier wool cloth (strouds). The prices of ready-to-wear shirts ranged from three pounds of leather for a plain white shirt to eight pounds of leather for a fine checked or ruffled shirt. Saddles, priced from thirty to sixty pounds of leather, were seldom purchased. More often, they were acquired as presents or given as rewards for service. Horse bridles cost four pounds of leather. Indians paid from six to ten pounds of leather for horse blankets called housing, depending on quality.[32]

The rapid transformation from a self-sufficient subsistence economy to one based on commercial hunting and trade worked to remake Creek society

Tariff of Trade in the Creek Nation Agreed upon between the Traders and Indians at a Congress Held at Augusta, Georgia, May 27, 1767
In Pounds of Dressed Deerskin

Beads, 5 strands barley corn	1
Beads, 30 strands common	1
Bells, hawks, 10	1
Binding, 4 yards	1
Blanket, plain duffel	8
Blanket, shag end	6
Bridle, snaffle	3
Bullets, 50	1
Buttons, 15 pea	1
Caddice, 1 piece	2
Caddice, 1 piece fine	3
Callico, 1 yard	3
Callico, 1 yard fine	4
Combs, 2 Horn	1
Cotton, striped, 1 yard	2
Cuteaux, 1 small	1
Cuteaux, 1 large	2
Dutch pretties, 1 piece	1
Earbobs, silver, 1 pair	2
Ferret, silk, 3 yards	1
Flannel, striped, 1 yard	2
Flints, 20 common	1
Flints, 15 fine	1
Garlix, 1 yard	1
Gun	16
Gun lock	6
Gunpowder, ¾ pint	1
Handkerchief, Romal	2
Handkerchief, large silk	4
Handkerchief, small silk	3
Hatchets	according to size
Hoe, broad	3
Housing, fringed and laced	according to quality
Kettles, brass or tin	according to size
Knives, 2	1
Linen, 1 yard checked	1
Osnaburgs, 1 yard	1
Plains, white, ½ yard	3
Razor	1
Saddles	according to quality
Scissors	1
Shirt, white	3
Shirt, checked	3
Strouds, 2 yards	8
Vermillion, 1 ounce	1
Wire, brass, 3 spans	1

Note: These prices generally represented a reduction in price from former tariffs.
Source: Journal of the Superintendent's Proceedings, April 24, 1767–June 6, 1767, Gage Papers, William L. Clements Library, Ann Arbor, Michigan.

in numerous ways. At the same time, the strength and adaptability of their culture sustained individual Creeks and provided ways to meet the challenges presented by the deerskin traders, the new hunting mentality, and the influx of manufactured products. Hospitality and the sharing of available goods had always been important in Creek life and remained so despite a new emphasis on material goods. Bartram, though he decried the excesses of the trade, was also quick to note the Muscogulges' most endearing qualities:

> I know a Creek Indian would not only receive into his house a traveller or sojourner, of whatever nation, color, or language (without distinction of rank or any other exception of person), and there treat him as a brother or his own child so long as he pleased to stay, and that without the least hope or thought of interest or reward, but serve him with the best of every thing his abilities could afford. He would divide with you the last grain of corn or piece of flesh, offer you the most valuable things in his possession that he imagines would be acceptable, nay, would part with every thing rather than contend for them, or let a stranger remain or go away necessitous.[33]

The new Muscogulge commercialism did little to alter concepts of property ownership. A hunter's gun, ammunition, and the produce of his hunt were his own, but that had always been so. Creek men traded individually with British traders, keeping the needs of themselves and their families in mind.[34] Communal ownership of land was not abandoned. The public granary continued, and in like manner, headmen redistributed presents from European powers among the people of their town.[35] Some Creeks even regarded the horses of the traders as Creek property, since the horses were "wholly employed in the Service of Trade to the Nation."[36] The practice of burning all "worn-out cloaths and other despicable things" during the Green Corn Celebration (Busk) persisted. Traders must have delighted in the fact that at least once yearly, their patrons found it necessary to "provide themselves with new cloaths, new pots, pans, and other household utensils and furniture."[37]

The custom of burying a man's property with him was maintained, though a few leading men sought to pass on their wealth to their children. Malatchi of Coweta made provisions to have his property transmitted to relatives after his death, a feat that was far from usual.[38] The Wolf of the Muccolossus distributed his herd of two hundred black cattle among his children in 1765 because he feared the cattle might be sacrificed at his death.[39] But most Creek men were buried in the traditional manner, taking their new tools and weapons with them. They were "buried in a sitting posture, and . . . furnished with a musket, powder and ball, a hatchet, pipe, some tobacco, a club, a bow and arrows, a looking glass, some vermillion and other trinkets, in order to come well provided into the world of spirits."[40] Some whites, tempted by the value of Creek grave goods, violated graves and robbed them of their wares.[41]

The significant fact about personal property was that some Creeks, through a variety of means, managed to acquire more than most of their neighbors. Some began to pass on their wealth to their relatives after death. Native society slowly began to exhibit signs of differentiation by wealth. Those who aspired to material wealth, more often than not, were of mixed blood. Yet, even those who were the wealthiest by Creek standards were never as materialistic and acquisitive as their Anglo-American neighbors. And material wealth continued to count for less among the Creeks than did family connection and clan ties. In 1784, Alexander McGillivray noted the limitations of economic power in the Creek country, "Since I cannot use wealth in this country and expect never to leave it, all that I want is a decent living."[42] And significantly, wealth had to be measured in personal property—not land. Land continued to be community property, but acquisitive Creeks could—and did—amass stocks of cattle, horses, and slaves and use land allotted to their matrilineage as if it were their own.

The Creeks welcomed the improved tools, weapons, and implements brought by the trade. Many goods merely replaced items of native manufacture, and Creeks continued their normal activities of farming and hunting, albeit greatly aided by European hoes, axes, hatchets, and knives. Creek women replaced their handmade tools and utensils with those furnished by the trader as well. Though they continued to manufacture ceramic pottery and still used the traditional mortar and pestle for grinding corn, they also began using brass and tin kettles. Metal spoons and plates appeared around Muscogulge firesides. The new housewares made boiling and other cooking tasks easier. In addition, they were valuable during the winter hunts, since they were easily carried and less fragile than pottery. Imported needles, thimbles, scissors, and knives made life easier and more productive.[43]

The improved tools meant that traditional tasks were completed faster and better. As a result, Creek craftsmen neglected their arts, and there was a decline in both quantity and quality of native manufactures. Metal replaced stone, bone, and shell. This replacement of Creek manufactures with the commensurate loss of native handicrafts was one of the most significant results of the deerskin trade and lay at the heart of the Muscogulges' economic dependence on imported goods.[44]

The abandonment of traditional training in native crafts and manufactures fractured the bond between generations of Creek men. Much high-quality interaction between young men and their elders disappeared as old skills and manufacturing techniques fell into disrepute and were not passed on to succeeding generations. Creek youths, enamored by the power of guns and the excitement of the chase and combat, grew weary of the old-fashioned probity of their elders. The pressures of commercial hunting, the long periods spent in hunting camps, the ready supplies of rum, and the influence of lawless traders combined to further erode respect for traditional authority and the virtues of restraint. The very nature of Creek society encouraged young warrior-hunters to be bold and reckless. Heedless of the admonitions of their more thoughtful elders, they were a volatile and head-strong force in Creek political life. They were often absent from their towns, away from the watchful eyes of their elders, and if they did not seek trouble, they often found it.[45]

Creeks roaming the forests in search of deer often clashed with their neighbors, both red and white. Young warriors drank themselves senseless and committed outrages against their own people and their white neighbors. Tensions increased all along the Creek frontiers, and respectable men on both sides of the border decried the "Boisterous & Wanton" nature of Creek youth.[46] Horse thievery became a lucrative, but dangerous, frontier activity. And the bravery and daring required to snatch horses from well-armed and hostile "Virginians" provided a way for young warriors to assert their manhood and strike back at whites who encroached on Creek hunting lands. In a society that placed the highest regard on sharing and scrupulous honesty, the prevalence of such activities was more than simply a dishonor. It also symbolized the breakdown of time-honored values as a result of trade dependence and the growing importance of personal wealth in Creek society.[47]

Traditional female activities, including the preparation of deerskins and the manufacture of clothing, were accentuated by the trade. The continued importance of subsistence agriculture and the reliance on native pottery as opposed to imported ceramic ware also reinforced female roles and strengthened the bond between generations of Creek women. Creek females, left to the care of their clanswomen and elder male relatives, noticed less disruption in their daily lives. The relative stability of the female role helped offset the ill effects of the trade and white contact on Creek men and bolstered traditional social institutions.[48]

This stability and traditionalism among Creek women was of tremendous importance in light of the many marriages and cross-cultural relationships between Creek women and the deerskin traders who came among them. Some traders ignored their offspring, but many, including such prominent men as George Galphin, Lachlan McGillivray, and James Germany, built close relationships with their Creek families. These men introduced a number of new notions into Creek family life, including ideas of patrilineal descent. But Creek mothers sought to maintain family values and raised their children in the traditional method. Outsiders were confused by the clan system, based on matrilineal kinship, and often recorded garbled and confused pictures of Creek society.[49] But the Creeks were not confused. Despite external and internal pressures, Creek society remained essentially matrilineal. "Children always fall to the woman's lot," related one early historian. "It even seems impossible for the Christians to get their children."[50] Though often a trader wished to send his mixed-blood progeny east for a "proper" education in Charleston or Savannah, he had to first obtain the permission of his wife and her matrilineage. Such permission was not always forthcoming. The matrilineal clan system absorbed the newcomers and remained the basis for Creek society.[51]

Trade goods were expensive, and Creeks of all ages and stations were aware of the need to procure large numbers of deerskins for the trade. Overhunting in home ranges led, of necessity, to an expansion of the Creek domain. Defense of traditional hunting grounds and the conquest of new ones became the Muscogulges' preeminent preoccupation. The Creeks were, as Bartram so eloquently noted, "a proud, haughty and arrogant race of men . . . brave and valiant in war, ambitious of conquest, restless and perpetually exercising their arms."[52] The Creeks slowly enlarged their effective hunting territory via wars against the Florida tribes, the Cherokees, and the Choctaws. The hunt, sandwiched on many occasions between raids against the enemy, ranged wider and lasted longer. Oftentimes, war parties specifically set out to engage the enemy in the field. Smoked venison, deer hides, and unarmed women and children became fair booty for rival parties of armed warriors. Depending on the state of affairs among the southeastern tribes, some hunting grounds lay unused as intertribal conflict rendered the land more dangerous for humans than for deer.

A series of protracted wars marred Creek-Cherokee relations between 1716 and 1754. The causes of the conflict were complex and sprang not only from the machinations of European powers but also from the nature of Indian society and warfare. In 1749, due to the intercession of South Carolina, the Upper Creeks and Cherokees managed to restore good relations. The Lower Creeks declined the peaceful overtures, and for them, the entire character of the war changed. No longer content to field limited war parties, whose aim was to seek retribution for attacks against their people, the Lower Creeks of Coweta and Cussita decided on a war of conquest aimed at acquiring valuable hunting territory from the Lower Cherokee towns. In April 1750, Malatchi of Coweta led five hundred Creek warriors against the Lower Cherokee towns of Echoi and Estatoe. The Cherokees suffered heavy casualties, and the Creek victors looted and burned the villages. Several border incidents resulted in a brief South Carolina trade embargo against the Cherokees in 1751. While their enemies were suffering from a shortage of guns and ammunition, the Lower Creeks stepped up their attacks. In 1752, Creek parties raided several major Cherokee villages, including Hiwassee. Keowee, Tugalo, and most other Lower Cherokee towns were destroyed, leaving numerous casualties and creating a refugee problem in the Overhill and Middle Cherokee villages. James Adair reported that near the end of the war, the Creeks had so thoroughly beaten their enemies "that in contempt, they sent several of their women and small boys against them, though, at that time, the Cheerake were the most numerous."[53]

In April 1754, aided by the intervention of Governor James Glen of South Carolina, Cherokee deputies visited Coweta to participate in peace ceremonies that formally closed the fourteen-year conflict and established a lasting peace between the two tribes. Creek peace terms were harsh, and the Lower Cherokees were forced to renounce claim to valuable hunting territory that lay between the Little and Broad rivers on the south side of the Savannah River above Augusta, Georgia.[54]

Creeks also looked westward, to the "plentiful borders of the Chactaws."[55] Though there were numerous clashes with other neighboring tribes, the war that erupted between the Choctaws and the Creek towns in 1763 was the longest—and the most disastrous—for the Creeks. Creek-Choctaw hostility was of long standing. Choctaw villagers had been easy targets for Creek slavers early in the century, and both nations claimed prime hunting grounds along the Alabama-Tombigbee river system. The Choctaws had been deprived of adequate supplies of trade goods, especially guns, by the inability of their French allies to sustain an adequate trade. The situation had suited the Creeks perfectly, for their ancient enemies thus lacked guns with which to threaten their security, and on occasion, Creeks acted as middlemen in the limited Anglo-Choctaw trade.[56]

The British were determined to establish peaceful relations with the Choctaws after the Seven Years' War. The Creeks, alarmed over the prospect that the Choctaws might be supplied with adequate weapons by British traders out of Mobile, attempted to thwart the Anglo-Choctaw rapprochement. In 1763, Britain held a general congress of all the southern tribes at Augusta in order to establish better relations in the wake of the French withdrawal from North America. Creeks stymied Choctaw participation at the congress by threatening to kill any Choctaw emissary traveling through their country. Only one Choctaw, the pro-British headman Red Shoes, traveling among the Chickasaws, managed to reach Augusta. To ensure his safety, the British sent him back to Mobile on a naval vessel. When it became clear that the British and the Choctaws had come to terms, Creek warriors instigated a war to disrupt the budding commercial relationship and to protect Creek claims to disputed hunting territory, particularly land on the east side of the Tombigbee River. The ploy backfired, and Britain profited from the ensuing carnage. The contested territory north of Pensacola, between the Alabama and Escambia rivers, was vividly described by William Bartram as "a solitary, uninhabited wilderness, the bloody field of Schambe, where those contending bands of American bravos, Creeks and Chactaws," often met "in dire conflict."[57]

As it became increasingly apparent that the Choctaw War was a bad thing, a group of Upper Creek headmen sent peace talks to the Choctaws in an attempt to negotiate a settlement, and even sought the assistance of the British and the Chickasaws.[58] Due to the nature of the Creek political process, their efforts failed.[59] Creeks who opposed peace simply continued to attack. Some micos, sensing an opportunity to keep "restless" young warriors so busy that they would not harass the traders, repeatedly thwarted peace negotiations. Those who lost clansmen to Choctaw guns and hatchets were duty-bound to seek blood vengeance and had little choice but to continue the carnage. Others simply enjoyed the opportunity to earn war honors. For some, war parties served as a convenient cloak for the plunder of Choctaw traders and West Florida plantations. And so the war continued. The costs of the war were staggering. In addition to the dead and wounded, the war disrupted winter hunting, thereby reducing productivity. And by its nature, warfare demanded excessive consumption of ammunition, imported war paint, and rum.

Some Creeks, seeking better hunting territory, moved southward into the Florida peninsula. There was little to oppose their progress in this direction, for the region's population had been decimated by disease and the Creek slaving raids of previous decades. Now, Creek settlers eagerly stalked the herds of the rich Alachua savannah. The ultimate result of this southward migration was the establishment of the Seminole Nation. The first Seminoles, led by the Cowkeeper, settled on the Alachua savannah near present-day Gainesville, Florida. Their town was called Cuscowilla. The Cowkeeper and his band were Oconee Indians. The remaining small Florida tribes in the area, as well as other Indians who had earlier fled South Carolina during the Yamasee War, resisted but were quickly defeated.[60] The Oconees triumphed, primarily due to the influx of Creeks seeking better hunting or a safe haven from clan vengeance. Yamasees and others who resisted their advance were enslaved. Hunters from other towns along the Chattahoochee soon joined the Oconees.[61] They established a number of other towns around the Alachua area. Talhasochte was established along the Suwanne River. Other new settlements sprang up in the territory that had belonged to the Apalachee Indians (near modern Tallahassee, Florida), whose towns the Creeks had destroyed in the early part of the century.[62] With their more northern brethren, Seminole warriors trooped westward to harass Choctaw warriors and track their game.[63]

The Lower Creeks were not happy with the defection of the Oconees, and Stuart reported that the nations wanted the Seminoles to return so that they could be properly supervised by the leading Lower Creek Towns.[64] The Oconee exodus was duplicated among the Upper Towns by the departure of a group of Alabama tribesmen from their towns along the Coosa and Alabama rivers. About forty Alabama gunmen and their families moved to Manchac, a small British settlement just east of the Mississippi River.[65] Their reasons were clear: they did not approve of the Creek-Choctaw war and were tired of being harassed by both belligerents.[66] There were various other Creek outsettlements.[67] The Mortar established a village on the upper reaches of the Coosa River where it met Coosawaitee Creek.[68] His settlement allowed access to the richer game lands of the mountainous regions and provided a place to conduct diplomacy with the Chickasaws and Cherokees unhampered by his Abeika opposition.

More distressing was the movement of less well-meaning groups to the frontier, away from the meddling of village elders. Semipermanent settlements by vagrant Creeks often protected illegal trading and liquor establishments. Here, rogues and horse thieves, both white and red, gathered to drink and do business.[69] One of the most infamous outsettlements was Buzzards' Roost, an illegal trading post on the Chattahoochee River about which Creek headmen repeatedly complained. Edmund Barnard, who was George Galphin's nephew, did a thriving business here with hunters from the Upper Towns. Primarily a tippling house, Barnard's business stocked mostly rum, and young hunters often returned home with little more than a hangover to show for their efforts.[70]

Pucknawheatly, or the Standing Peach Tree, a detached village located on the Ocmulgee River about seventy miles from the Georgia boundary, was another infamous settlement. It was peopled primarily by Cowetas, but Creeks from other Lower Towns lived there as well. The leader of the village was Houmahta, a notorious Creek outlaw.[71] The White Boy, the town's mixed-blood storekeeper, was supplied from George Galphin's Silver Bluff store. There he traded the undressed deerskins he received from the hunters for trade goods and rum.[72] The village's location was an ideal staging site for horse-stealing raids against Georgia farms.

Despite the efforts of Creek hunter-warriors to acquire better hunting ranges, consumption always outstripped production in the Creek country. As John Stuart observed, "The best hunter can do very little more than supply himself & Family with bare necessaries."[73] As a result, hunter and trader alike turned to the use of credit. Creeks quickly grasped the meaning of credit and debts, and when possible, they were eager to discharge their obligations. At death, a man's relatives attempted to pay off whatever he owed, since Creeks traditionally did not repeat the name of a dead loved one and did not care to have traders do it either.[74]

All the colonies that traded with the Creeks established certain well-defined and narrow limits for the extension of credit in order to protect both Indians and honest traders. The usual credit limit was thirty pounds' weight of dressed deerskin per year, with any extension of the limit rendered unrecoverable. Also, traders were limited to crediting Indians with no more than five pounds of powder and twelve pounds of bullets per hunting season in order to preclude the formation of armories by the Indians.[75] Such restrictions were, of necessity, widely ignored. To conduct trade, Indians required credit, and they routinely received more goods than they paid for. The practice of "trusting" a customer with more than the legal credit limit was widespread. Indeed, Indians often demanded credit, and many times the trader was forced to accede to their request or the goods would be forcibly removed from his store. Even the most respectable traders "deviated" from established guidelines.[76] During the Choctaw War, a party of forty Seminole warriors assured James Spalding's factor, Charles McLatchy, that their proposed expedition to the Tombigbee region would result in hides "sufficient not only to pay their debts, about to be contracted, but be able to make other considerable purchases." The terms McLatchie offered them were about what most Creeks could expect from their village traders: "one half to be paid for directly, and the remainder to stand on credit until their return from the expedition."[77]

Creeks, regardless of their success at the hunt or their gain from other economic enterprises, acquired greater debts year after year.[78] The causes of the Creeks' growing national debt were complex. Wars against the Cherokees and the Choctaws frequently curtailed the hunting season and resulted in higher expenditures of powder and shot. As deer populations shrank, even the most determined hunters found it difficult to gather enough deerskins to cover the goods they received on credit. Rum, watered down or not, consumed plenty of hard-won deerskins. It is impossible to calculate the monetary cost of the rum trade to Creek society, but it can be affirmed that the huge debts the Creek people had accumulated by the last quarter of the eighteenth century were largely due to excessive consumption of rum.[79] The personal cost of the rum trade is also inestimable. The Creeks found it impossible to maintain their new standards of living without credit. Traders, eager to gain and maintain customers, readily acquired debts of their own to supply the Creeks, and the chain of debt extended from Little Tallassee to London.[80] Economic dependence and individual debt became the most important consequences of Creek participation in the market exchange economy.

During the eighteenth century, the Muscogulges embraced a new trading economy and, to the best of their ability, molded the commerce to suit their culture and condition. Their most commendable traits, firmly rooted in tradition and interwoven into the moral fiber of the people, could be neither erased nor diminished by the "mercenary empirics" who came among them.[81] "Progress," as always, carried a heavy price, and increasingly the Muscogulges came to realize that their reliance on foreign technology had serious drawbacks. Once, the Creeks had obtained every item they needed for a plentiful and wholesome existence with tools made by their own hands. Now, Creek producers depended on outsiders for guns and ammunition—

their means of production and the basis of their power. With every exchange of deerskins for duffels, Creeks bartered away their economic self-sufficiency. And in spite of all the new strategies they developed to obtain foreign manufactures, Creeks always consumed goods that were worth more than those they produced. Debt, excessive use of alcohol, a growing inequality of wealth among the people, war, and a breakdown of traditional authority were of grave concern to all Creek people. It was left to the Muscogulge leadership to deal with the consequences of Creek consumerism.

CHAPTER 8

Politics and
the Trade Alliance

The steady conduct of the deerskin trade required patient negotiation and accommodation between the Creeks and the British. Yet the loosely structured, ill-defined collection of independent towns that constituted the Muscogulge Confederacy lacked a delegated apparatus for the conduct of foreign relations, and no new political institutions emerged during the eighteenth century to address these concerns. Instead, after the establishment of European settlements, the town unit retained its primacy as the most important Muscogulge political division. It fell to town leaders to devise foreign policy and provide the "official" response to the new economic and political world developing around them.

This enormous responsibility was hampered by the decentralized nature of the Creek Confederacy of towns as well as by a number of other factors, including Creek relations with France and Spain and other southeastern Indian tribes. Domestic unrest and unruliness, largely the consequences of commercial hunting and the out-migration of sizable numbers of Creeks, further complicated matters. Despite such difficulties, the men who directed Muscogulge foreign affairs were highly talented and astute politicians who achieved remarkable success in their dealings with Anglo-America. Leading micos (also called *miculga*) and other high officials negotiated trade treaties, established boundaries with their expanding neighbors, and were continually employed in maintaining peace by accommodating differences between their towns and the British.

At first, Creek towns conducted business singly with the newcomers. Coweta, as the largest town on the Chattahoochee, was the most eagerly courted. A succession of powerful micos during the early eighteenth century assured Coweta's ascendancy.[1] But by mid-century, vigorous leadership at Coweta had weakened, and the smaller non–Muskogean-speaking tribes of the Chattahoochee Valley began to assert their independence. Nor could Coweta speak for the Abeikas, Tallapooses, and Alabamas, whose towns lay farther west.[2] Geography partitioned the Muscogulge towns into two regional groups, commonly called nations. There was a sense of common identity, and both divisions acknowledged they were "one People."[3] But Upper Creeks made it clear again and again, "As we look upon the lower Creeks to be a different nation from us; we cannot intermeddle with them."[4] Nor did the Lower Creeks attempt to direct Upper policy. It was this unity of spirit and division of authority that constituted the Creek Confederacy.

Still, there was a need for discussion and agreement among towns and between the two geographic divisions as Europeans and an increasing dependence on imported trade goods presented new opportunities and problems for the Muscogulges. In the absence of a mechanism for devising or implementing a unified position, leadership at the town level was forced to assume new regional and national authority. For most of the eighteenth century, Muscogulge foreign relations were conducted by assemblies of headmen who spoke as representatives for their towns in the regional councils of the Upper and Lower towns, thereby confirming the geographic reality of a bipartite division among Creek towns. Individual town autonomy suffered as regional coalitions and collective negotiation became a necessity.

Though they exchanged emissaries and kept each other informed of their positions, there was no single, organized national council of Upper and Lower towns during the colonial period. Instead, the two divisions conducted their meetings at different times and places as events demanded. Leading men communicated frequently by conducting informal visits, dispatching messengers to other towns, or attending regional meetings to discuss pressing concerns. Though this conservatism hindered the development of a unified Creek approach to European encroachment and economic dependence, it was largely successful in steering Creek policy until the end of the eighteenth century.

The regional conferences were not held on a regular basis. Tribes, such as the Abeikas or Alabamas, came together yearly to review their history and ponder their future.[5] Of more importance were assemblies that were called by a particular headman or group of headmen due to a crisis or matter that demanded attention. The arrival of a diplomatic representative from the colonies also required that the headmen assemble.[6] Runners, carrying bundles of canes denoting the number of days before such a meeting was to be held, were dispatched to leading men throughout the region.[7] The mico usually spoke for his town at such gatherings, but occasionally war leaders or Second Men represented their town.

The meetings were conducted according to established ceremony, with specific seating and speaking arrangements based on the relationship among the towns. Lower Creek headmen met most often at Chehaw and Apalachicola, both white towns. Apalachicola had the distinction of being regarded as the oldest town in the confederacy. Conferences were seldom held at Coweta, since it was a red town. Okchai, Little Tallassee, and Tuckabatchee were the most prestigious Upper Towns where conferences were held. Sometimes the Abeikas, Tallapooses, and Alabamas, the three tribes that constituted the Upper Nation, met together. At other times, they met separately.[8] The result of these innate divisions in Creek governance was differing perceptions of the proper course of action. The town, tribal, and regional divisions sometimes resulted in factionalism and more difficult negotiation as each group interpreted its interest in a different light. This was particularly true before 1763, when French spokesmen were always eager to present alternative points of view for Creek consideration.

What is important is that the Creek people came to be recognized by the British on a regional basis during the eighteenth century. A coterie of the most talented and respected leading men from the most prominent towns of the two geographic divisions within the Creek Confederacy determined the Creek response to the European intrusion. The historian David Corkran believed that the Creeks withstood the perils that confronted them during the eighteenth century better than any other southern Indian nation. According to Corkran, their "success was a triumph of their well-developed system of council and consensus—republican rather than democratic, a congeries of semi-representative and hereditary oligarchs which functioned in a rude parliamentarianism."[9] By the nineteenth century, Creek political institutions had undergone subtle changes, but leading men still made all the important decisions. One mixed-blood Creek labeled the nineteenth-century Muscogulge government "a tyrannical oligarchy in its principles and practiced under that head to the full extent." He explained, "For all public business whether of a national or private character is done by the chiefs."[10] Power was based on one's position, usually hereditary, in the town government. Powerful oratory and forceful actions buttressed the leading men's authority, British attention ratified their prominence, and their ability to secure trade goods and presents sustained it. The new regional leaders relied heavily on the support of their clansmen from all towns in the confederacy to help them implement the treaty agreements they made. Although these men were directed by their towns to represent villagers at regional meetings, they lacked an effective mechanism for implementing any course of action the council might decide on.

The most influential Creek spokesmen who directed the regional councils usually supported close ties to the British colonies because of Britain's strength and reliability as a trade partner. For their part, the British were eager to reward friendly headmen, especially before 1763. When the wives of Captain Allick, the mixed-blood mico of Coweta, openly complained that they were impoverished, British officials took steps to secure a herd of cattle for the mico.[11] Other leaders were regularly clothed, armed, and inebriated at crown expense. Many of the presents that Britain distributed to Creek micos "trickled down" to the warriors and others who supported the headmen in council. Yet though British favor was important, it was not paramount. The support of a foreign government could help a man rise in the ranks, but foreign disfavor could not unseat a legitimate Creek mico.[12] Indeed, the British consistently sought the advice and council of leading Creek headmen when appointing medal chiefs and dispensing commissions.[13]

Once they had established their course at regional conclaves, the leading headmen, together with their warriors and junior partners, prepared to parley. Those with the ability to directly and forcefully communicate the ideas of the Creek councils became the authorized spokesmen for their fellow headmen. In 1765, the Mortar told the British, "I am the Voice of my People who are all to abide by what I say or do."[14] Tallachea of Ockmulge was known among his people as "Tama, flame of the tongue." He stated, "My people always employed [me] to talk for them." In 1768, he claimed to represent the interests of ten Lower Towns.[15] Recognition and prestige followed a man's appointment as a spokesman for the other headmen. But by then, the spokesman had already acquired power in his own right. The Mortar, of the Bear clan, was the mico of Okchai; Tallachea was the headman of Ockmulge.[16] The Creek oligarchs, nervous that one man might acquire too great a voice in their relations with the British, constantly enjoined their allies to transact business only with those duly authorized by general consent of all the headmen.[17]

The headmen met with colonial and imperial officials at congresses or conferences to discuss their relationships and resolve their differences. Their most common destinations were Charleston and Augusta, although Savannah, Pensacola, and Picolata, in East Florida, were also the sites of important gatherings. The results of the conferences were spelled out in treaties, which both sides agreed to uphold. The Muscogulge oligarchs undertook a threefold obligation in their dealings with the British colonies: to establish procedures and regulations for the deerskin trade, to preserve the Creek domain while at the same time granting land for the colonists, and to accommodate all differences between the two peoples.

The establishment of Augusta, Georgia, and the emergence of specialty trading companies ensured a plentiful flow of trade goods into Creek towns, and during the remainder of the colonial period, Creek headmen espoused two concerns about the trade: better trade prices and better traders. It was the English, first in South Carolina and then in Georgia, who established the Creek exchange rates. The Creeks complied and gladly accepted what they considered to be a fair exchange. The schedules listing the value of English goods in pounds of dressed leather were attached to most Anglo-Creek treaties. The rates set for the Creeks were more favorable than those established by the British for the Choctaws and Chickasaws and were much better than those offered by the French.

It was not until the Creeks realized that it was possible for trade rates to be even lower that they became dissatisfied with the established prices. This happened in the late 1740s, when leading Creeks discovered that the exchange rates for the Cherokee towns were markedly better than their own. During a tense meeting between Creeks and South Carolina officials in 1753, incensed headmen demanded that the governor use his influence to lower trade prices. Governor Glen responded: "Trade is a Plant of a very tender and delicate Nature. It delights in Freedom and will not be forced." This weak reply neither amused nor convinced the ruffled headmen.[18] When pressed, the governor noted that the Cherokee leather was thicker than the Creek leather and that the distance between the Creek towns and Charleston contributed to the high prices. The Creeks were still unconvinced. One headman stated that the traders charged such high prices to make up for the large quantities of goods they dispensed free "to their Wives and Women which they keep." Other warriors, disgruntled and convinced they had been cheated, stalked out of the room.[19]

With the establishment of peace after the bitter war between the Creeks and the Cherokees in the 1750s, the Gun Merchant of Okchai and thirty

Okchai warriors, along with their wives and children, traveled to Cherokee territory to affirm the peace. During discussions with leading Cherokees, trade prices proved a popular topic. The Cherokees explained that their rates had been lowered after they made war on Carolina, and they advised the Creeks to pursue the same course. The argument failed to convince the Creeks, at least the important ones, and the Gun Merchant of the Okchai decided on a different course. He invited the Cherokee traders to his hunting camp to do business—at Cherokee prices. When the Gun Merchant returned home the following spring, he immediately called a meeting of all headmen and deerskin traders in the Upper Towns and vigorously presented his views to the assemblage. "Before I had an Opportunity of coming to the Knowledge of a Cherrockee Trade I was easy without it, and had no Thought of it, but now that I am, I cannot be easy till I obtain it."[20]

The Gun Merchant and a host of other micos pressed the issue for a number of years and even expressed a willingness to make significant concessions in order to obtain better prices. Over the course of their negotiations, Muscogulge headmen developed a number of worthwhile arguments designed to win price abatements. All were quick to point out that English settlements lay on former Indian hunting grounds and that therefore the English should be willing to reduce their prices in gratitude for the land the Creeks had so generously granted to them. Governors cared little for the rhetoric, and their merchants and traders always countered by reminding the Creeks that the transportation costs to the Creek towns were high. After 1763, when the headmen retorted that goods from West Florida should cost less because of easier transportation, they were ignored.[21] These and countless other logical observations by the Muscogulge oligarchs failed to roll back the Creek price schedule until 1767, when prices were finally adjusted to Creek advantage at the Augusta trade conference sponsored by John Stuart. The conference reflected the demands of the market rather than those of the headmen, for after 1763, the Creek country was flooded with traders who were eager to undercut the prices of competitors. The new tariff was designed to stabilize falling trade prices in order to save established merchants. Overall, the prices of the most popular goods were reduced by an average of one pound of dressed leather. Even so, prominent headmen rightly viewed the concessions as a victory and immediately redoubled their efforts to maintain peaceful relations with the colonies.[22]

Besides complaining about the high cost of manufactured goods in relation to deerskins, Creeks condemned the unethical practices of their traders. Creeks loathed the tactics of traders who swapped rum for raw skins "in the woods" and operated tippling joints along the Creek-Georgia frontier. Indians who fell prey to the scams blamed the rum and those who peddled it for their troubles. Whites who scoured Creek lands for game were particularly detested, and Creek townspeople consistently enjoined their headmen to clear the riffraff from their territory. The Muscogulge oligarchs passed their complaints along to any British official who would listen. Governors were quick to agree that the accusations were true and the annoyance real, but they never devised a means of enforcing rules against such behavior. John Stuart's 1767 Augusta accord incorporated virtually all the Muscogulges' demands for the regulation of deerskin traders. The ambitious licensing program was warmly received by the Creeks. But when the British ministry withdrew the plan, the agreements were effectively nullified, especially those concerning the sale of rum and the extension of credit.[23]

Unable to implement an imperial system for effectively controlling the traders, John Stuart recommended to the Muscogulges that they take matters into their own hands. At the 1771 Congress of Pensacola, he bluntly told the headmen:

> When you meet white hunters in the woods you have a right to the skins of your own deer and the guns with which they were killed. As to persons unlicensed carrying on an illicit trade in the woods, your people have in their power to discourage that practice by taking their skins, for men breaking the laws of their country are not entitled to their protection. Settling stores in the woods, distant from any town or settlement, is contrary to the King's orders and an infringement on your right, which is in your own power to prevent by obliging such offenders to remove.[24]

But most attempts by headmen to police their frontiers simply resulted in more problems, usually charges by whites of unfair harassment or outright violence. At Buzzards' Roost, a notorious frontier tippling house, it was possible on any given day to find "great numbers of white and Red people, who had been trading in the Woods, lying drunk with bottles in their Hands."[25] Emisteseguo, of Little Tallassee, raised the ire of both his own people and the Georgia trading establishment when he stormed Buzzards' Roost in 1771, confiscated the goods and deerskins, and distributed them to impoverished Upper Creeks. The respected headman was forced to apologize and defend his actions while unscrupulous traders simply restocked.[26]

Headmen, ethical traders, and government officials alike wanted the rum traffic regulated. Headmen thought it reasonable that traders be allowed to bring rum into their towns for their personal use, as well as a "small Quantity sufficient to Procure Provisions & Pay for the Building of Stores & Houses." They were also happy to accept presents of rum for services rendered or as a mark of British recognition. John Stuart's regulations reflected these sentiments: licensed traders could carry fifteen gallons or four small kegs into the Indian villages every three months with the superintendent's blessings. Any amount over this was subject to confiscation.[27] But these regulations were first ignored and then overturned with the abrogation of imperial control of the trade in 1767. With the proliferation of traders, Creek headmen suggested a more effective scheme whereby limits would be set "per town" rather than for individual traders. In 1772, after a particularly violent bacchanal in which some of their young men were killed and others severely burned, Tallapoose headmen demanded that no more than four kegs of rum be brought into their towns at one time by all traders. The Abeikas, who had seen less trouble, were willing to allow ten kegs into their towns.[28] The suggestions, of course, had no effect at all on the rum peddlers, who simply moved their business to the hunting camps or along the trading paths away from the disgruntled nattering of a town's prohibitionists.

Faced with a lack of regulation and enforcement by the Anglo-Americans, somber headmen took the matter into their own hands. On his travels, William Bartram met two traders from Pensacola who were illegally transporting forty kegs of Jamaican rum into the Upper Creek country. According to the usual practice of "dashing it," or diluting it with water, the pair would have been able to produce at least eighty kegs for distribution to the Indians. The traders were soon overtaken by a party of Creek warriors, "who discovering their species of merchandize, they forthwith struck their tomahawks into every keg, giving the liquor to the thirsty sand, not tasting a drop of it themselves; and they [the traders] had enough to do to keep the tomahawks from their own skulls."[29] But in the long run, there were more kegs than temperate warriors, and the rum trade suffered such minor setbacks as a regular part of business. The Creek headmen may have been among America's earliest prohibitionists, but their efforts to impose sobriety and to control the sale of spirits were as ineffectual as those of the British colonial establishment.[30] In the absence of specifically appointed law-enforcement officials—either white or Indian—even the most dedicated headmen and leading warriors could not effectively patrol and police the hundreds of square miles of Creek hunting territory.

Trade presented new economic opportunities for some, especially those of mixed blood. Creek factors and traders gained prestige and authority from their economic position within the community. The support they could expect from their clan members meant that it was impossible for Creek headmen to halt the unsavory practices in which many indulged, particularly the rum trade. This new economic class of factors presented real threats to traditional authority.[31] Formerly, micos had protected the trader and benefited from the patronage. With the advent of Indian factors, headmen lost prestige as well as their link to "presents" from the village traders. The distribution of presents from the mico to his followers assured support for his positions in the town square. Now, many factors controlled the distribution of free trade goods. By the end of the century, a class of mixed-blood traders had emerged who were able to exercise tremendous influence in the direction of national affairs. Coupled with this was the fact that Indian factors tended toward unlawful behavior. It is no wonder many headmen turned against their fellow entrepreneurs and constantly lobbied against the employment of Indians as factors and packhorsemen. Like most other trade evils, the practice continued unabated even though prohibited by the British.[32]

Although eager for trade, the Creeks were apprehensive about the growth of their colonial neighbors. John Stuart, one of the most knowledgeable observers of the Creeks, wrote, "The jealousy of the Indians upon account of their lands, I have always considered as the principal source of their discontent and uneasyness."[33] The Creeks recognized the absolute necessity of transferring title to some of their lands to the newcomers, for without settlements, there could be no trade. At the same time, they sought to limit the expansion of the white settlements in order to preserve their own hunting grounds.

Theoretically, Creek lands were owned equally by all members of the confederacy as their "natural Inheritance."[34] Emistesequo, speaking on behalf of the Upper Towns in 1771, said, "Every child [in the nation] has an equal property in the land with the first warrior."[35] The natural inheritance or equal property of which the headmen spoke was the right to use the land. But neither warriors nor children were empowered to alienate their share of the Creek domain. Land was controlled or owned by the various tribes, or towns, of the confederacy. Each tribe held title to specific regions. The headman in each town allocated land to the various clans in his town based on need, and the clan elders further divided the land among the matrilineages. The hunting reserves were open to all. Basing their actions on their ancient prerogative to apportion cropland among the matrilineages of their towns, headmen conducted negotiations with European powers regarding the transfer of Creek lands. As in other matters, their decisions were founded on general consensus and widespread popular support.[36]

As a result, there were few Creek cessions during the colonial period. The initial tract from the Lower Towns to Oglethorpe for the establishment of Georgia was confined to the tidewater. Georgians were merely granted the "use of" the land, and the treaty required that each new white settlement established by the colony set aside some area for the use of the Indians, for which they would retain title.[37] During the ensuing years, there were minor alterations in the grant.[38]

After the removal of the French and Spanish from the Southeast in 1763, Britain's southern colonies were freed from the threat of war along their boundaries, and white populations surged upward. In addition, Britain took control of East and West Florida, necessitating meetings and negotiations with the Creeks for a confirmation of the transfer. When the British first assumed control of the lands formerly occupied by the French and Spanish, the Creeks quickly pointed out that the land in question had only been "loaned" to the defeated Europeans and demanded that Creek permission be obtained in order to ratify the transfer of empires. The British recognized the legitimacy of Creek claims to the lands and were eager to secure legal grants of territory. This was accomplished at congresses held in Augusta, Georgia, in 1763, at Pensacola, West Florida, in 1764, and at Fort Picolata, East Florida, in 1765.[39]

Between 1763 and 1783, the Creek headmen negotiated more land grants than in the previous thirty years. Though sizable areas were ceded, most of their territory was retained. To protect the deerskin trade and limit conflict between the Indians and colonials, the British government sought to impose limits on unchecked colonial expansion and to protect the Indians' land by the establishment of an Indian boundary line, a no-man's-land designed to divide two potential adversaries.[40]

For their part, Creek headmen often proved to be expert negotiators. The Upper Towns claimed the land bordering West Florida, and negotiations with the British for territory in that area were undertaken by Upper headmen. Lower Creeks owned the land bordering East Florida and Georgia. Still, widespread agreement among all the towns was necessary before land could be alienated. The Upper Towns were especially blessed with stalwart chiefs and weak neighbors. The Lower Towns, hindered by a wavering leadership and more vulnerable to a growing and greedy Georgia, parted more readily with their land, often to the chagrin of their Upper Creek fellows. More than once, headmen hinted that they wished to check colonial expansion, referring to their trade partners as "the white People who live upon the Coast." Their British friends, however, were eager to escape their coastal limits and possess the piedmont.[41]

These land cessions resulted in a series of new boundary lines between the Creeks and their colonial neighbors. Ideally, the Creeks preferred natural boundaries, such as rivers and streams, but where this was not possible, the Indians eagerly agreed to help clear and mark the boundaries by blazing trees and removing brush.[42] A marked boundary line was necessary to clearly delineate Creek and British lands, and the Creeks made it clear that they would not welcome border jumpers. They frequently asserted that they intended to seize the property of trespassers and kill cattle that strayed across the line, and they demanded that Britain support their right to protect their property. Instead, the British preferred to reward them for driving cattle back across the line and asked that they report boundary violations to the proper authorities. This difference of opinion over the best way to handle trespassers upset Creek-British relations throughout the colonial period.[43] The trouble was that once the boundary was marked, some colonials believed it would be difficult to induce the Indians to part with more land. With that in mind, the governors of both Floridas resisted having their boundaries surveyed. Georgia, constantly bothered by border clashes, was more eager to mark the line.[44]

Far from becoming a "stone wall" that kept settlers at bay, the British-Indian boundary line proved to be an ever advancing zone of white settlement from New England to Florida. Some Creek and Cherokee headmen, hoping to end intertribal jealousies and warfare, sought to form an alliance of Indian nations to halt the onslaught of white settlers. By the 1770s, intertribal diplomacy to plot a response to repeated encroachments by white hunters, herders, and settlers on Indian hunting grounds was in full swing. Creeks and Cherokees welcomed Shawnee and Delaware emissaries who faced the same problems. Militant headmen sought to "form a Confederacy of all the Western and Southern Nations" to halt the spread of Anglo-America. As General Thomas Gage observed, it was "a notable piece of Policy."[45]

The Mortar of Okchai, whose early career had been largely devoted to anti-English and antiexpansionist activities, was the most prominent Creek to support the movement. He and his deputies worked steadily to end intertribal conflicts, such as the Creek-Choctaw war, and to form a pan-tribal resistance to British advance. Ominous-looking wampum belts colored red, black, and blue were passed around Creek council meetings in the decade before the American Revolution. And more than a few headmen were interested in mutual defense agreements whereby tribes whose lands were threatened would be assisted by warriors from other nations. Creek representatives were sent to Chickasaw and Choctaw towns to secure peace agreements, but their efforts were frustrated by the never-ending Creek-Choctaw war.[46]

The Muscogulges were "jealous" of their land with good reason. All accounts of the Creek country described "a noble and fruitful country," and white people were eager to possess the "empty" lands.[47] It is no surprise that Augusta's practical-minded, debt-laden merchants, long accustomed to thinking in terms of debits and resources, would ultimately link tribal trade debts to Indian real estate, although there is no evidence they purposely encouraged debt in the hope of gaining territory.[48] In the early 1770s, the Creek traders, following the example of the Cherokees and their traders, introduced a solution to the staggering Creek national debt by attempting to arrange a cession of land to Georgia in return for cancellation of the Creek debt. The proposal pitted the Superintendent of Indian Affairs against Governor James Wright, for under British law, individuals were prohibited from conducting their own negotiations with Indians for land. But this, in addition to the fact that Indian debts were legally unrecoverable, made no difference to the Georgians.[49] Wright, eager to expand his colony's dominion, let it be known that if the merchants and traders could persuade the Creeks and Cherokees to deed their land to Georgia, he would do all in his power to secure crown approval. Wright left for London to present his case. The traders, laden with rum, threats, and promises, descended on the Creeks. They asked for lands along the Little River as well as tracts along the east side of the Oconee River. The traders explained their unprecedented attempt to obtain land by telling their customers that it was "not the Superintendent nor Governors that supplied [the Creeks] with goods and unless they gave them the land they would not be able to supply them."[50] The traders pressed their debtors and explained that unless they were paid, they would go out of business and the Creeks would be left without supplies and trade partners. The Creeks were incredulous when informed that the Cherokees had instigated the deal. Enraged headmen sent messengers to the Cherokee towns to ascertain the state of affairs there and to demand an explanation of how Cherokees could talk of ceding Creek lands.[51]

Wright, supported by a number of prominent London merchants, secured royal approval for the transfer.[52] Back in the Creek country, free rum and other presents, promises of extraordinary abatements in prices for guns and blankets, and pressure from George Galphin and other Augusta merchants on prominent Lower Creek debtors won Creek consent. There was considerable opposition in both the Upper and Lower towns, and many listened more intently to talk of a pan-tribal confederacy to protect Indian land from white greed. But even those reluctant to part with the land were easily convinced of the necessity when trade partners brought pressure to bear. In 1772, traders overheard Emisteseguo and the Second Man of Little Tallassee passionately discussing the proposed cession to Georgia. Emisteseguo declared he would go to war rather than part with the land. He blamed the Augusta merchants "for trusting their young men with such quantities of goods and then taking their lands from them in payment." The Second Man said that it "would not do for them to go to war except they could make guns, ammunition etc." Emisteseguo was forced to admit what he already knew—that the cession must be secured and that many Creeks would resent it. It was a question of either no guns and cloth or loss of land.[53] The final decision regarding the cession was left to Coweta, since it was widely agreed that most of the territory, conquered by Coweta's warriors during the Cherokee War, was under that town's jurisdiction. Leading Cowetas, among the heaviest debtors to George Galphin, folded under the relentless pressure of Galphin's underlings.

The transfer of both Cherokee land and Creek land was finalized under the auspices of Stuart and Wright at Augusta on June 1, 1773. The cession amounted to nearly 2.5 million acres of land and consisted of two portions. The first extended north and west from Augusta and was considered to be the most valuable part of the cession. The southern portion of the grant fell between the Ogeechee and Altamaha rivers. Despite the large cession, the Creeks did not give the Georgians all they wanted—the Indians adamantly refused to part with valuable hunting lands along the Oconee River.[54]

It was a bitter day for the Creek oligarchs. Creek headmen and warriors, some three hundred strong, stoutly faced nearly one hundred assembled Cherokees in the presence of Georgia's merchant community. Passions ran hot, and one unnamed Creek, spokesman for the others, "with an agitated and terrific countenance, frowning menaces and disdain," boldly insulted the Cherokees and demanded that they withdraw their claims to lands won with Creek blood during the late Creek-Cherokee war. The Cherokees, burdened by debt and mindful of their bitter defeat, "amidst the laugh and jeers of the assembly . . . were obliged to bear the stigma passively, and even without a reply."[55]

Although all Creek debts had been forgiven by the cession, many tribesmen resented the loss of their land and blamed the traders for extending credit in the first place.[56] John Stuart told William Bartram, who attended the Augusta conference formalizing the transfer, that he did not think it "alltogether safe" for the naturalist to travel in the Indian country.[57] Even so, Bartram joined the "surveyors, astronomers, artisans, chain-carriers, markers, guides & hunters, besides a very respectable number of gentlemen" speculators and twelve Creek representatives, nearly ninety men altogether, who constituted the party that marked the New Purchase boundary.[58]

Though the New Purchase eventually received widespread, if grudging, support among the Creeks, it was neither a pleasant nor easy decision. The conduct of the traders and the Georgia government alienated many Creeks. The fact that the goods they had been promised as part of the deal did not meet their specifications served to heighten tensions, especially when the traders failed to send the proper quantity of ammunition into the Creek towns and watered down the promised rum. Such actions reinforced Creek notions that they had been doubly cheated by their traders.[59]

Nor did the cession satisfy the Creek traders. The manner in which Georgia proposed to compensate them for their debts proved lengthy and was calculated to try the patience of even the most honest. Frontier accounts books were meticulously examined and those found questionable rejected. According to John Stuart, "[This] has filled [the traders] with discontents which they have communicated to the Indians who are made to believe that they have ceded their lands to the Crown without bettering the condition of their trader or reaping the advantages which they expected to their nation by it."[60] Even if Georgia had immediately paid the legitimate debts of many traders, the money would not have been sufficient to pay their creditors.

With the ratification of the New Purchase, the Creek oligarchs temporarily solved the problem of the Creek debt. But they could not begin to address the problems of the Creek economy. Though stock raising and other methods of obtaining trade goods were being more widely practiced, commercial hunting remained the primary mode of production in the Creek country. Yet the large deer herds of the early eighteenth century had been drastically reduced, so that hunters were finding it more and more difficult to harvest adequate numbers of hides to satisfy their growing needs. Creek hunters were forced to harvest younger and younger animals.[61] In addition, though the prices paid by the Creeks for trade goods remained relatively stable during the eighteenth century, by the time of the American Revolution, a glut of deerskins and cattle hides on the world market and the disruption of commerce caused by the numerous European wars meant that the deerskin-to-goods exchange rate was slowly eroding.[62] Moreover, the Creek population was increasing.[63] Thus, more Creeks were searching for fewer deer on less land to satisfy greater demands for European goods on which they had become totally dependent. The influx of farmers, cattle, and white hunters into the newly ceded lands placed further demands on the winnowed deer herds and brought Creeks and Georgians into closer, and more competitive, contact.

Creeks were determined to resist further demands for their land. When West Florida decided to request an enlargement of its boundary around the same time that Georgia's merchant community was lobbying for the New Purchase, Upper Creeks balked. They did grant a small cession but refused to relinquish control of the large tract desired by West Florida. Upper Creek headmen deliberated and sent word to West Florida: "we Cannot nor will not give [land] as we want that for our hunting Land, the former boundary must stand. . . . The Land is ours and we have given what we think we Can spare . . . too many demands of this kind may Cause friends to lean one from another."[64]

Even though there was considerable disquiet over the New Purchase and other cessions during the late colonial period, it would be wrong to assert that hapless Creeks "lost" their land or had it taken from them by force. Although Muscogulges were not adverse to parting with land on their periphery, they absolutely refused to allow the British to establish forts in their midst and constantly lobbied against the plantations established by their traders. If they believed certain lands had lost value due to lack of game or conflict with colonists, the Creeks made the best use of the land and traded it off. Most of the land alienated by the Creeks was land they had acquired by conquest or absorption of the traditional owners. They received substantial trade goods in return for their property, and with the 1773 cession, land became a way to ease the burden of debt. Even after the New Purchase, the Muscogulge people still retained most of their territory. Though they disapproved of the heavy-handed methods the British sometimes used to inveigle cessions, they were practical enough to realize that they could not effectively police the land or turn back the tide of white settlement.[65]

Whether they were negotiating for better trade terms or settling boundaries, every peace treaty entered into by the headmen bound them to maintain peace along the frontier and provide satisfaction for injuries committed by their people. Failure to bring offenders to justice threatened the continuance of trade and peaceful relations. Creek headmen often found that their powers were most severely tested when it was necessary to "observe Treaties & Agreements and Render each other Strict Justice."[66]

Dispensing justice was made difficult by the Creek system of clan retribution. In Creek towns, headmen had no say in the resolution of internal crimes, for the clan was the instrument of justice in Creek society. When one Indian killed another from a different clan, the clan of the deceased had the right to demand immediate and like satisfaction for its loss. There was no official law-enforcement body. Instead, each clan stood prepared to avenge its losses. According to John Stuart, "Revenging the Death of a Relation is esteemed the point of honor . . . the Sentence of the whole Nation for the most heinous Crime cannot be carried into execution but by a Near Relation only, and Drunkeness, accident, or self defense are not considered as any attenuation."[67] One colonial governor observed, "[Indians] calculate Debts of Blood as exactly as any Banker does his Guineas."[68]

The offended clan at first demanded satisfaction be done by the murderer's clan. Sometimes, especially if the death was accidental, the perpetrator's clan paid compensation, usually in leather or trade goods. If the victim's family refused to accept compensation, the guilty man's clan members were responsible for his execution. If they failed or refused to carry out the sentence, the victim's clan had "a right to kill any of the aggressors family they first meet, without being called to any Account for it."[69] Grieving clansmen were not particular about whose death relieved the tortured soul of their deceased. It was not uncommon for an uncle or other elder relative of a young criminal to die in his place.[70]

In every treaty that they signed, Creek headmen, though they lacked the means of enforcement, readily agreed to secure punishment of those who committed crimes against the British, thereby substituting the British concept of individual guilt for their own. Even so, the new concept had to be enforced by traditional methods. But before a father or an uncle would "become the Executioner of his own Son or Nephew," the British found it necessary to "render them sensible of their own situation with respect to

[England] and the Neighboring Nations."[71] There was the threat, real and implied, that should those guilty of crimes against the colonies go unpunished, the trade would be interdicted and war could possibly result. Sensible Creeks everywhere agreed to the necessity of executing a few guilty criminals rather than losing British friendship.[72] But reason often took second place to emotion when Muscogulges were faced with the execution of their loved ones.

Creek justice was slow and unsure, for headmen preferred making promises for satisfaction more than they enjoyed carrying them out. If the atrocities were committed by Lower Creeks, Upper headmen quickly disavowed responsibility. The reverse, of course, was also true.[73] Crimes were more prevalent during the winter when hunters were ranging on their hunting territories. Thus, it was sometimes months before headmen returned to their villages to discuss demands for satisfaction by the British.[74] After colonial officials stated that justice should be done and executions carried out, plotting ensued.[75]

The scheming surrounding the execution of the Acorn Whistler in 1752 was typical. The two most powerful men in the Lower Towns agreed

> to the Justice and Reasonableness of the Acorn Whistler's suffering Death, but added that he was a great Man and had so many Relations both in the Upper and Lower Creek Nation that might not be of the same Opinion with them. That the Execution thereof would be very difficult and dangerous. That if it was to be publickly known that he was to die on the white People's Account, he had Warriors enough at Command to kill all who came to hear the Talk that the white People would not be safe.[76]

The headmen chose one of the Acorn Whistler's nephews to do their deed to avoid his clan's wrath. Still, the leading men feared retaliation for simply ordering the death and instructed the young man to say that he killed his uncle in his own defense. They later had the nephew killed to make sure their dealings were never found out.[77] The demand for a formal execution with white witnesses was not a real possibility in the Creek country. If witnesses were present, they were usually relatives of the guilty party. Some family members simply watched; others were the executioners, holding and knifing their kin.[78]

Headmen always worked within the clan system to obtain satisfaction for crimes against the British. Thus, if Bears were among the guilty, headmen of that clan were responsible for securing justice. On one occasion, it was suggested that the Cussitas, who carried the title of leading warriors in the nation, should execute those guilty of murdering whites. Clan elders balked at the idea as being too dangerous.[79]

Peace-threatening incidents along the Creek-British frontier can be divided into three categories. First, there were politically motivated murders. These had predominated during the Seven Years' War and had been aimed at drawing the Creeks into the fray against the British. It was long a custom among the southern Indians to declare war by killing any members of the enemy's tribe who lived among them. The murders of at least five traders in early 1763 were designed to rouse opposition to the British takeover of the Floridas. But the incident failed to draw the Creeks into war because the majority of Creek headmen quickly disavowed the acts and took steps to protect the traders in their region.[80] The murders were also glossed over by the British, who dreaded the prospect of an Indian war in the South to match Pontiac's Rebellion in the North. Eager to start anew after 1763, Britain forgave all former offenses at the 1763 Congress of Augusta and again at the 1765 Congress of Pensacola and promised to renew the trade that had been disrupted by war. The Creek oligarchs, of course, traded land for the favor.[81]

The second category involved unprovoked or unjustifiable criminal activities, which both Creeks and Britons condemned, particularly the murder of traders or other whites. In virtually every instance of unjustifiable homicide, Creek headmen, working through their clans, obtained satisfaction for the murders. If the murderer fled, runners were sent after him.[82] If the guilty person could not be found, his clan sometimes offered another of its members to settle the debt. For example, when Stichey, the mico of Apalachicola, killed the trader Elliott for stealing his gold watch and debauching his wife, Creeks resented British demands that treaty obligations be carried out, since Elliott had provoked the brawl. Stichey, unsure of his relations, fled to St. Augustine. His clan, on reflection, decided Stichey had overreacted, and Stichey's sister was put to death to atone for the crime and settle the clan's obligation.[83] On some occasions, older men, eager to spare the life of their young nephews, sacrificed themselves to pay their clan's debt.[84] The British were loath to accept such satisfaction, but once rendered, they had little choice. In the case of robberies, headmen made attempts to return stolen goods or provide compensation.[85]

Border incidents constitute the final category. Along the frontier, thievery, rum, and bellicose settlers combined to incite trouble. Indeed, it often seemed that highly mobile, armed parties of Creeks and white settlers and travelers—ostensibly spread out along hundreds of miles of territory—attracted each other like magnets. As a rule, whites and Indians frequented the same trails and paths, the same rich game fields, watering holes, and salt licks, and the same hastily constructed tippling joints that dotted the boundary lines. Curious about the activities of their neighbors and eager to see the changes wrought by the new white inhabitants, parties of Creeks cruised the borders of their territory. Backcountry clashes between Indians, white hunters, settlers, and illegal traders became almost commonplace on both sides of the Anglo-Creek border.[86]

Creeks acquired a reputation for thievery among white settlers during the late colonial period. Perhaps part of the problem was differing perceptions of hospitality, since visiting Creeks sometimes took what they needed.[87] Hungry Creek hunters, observing that the white people with their horses and cattle had usurped Indian hunting grounds, considered livestock that wandered over the boundary line as fair game. For the Creeks, taking property belonging to traders and settlers was commonly viewed as a way to obtain satisfaction for the real or imagined wrongs. Creeks considered it fair compensation for insults and injuries; whites always considered such action to be theft. Travelers too were occasionally robbed by contentious hunters who looked on them as intruders on Indian hunting grounds.[88] Warriors on the way home from raids against the Choctaws were not adverse to robbing and even killing Choctaw and Chickasaw nation traders who carried ammunition.[89] White vagrants poaching on Creek lands occasionally bumped into Creek hunting parties, with deadly results.[90]

Resolving these annoying incidents placed tremendous strains on Creek political institutions. When Creeks abused trespassers or slaughtered pigs and cattle that wandered across the boundary line, their people found it difficult to view such actions as anything other than defense of property.[91] Young Creeks guilty of outrages against trespassers found sympathetic ears when they asserted that they had done no wrong by killing Creek "enemies."[92] Often, those who murdered whites did not linger and put their relatives to the test but absconded to live among the Cherokees or to live in a remote settlement along the frontier—a common and obliging way to avoid one's punishment. Clansmen would not follow.[93] It was never easy to put one's kin to death simply because they had killed border jumpers. On one occasion, members of the Tyger clan decided that the death of one of their relatives, who was shot and killed while stealing horses from the Georgia settlements, would count as satisfaction for earlier frontier murders committed by some of their kinsmen. Their decision made sense in light of Creek custom, and the British were forced to accept the logic.[94] Rather than execute powerful men involved in such incidents, many Creek headmen opted for banishment of the guilty party.[95] Nor would Creek headmen supervise the execution of those who committed crimes outside the Creek country.[96]

Creek headmen blamed the epidemic of lawlessness on the bad example of the white people in their midst, and there was much truth in the assertion. White hunters declared open season on native game. Many, employed by plantation owners, seaboard merchants, and government officials, were ostensibly charged with supplying venison and were allowed to keep the deerskins as part of their wage. But such men did more than supply white households with fresh meat. In East Florida, Denys Rolle found to his horror that such men destroyed, "for the Sake of the Skins, ten Times as much Deer" as they needed for venison.[97] Profits from the sale of deerskins were quickly converted to rum at St. Augustine, Pensacola, and Augusta and then returned to the frontier to be peddled to thirsty backcountry farmers, white servants, and Indian hunters searching for deer. West Florida enacted statutes prohibiting "vagabonds and other idle and disorderly persons" from hunting and herding on Indian land, but the law was worthless, and travelers, hunters, and herders regularly invaded Creek lands from all sides. The Young Lieutenant of Coweta cogently observed: "Whenever the Virginia people [backcountry settlers] are told by our people that they are over the Line and if they dont keep in the Bounds they will Burn their Houses, they make answer they will burn the Governors house over his Head. If the Governor cannot keep these Virginia People under, how can we keep our young people under?"[98]

Creek headmen were aware that their failure to uphold their treaty agreements could result in a trade embargo or even war. They were dependent on British goods, and they knew it. But British power, at least in Georgia and the Floridas, was weak. Colonial officials were afraid that if they interdicted Creek trade, war could result. And even the hint of an Indian war could damage a colony's economy. Potential investors and settlers were frightened off, and farms were abandoned. Wars, even winnable ones, were unacceptable to colony builders. The result was a mad mix of confrontation and patient accommodation between the Creek oligarchy and the British colonial establishment. The British, unconvinced of their own superiority of arms and fearful of war, often wavered, as was the case in late 1763 when Creeks were involved in the murders of eleven whites in South Carolina. And there were many other such incidents.

Trade dependence, disputes with traders over prices and practices, the loss of hard-won lands, and frequent clashes with their white neighbors were the unpleasant realities confronting all Creeks. The Muscogulge oligarchs, mediators between their own towns and their white trade partners, walked a fine line as they attempted to preserve their culture and territory and satisfy their trade partners. At the little detached village called Pucknawheatly by the Muscogulges and the Standing Peach Tree by Georgians, a series of events unfolded that presented the Muscogulge oligarchs with a daunting task: preventing an all-out war with Anglo-America.

The trouble began in late December 1773. For a number of weeks, Ogulki of Coweta had been in pursuit of another Creek whom he intended to kill for "witchcraft." Ogulki finally caught his adversary near the Georgia boundary line and killed him. Ogulki, hoping to avert suspicion from himself in order to avoid conflict with the victim's clan, made a bloody path from the body to William White's farm, which had been established near the head of the Ogeechee River on New Purchase land. He returned to Pucknawheatly, where he found Houmahta and five other Cowetas. Together, they returned to the scene of the murder. From there, they followed the tracks to the White farm. Ogulki's evidence was enough to convince them that White had killed their companion, and on Christmas Day, the Coweta hunters attacked the White household, killing Mr. White, his wife, and four children. At least, that is what most people came to regard as the truth. Ogulki always maintained that White struck the first blow.

The renegades returned to Coweta, where they proudly displayed their war trophies and recounted their actions. Troubled headmen believed that war with Georgia was now inevitable. Resentment over the New Purchase swelled Ogulki's band, and the renegades prepared for war. White's neighbors, fearing more trouble, began at once to fortify their cabins. Their fears proved to be well-founded: the Sherrill family was surprised by another body of warriors about two weeks later. William Sherrill, four other white men, and two black slaves were killed as Pucknawheatly warriors, stripped naked and painted black, laid siege to the farm. Two of Sherrill's sons and another slave managed to fend off their attackers, killing two Creeks and wounding four.[99]

The whole party of Creeks, no more than about twenty in number, waited. The Georgia militia eventually arrived to help the Sherrill survivors carry away their belongings. The party of thirty-five troopers was fired on by the Creeks, and the commander, Lieutenant Grant, fell wounded from his horse. He was tortured and scalped. The Georgia militia abandoned the field without firing a shot.[100] Elated with their rout of the Georgia militia, the "strayed Cowetas" returned home, where the leading men were awed by their brashness and numbers and kept quiet. In private, the headmen let it be known that they were horrified by the unprovoked attacks, did not want war, and were willing to make satisfaction: "no lands must be given up but blood for blood." The headmen found it convenient to blame George Galphin for the incident. After all, if he had not supplied the trader at the Standing Peach Tree, the young men might have stayed closer to their villages under the watchful eyes of their elders.[101]

Leading men on both sides of the boundary line immediately began to assess their positions and plan their response. This was a crisis of immense proportions and was the first large-scale attack ever suffered by Georgia. There were no extenuating circumstances. Detached and unruly warriors had crossed the boundary line and killed fifteen Georgians and two black slaves in three separate attacks during peacetime. Frontier farms had been abandoned, and it seemed to many that war would be the inescapable result. Yet war, fortunately for both sides, did not come.

What made this crisis different was Georgia's response. Georgia's population had risen from 8,500 in 1761 to 33,000 in 1773. It was no longer a fledgling colony. And though Creek populations were also rising, there were now more Georgians than Creeks.[102] Wright and the rest of the colonial administration realized that to maintain Georgia's growth, they had to stop the atrocities along the border. There was no way, as Governor Wright so aptly put it, "to skin this over."[103]

Halting the trade until justice was "rendered" seemed the best solution. Besides, the Indian trade was no longer Georgia's primary source of income. Agriculture and lumbering had assumed important positions in the economy. Exports of timber, staves, and shingles had increased significantly from the mid-1750s to the 1770s. Rice and indigo production had risen dramatically. Pork, beef, and corn found ready markets in the West Indies. Farmers, both large and small, disapproved of the Indian trade, since it placed arms and ammunition in the hands of potential enemies and caused conflict over land. Resolute, the Georgians declared an embargo on the Creek trade until the Coweta renegades were executed. All the traders left the Creek country at first word of the frontier trouble. Most now waited in Augusta for the opportunity to return to their stores.[104]

Creek headmen pleaded in vain for a return of their traders with supplies. Hard pressed, they admitted their dependence on the trade: "We know what poverty it would bring us whenever that [trade] path shall grow up."[105] There was a subtle shift in the way the participants viewed themselves and a very real shift in the balance of power. For Georgia, the trade had become an instrument rather than an investment. The Creeks, still entangled in a purposeless war with the Choctaws, were desperate for arms and ammunition for their defense. The Choctaws, emboldened by British encouragements and presents of ammunition, stepped up their attacks. The Creek death toll rose precipitously.[106] The Cherokees, recalling their bitter defeat in the protracted Creek-Cherokee war and their humiliation by the Creeks at the New Purchase cession months earlier, offered no assistance. Indeed, there was every indication that if the Creeks made war on Georgia, the Cherokees would gladly join the Georgians against them.[107]

It was a dilemma of the highest order. At a meeting with Creek representatives in Savannah in April, Governor Wright was blunt: "And what can you do? Can you make guns, gunpowder, bullets, glasses, paint and clothing etc.? You know you cannot make these things, and where can you get them if you quarrel with the white people and how will your women and children get supplied with clothes, beads, glasses, scissors and all other things that they now use and cannot do without?"[108] Sadly, Emisteseguo of Little Tallassee agreed that stopping the flow of trade goods would be the only way to force the Creek towns to execute those responsible for the atrocities.[109]

The speedy acquisition of new trade partners became essential. Upper Creeks who had earlier spurned a trade with West Florida now pleaded that their towns be allowed to receive ammunition while guilty Coweta was made to suffer by the Augusta embargo.[110] But the embargo was extended to East and West Florida. Though leaky, it created severe hardships for the Creeks.[111] The Mortar of the Okchai, seeking another outlet of arms for his goods-starved people, set out for New Orleans with eighty-five warriors to arrange a Spanish trade. His party was ambushed by well-armed Choctaws, and the Mortar died on the path.[112]

A number of Lower Creek headmen entered into a bizarre series of negotiations with the Georgian Jonathan Bryan. In return for meager presents and one hundred bushels of corn per year, Bryan promised to build a city to rival Savannah and to open trading stores to supply the Creeks cheaply.

Thereupon the Lower Creeks with whom he was negotiating agreed to "lease" Bryan nearly five hundred acres of land in what the British regarded as East Florida. The proceedings were rife with chicanery, for most Creeks abhorred the thought of granting new lands for settlement. And Creeks had never found it necessary to exchange land for corn before. Bryan's efforts were aided by the trade embargo, well-known interpreters, and plenty of rum. When later confronted with Bryan's deed, those who had signed the lease claimed to have been hoodwinked. When they returned and signed a second lease, after receiving more presents and rum, perhaps they intended to hoodwink Bryan. Whatever the truth concerning the Bryan leases, they pointed to a desperate need for trade goods and the willingness of some Creeks to do almost anything to obtain them.[113]

Georgia's high moral position regarding the execution of those involved in the affair was somewhat weakened when Thomas Fee, harboring old grudges against Indians, struck a Creek, the Mad Turkey, over the head with an iron bar at an Augusta tavern, killing him. Wright ordered Fee's arrest, and he was apprehended, but friends and neighbors rallied to his aid and freed him from the Augusta jail. From there he escaped into South Carolina, where the authorities were unable to recapture him.[114]

Georgia's embarrassment at being unable to successfully prosecute Fee, the growing stress between the colonies and the home government, the machinations of Bryan, and the difficulty in policing the embargo meant there was a need to accommodate differences as soon as possible. Georgia compromised. At a meeting held in Savannah in late October, Emisteseguo, representing the Upper Creeks, and Tallachea of Ockmulge, representing the Lower Creeks, agreed to execute the ringleaders as the token satisfaction. It was a momentous occasion. The primary offender, Ogulki, was a member of the Tyger clan. Heretofore, that clan had stoutly refused to provide satisfaction for wrongs committed along the border. But now the entire population suffered, and pressure was brought to bear. A general council of all Creek towns was convened. Upper and Lower headmen, working within the traditional political framework, debated the issue. Headmen representing twenty-six towns ordered the Tyger headmen to do their duty. Emisteseguo, of that clan, took the lead in negotiations among clan elders.

Ogulki was executed by his kinsmen. Another execution followed, and two more Creeks were condemned and would have been executed but for their timely escape to the Cherokee towns. Two Alachua Seminoles were also executed for their part in an unrelated incident in which whites had been killed. Muscogulge headmen pledged to return all goods stolen from the white people, to return fugitive slaves who had sought refuge in the Creek country, and to prohibit their young from establishing outsettlements. Georgia reopened the trade.[115]

By the end of 1774, the crisis in Creek-Georgia relations over the White-Sherrill murders had passed. British authorities blamed the whole affair on the troubled state of the trade. The traffic in undressed skins for rum, too-liberal credit, and the proliferation of detached villages where stolen horses were exchanged and brawls were common were seen as the basis for the discontent. The Georgia assembly, panicked by the December 1773 terrorism, passed provisions designed to end the abuses of the deerskin trade. South Carolina implemented the same ordinances. The new colonial trade laws were virtually identical to John Stuart's defunct 1767 regulations and included provisions for Stuart to appoint commissaries to enforce them. West Florida and East Florida seemed inclined to follow with similar acts.[116] Stuart, jubilant over the prospect of seeing his pet project accepted, wrote to his superiors in London, "The clashing and confusion which for several years past have prevailed will be prevented."[117]

No doubt all the Muscogulges rejoiced at the news that the colonies intended to police the trade. But by 1774, most Creeks realized that their problems could not be remedied by ordinances alone, and the episode forced all Creeks to face the harsh reality of their heavy dependence on imported trade goods. War with the British colonies had been out of the question because without guns and ammunition, Creeks far and wide agreed they could not possibly win. Even more distressing was the willingness of their trade partners to supply their enemies and encourage attacks. On that basis, the oligarchy garnered support for the Savannah treaties, manipulated the clan system to uphold the agreement, and preserved peace with the British. It was a hard and bitter lesson, and it alienated many Muscogulges, especially those who perceived the very real shift in the balance of power from their towns to Anglo-America.

CHAPTER 9

Old Needs and New Partners: The American Revolution and Beyond

In October 1774, the *South Carolina Gazette* reported that the Creeks had complied with most of the terms set forth by Georgia for the restoration of the trade after the White-Sherrill affair and seemed entirely peaceable. The author of the piece noted that there was therefore little need for the royal troops that the governor of Georgia had repeatedly requested, and that Georgians, freed from the fear of Indian attack, had no reason to refrain from "such Resolves and Measures as appear[ed] to be absolutely and indispensable for the Restoration and Preservation of the common Rights of His Majesty's subjects in America."[1] Many Georgians were beginning to see the wisdom of such sentiments, and events far removed from Creek square grounds were soon topics of conversation not only in Charleston, Savannah, and Augusta but in the Indian country as well.

The growing revolt pitted the southern colonies not only against the home government but also against each other as loyalists and rebels vied for control of the backcountry. Both sides quickly eyed the Creeks and the other southern tribes and began sizing them up as either allies or adversaries. Both the British and the Americans courted the Creeks, and the contest divided the Indians as sharply as it did their white neighbors. As with other things Muscogulge, trade dependence determined the Creek course—although not all Creeks could agree exactly what that course should be. The war reordered the Creek world. By the end of the conflict, Creek commerce ran in new channels and was directed by new trade partners. But the Creeks were left to contend with the same problems as before, as well as many new ones presented by the growth and development of the American nation.

With the peaceful settlement of the White-Sherrill affair, the Creeks eagerly awaited the return of packtrains from Augusta. None appeared, even though the interdiction of the Creek trade had ended. The absence of the traders was due to a general shortage of trade goods in Charleston and Savannah. The series of trade laws that the British Parliament had paraded before the colonies beginning in 1764 had begun to take a toll. Shipping regulations, taxes on certain imported goods, and the colonial uproar over loss of commercial freedom meant fewer British manufactures and other imported goods for the southern Indian trade.[2] The nonimportation agreements entered into by Charleston merchants in the early 1770s also disrupted the flow of trade goods, despite the fact that certain items, such as duffel blankets and some kinds of trade cloth, were exempted from the provisions.[3] As a result of the troubles in Boston over the Tea Act, the First Continental Congress created an association with committees throughout the colonies to enforce boycotts of British goods. George III, in response to the grumbling of the colonists, prohibited the export of gunpowder and arms to the colonies.[4] Taken together, these measures severely crippled the Creek economy. The shortage of powder was especially hurtful, since it hampered the Creek war effort against the Choctaws and curtailed winter hunts.[5]

By late 1775, the Revolution had begun in earnest. Liberty men from South Carolina fitted out three privateers, each armed with eighteen guns, and seized inbound vessels from London carrying gunpowder meant for loyal governments, approved merchants, and the Indian Department. In one raid alone, the rebels pirated thirty thousand pounds of gunpowder meant for the smooth-bore muskets of Muscogulge hunters.[6] Rebel activity in Charleston stanched the established supply routes, and Savannah merchants still loyal to the British government attempted to bypass the commotion in South Carolina by instructing their London suppliers to forward their orders directly to Savannah.[7] In a prophetic move, John Stuart was forced to abandon his headquarters in Charleston for the safer soil of East Florida.[8] In addition to the shortage of goods, the trade was hampered by a fall in the price for deerskins on the English market, making it even more difficult for merchants to obtain scarce trade goods at reasonable prices.[9] As the revolt escalated in South Carolina and Georgia, Stuart attempted to shift the center of the Indian trade from Augusta to the calmer colonies of East and West Florida, particularly Pensacola.[10]

The Creek oligarchs, who had put their reputations and even lives at risk by their acquiescence in Georgia's demands for the execution of the White-

Sherrill killers, demanded to know why their traders had not returned. At a meeting of the Upper Creek headmen held at Little Tallassee in the fall of 1775, Emisteseguo demanded an explanation for Britain's failure to resume the deerskin trade. Holding his Great Medal aloft, the chief recalled Stuart's injunction to hold fast to Great King and Stuart's assurance that "while I held this [commission], I should not be poor." The headman added, "I do not know any reason for the Shipping now being stopt."[11] Nor were the Creeks pleased by Stuart's request that they come to St. Augustine to fetch supplies for themselves. The headmen claimed they had no horses to send to East Florida, which was a long way indeed from the Upper Creek Towns. As they pointed out to Stuart, the best trails from the Creek villages led to Augusta and Pensacola. Emisteseguo chided the superintendent, "We did not expect that you was at St. Augustine, but expected you to be at Pensacola where we made you a King and where you promised to take care of the Red People."[12] Laboring under shortages caused by the loss of trade, which by now had extended for two years, the headmen had no choice and eventually agreed to protect and defend the new trading paths that Stuart sought to open from the Floridas.[13]

John Stuart's efforts to maintain the trade were doomed. The war completely disrupted transatlantic commerce. West Indian rum, however, did reach West Florida traders. It was such a profitable item that merchants refused to consider any regulations that might hinder their business. Stuart reckoned that for every deerskin bought with British goods, five were taken in exchange for West Indian spirits. On one occasion, some thirty thousand gallons of rum were dispensed within a three-month period, the outcome of which, Stuart observed, was that the Indians were "poor, wretched naked and discontented."[14]

With trade goods scarce and tensions high, the Muscogulge towns divided into factions based on old loyalties, old grudges, and the old need to obtain trade goods. Stuart's personal ally, Emisteseguo, was convinced it was better to trust the king's men than the Virginians, as the frontiersmen were called, and rallied support for the British cause. He was sure that, given time, the Great King would triumph. His fellow Tyger clansman at Coweta, Escochabey (the Young Lieutenant), still smarting from the affront to his clan by the execution of his kinsman, chose the other side. Escochabey, who had never forgiven the British for their failure to award him a medal, renewed old ties with Spanish Cuba and was pleased to hear from the Americans that the French and Spanish would soon return to their old haunts along the Gulf Coast. Support for the British cause was further hampered by the efforts of the American agents, notably George Galphin and Robert Rae, to maintain Creek neutrality.[15] Galphin, whose commercial and familial ties extended from Coweta to nearly every Lower Town, worked feverishly to persuade Creek headmen to ignore Stuart's request for aid. Robert Rae found support among the Okfuskees, especially their headman the Handsome Fellow, his personal friend.

The Americans, aware that loyalty hinged on supplies, made more raids on Stuart's supply line and hurried what goods they could to the Creek frontier.[16] Galphin was especially concerned over the need to supply the Lower Towns with an American trade. Although he conceded that the majority of the Upper Towns were firmly linked to Britain by a royal supply of goods coming from West Florida, he was convinced that a steady trade to the Lower Towns would prevent a war: "The Uper Towns will do us no hurt without the Consent of the lower Towns . . . & if the Trade is stop'd from them here they will go all to Florida, & then we may Expect an Indian War, when Thirty or forty stragling Indians made the Greatest part of Georgia run, what must the whole Nation do."[17] But a block on the export of deerskins and other American produce by the Continental Congress seemed bound to doom any hope of establishing a trade with the Creeks. Galphin, declaring his commission useless without the benefit of an American trade, threatened to resign if some solution could not be found. In the end, he persevered and attempted to convince the Creeks that the shortage of American-supplied trade goods was due to the interference of the royalists.[18] In the meantime, Galphin and the other rebel officials worked to keep the Creeks neutral and to intercept Stuart's supplies until the Continental Congress could provide goods for the Creeks.[19]

Stuart and his agents also worked feverishly to maintain their support among the Creeks and other southern Indians. Ultimately, the British command hoped to use the Indians in conjunction with loyalist militias and army regulars when the time seemed right. Until then, the Indians were urged to remain on the sidelines.[20] To that end, Stuart arranged an end to the Creek-Choctaw war so that warriors from both sides would be able to go into action when called on.[21] The Cherokees, harboring resentment against repeated encroachments by settlers from Virginia and North Carolina, did not listen to the British advice that neutrality was the best policy. In 1776, Cherokee warriors attacked the Carolina backcountry, and Americans responded with a series of violent raids. By the end of the year, Creeks looked on in horror as destitute Cherokees, fleeing from their burned-out towns, sought food and shelter among the Muscogulges.[22] Creeks did not need to hear Georgia spokesmen point out the obvious: "And now they see, when they are drove out of their Country, like a Gang of Cattle & their Corn all destroyed, that the people over the great Water cannot help them."[23] The Creek people took the Cherokee example to heart. Throughout the war, the Creek towns maintained an official—and precarious—peace with their rebellious neighbors.

This did not mean that individuals and war parties did not rally to the British cause when it suited their purpose. War along the Georgia-Florida frontier meant forays and raids, and Creeks used the opportunity to plunder settlements, carry off horses and slaves, destroy livestock, and kill Georgians who worked against the British cause.[24] Alexander McGillivray, the son of the trader Lachlan McGillivray and a woman of the Wind Clan, assumed Emisteseguo's place as the leading spokesman for the British view among the Upper Towns. McGillivray acquired position and prestige through his mother's matrilineage.[25] His father had sent him to Charleston for schooling, and the combination of education and birth ensured his rapid advancement in Creek politics, especially after John Stuart gave him a position in the British Indian Department.

During the Revolution, McGillivray found his influence counted for very little when trade goods were absent. Nonetheless, he managed to lead a handful of Creek warriors to Pensacola to help defend against Spanish attacks in that quarter. But even aid from the southern Indians could not save Britain's beleaguered colony, and Pensacola fell. Spain, America's cobelligerent, won the Floridas.[26] Near the end of the war, Emisteseguo, determined to reach British-held Savannah to exchange deerskins for ammunition, gathered his warriors, and they attempted to push through American lines around the town. Emisteseguo paid the ultimate price for his loyalty. The Georgians left the bodies of the slain "to the ravenous wolves and the birds of the air."[27] It was a foreboding omen.

In Georgia, the war against Britain developed into civil war as a complicated set of circumstances aligned the frontier people against each other. In 1774, frontier-dwellers believed more land should have been taken from the Creeks as payment for the White-Sherrill murders. The Augusta merchants and traders fought the idea, and Governor James Wright sided with them.[28] Thus, when the "Troubles" came in 1776, the great majority of those involved in the Indian trade remained faithful to the British government. In a fit of pique, the rebel Georgia legislature, noting that most of the traders and members of the British Indian Department were Scots, retaliated for this treachery by passing an act prohibiting natives of Scotland from settling in the province or conducting commerce.[29]

A few traders did side with the rebels. Lachlan McGillivray claimed that George Galphin joined the Americans simply to prevent the Creeks from being drawn into the fray, and there is much merit in the assertion. Some Indian trading firms, including Galphin's, had partners on each side, which begs the conclusion that the partners were courting the odds and hoped to have a representative on the winning side. Such schemes were to no avail, for in Georgia the fight turned into a contest between settlers and Indian traders. No matter their position during the war, both the Creeks and their traders found that when the fighting ended, they were among the losers.[30]

By the time peace was achieved, the decades-old pattern of trade that linked Georgia and the Creeks had been destroyed. An overwhelming majority of those who had been involved in the trade, both loyalist and rebel, abandoned their businesses during the war years. Some simply perished of disease or old age, as did George Galphin, who died during the war at the age of seventy-one.[31] Others were hounded from their homes and businesses by their adversaries. Georgia confiscated the property of many loyalist traders.[32] One of the most famous Georgia exiles was Lachlan McGillivray, who abandoned everything and returned to Scotland. Many, like the Savannah merchant Basil Cowper, fled to the Bahamas. Some, including James Spalding, William Panton, and a host of others, moved south into East Florida. Substantial numbers sought refuge with their Indian families in the Creek country. Augusta, once the center of the southern Indian trade, became the new capital of expansionist-minded Georgia. The state's population rose nearly 70 percent during the war years. New Georgians, eager to till the land so recently gained from the Creeks, changed the character of the backcountry. The new merchants who took up residence in Augusta hawked farm implements, not trade guns.[33]

The Indian traders and merchants who remained in America found it difficult to continue their trade. The Treaty of Paris prohibited commercial arrangements between the United States and Great Britain. More important, the lines of credit and supply had been irreversibly broken by the bitterness of the war. Though some illicit commerce was conducted with Britain's West Indian islands, it was unrelated to the deerskin traffic. The sources of credit, trade goods, and the markets for deerskins vanished. Indian trade goods, especially textiles, were manufactured in England and could not be had for any price in America. Moreover, the United States lacked a market for native deerskins. Credit, due to the unstable financial situation, was impossible to secure, and there was little currency in circulation. In any case, the victorious settlers in the Georgia backcountry had no desire to carry on the trade. They were more interested in acquiring Indian land than in bartering for Indian deerskins. Edward J. Cashin, the historian of Augusta during the Revolution, has aptly observed that the "century-old British policy of trading with the Indians ended and a century-long policy of Indian removal began."[34]

For the Creeks, the war had been an economic disaster. Wartime disruption of trade had left them short of guns, ammunition, and clothing. The war had been politically disabling as well. During the eighteenth century, frequent wars had led to a predominance of head warriors as spokesmen for many Creek towns. But these same wars resulted in a high mortality rate for town leaders. The two most prominent Upper Creek chiefs, Mortar of Okchai and Emisteseguo of Little Tallassee, both were victims of the Creek involvement in war. Others, like the Handsome Fellow of Okfuskee, died of natural causes. The aged and infirm were replaced by their young protégés. Thus, by 1783, the Creeks were deprived of many talented leaders, their British allies, and their Augusta connection to the world market. Economically and politically drained, they still needed guns and cloth. Of even more importance were the forces that moved Creek history in new directions, especially the power and rapacity of their former enemies, the irate and land-hungry Georgians.[35]

Back in the Creek towns, a new generation of relatively young and inexperienced men took up the burdens of leadership. Many were of mixed blood, the result of trader marriages to Creek women. They often possessed many skills that the new times demanded but that many older Creek leaders lacked, such as literacy, a knowledge of Spanish or English, and an understanding of white culture. One might add that Europeans and Americans were more willing to deal with a white man's son, even if his mother was an Indian, than they were to deal with a full-blood Indian.[36]

Alexander McGillivray was the most powerful of these new leaders. After the war, McGillivray's literacy, experience, natural ability, and clan connections made him the most successful man in the Upper Nation. He soon emerged as the leading spokesman for the Upper Towns, and by 1783, outsiders had begun to refer to a Creek National Council directed by Mc-

Gillivray. There was no such body. Instead, McGillivray took control of the meetings of Upper Creek (Abeika, Tallapoose, and Alabama) headmen and transformed their erratic and crisis-oriented meetings into a proper noun and little more. McGillivray, whose office was that of Great Beloved Man, became the spokesman for a sizable faction of Upper Creek headmen. The White-Sherrill crisis had generated a meeting of twenty-six Creek towns. McGillivray was never able to do better. He could not speak for the Lower Towns, and the Seminole towns were too far away. In his dealings with the British, Americans, and Spanish, he asserted no more than earlier spokesmen for the Creek oligarchs had—what was important was that he asserted it in English rather than Muskogee. He looked, acted, and spoke like a white man. Other powerful white men took notice.[37]

Still, McGillivray was careful to respect Creek conventions. Like earlier Creek statesmen, he allowed himself to be courted by all sides. He drove hard bargains at treaty time and demanded that Creek sovereignty be respected, just as earlier headmen had done. And like his predecessors, he accepted foreign titles and "presents" as his due. His formation of a force of constables to handle political executions was reminiscent of earlier suggestions that Cussita warriors be assigned to perform such tasks. But not even the suave McGillivray could control the renegade elements or speak for all the Creek towns. Nor could he halt the movement of individuals and groups away from Creek control, a change that had begun in the previous decades. The Seminole towns grew, and many non–Muskogean-speaking tribes continued to drift farther from Creek councils. In addition, many Indian countrymen, white men with Indian wives, built their homes outside the limits of their wives' villages and away from the authority of Creek town government.[38]

In May 1783, a group of pro-British Creek warriors and headmen traveled to St. Augustine to ascertain the validity of the rumors that Great Britain intended to evacuate the Southeast. Distraught over the loss of their trading partners and fearful that Georgia would demand land to compensate for damage done by Creek war parties during the Revolution, the loyalist Creeks were unable to decide on a course of action. Pro-American and neutralist headmen from both the Upper and the Lower towns did not. In November, sensing the need for rapprochement and desperate for a renewal of trade, they headed east along the "old beloved path" to Augusta in response to an invitation by the Georgians. The resulting Treaty of Augusta in 1783 concentrated on two issues: trade and land. Georgia promised to forget the depredations committed by pro-British Creek warriors during the war and to renew the old system of trade. In return, the headmen turned over eight hundred square miles of Creek real estate—prime hunting lands along the Oconee River.[39] Slowly, a few traders began operating out of Augusta.

The 1783 Treaty of Augusta enraged many Creeks. Those who opposed the treaty denounced the chiefs who had signed it and claimed that the signers had not been authorized to speak for the entire nation. They also asserted that Georgia had used force to obtain the cession. Alexander McGillivray assumed the leadership of those who opposed the treaty.[40] Georgia persevered. In 1785 and 1786, the state managed to obtain an additional parcel of land and secure confirmation of the 1783 boundary.[41] Georgia settlers lost no time in occupying the newly ceded territory.

By 1786, eastern land speculators were casting covetous eyes toward the Mississippi. Settlers soon followed their gaze and moved up the Alabama River, spreading over hunting grounds belonging to the Upper Towns. Faced with unprecedented encroachments, McGillivray and his Upper Creek supporters assumed extraordinary powers. If "peaceable remonstrances" failed to remove the squatters, McGillivray asserted that his people would not be "quiet Spectators."[42] The Upper Creeks had no jurisdiction over the Oconee or Okmulge lands of the Lower Towns. But sensing a need for swift and concerted action, McGillivray castigated the Lower Creek headmen for their dilatory attitude toward the Georgia treaties and the ever growing numbers of white settlers on the land. He convened the headmen opposed to the Georgia treaties and called on them "to take arms in our defence & repel those Invaders of our Lands, to drive them from their encroachments & fix them within their own proper limits."[43] The council agreed, and the "red hatchet" was raised. McGillivray was instructed to call up war parties and direct them "to Set out without loss of time & to traverse all that part of the Country in dispute & whenever they found any American Settlers to drive them off & destroy all the buildings." He directed that no violence was to be used against the settlers themselves, unless in self-defense.[44] In June 1787, McGillivray met with representatives from several northern tribes, including the Iroquois, Hurons, and Shawnees. In the Cumberland, Creek warriors combined forces with Chickamauga Indians, and in the spirit of earlier anti-expansionist gatherings, the tribes agreed to coordinate attacks against the American frontier "wherever they Shall pass over their own proper Limits, nor never to grant them Lands, nor Suffer Surveyors to roam about the

Country."[45] By July 1787, McGillivray claimed he had sent between five hundred and six hundred warriors to "ravage the Settlement of Cumberland." After the annual Busk, the warriors planned to raid the Georgia frontier.[46]

What set McGillivray apart from the other Creek headmen and made him so powerful was his connection with a group of exiled merchants through whom he managed to secure trade for his people. Early in the Revolution, a number of Georgia traders had sought haven in East Florida and from there had managed to supply the Indians, albeit sporadically, during the war years. As the British abandoned their footholds in East Florida to the victorious Spanish, even this avenue of trade seemed likely to close. But the Spaniards realized that close commercial relations with their new Indian neighbors were essential to their own security.[47] McGillivray told them so: "For Indians will attach themselves to & Serve them best who Supply their Necessities."[48] In late May 1784, the new masters of the Floridas had met with Alexander McGillivray and other Upper Creek headmen and negotiated a trade treaty. In the absence of suitable Spanish replacements for experienced factors, a group of astute loyalist exiles—William Panton, John Leslie, and William Alexander—was able to convince the Spanish government that their decidedly Scottish firm should be granted a special dispensation to trade with the Indians. Establishing the company as the preeminent trading firm in the Creek country cost William Panton dearly, and he claimed that the company sustained more than thirty thousand dollars in losses in its first two years of business when it dropped prices in order to run American competitors out of business.[49]

The firm eventually prospered, in part due to the efforts of Alexander McGillivray, who became a silent partner. At the same time, McGillivray's control of the trade augmented his political power among the Creeks.[50] Despite Georgia's promises to renew the trade, by 1786 the only traders in the Creek towns were those licensed by McGillivray.[51] McGillivray, as Georgia had done earlier, threatened and actually embargoed the trade to towns that did not support his position.[52]

Old trade paths to Augusta were abandoned and new ones forged to Spanish Pensacola, which became the heart of the Panton, Leslie, and Company trading empire. Prices were slightly higher than before the war, but the Creeks had managed to secure a source of supplies. Panton, Leslie, and Company played a complicated game of give-and-take with its Spanish hosts and British trade partners. European wars, declining British deerskin markets, and economic rivals made the firm's job harder and resulted in uncertain supplies and higher and higher prices for its customers. And the deerskin trade remained a tool to secure Creek loyalty.[53] U.S. representatives told the Creeks, "[American] traders are very rich, and have houses full of such goods as you used to get in former days." It made little difference.[54] Panton, Leslie, and Company quickly "engrossed the greatest part" of the Creek trade.[55] Panton's traders, operating stores in virtually every Creek village, conducted business in the same manner that Indian traders had managed their affairs for nearly a century. The company also served as a quiet conduit for the presents of arms and ammunition that the Spanish sent to McGillivray for his war against illegal American settlements. In turn, the frontier raids eliminated most of Panton, Leslie, and Company's Georgia competition.[56]

Among those who obtained supplies from Georgia merchants and attempted to trade with the Creeks was John Galphin, the son of George Galphin, who built a trading house on the Oconee River. Timothy Barnard, like Galphin, worked for Georgia as an interpreter and messenger and also traded in the Lower Towns. Elijah Clarke had a store on the Ogeechee River, and a host of others established tippling houses and trading posts all along the frontier.[57] For a time, Lower Creeks traded with William Augustus Bowles, who hoped to establish an independent Indian state with trade ties to loyalist merchants in the Bahamas.[58] Jack Kinnard, "a rich Scotch half-breed" according to one American agent, carried on a lucrative cloth and rum trade with the Lower Creeks and also built up a stock of cattle that he sold for considerable profit in Pensacola.[59] In time, most of these men either did business with Panton, Leslie, and Company or were driven out of business.

Meanwhile, the border clashes and repeated waves of settlers crowding onto Creek lands undermined the already weak trading economy by increasing military spending, driving off game, and curtailing the hunting season.[60] The beleaguered Creeks had no choices. McGillivray viewed the situation in light of harsh geographic fact: "We were not situated as several other Indian nations were, with immense wildernesses behind us. On the contrary we were surrounded from west to north, by the Choctaws, Chickasaws, Cumberland, and Cherokees, and on every other side by the whites, so that our hunting grounds were already very insufficient for our purposes."[61] The Hallowing King of the Cowetas was more passionate. In the spring of 1789, he recounted the progress of Georgia from his own memory and the stories passed down by older generations of Creeks. He told a gathering of Lower Creek headmen: "These last strides tell us they never mean to let their foot rest; our lands are our life and breath; if we part with them, we part with our blood. We must fight for them."[62]

And many Creeks did fight. The Spanish, fearing American reprisals, halted the flow of free ammunition, but the fortuitous arrival of William Augustus Bowles with a large shipment of free goods from the Bahamian firm of Miller, Bonnany, and Company saved the day.[63] By 1789, Muscogulge war parties had killed 72 settlers, wounded 29, and taken 30 prisoners, killed 10 black slaves and taken 110 prisoners, taken over 640 horses and 984 cattle, killed 387 hogs, and burned 89 houses on the disputed lands.[64] Georgia politicians, seeking a remedy, pondered the possibility of restoring the property confiscated from the McGillivray family during the war if the Great Beloved Man would halt the hostilities.[65] Spanish officials and Panton, Leslie, and Company, worried lest Bowles and his companions undermine their established trading system, began to plot his arrest.

The Washington administration, in an attempt to settle the troubled Georgia frontier and lessen the Spanish threat by diffusing the alliance with the Creeks, invited Alexander McGillivray and other leading Creeks to the temporary capital at New York in 1790. The fact that trade and military alliances were closely related concerned George Washington. The president noted that the control of the Creek trade by British merchants operating from Spanish soil had "caused much embarrassment." Washington believed that it was "obvious" that the United States could not "possess any security for the performance of treaties with the Creeks" while their trade was likely "to be interrupted or withheld at the caprice of two foreign powers."[66] Washington's determination to stabilize Creek-American relations and to counteract the influence of Spain led to three important events: the Treaty of New York in 1790; the establishment of a government trading system; and the appointment of Benjamin Hawkins as the federal representative to the southern tribes in 1796.[67]

The Treaty of New York settled old anxieties for both sides. Alexander McGillivray, who served as the Creek spokesman, settled the disputed Creek-Georgia boundary by a cession of some three million acres lying between the Ogeechee and Oconee rivers. The land in question had been granted to Georgia by the three treaties negotiated during the 1780s and had been heavily settled, thereby losing its value as a hunting range. The cession merely confirmed established fact and offered the hope of a defensible border.[68] More important, the cession was made under the auspices of the federal government—not the state of Georgia.

In return for the land, the Creeks were given a perpetual annuity of fifteen hundred dollars in addition to an allotment of trade goods. The treaty also contained a secret article pledging that in any one year, up to sixty thousand dollars of trade goods, exempt from duties, could be transported into the Creek country through American territory. The provision was valuable insurance for the Creeks, who were completely dependent on Anglo-Spanish friendship for their supplies. Political implication aside, Creek economic interest was well served by the treaty. The United States also agreed to protect Creek territory, and the treaty legally prohibited individual states from concluding treaties with the Indians. In addition, the Creek towns retained the right to deal with intruders who crossed the new boundary, white hunters were banned from the remaining hunting lands, and federal passports were to be required for American visitors.[69]

One of the most significant provisions of the 1790 Treaty of New York represented the desire of leading Americans to end Creek dependence on the deerskin trade and recast the Indian socially, politically, and culturally. By Article 12, the United States agreed to "furnish gratuitously . . . domestic animals and implements of husbandry" so that the Creeks might "be led to a greater degree of civilization, and to become herdsmen and cultivators, instead of remaining in a state of hunters." Provisions were also made for interpreters and federal agents to reside among the Creeks in order to supervise and direct the transformation.[70]

Though the 1790 treaty did not directly establish trade relations with the Creeks, this was clearly Washington's goal. In 1793 and 1794, he called for the establishment of government posts to conduct a fair and equitable trade with the Indian tribes. In 1795, Washington's hopes were realized with the appropriation of money with which to purchase goods for trade with the Cherokees and Creeks.[71] After 1795, the United States established government trading posts at a number of locations along the Georgia-Creek border to help offset Spanish influence among the southern Indians. The first post or factory was located at Colerain, on the St. Mary's River in Georgia. The Creek factory was later moved to Fort Wilkinson on the Oconee River and still later to Fort Hawkins on the Ocmulgee River near present-day Macon, Georgia. The government trading system or factory system was a new concept in southeastern Indian commerce. The aim of the factory system was to provide Indians with trade goods, at cost, in order to establish a measure of political and economic control over the tribes. Creeks were quick to point out that the factory system was not without drawbacks. Journeying to the factory was not as convenient or as popular as having a resident storekeeper. In addition, prices were sometimes higher at the factory, whereas quality and quantity of goods were unpredictable. More often than not, rum and ammunition were absent from the government's stocks.[72] But there were some benefits. Although these establishments did little to change the economic situation in the nation, they did provide Creeks with an alternative source of supplies and a market for their agricultural produce.[73] Moreover, their existence tended to moderate the prices charged by Panton, Leslie, and Company.[74]

Since the factory was supposed to be self-sufficient, a cash-and-carry policy was attempted, but the factory storekeepers found it impossible to operate without allowing credit.[75] The American agent Benjamin Hawkins, who arrived in the Creek country in 1796, was convinced that credit lay at the heart of all Creek woes, especially what he saw as the "idle beggarly habits" of attempting to live by the hunt and asking for "presents."[76] Although he constantly advised the various storekeepers at the Creek factory to restrict credit, they found it impossible to do so. Inevitably, Creek debts grew. In 1789, U.S. commissioners estimated that the annual Creek sale of deerskins and other furs was £10,000, whereas the goods consumed in the nation were worth approximately £12,000.[77] The Creeks' largest creditor was Panton, Leslie, and Company, whose claims dated back to the 1780s. In 1797, William Panton estimated that the amount due his company by all the southern tribes was $282,445, of which $122,445 had been contracted by the Creeks and Seminoles.[78] These figures were accepted as legitimate by American agents as well as native headmen.

During the Adams administration, the American government tacitly agreed to help Panton, Leslie, and Company collect the debts owed by the Indians in return for the firm's support of the United States in the event of a break in Anglo-Spanish relations.[79] Nothing came of the notion. But by 1798, Benjamin Hawkins and William Panton were corresponding regarding the company's claims against the Creeks.[80] Hawkins and Panton agreed that the Creeks had no resources, other than their land, to apply toward the debts. Hawkins then put the matter to a number of leading Creeks and suggested a land cession as a way to clear their obligation to the company and to others who had claims against them. He wrote Panton in January 1799: "The bare mention excites very disagreeable emotions . . . I have explained the mode among civilized people, of taking property of every description, even land, to satisfy just claims. They are pleased with the mode, so far as it respects personal property, but land they say should not be touched."[81] Creeks feared that new cessions of land would become necessary to clear their debts, whereas Americans relished the prospect.[82]

Under the Jefferson administration, the government's view on credit took a new and menacing turn. Jefferson believed that as deer herds continued to decline, the Indians would be forced to depend on agriculture to support themselves. Once they took up the plow, Creeks would realize that their large hunting ranges were superfluous, and they would willingly sell the land to purchase agricultural implements and livestock.[83] With that in mind, the president charged Hawkins with the task of promoting "among the Indians a sense of the superior value of a little land, well cultivated, over a great deal, unimproved."[84] To hasten the process, the administration would widely extend credit to the Indians at the government factories "beyond their individual means of paying." Once they became indebted, they would be forced to sell their land to pay their debts, thereby hastening the day when they would abandon hunting.[85] Thus, the extinction of title to tribal hunting grounds became a prerequisite for "civilization."[86]

But the Creek people already faced hard economic times. Deer had become exceedingly scarce. Hawkins scoured the Creek hinterland in early 1797, and even his trained hunting dogs could find no game.[87] The agent reported in February 1799 that hunters in the Upper Towns had not been very successful. "Some . . . have returned from hunting without any skins and I have heard from one town who have not killed fifty."[88] The following month, he wrote to the factor at the government factory: "The skin trade is in decline. The hunts have been much less than they have ever been known to be in any season before."[89] Old bear grounds, long vacant, were grudgingly turned over to pigs and cattle.[90] A bad situation was made even worse by a concurrent rise in the price of trade goods. The prices established for European goods in Pensacola in 1784 were slightly higher than prewar prices. By 1792, the value of deerskins had dropped by almost 50 percent from their prerevolutionary levels. Panton was forced to adjust his exchange rates accordingly. Chronic shortages of powder, ball, flints, and salt at the American factory meant Creeks had no choice but to frequent the stores of Panton's traders. The Creek debt reached new heights. Many Creeks suffered from a lack of clothing.[91]

This problem was compounded by the refusal of the American government to reward its supporters with presents. Their political value aside, the influx of free guns, clothing, and other goods had been a tremendous boon to the Creek economy and had helped offset the trade imbalance in the Creek country. In 1802, Efau Haujo, a leading headman, reminded Hawkins of the government's obligation to help support its allies and reward leading men with presents. Hawkins chided the headman, "I am here to remedy the past, to assist the Indians as the game is gone to clothe and feed themselves by farming, spinning and stockraising & to help all who well help themselves but not to tollerate or support sturdy beggars." Hawkins was direct, "Sell some of your waste lands . . . I see no other resource and that is very abundant."[92]

Under Hawkins's constant pressure, the Creeks soon "acquired correct ideas of the value of property, and the importance of some permanent annual revenue" to offset the decline in the trade.[93] In June 1802, the federal government secured two minor land grants from the Creeks. In return, the Creeks received a three-thousand-dollar perpetual annuity plus a ten-year annuity of one thousand dollars for the headmen. They were also awarded twenty-five thousand dollars. Of that amount, the Creeks received only ten thousand dollars in the form of trade goods. The remainder went toward retiring the Creek debt to the government factory (ten thousand dollars) and for damages claimed by Georgia citizens before 1796.[94]

The 1802 cession, like the earlier 1773 New Purchase, was merely a temporary solution for the Creek debt. It brought sorely needed trade goods to the Creek towns and cleared their account books but did not address Creek economic woes. Still, Hawkins and the federal government did not abandon their civilization schemes nor realize the deficiencies in their theories.[95] In addition, American officials began obliging the tribes' primary creditor, Panton, Leslie, and Company, by encouraging the Indians to sell land to the United States in order to raise money to clear their obligations to the company and its successor firm, John Forbes and Company.[96]

Though the Creeks found that parting with their territory was "most disagreeable," the collapse of the hunting economy left little choice.[97] The Seminole towns ceded about one million acres in 1804 to cover their debts to Panton, Leslie, and Company. In 1805, after three years of negotiations, a Creek delegation traveled to the American capital and relinquished title to two million acres and authorized the American government to build a road through their country for a yearly annuity.[98] The annuity money, like presents from the British in an earlier period, was distributed to chiefs and then divided among the townspeople. "All the Indians had an equal right; and . . . whenever land was sold, all would expect to receive something."[99] Even so, stiff opposition by Upper Creeks delayed the construction of the Federal Road until 1811.[100] As Florette Henri, the biographer of Benjamin Hawkins, succinctly observed, "Little by little, treaty by treaty, the acre replaced the deerskin as the unit of trade."[101]

Though the United States had gotten land and encouraged the Creeks to settle their just debts, John Forbes and Company was not reimbursed by the 1805 cession.[102] By 1812, company representatives were again in the Creek towns urging headmen to pay their old debts with another cession or with their annuity from earlier sales. The company also demanded that interest be paid on the uncollected debts. Creek headmen were aghast and adamantly refused to pay interest. Usually polite and civil in council, the leaders abruptly changed their tone. The Creek spokesman accused the company's representative of trying to "tear the very flesh off their backs." John Innerarity, the company's representative at the meeting, recorded in his journal, "They had told me they were poor, that they knew nothing about interest, about what it meant, it might be a custom, a law among us white people, but poor Indians did not understand it, there was no word for it in their language, we were the first who ever talked of such a thing to them."[103] In the end, the company was forced to forgive the interest, and the Creek headmen agreed to retire the principal by 1814 with their annuity money.[104]

While the trade continued its drain on Creek land, game, and morale, there were other economic and social forces at work in the Creek Nation. One of the most significant changes resulted from the increasing numbers of white and black residents in the Creek country and the adoption, by the white men and their mixed-blood progeny, of commercial agriculture. Almost all of the whites were or had been connected in some way with the deerskin trade, either as traders or packhorsemen. The Revolution cut them off from their established suppliers at Augusta, leaving them to find other means to advance themselves after the war. Although no official census was made during this period, it is likely that between three hundred to four hundred white men made their homes in the Creek Nation during and after the American Revolution.[105] The influx of white men continued after the war and significantly altered the racial composition of the Creek people.

Some were able to continue their profession as associates of Panton, Leslie, and Company. However, keen competition barred many from this employment. Others adopted the only other economic ventures open to them: farming and cattle raising. After marrying Creek women, these men asked local village headmen to allocate land for their use, as they were entitled to do under established custom. Creeks grumbled but did not stop the new farming and herding activities of their compatriots.

One of the most successful "plantations" belonged to the trader Richard Bailey, who had resided in the Upper Creek town of Otassee for forty years by the time Hawkins visited him in 1796. With his family and slaves, Bailey had built an impressive farm. Bailey proudly showed the agent his fences, stables, peach orchard, beehives, and his large stock of cattle, horses, and hogs. Yet the people of Otassee were not pleased with Bailey's "improvements." After his livestock had repeatedly damaged the town's communal cornfields, the inhabitants had forced him to leave. But after three years without a trader, the Creeks had invited him back, and the people of Otassee agreed not to damage his fences or stock, since the farm was acknowledged to be the property of Mrs. Bailey, a woman of the Wind clan, and her children.[106]

By 1798, commercial production of cotton had begun on a small scale in the Creek territory.[107] The use of black slave labor to plant, cultivate, and harvest the crop soon followed. Black agricultural know-how contributed greatly to the cultivation of cotton and corn for market. Indian traders, as a rule, were not the best farmers and depended heavily on the agricultural expertise of their slaves. They also sought advice from Hawkins, who was delighted at their efforts. In addition to planting, hoeing and harvesting cotton, the slaves of Indian countrymen and mixed-bloods sacked it and escorted packhorses laden with the harvest to St. Augustine, Pensacola, Savannah, or towns in Tennessee—wherever there were buyers. Corn, honey, horses, dried beef, and cattle hides were marketed as well. Slaves were also used to produce food crops and tend growing herds of cattle, hogs, and even sheep. The growing emphasis on commercial farming assured the continuance of black slavery in the Indian country.[108]

Until the American Revolution, blacks had been relatively rare among the Creeks. Many traders had kept slaves, in spite of official protest, but the numbers had been inconsequential. During the colonial period, escaped slaves from South Carolina and Georgia were usually returned to white colonists by the Creeks, who were bound to do so by treaties. But some blacks were retained as slaves, by both traders and Indians. David George fled a cruel Virginia master in the 1770s and eventually reached the Ocmulgee River. Blue Salt of Cussita happened upon the runaway while the slave was fashioning a raft and made George his "prize." For five months, from December to April, George labored for the Cussita headman. His rare account of life as a Creek slave is terse, "I made fences, dug the ground, planted corn, and worked hard; but the people were kind to me."[109] Unlike George, some slaves avoided returning to their white masters by being adopted into a Creek family, usually by marriage.

During the Revolution, the numbers of blacks coming into the Creek country increased dramatically. Traders and other loyalists fleeing the brutal fighting in Georgia and the Floridas sought refuge in Creek towns and brought their slaves with them. Sizable numbers of Muscogulges also began keeping slaves. Creek warriors captured many slaves on their raids into neighboring colonies during the war. Their British allies encouraged such tactics and allowed the Creeks to keep captured slaves, who thereby became known as the "king's gifts."[110] The mixed-blood Jack Kinnard, who earned his property "entirely by plunder and freebooting, during the American war, and the late Georgia quarrel," had forty black slaves and some Indian slaves.[111]

The logical result of the influx of blacks and whites was a mixing of red, black, and white. More than one observer noted the "strange medley of people . . . Caucasians, Mongolians or Indians, Africans & several new breeds manufactured by judicious crossing!"[112] All sorts of racial mixtures were the result. In general, a person of Indian-white extraction was known as a *mestizo,* whereas intermixture with a black resulted in a *mulatto* offspring. In addition to acquiring a decidedly Scottish character, Creek culture began to take on some African aspects as well. By the same token, southern slave society incorporated many Creek and other southern Indian characteristics as the children of Creek-black relationships moved into black slave society. Indeed, many myths believed to have originated in Africa have distinct Creek counterparts. As one traveled through Creek towns, it was possible to hear Chickasaw, Muskogee, Yuchi, and the many other diverse native tongues that had become part of the Muscogulge confederacy. Now, strains of Scottish brogue, French and Spanish, and a variety of African dialects filled the air too.[113]

The saga of the Grierson family exemplifies the changes in Creek economic and social development after the American Revolution. Robert and his brother Thomas were both traders to the Creeks before the war. Thomas, who served as an officer in the rebel militia, died in 1775. His death left the Eufaulees without a trader, but his mixed-blood son continued to reside in their town with his maternal relatives. Little is known of him. Another brother, James, was a prominent citizen of Augusta and colonel of the Augusta militia. James Grierson was also a merchant at Augusta and benefited from the transfer of Creek lands to their traders in 1773. James's two brothers most likely received their trade goods from him. When the Revolution came, James Grierson remained loyal, since he was an "officer of the Crown." In 1781, after the surrender of loyalist forces at Augusta to the rebel army, James Grierson was executed by Georgia militia before the eyes of his children.[114] Robert Grierson, like his brother James, was a Loyalist and remained in the Upper Nation near Okfuskee after the war. He continued to operate a trading establishment, but of more importance, he and his Creek wife and five children engaged in cattle herding and cotton cultivation. Grierson's family was assisted in their commercial endeavors by some forty slaves. Grierson acquired a spinning wheel from Hawkins after the agent arrived in 1796, and the trader promptly set his wife and daughters to work spinning their home-grown cotton fibers into cloth.[115] Grierson's mixed-blood progeny were reared as Indians. His mestizo daughter bore two children by a black father, and one of his sons married one of the family's black slaves, producing a large family. Although such mixing was of little consequence during the early nineteenth century, one of Grierson's Creek-white descendants, who became head chief of the Creek Nation in Oklahoma in the early twentieth century, later lamented the "lasting cloud" over the family name caused by this mingling of Creek and black blood.[116]

Early in the nineteenth century, Creeks showed little concern about the color of a person's skin. As time passed, Creek attitudes toward blacks tended to mimic the prejudices of their white neighbors. It was not until the 1830s that the offspring of Creek-black unions faced discrimination. As the nineteenth century progressed and black slavery became more entrenched in the interior, white society was likely to label anyone with any degree of African blood as a black. As a result, many mixed-blood Creeks were classified as black, and many mulatto Creeks were slaves on southern plantations by the mid-nineteenth century.[117]

James McQueen, another native of Scotland, entered the Creek trade in the late 1750s and established himself at Little Tallassee in the Upper Nation. He remained there after the war, accumulating land, cattle, and slaves. His son Peter eventually rose to the position of Head Warrior at Tallassee. The young mixed-blood also took up the merchant's mantle, receiving goods from Panton, Leslie, and Company. Like his father, he was a slave owner and participated in commercial farming to some extent.[118] The elder McQueen was reputed to be the grandfather of Osceola, the famous Seminole leader. There are some who believe that Osceola had African forebears, and it should come as no surprise that one of Osceola's wives was most likely a black woman.[119]

Like Grierson and McQueen, Alexander McGillivray and his sisters established several plantations and were the largest slaveholders in the Creek country. By the end of the first decade of the nineteenth century, it was often hard to tell exactly who was an Indian and who was not. Many mixed-blood mestizo Creeks spoke, dressed, lived, and worked in the same manner as the increasing numbers of white settlers on the edges of Creek territory. Names were of no use: the Woodwards, Weatherfords, Mims, Tates, Baileys, Kinnards, and McIntoshes were Creeks, not just ordinary settlers. Those who adopted white culture so thoroughly are often labeled "acculturated" or "progressive" rather than traditional. But nonetheless, they were still Creek.

As the progressive Creeks assumed the life-style of their white neighbors, important changes occurred. The nuclear family, composed of immediate family and slaves, tended to supplant the matrilineage, thereby undermining the authority of elders and the social and political functions of the clan. Moreover, there was an increasing tendency toward patrilineal rather than matrilineal descent, which further eroded the clan system. Cash-crop farming encouraged competition to gain control of the best agricultural land. Communal ownership of land was the Creek way, but this fact was, of necessity, ignored by those who engaged in the new ways. For the progressives, self-interest supplanted community spirit. But as always, Creek culture proved to be remarkably persistent, and many mixed-bloods used Creek names and continued to live as their Creek ancestors had always done. As time passed, the differences between those who accepted and those who rejected traditional Creek life-styles became more pronounced.[120]

Benjamin Hawkins hoped to exploit these differences in order to achieve the goals of American policymakers who wished to "civilize" the Creeks. Like many of his American contemporaries, Hawkins believed that the best hope for Creek survival lay in a shift away from their traditional pattern of subsistence agriculture and commercial hunting. The success of the civilization program depended on the widespread adoption of individual self-sufficient farms. The agent chafed at the unprofitable nature of the communal cornfield and was horrified that Creek slaveholders did not properly manage their work force. Hawkins was a fount of advice, "Put your negros and family to work, make them pen and milk your cattle, let me see your fields enlarged and well fenced." He promised "axes, grubing hoes, wedges and ploughs" to those who would use them. He encouraged men like Grierson and their mixed-blood offspring, repeatedly pointed to their example, and urged their Creek neighbors to mimic their efforts. He supported new crops and farming techniques. Creek women were encouraged to spin cloth from their own cotton rather than buy imported fabrics from the traders.[121] The plough, though it was not widely accepted, became the symbol of the "civilization" experiment.

Hawkins encouraged not only the establishment of private farmsteads and the abandonment of the communal fields but also the dissolution of the village community. But moving away from the town meant a disruption of the matrilineal household and social control by clan convention. This was the ultimate ethnocentric blind-spot. In effect, by attempting to change the economic basis of Creek life, the philanthropists undermined the traditional foundation of Creek society. The fences that Hawkins enthusiastically promoted divided the land into individual parcels and established visible reminders that some now lived apart and treated the land as if they owned it outright. This was a revolution—agricultural as well as cultural.[122]

Coping with change was as difficult for those of mixed parentage as it was for full-blooded Creeks. Richard Baillie, whose father of the same name had been a trader, was educated by Philadelphia Quakers. But he was "neither an Indian or white man." His contemptuous attitudes regarding such customs as land ownership earned him the censure of his fellow Creeks, and Hawkins had little hope for his farming ability. Baillie was only one of many who could not find a place in the new order.[123]

A lack of markets, the uncertain political situation in the Creek Nation, foreign intrigues, and the human psyche frustrated Hawkins's attempts. Change was very difficult. The Creeks found themselves swirling in a cultural and economic storm over which they had no control. Traditional economic pursuits were unprofitable, and new ones meant a realignment of traditional sex roles, for Creek men were hunters and warriors—not ploughmen. As Hawkins explained in a letter to the secretary of war in 1798: "They told me they did not understand the plan, they could not work, they did not want ploughs, it did not comport with the ways of the red people, who were determined to persevere in the ways of their ancestors. They saw no necessity why the white people should change the ways of their ancestors."[124]

Into the maelstrom entered Tecumseh, who with his brother Tenskwatawa, the Shawnee Prophet, hoped to forge a pan-Indian confederacy to oppose the whites and their demands for land. The idea was not a new one; such talk had circulated among Creek councils since the mid-eighteenth century. Now the effort took on new urgency. Although the Shawnees' basic goal was to oppose American expansion, the movement also sought to revitalize Indian society. Stock raising, cloth manufacturing, and new farming methods became symbols of the decay of Indian culture, and their followers were urged to return to the ways of their ancestors.[125]

Tecumseh visited the Creek Nation in 1811 and was warmly received. He should have been, since his mother was of Creek extraction. His visit was followed by intense religious and prophetic activity. Mixed-blood Creeks were not immune to the revitalization movement. The most important of the Creek prophets, Hildis Hadjo, was better known to his American enemies as Josiah Francis. Peter McQueen and William Weatherford felt the same stirring of Muscogulge heritage when they aligned themselves with the prophets.[126] There was frequent talk of the return of the British to Pensacola and a renewal of the old trade alliance. Warriors visited Pensacola to consult with British agents and receive ammunition for the coming war against the land-hungry Americans. According to one Creek mixed-blood, "The whole nation was in commotion and excited . . . the ferment and agitation was almost a general thing and superlatively progressing from bad to worse."[127] The eventual result of such agitation was the Creek civil war of 1813–14.

The changing economic conditions that confronted the Creek people are the key to understanding the Creek war. Dependence on foreign technology, the scarcity of trade goods, poverty, indebtedness, and white encroachment contributed as much to the war as did political factionalism and spiritual awakening.[128] Antagonism toward the new social and economic order promulgated by the mixed-bloods and promoted by Hawkins effectively divided the Creeks. More than one "town divided against itself" as some Creeks, usually of mixed blood, took Hawkins's advice to heart.[129] The competition for political and economic power accentuated old divisions within the Muscogulge alliance. The new roads so recently cut through the Creek domain served only to excite tensions. Encroachment by white settlers and hunters and concern over the steady alienation of lands meant that many Creeks listened eagerly to Tecumseh's plans for an Indian confederacy to oppose American expansion and revitalize Indian culture. Hounded from without and convulsed from within, the Creek people turned on themselves.

It was more than coincidence that the Red Sticks, as the hostile Creeks have been called, slaughtered hogs and cattle wherever they found them. Cattle had always been viewed as the enemy of traditional Creek economic life, for they trampled unfenced communal cornfields and intruded on traditional grazing areas, canebrakes, and mineral licks, thereby driving deer and other game away. As a symbol of the new economic and social thrust of the "civilization program," livestock was especially detested.[130] But the hostiles slaughtered more than cattle, and their leaders called for the destruction of "everything received from the Americans, all the Chiefs and their adherents . . . friendly to the customs and ways of the white people."[131] The massacre of mixed-bloods and white settlers at Fort Mims in 1813 provided an excuse for American frontiersmen to join the fray. Black slaves in the Creek country were drawn into the hostilities as well, and it was reported that many "run-away negroes . . . went and joined the hostile Indians to assist in exterminating the white people and be free."[132] Such red-black combinations had long been feared and only gave the white slaveholding neighbors of the Creeks another reason to intervene. The Creek people, no matter which side they supported, were the losers.[133]

American intervention after the outbreak of the Creek War in 1813 spelled doom for the Creeks. Andrew Jackson, who led the American war effort, soundly defeated the natives. The final—and greatest—battle came at Tohopeka, a well-known bend in the Tallapoosa River shaped like a horseshoe. Over one thousand Red Stick warriors, plus numerous women and children, barricaded themselves in the hollow of the bend and erected breastworks across the open end, leaving it to the Tallapoosa to protect their flanks and rear. Jackson's army, including "friendly" Creeks and Cherokees, was twice the size of the Creek force. The Red Sticks staged a valiant, but vain, defense. Their defeat was as thorough as it was brutal. At day's end, an estimated nine hundred Creeks lay dead.[134]

As the American soldiers celebrated at Horseshoe Bend on that March day in 1814, the economic roots of Creek distress sprouted forth bitter fruit. Muscogulge hunters had preyed on the white-tail, and it had made them powerful. But their dependence on the trade of deerskins for manufactured goods ultimately made them weak. It seems a tragic irony that Jackson's men, eager to remember their great victory, stripped the flesh from the backs of the dead and fashioned Creek skin into souvenirs.[135]

The Treaty of Fort Jackson in 1814, which ended the war, was clearly designed to destroy Muscogulge power in the Southeast. The treaty terms, dictated by Jackson, were presented to the chiefs who had assisted the

United States in the war against the Red Sticks. Jackson explained to the stunned headmen and warriors gathered at the site of the abandoned Fort Toulouse, now called Fort Jackson, "We bleed our enemies in such cases to give them their senses."[136] All other issues paled as the Creek people were dispossessed of over thirty million acres—roughly one-half the Creek domain—by the harsh treaty that Jackson thrust on them.[137] The southern part of the cession cut through the hunting grounds of both the Upper and Lower towns, creating a broad band of American territory that severed the Muscogulges from foreign merchants operating out of Spanish ports—"our Enemies," as Jackson termed them. Poorly armed, poorly clothed, and hungry, the ragged and wretched survivors scarcely knew what to mourn first.

The treaty decreed that the deerskin trade would continue but that henceforth all traders would operate strictly under American supervision. By Article 7, America promised that conveniently located "trading houses" would be established so that Creeks would be able, "by industry and economy, to procure clothing."[138] After the war, Muscogulge men still hunted and killed deer for subsistence and for a limited trade. Many, like Hildis Hadjo, who traveled to England to present his people's case to the king, continued to hope that the British would return to the Southeast, reestablish the trade, and help the Creeks regain their land.[139] But the deerskin trade—as a viable economic activity and as a symbol of a larger alliance between two peoples—was finished. With Jackson's total victory, "the Original great tye" that had bound Anglo-Americans and Muscogulges for over a century was forever broken. The confident military rifle of a rising economic power replaced the overworked smooth-bore trade gun as the harbinger of Creek destiny.

Appendix

Regulations for the Better Carrying on the Trade with the Indian Tribes in the Southern District*

1. No trader shall employ any person as clerk, packhorseman, or factor, in his service, before an agreement be first entered into between them, specifying the time and conditions of service, and having his or their names inserted or endorsed on the back of the license, so that the principal trader shall be rendered responsible for, and subjected to, the penalties which may be incurred by his or their bad conduct.

(Stuart's comment: It is a practice with the traders to entice away each other's servants, when on the point of carrying their peltry to market which suggested the two following articles.)

2. No trader, while in any Indian nation, shall employ in his service any clerk, packhorseman, or factor, who may have formerly been engaged with any other trader, until the time of service stipulated by his said agreement be expired, or a regular discharge from such former master shall first have been had and produced to the person hiring such servant, showing that the former contract had been dissolved by mutual consent, or else till said servant shall have produced a certificate from the commissary showing that the former contract had been dissolved for good and sufficient reasons, shown before him the said commissary.

*The Creek merchants and traders agreed to these regulations at the Augusta Conference of 1767. On the copy sent to London, Stuart added handwritten explanatory comments, which are indicated above in parentheses. The original document is found in Stuart's letter to Shelburne, April 1, 1767, Colonial Office, Class 5/68, fo. 110, Great Britain Public Record Office. Another printed version of these regulations appears in Colonial Office, Class 5/68, fo. 144. Punctuation and spelling have been modernized here. The West Florida traders' regulations, which are similar to the above, can be found in John R. Alden, *John Stuart and the Southern Colonial Frontier*, pp. 341.

3. Every trader on employing any clerk, packhorseman, or factor, while residing in any Indian nation, shall give notice within ten days thereafter to the commissary residing in said nation, whose permission for employing such clerk, packhorseman, or factor, must be obtained, and if not obtaining such permission in the space of six weeks, after giving notice as above, and such clerk, packhorseman, or factor, still continuing in the service of said trader, the bond and license to be forfeited.

(Stuart's comment: The intention of this article is to prevent vagrants and men of bad character being employed in the quality of clerks, etc. to the traders.)

4. No trader shall employ any Negro, Indian, or half-breed, professing himself an Indian, or under Indian government, as a factor or deputy, to trade in any town or village, on account of said trader.

5. No Indian trader shall harbour in his house, any white person, for a time exceeding fourteen days, unless under the foregoing regulations, or by virtue of a particular permission from the commissary.

(Stuart's comment: Intended to discourage idlers and vagrants in the Indian nations.)

6. All factors, clerks, packhorsemen and traders, shall, when regularly and legally called upon, be aiding and assisting to the commissary in apprehending any offender.

7. No trader shall by himself, servant, or substitutes, sell to the Indians, swanshot or rifle barrelled guns.

(Stuart's comment: Swanshot spoils the skins, and rifle barrelled guns are too good arms.)

8. All goods shall be sold to the Indians, according to a certain tariff, hereunto annexed, and any trader by himself, servants, or substitutes, selling goods to Indians at any other prices or rates, than what are contained in said tariff, shall forfeit his bond and license, unless in consequence of any alteration hereafter made and agreed to at a general meeting.

(Stuart's comment: The tariff to be settled at different meetings of Indians and traders by the parties themselves.)

9. No trader shall credit any Indian for more than thirty pounds' weight of Indian dressed deerskins, and all debts due by Indians, above that sum, shall be considered as not recoverable, neither shall any trader credit an Indian for more than five pounds of gunpowder, and twelve pounds of bullets, in one hunting season.

10. The weights and measures of every trader in the Indian nations, shall

conform exactly to the standard weight and measure lodged with the commissaries residing in the respective nations, and if any weight or measure shall be found, upon comparison, to differ therefrom, one half ounce in weight, or one half inch in length, then such difference shall subject said trader to the forfeiture of his bond and license.

(Stuart's comment: Weights and measures properly marked to be lodged with the commissary by the superintendent.)

11. No trader shall by himself, servants, or substitutes, propagate any false report or reports among Indians; and no trader shall convene any meeting with them, or deliver any message or talk to them, without the concurrence and consent of the commissary first obtained in writing.

(Stuart's comment: The Indians complained of being often imposed on by pretended talks. The commissaries have orders to deliver all talks to the Indians from the governors.)

12. All traders, their packhorsemen, clerks, deputies and servants, shall communicate all intelligence, any way relating to peace or war, or by which his Majesty's service can be in any degree affected, to the commissaries in the respective nations where such traders shall reside.

13. Any trader refusing or neglecting to appear at any Congress, or general meeting of the Indians with the commissary, when duly summoned by the commissary, except in case of [sickness, or for other lawful, unforeseen or unavoidable cause] shall forfeit his bond and license.

14. No trader shall himself, or permit any of his servants to, hunt deer or bear, or set traps for beaver, in any of the Indian hunting grounds, or shall by himself, servants, or substitutes, purchase deerskins, fur, or peltry of any sort, from any white person hunting or laying traps as aforesaid, or in any way deal for such goods, by barter with, or receive the same from, or dispose of, or carry the same to market, for such hunters.

(Stuart's comment: White men who live by hunting in the Indians' grounds [are] much complained of.)

15. Any trader who shall by himself, servants, deputies, or substitutes, be convicted of selling to, or bartering rum, or other spirituous liquors, with any Indian or Indians, for half-dressed or raw deerskins, bearskins, fur, or peltry of any sort, shall forfeit his bond and license.

16. Any trader who by himself, substitute, or servant, shall carry more than fifteen gallons of rum, at any one time, into any nation of Indians, or who shall upon the evidence of two white men, be convicted of having any more than fifteen gallons of rum in his or their possession, at any one time,

shall forfeit his bond and license; and said rum shall be liable to seizure by the commissary, who shall distribute the same among the Indians. Such importation of fifteen gallons of rum aforesaid, shall not be repeated till after an interval of three months.

(Stuart's comment: While Indians can get spirits for their peltry they will not purchase other necessaries, and they often supply themselves by plundering the traders.)

17. No trader, clerk, factor, or packhorseman, shall beat or abuse any Indian, but shall, on the contrary, pay a proper respect to the medal chiefs, and captains bearing commissions.

18. No trader by himself, servants, or substitutes, or any of them, shall trade with any of the Indians, in the woods, or before their return to their respective towns from hunting, under any pretence whatsoever.

19. No trader shall buy or take in barter for their goods, any hides, or deerskins in the hair, or before they are dressed by the Indians, except in the proportion of four undressed skins in the hair to one hundred and fifty pounds of weight Indian dressed deerskins; and any trader who shall be convicted of transgressing this regulation by purchasing skins in the hair as aforesaid, by himself, servants, or deputies, or any of them, shall forfeit his bond and license.

(Stuart's comment: Trading for skins in the hair leaves room for great imposition of the Indians. Skins are then bought by tale [tally or count]. When half-dressed, the labor of the Indians is paid in British manufactures.)

20. All traders immediately upon their arrival in the nations, towns, or tribes, for which licenses have been granted them, before any goods are sold or bartered with the Indians, shall produce such licenses to the commissaries appointed for direction and inspection of the trade at such posts, or truck-houses, or in such tribes, towns, or nations, to whom they shall give an exact list of their servants, clerks, and packhorsemen.

21. All traders employing Negroes or mulattoes, in any capacity, shall give a list of their names and employments to the commissary in the nation to which they trade, and become bound in a sufficient sum for their good behavior and traders employing such Negroes or mulattoes one month without giving notice to the commissary as aforesaid, shall forfeit their bonds and licenses.

(Stuart's comment: Negroes and mulattoes are employed by traders to plant in the nations and may form dangerous connections with the Indians.)

Notes

PREFACE

1. *Travels of William Bartram,* edited by Mark Van Doren (New York: Dover Publications, 1955), p.383 (hereafter cited as Bartram, *Travels*).

CHAPTER 1: *The Eighteenth-Century Muscogulges*

1. The term *Muskogean* is used to describe a family of related languages, including Choctaw, Chickasaw, Alabama, Hitchiti, and Muskogee. *Muskogee* refers to people who speak the Muskogee language. But since Muskogees are of composite origin, not all spoke the dominant dialect, or at least they did not claim it as their mother tongue. Robert F. Spencer et al., *The Native Americans: Ethnology and Backgrounds of the North American Indians,* 2d ed. (New York: Harper & Row, 1977), pp.412–14. The term *Muskogee* was most likely given to these people by the Shawnees and is related to the Algonquian word *muskeg*. The Algonquian and Muskogean language families are distantly related. Since the Muskogees claim to have originated in the drier lands to the west, their designation as *Muskogee* is a relatively new one. William Bartram, "Observations on the Creek and Cherokee Indians, 1789, with Prefatory and Supplementary Notes by E. G. Squier, *Transactions of the American Ethnological Society,* vol.3, part 1 (New York: American Ethnological Society, 1853), pp.11–12; Albert S. Gatschet, *A Migration Legend of the Creek Indians, with a Linguistic, Historic, and Ethnographic Introduction,* vol.1, Brinton's Library of Aboriginal American Literature, no.4 (Philadelphia: N.p., 1884; reprint, New York: AMS Press, 1969), pp.58–62.

2. James Adair, *Adair's History of the American Indians,* edited by Samuel Cole Williams (Johnson City, Tenn.: Watauga Press, 1930; reprint, New York: Argonaut Press, 1966), p.274 (hereafter cited as *Adair's History*).

3. J. Leitch Wright, Jr., *Creeks and Seminoles: The Destruction and Regeneration of the Muscogulge People* (Lincoln: University of Nebraska Press, 1986), p.2; *Letters, Journals, and Writings of Benjamin Hawkins,* edited by C. L. Grant, 2 vols. (Savannah: Beehive Press, 1980), 1:285.

4. Bartram, "Observations," pp.11–12, see also pp.59–60.

5. For the derivation of the name *Creeks,* see Verner W. Crane, "The Origin of the Name of the Creek Indians," *Mississippi Valley Historical Review* 5 (December 1918): 339–42.

6. David H. Corkran, *The Creek Frontier, 1540–1783,* Civilization of the American Indian Series, no.86 (Norman: University of Oklahoma Press, 1967), p.4; Charles M. Hudson, *The Southeastern Indians* (Knoxville: University of Tennessee Press, 1976), pp.94–95.

7. The political importance of ball play is discussed by Mary R. Haas, "Creek Inter-town Relations," *American Anthropologist* 42 (1940): 479–89.

8. Depopulation predated actual contact in many cases. See George R. Milner, "Epidemic Disease in the Postcontact Southeast: A Reappraisal," *Mid-Continental Journal of Archaeology* 5 (1980): 39–56. A concise summary of early European exploration is found in Jerald T. Milanich, "The European Entrada into La Florida: An Overview," in *Archaeological and Historical Perspectives on the Spanish Borderlands East,* pp.3–29, vol.2 of *Columbian Consequences,* edited by David Hurst Thomas (Washington, D.C.: Smithsonian Institution Press, 1990).

9. Marvin T. Smith, *Archaeology and Aboriginal Culture Change in the Interior Southeast: Depopulation during the Early Historic Period,* Ripley P. Bullen Monographs in Anthropology and History, no.6 (Gainesville: University Presses of Florida/Florida State Museum, 1987), pp.135–37. These same sentiments were earlier expressed by Gregory A. Waselkov and John W. Cottier in "European Perceptions of Eastern Muskogean Ethnicity," in *Proceedings of the Tenth Meeting of the French Colonial Historical Society, April 12–14, 1984,* edited by Philip Boucher (Lanham, Md.: University Press of America, 1985), p.23: "Even deep in the interior, the introduction of guns and the colonial demand for slaves so intensified inter-tribal warfare that previously distinct, geographically dispersed peoples sought mutual protection by concentrating their villages in a few selected river valleys. The resultant confederacies were unions of convenience, often temporary and entailing few mutual obligations, which joined peoples who differed in language, material culture or social custom."

10. Converse D. Clowse, *Economic Beginnings of Colonial South Carolina, 1670–1730,* South Carolina Tricentennial Commission Studies, no.3 (Columbia: University of South Carolina Press, 1971), pp.83–86. According to

Clowse, p.86, "Even before 1690 and until 1715, this trading arrangement with the Lower Creeks was the single most important link to the tribes in the interior." Creeks, almost from the beginning, were the hunters and not the hunted. Even so, they did incorporate some of the very peoples they pursued.

11. Bartram, "Observations," p.12.

12. Bartram, *Travels,* pp.366–67. In his "Observations," p.12, he reported that thirty of the sixty Creek towns spoke Muskogee as their primary language. See also p.37. See Benjamin Hawkins, *A Sketch of the Creek Country in the Years 1798 and 1799 and Letters from Benjamin Hawkins, 1796–1806,* a one-volume reproduction of vol.3, part 1, and vol.9 of *Collections of the Georgia Historical Society* (Spartanburg, S.C.: Reprint Co., 1982), pp.13–15, for Gallatin's reflections on Creek language. For information on Gallatin's work on Indian languages, see Robert E. Bieder, *Science Encounters the Indian, 1820–1880: The Early Years of American Ethnology* (Norman: University of Oklahoma Press, 1986; reprint, 1989), pp.16–37.

13. *Adair's History,* p.285.

14. Ibid.

15. Spencer, *Native Americans,* pp.413, 424.

16. John H. Hann, *Apalachee: The Land between the Rivers,* Ripley P. Bullen Monographs in Anthropology and History, no.7 (Gainesville: University Presses of Florida/Florida State Museum, 1988), p.288. The Apalachee were also most likely Hitchiti speakers.

17. Vernon James Knight, Jr., "Tukabatchee: Archaeological Investigations at an Historic Creek Town, Elmore County, Alabama, 1984" (Report of Investigations 45, Office of Archaeological Research, Alabama State Museum of Natural History, University of Alabama, Tuscaloosa, 1985 mimeographed report), p.27.

18. John Phillip Reid's observations about the Cherokees can be extended to include the Creeks. "As a body politic the Cherokees may not have yet been welded into a 'state,' but as a people they were a 'nation': an ethnic group that possessed a fund of shared experience and had accumulated an identity of interest providing them with a distinctive character and a common culture." *A Better Kind of Hatchet: Law, Trade, and Diplomacy in the Cherokee Nation during the Early Years of European Contact* (University Park: Pennsylvania State University Press, 1976), p.7. Richard White says much the same for the Choctaws. "The term 'nation' here is a fitting one for the Choctaws. It does not signify the existence of a centralized political unit but rather denotes the linguistic, cultural, and kin connections which made the Choctaws a people." *The Roots of Depen-*

dency: Subsistence, Environment, and Social Change among the Choctaws, Pawnees, and Navajos (Lincoln: University of Nebraska Press, 1983), p.2.

19. Thomas M. Hatley, "The Dividing Paths: The Encounters of the Cherokees and the South Carolinians in the Southern Mountains, 1670–1785" (Ph.D. dissertation, Duke University, 1989), p.458.

20. David Taitt to John Stuart, March 16, 1772, in Great Britain, Public Record Office, Colonial Office, American and West Indies, Indian Affairs, Class 5, vol.73, folio 259. Class 5 material will hereafter be cited using the following form: CO5/vol. number, folio number. The folio number cited refers to the first page of the letter or document. Bartram, *Travels,* p.366.

21. Report of John Stuart to the Lords Commissioners of Trade & Plantations on the Southern Indian Department, March 9, 1764, Great Britain, Public Record Office, Colonial Office, Colonies General, Class 323, vol.17, pp.22–23. Page numbers for this report refer to the handwritten number given the report by Stuart and not to the folio number. Class 323 material will hereafter be cited using the following form: CO323/volume number, folio or page number.

22. The Creek explanation of the importance of these towns can be found in Gatschet, *Migration Legend,* pp.250–51.

23. This division into four primary tribes—Alabama, Abeika, Tallapoosa, and Coweta—is based on Creek usage. These divisions were also recognized by Europeans. A French census of Creek towns is found in Dunbar Rowland, ed., *Mississippi Provincial Archives, English Dominion, 1763–1766: Letters and Enclosures to the Secretary of State from Major Robert Farmar and Governor George Johnstone,* vol.1 (Nashville: Brandon Printing Co., 1911), pp.94–97 (hereafter cited as Rowland, MPAED). Another is by Major Francis Ogilvie, dated July 8, 1764. Ogilvie used the French census as a guide. Major Francis Ogilvie to General Gage, July 8, 1764, General Thomas Gage Papers, William L. Clements Library, Ann Arbor, Michigan (hereafter cited as Gage Papers). Both documents erroneously label some Abeika villages as Tallapooses and some Tallapoose villages as Abeika. Allen D. Candler, Kenneth Coleman, and Milton Ready, eds., *The Colonial Records of the State of Georgia,* 28 vols. (Atlanta: C. P. Byrd, 1904–16; Athens: University of Georgia Press, 1974–76), 8:432 (hereafter cited as CRG). A wealth of information on Creek towns and tribes is available in John R. Swanton, *Early History of the Creek Indians and Their Neighbors,* Bureau of American Ethnology Bulletin no.73 (Washington, D.C.: Government Printing Office, 1922; reprint, New York: Johnson Reprint Co., 1970).

24. The Upper and Lower towns were frequently referred to as "nations" during the seventeenth and eighteenth centuries, and that practice will also be

followed in this study. For information on the early Seminoles, see Stuart to Hillsborough, January 27, 1770, CO5/71, part 1, fo.69; Robin F. A. Fabel, "St. Mark's, Apalache, and the Creeks," *Gulf Coast Historical Review* 1 (Spring 1986): 4–22.

25. Hudson, *Southeastern Indians,* p.235–38.

26. Emisteseguo's speech at the Congress of Pensacola, in Rowland, MPAED, p.201.

27. J. Anthony Paredes and Kenneth J. Plante, "A Reexamination of Creek Indian Population Trends, 1738–1832," *American Indian Culture and Research Journal* 6 (1983): 13, mentions the possibility of a smallpox epidemic in 1738. Corkran, *Creek Frontier,* does not mention the epidemic, pp.98–100.

28. Report of Sir James Wright to Lord Dartmouth on the Condition of the Province of Georgia, September 20, 1773, in *Letters from Governor Sir James Wright to the Secretaries of State for America, August 24, 1774, to February 16, 1782,* Collections of the Georgia Historical Society, vol.3 (Savannah: Georgia Historical Society, 1873), p.169. It is of interest that in 1764, Wright used a ratio of five inhabitants per gunman to calculate the total Lower Creek population. Governor James Wright to the Board of Trade, November 10, 1764, CO323/20, fo.70. The best modern attempt to calculate the population of the entire region is Peter H. Wood, "The Changing Population of the Colonial South: An Overview by Race and Region, 1685–1790," in *Powhatan's Mantle: Indians in the Colonial Southeast,* edited by Peter H. Wood, Gregory A. Waselkov, and M. Thomas Hatley (Lincoln: University of Nebraska Press, 1989), pp.35–103. Wood uses a factor of three and one-half (3.5:1) to calculate aboriginal populations.

29. Caleb Swan, "Position and State of Manners and Arts in the Creek or Muscogee Nation, 1791," in Henry Rowe Schoolcraft, ed., *Information Respecting the Historical and Statistical Information Respecting the History, Condition, and Prospects of the Indian Tribes of the United States,* 6 vols. (Philadelphia: J. B. Lippincott Co., 1852–57), 5:263.

30. *Adair's History,* p.241.

31. Hawkins, *Sketch,* p.32.

32. *Calendar of State Papers, Colonial Series, America and West Indies, Preserved in the Public Record Office,* vol.31, *January, 1719, to February, 1720,* edited by Cecil Headlam (London: HM Stationery Office, 1933; reprint, Vaduz: Kraus Reprint, 1964), p.302. The tribes enumerated that were part of the Creek Confederacy were the Apalatchicolas, Apalatchees, Savanos, Euchees, Ochesees, Abikaws, Tallipooses, Albamas. This census also lists women, boys, and girls.

The ratio of gunmen to others is 3.3:1. The French information, dated 1726, is from Dunbar Rowland and A. G. Sanders, eds., *Mississippi Provincial Archives: French Dominion, 1729–1748*, 3 vols. (Jackson, Miss.: Mississippi Department of Archives and History, 1927–32), 3:536–37 (hereafter cited as Rowland and Sanders, MPAFD). Adair counted 3,500 Creek gunmen. *Adair's History*, p.257. For other estimates, see Bernard Romans, *A Concise Natural History of East and West Florida*, facsimile reproduction of the 1775 edition, Florida Facsimile and Reprint Series (Gainesville: University of Florida Press, 1962), p.62. See also Governor Lyttelton to William Pitt, November 4, 1758, in Gertrude Selwyn Kimball, ed., *Correspondence of William Pitt When Secretary of State with Colonial Governors and Military and Naval Commissioners in America*, 2 vols. (New York: Macmillan, 1906; reprint, New York: Kraus, 1969), 1:188–89; Elam Potter, "An Account of Several Nations of Southern Indians, in a Letter from Reverend Elam Potter to Reverend Dr. Stiles, A.D. 1768," *Massachusetts Historical Society Collections*, 1st ser., 10 (1809): 119–21. In 1749, Creek population had been estimated at 2,565 gunmen. See *The Appalachian Indian Frontier: The Edmund Atkin Report and Plan of 1755*, reprint edition of *Indians of the Southern Colonial Frontier*, edited by Wilbur R. Jacobs (Columbia: University of South Carolina Press, 1954; reprint, Lincoln: University of Nebraska Press, 1967), p.43 (hereafter cited as *Atkin Report*).

33. Report of John Stuart to the Lords Commissioners of Trade and Plantations on the Southern Indian Department, March 9, 1764, CO323/17, p.7. Stuart's information was derived from trader information. A French Census of Creek Towns, in Rowland, MPAED, pp.94–97, lists 3,655 gunmen. Ogilvie's translation of the same data is found in Major Francis Ogilvie to General Gage, July 8, 1764, Gage Papers.

34. Report of Sir James Wright to Lord Dartmouth on the Condition of the Province of Georgia, September 20, 1773, in *Letters from Governor Sir James Wright*, Collections of the Georgia Historical Society, vol.3, p.169.

35. James Wright calculated populations for these tribes as follows: Choctaw at 2,500 gunmen for a total of 7,500; Cherokee at 3,000 gunmen for a total of 9,000; and Chickasaw at 450 gunmen for a total of 1,350. These figures were based on a ratio of three others per number of gunmen. The higher figures given here are based on five others per number of gunmen. Report of Sir James Wright to Lord Dartmouth on the Condition of the Province of Georgia, September 20, 1773, in *Letters from Governor Sir James Wright*, p.169. Bossu claimed that the Choctaws could muster 4,000 warriors in 1759, but this seems unduly high. Jean Bernard Bossu, *Jean Bernard Bossu's Travels in the Interior of North America*,

1751–1762, edited and translated by Seymour Feiler (Norman: University of Oklahoma Press, 1962), p.163. Likewise, the Atkin report, citing captured French documents, gave the Choctaw population at 3,600 gunmen in 1755. *Atkin Report,* p.44. John Stuart estimated 5,000 Choctaw gunmen in 1764. Clarence E. Carter, ed., "Observations of Superintendent John Stuart and Governor James Grant of East Florida on the Proposed Plan of 1764 for the Future Management of Indian Affairs," *American Historical Review* 20 (July 1915): 825, but later modified his estimate when better information was provided by traders.

36. James Wright to Board of Trade, April 15, 1761, in CRG, vol.28, pt.1, p.309; Ellis to Board of Trade, January 28, 1759, in CRG, vol.28, pt.1, p.178; Report of Sir James Wright to Lord Dartmouth on the Condition of the Province of Georgia, September 20, 1773, in *Letters from Governor Sir James Wright,* pp.167–69.

37. How Swan arrived at this figure is not clear. He favored a ratio of 3:1 and stated that the number of gunmen stood at "between 5000 and 6000." Thus, either his mathematical skills were poor, or he was also including the Seminole villages in the total count even though he purposefully excluded them from the gunmen tally. Swan, "Position and State of Manners," p.263. See also *American State Papers: Documents, Legislative and Executive of the Congress of the United States, from the First Session of the First to the Third Session of the Thirteenth Congress, Inclusive: Commencing March 3, 1789 and Ending March 3, 1815,* vol.1, Class II, Indian Affairs, edited by Walter Lowrie and Matthew St. Clair Clarke (Washington, D.C.: Gales & Seaton, 1832), p.15 (hereafter cited as *American State Papers, Indian Affairs*). And see Paredes and Plante, "Creek Indian Population Trends," for a general discussion of the topic.

38. Lord Adam Gordon, "Journal of an Officer's Travels in America and the West Indies, 1764–1765," in *Travels in the American Colonies,* edited by Newton D. Mereness (New York: Macmillan, 1916), p.385.

39. Bartram, *Travels,* pp.380–81; Robin F. A. Fabel and Robert R. Rea, "Lieutenant Thomas Campbell's Sojourn among the Creeks, November, 1764–May 1765," *Alabama Historical Quarterly* 36 (Summer 1974): 108.

40. Bartram, "Observations," p.19.

41. *Adair's History,* pp.7–9.

42. Swan, "Position and State of Manners," p.262.

43. Corkran, *Creek Frontier,* p.26. The Wind and the Bear were the most prominent Muskogee clans. Other clans appeared in non–Muskogee-speaking towns, including the Deer, Beaver, Potato, and Alligator. John R. Swanton, *Social Organization and Social Usages of the Indians of the Creek Confederacy,*

Bureau of American Ethnology Bulletin no.42 (Washington, D.C.: Government Printing Office, 1928; reprint, New York: Johnson Reprint Co., 1970), pp.107–241, should be consulted concerning matters pertaining to clan affiliation and organization.

44. Theron A. Nuñez, Jr., "Creek Nativism and the Creek War of 1813–1814 (George Stiggins Manuscript)," *Ethnohistory* 5 (Winter 1958): 133 (hereafter cited as Nuñez, "Stiggins Narrative").

45. Thomas Nairne, *Nairne's Muskhogean Journals: The 1708 Expedition to the Mississippi River,* edited by Alexander Moore (Jackson: University Press of Mississippi, 1988), pp.60–61.

46. Swanton, *Social Organization,* pp.156–66.

47. Nuñez, "Stiggins Narrative," pp.132–33.

48. For a concise description of the Creek clan system, see Hudson, *Southeastern Indians,* pp.185–96; Spencer, *Native Americans,* pp.432–37; Vernon James Knight, Jr., "Social Organization and the Evolution of Hierarchy in Southeastern Chiefdoms," *Journal of Anthropological Research* 46 (Spring 1990): 16–17. See also Alexander Spoehr, "Changing Kinship Systems: A Study in the Acculturation of the Creeks, Cherokee, and Choctaw," *Publications of the Field Museum of Natural History, Anthropological Series* 33, no.4 (January 1947); Frederick R. Eggan, *The American Indian: Perspectives for the Study of Social Change* (Chicago: Aldine, 1966), pp.36–40.

49. *Letters, Journals and Writings of Benjamin Hawkins* 1:320–21. In *Adair's History,* p.147, James Adair related much the same, noting that before a marriage was valid, a man had to plant the cornfields and provide a deer for the new bride.

50. *Adair's History,* pp.93–94, 147.

51. "David Taitt's Journal to and through the Upper Creek Nation," Appendix A, in Kenneth G. Davies, ed., *Documents of the American Revolution, 1770–1783,* 20 vols. (Dublin, Ireland: Irish University Press, 1972–79), 5:260 (hereafter cited as Davies, DAR); Bartram, *Travels,* pp.402–3.

52. Nuñez, "Stiggins Narrative," p.38; Swan, "Position and State of Manners," p.273.

53. "David Taitt's Journal to and through the Upper Creek Nation," in Davies, DAR, 5:268–271; Nuñez, "Stiggins Narrative," *Ethnohistory,* 5:38–40.

54. Swanton, *Social Organization,* p.385; Charles M. Hudson, *The Southeastern Indians* (Knoxville: University of Tennessee Press, 1976), pp.260–269. For a fuller discussion of the roles of Creek women, see Kathryn E. Holland Braund, "Guardians of Tradition and Handmaidens to Change: Women's Roles in Creek Economic and Social Life during the Eighteenth Century," *American Indian Quarterly* 14 (Summer 1990): 239–58.

55. Swanton, *Social Organization*, p.384.

56. Swan, "Position and State of Manners," p.272; see also Hudson, *Southeastern Indians*, p.260.

57. See Hudson, *Southeastern Indians*, pp.317ff., for the best discussion of this concept and its practice.

58. *Adair's History*, pp.129–30; Fabel and Rea, "Lieutenant Thomas Campbell's Sojourn," p.109. Amelia R. Bell, "Separate People: Speaking of Creek Men and Women," *American Anthropologist* 92 (June 1990): 332–45, explores this theme and gender roles among modern Creeks. See also J. Anthony Paredes, "Some Creeks Stayed: Comments on Amelia Rector Bell's 'Separate People: Speaking of Creek Men and Women,'" *American Anthropologist* 93 (September 1991): 697–99.

59. Hudson, *Southeastern Indians*, p.321.

60. *Adair's History*, pp.129–30, 171. Bartram, *Travels*, p.399, noted that gender separation occurred during the Green Corn Ceremony.

61. Europeans tended to view such male occupations as hunting and fishing as sport and often took pains to point out the inequality of the female work load. However, male pursuits, especially commercial hunting, were exceedingly taxing. Conversely, the hill agriculture of the southeastern Indians was not particularly labor intensive. See Theda Perdue, "Southern Indians and the Cult of True Womanhood," in *The Web of Southern Social Relations: Women, Family, and Education*, edited by Walter J. Fraser, Jr., R. Frank Saunders, Jr., and Jon L. Wakelyn (Athens: University of Georgia Press, 1985), for an excellent discussion of European perceptions of Cherokee women and an analysis of gender roles in native society.

62. *Adair's History*, p.274.

63. "David Taitt's Journal to and through the Upper Creek Nation," in Davies, DAR 5:254. See also William Bartram's vivid and lengthy description of the town square and the cabins in *Travels*, pp.359–61. In his "Observations," Bartram provides diagrams of the town layout, pp.38, 52–56.

64. Bartram, "Observations," pp.18, 19; Hudson, *Southeastern Indians*, pp.378–79.

65. The method of preparation and ceremony associated with black drink are described by Taitt: "David Taitt's Journal to and through the Upper Creek Nation," in Davies, DAR 5:254. See Charles M. Hudson, ed., *Black Drink: A Native American Tea* (Athens: University of Georgia Press, 1979), for the complete story of the drink and its associated rituals. The leaves of the *Ilex vomitoria Ait.* do not act as an emetic when prepared according to the Creek manner. Rather, the Creeks voluntarily purged themselves. John Bartram, the naturalist

father of William Bartram, related that the Creeks planted the shrub in all their settlements and that the tea was "very wholesom & far more salutary than any from ye east indies[.] its pitty it was not more used." John Bartram, "Diary of a Journey through the Carolinas, Georgia, and Florida from July 1, 1765, to April 10, 1766," edited by Francis Harper, *Transactions of the American Philosophical Society*, n.s., 33, part 1 (Philadelphia: American Philosophical Society, 1942), p.27. James Adair's sentiments were much the same, especially in view of the Tea Act. "It is well tasted, and very agreeable to those who accustom themselves to use it: instead of having any noxious quality, according to what many have experienced of the East India insipid and costly tea, it is friendly to the human system. . . . it perfectly cures a tremor in the nerves." *Adair's History*, p.388. See Bartram, *Travels*, pp.357–59, for a description of the ritual surrounding the brewing of the tea and the yahola singers.

66. "David Taitt's Journal to and through the Upper Creek Nation," in Davies, DAR 5:254.

67. Bartram, *Travels*, p.357; Swan, "Position and State of Manners," p.265, says the old men and women without adequate winter clothing were allowed to sleep in the hot houses in their villages. See pp.264–67 for information on town squares and hot houses.

68. Hudson, *Southeastern Indians*, pp.408–26.

69. "David Taitt's Journal to and through the Upper Creek Nation," in Davies, DAR 5:254, 263–64.

70. *Adair's History*, pp.147, 276, 462; Bartram, "Observations," p.31, says that more men than women worked in the fields. Nuñez, "Stiggins Narrative," p.32. There was a famine in 1755. William L. McDowell, Jr., ed., *Documents Relating to Indian Affairs, 1754–1765*, Colonial Records of South Carolina, series 2 (Columbia: South Carolina Department of Archives and History, 1970), p.255.

71. Douglas R. Hurt, *Indian Agriculture in America: Prehistory to the Present* (Lawrence: University of Kansas Press, 1987), pp.29, 40; Kristian Hvidt, ed., *Von Reck's Voyage: Drawings and Journal of Philip Georg Friedrich Von Reck* (Savannah: Beehive Press, 1980), 38.

72. *Letters, Journals, and Writings of Benjamin Hawkins* 1:307.

73. Descriptions of Creek agriculture and cuisine can be found in Fabel and Rea, "Lieutenant Thomas Campbell's Sojourn," p.107; "A Ranger's Report of Travels with General Oglethorpe, 1739–1742," in *Travels in the American Colonies*, edited by Newton D. Mereness (New York: Macmillan, 1916), p.220; Bartram, "Observations," pp.39–40, 47–48. For Bartram's mention of rice, see

William Bartram, "Travels in Georgia and Florida, 1773–1774: A Report to Dr. John Fothergill," annotated by Francis Harper, *Transactions of the American Philosophical Society,* n.s., 33, part 2 (Philadelphia: American Philosophical Society, 1942), p.158 (hereafter cited as "Travels in Georgia and Florida"). Hvidt, *Von Reck's Voyage,* p.41, relates that the Creeks traded deerskins for rice. Hudson, *Southeastern Indians,* pp.300–309, provides a detailed description of southeastern Indian food-preparation techniques. See also G. Melvin Herndon, "Indian Agriculture in the Southern Colonies," *North Carolina Historical Review* 44 (Summer 1967): 283–97.

74. Nuñez, "Stiggins Narrative," pp.32–33. Many towns had several micos.

75. *Nairne's Muskhogean Journals,* p.34. For information on Nairne's visit, see Alexander Moore, "Thomas Nairne's 1708 Western Expedition: An Episode in the Anglo-French Competition for Empire," in *Proceedings of the Tenth Meeting of the French Colonial Historical Society, April 12–14, 1984,* edited by Philip P. Boucher (Lanham, Md.: University Press of America, 1985), pp.47–58.

76. Report of John Stuart to the Lords Commissioners of Trade and Plantations on the Southern Indian Department, March 9, 1764, CO323/17, p.28.

77. Corkran, *Creek Frontier,* p.14; Reid, *Better Kind of Hatchet,* pp.20–21; Swanton, *Social Organization,* pp.194–99; *Letters, Journals, and Writings of Benjamin Hawkins* 1:318.

78. Bartram, "Observations," p.24n. See also, Bartram, *Travels,* p.389.

79. *Letters, Journals, and Writings of Benjamin Hawkins* 1:318.

80. The best illustration of this is a 1747 statement by Mary Musgrove: "That She is by Descent on the Mothers Side, (who was Sister to the Old Emperor) of the Same Blood of the Present Mico's [Malatchi] and Chief's now in that Nation." If Malatchi had been the biological son of Brims, then he and Mary would not have been of the "same blood." John T. Juricek, ed., *Georgia Treaties, 1733–1763,* vol. 11 of *Early American Indian Documents: Treaties and Laws, 1607–1789,* edited by Alden T. Vaughan (Frederick, Md.: University Publications of America, 1989), p.140. These assertions appear in numerous other speeches; for example, see ibid, p.152.

81. Hvidt, *Von Reck's Voyage,* p.41. See also *Letters, Journals, and Writings of Benjamin Hawkins* 1:318, for a discussion of the duties of a mico.

82. *Nairne's Muskhogean Journals,* p.32.

83. See Bartram, "Observations," pp.24, 40, 62–64, for a discussion of various ranks. Caleb Swan, "Position and State of Manners," pp.264–67, 279–82; Swanton, *Social Organization,* pp.293–95.

84. Hudson, *Southeastern Indians,* pp.225, 371.

85. *Letters, Journals, and Writings of Benjamin Hawkins* 1:319.

86. Mortar's Speech, Congress of Pensacola, 1765, in Rowland, MPAED, p.199; Emistesiguo's Speech, Proceedings of a Congress with the Upper Creeks, 1771, in Davies, DAR 3:217. Bartram, "Observations," p.37.

87. James F. Doster, *The Creek Indians and Their Florida Lands, 1740–1805,* 2 vols., Garland American Indian Ethnohistory Series: Southern and Southeast Indians (New York: Garland Publishing, 1974), 1:62.

88. Lord Dartmouth to Thomas Hutchinson, December 9, 1772, in Davies, DAR 5:239.

89. In contrast, Corkran, in *Creek Frontier,* p.61, wrote, "The doctrine of neutrality . . . was to be the most clearly defined and influential Creek national diplomatic policy during the remainder of the colonial period." James Adair noted that the Creeks gained by switching their allegiance. *Adair's History,* pp.277–83.

90. Bartram, "Observations," p.32.

91. Meeting at Sugar Town, February 24, 1774, CO5/75, fo.85; William L. McDowell, Jr., ed., *Documents Relating to Indian Affairs, May 21, 1750–August 7, 1754,* Colonial Records of South Carolina (Columbia: South Carolina Archives Department, 1958), p.270.

92. McDowell, *1750–1754,* p.410; "Journal of the Augusta Congress, 1763," in William Saunders, ed., *The Colonial Records of North Carolina,* 16 vols. (Raleigh: Josephus Daniels, 1886–90), 11:175 (hereafter cited as Saunders, CRNC).

93. Creek women were sent against the Cherokees during the closing phases of the Creek-Cherokee war. *Adair's History,* p.275. Cherokee women who accompanied war parties and determined the fate of captives were titled War Women. Some Cherokee women participated in councils. Theda Perdue, "Southern Indians and the Cult of True Womanhood," p.38.

94. Corkran, *Creek Frontier,* pp.30–31. See McDowell, *1754–1765,* pp.363–64, for information that women would be disturbed by a proposal to give rewards for scalps, since it might lead to war. Women dispatched captive warriors by first beating them with dry cane bundles and then by setting the canes, and captives, alight. *Adair's History,* pp.418–19, describes the process; see also pp.101, 127. Hvidt, *Von Reck's Voyage,* p.47, supports this. Fabel and Rea, "Lieutenant Thomas Campbell's Sojourn," p.108. Regarding the treatment of war captives, see Kathryn E. Holland Braund, "The Creek Indians, Blacks, and Slavery," *Journal of Southern History* 57 (November 1991): 602–4.

95. Corkran, *Creek Frontier,* pp.39–40, 168, 216.

96. Bartram, "Travels in Georgia and Florida," pp.157–58. Quotations is on p.158.

97. Ibid., pp.157–60, and Bartram, "Observations," pp.41–42.

98. Bartram, *Travels*, p.396.

99. "David Taitt's Journal to and through the Upper Creek Nation," in Davies, DAR 5:261, 265.

100. An excellent account of the Green Corn Ceremony is found in a lengthy letter by John Howard Payne to his sister. See Payne, "The Green Corn Dance," edited by John R. Swanton, *Chronicles of Oklahoma* 10 (1932): 170–95. Part of Payne's account is reproduced in Corkran, *Creek Frontier*, pp.36–39. Adair's account is colored by his attempt to equate the Busk with Hebrew Passover. *Adair's History*, pp.101–19. See James H. Howard, *The Southeastern Ceremonial Complex and Its Interpretation*, Memoir no.6, (Columbia: Missouri Archaeological Society, 1968), for information about the historic and modern Busk.

101. Speech of Emisteseguo, June 6, 1767, in Journal of the Superintendent's Proceedings, April 21, 1767–June 6, 1767, Gage Papers.

102. Bartram, "Observations," pp.20–21. See John R. Swanton, "Religious Beliefs and Medical Practices of the Creek Indians," in *Forty-Second Annual Report of the Bureau of American Ethnology* (Washington, D.C.: Government Printing Office, 1928), pp.473–672.

103. Johnstone's Speech, Congress at Pensacola, 1765, in Rowland, MPAED, p.193.

CHAPTER 2: *Trade: "The Original Great Tye"*

1. Report of John Stuart to the Lords Commissioners of Trade and Plantations on the Southern Indian Department, March 9, 1764, CO323/17, pp.46–47.

2. See Sharon Goad, "Exchange Networks in the Prehistoric Southeastern United States" (Ph.D. diss., University of Georgia, 1978); Peter A. Brannon, "The Pensacola Indian Trade," *Florida Historical Quarterly* 31 (July 1952): 6–7; John R. Swanton, *The Indians of the Southeastern United States*, Bureau of American Ethnology Bulletin no. 137 (Washington, D.C.: Government Printing Office, 1946; reprint, New York: Greenwood, 1969), pp.738–39; Hudson, *Southeastern Indians*, p.316; John A. Walthall, *Galena and Aboriginal Trade in Eastern North America*, Illinois State Museum Scientific Papers, no.17 (Springfield: Illinois State Museum, 1981).

3. A recent study suggests that Cofitachique was located on the Wateree River near Camden, South Carolina. See Steven G. Baker, *Cofitachique, Fair Province of*

Carolina: History and Archaeology of the Carolina Indians (Ann Arbor, Mich.: University Microfilms, 1983). James D. Scurry, Joseph J. Walter, and Fritz Hamer, *Initial Archeological Investigations at Silver Bluff Plantation, Aiken County, South Carolina,* Research Manuscript Series 168, Institute of Archeology and Anthropology (Columbia: University of South Carolina, 1980), p.7; J. Leitch Wright, Jr., *The Only Land They Knew: The Tragic Story of the American Indians in the Old South* (New York: Free Press, 1981), pp.4–6; Gary B. Nash, *Red, White, and Black: The Peoples of Early America* (Englewood Cliffs, N.J.: Prentice-Hall, 1974), p.236.

4. James M. Crawford, *The Mobilian Trade Language* (Knoxville: University of Tennessee Press, 1978), pp.6–7; Mary R. Haas, "What is Mobilian?" in *Studies in Southeastern Indian Languages,* edited by James M. Crawford (Athens: University of Georgia Press, 1975), pp.257–61.

5. A good introduction to this concept is Christopher L. Miller and George R. Hamell, "A New Perspective on Indian-White Contact: Cultural Symbols and Colonial Trade," *Journal of American History* 73 (September 1986): 311–28. Mary W. Helms also explores these themes in *Ulysses' Sail: An Ethnographic Odyssey of Power, Knowledge, and Geographical Distance* (Princeton: Princeton University Press, 1988) and "Native Cosmology and European Trade," paper delivered at Forty-sixth International Congress of Americanists, Amsterdam, the Netherlands, July 1988.

6. Hann, *Apalachee,* pp.15–16, 147–48, 183–84; Gregory A. Waselkov, "Seventeenth-Century Trade in the Colonial Southeast," *Southeastern Archaeology* 8 (1989): 117–33.

7. Verner W. Crane, *The Southern Frontier, 1670–1732* (Ann Arbor: University of Michigan Press, 1919; reprint, New York: W. W. Norton, 1981), pp.34–36; Corkran, *Creek Frontier,* pp.48–51; *Nairne's Muskhogean Journals,* p.50. An interesting account of early Coweta-Georgia relations is found in Walter A. Harris, *Here the Creeks Sat Down* (Macon, Ga.: J. W. Burke Co., 1958).

8. See Louis R. Smith, Jr., "British-Indian Trade in Alabama, 1670–1756," *Alabama Review* 27 (January 1974): 65–68, for information on Woodward. Herbert E. Bolton, "Spanish Resistance to the Carolina Traders in Western Georgia (1680–1704)," *Georgia Historical Quarterly* 9 (June 1925): 115–30; Marion Eugene Sirmans, *Colonial South Carolina: A Political History* (Chapel Hill: University of North Carolina Press, 1966), pp.22–23; Crane, *Southern Frontier,* pp.34–36.

9. Philip M. Brown, "Early Indian Trade in the Development of South Carolina: Politics, Economics, and Social Mobility During the Proprietary Period, 1670–1719," *South Carolina Historical Magazine* 76 (July 1975): 118–28.

Crane, *Southern Frontier,* pp.108–12; Corkran, *Creek Frontier,* pp.48–60; John J. TePaske, "French, Spanish, and English Indian Policy on the Gulf Coast, 1513–1763: A Comparison," in *Spain and Her Rivals on the Gulf Coast: Proceedings of the Gulf Coast History and Humanities Conference,* edited by Ernest F. Dibble and Earle W. Newton, (Pensacola: Pensacola Preservation Board, 1971), pp.9–39.

10. Clowse, *Economic Beginnings of Colonial South Carolina,* pp.120, 162–63. See also Converse D. Clowse, "Charles Town Export Trade, 1717–1737" (Ph.D. diss., Northwestern University, 1963).

11. Corkran, *Creek Frontier,* pp.50–51.

12. The Creeks did not soon forget their role as porters; as late as 1764, they were still reminding the British of it. Upper Creeks to John Stuart, April 10, 1764, Gage Papers.

13. Crane, *Southern Frontier,* pp.36–37, 116–18; Sirmans, *South Carolina,* p.187; Wright, *Only Land They Knew,* pp.102–10, for more details on the early trade from Carolina.

14. Bartram, *Travels,* p.392.

15. Report of John Stuart to the Lords Commissioners of Trade and Plantations on the Southern Indian Department, March 9, 1764, CO323/17, p.47.

16. *Nairne's Muskhogean Journals,* pp.75–76.

17. See Braund, "Creek Indians, Blacks, and Slavery," for a fuller discussion of slave raiding and the fate of captive slaves. Surviving evidence does not relate who profited from the sale of captives to Europeans. Since Creek women traditionally played a part in determining the fate of captives, it is likely that women were involved in the decision to sell captives for trade goods.

18. Crane, *Southern Frontier,* pp.74–75; Corkran, *Creek Frontier,* p.54; Daniel H. Usner, Jr., *Indians, Settlers, and Slaves in a Frontier Exchange Economy* (Chapel Hill: University of North Carolina Press, for the Institute of Early American History and Culture, Williamsburg, 1992), pp.17–20.

19. See Corkran, *Creek Frontier,* pp.52–56. Speech of Sempyoffe at Congress of the Principal Chiefs and Warriors of the Creek Nation held at Fort Augusta the 12th of November 1768, by John Stuart in Journal of the Superintendent's Proceedings, CO5/70, fo.386.

20. Hann, *Apalachee,* pp.264–317, is the best treatment of the 1704 raids. An earlier study is B. Calvin Jones, "Colonel James Moore and the Destruction of the Apalachee Missions in 1704," *Bureau of Historic Sites and Properties Bulletin no.* 2 (Tallahassee: Florida Department of State, 1972). Crane, *Southern Frontier,* pp.76–81, 85–86; Wright, *Only Land They Knew,* pp.112–16; Mark F. Boyd, Hale G. Smith, and John W. Griffin, *Here They Once Stood: The*

Tragic End of the Apalachee Missions (Gainesville: University of Florida Press, 1951). William R. Snell, "Indian Slavery in Colonial South Carolina, 1671–1795," (Ann Arbor: University Microfilms, 1973), explores the topic of Indian slavery in detail. James W. Covington, "Apalachee Indians, 1704–1763," *Florida Historical Quarterly* 50 (April 1972): 366–84, discusses the postraid period. Known in America as Queen Anne's War and in Europe as the War of the Spanish Succession, the conflict lasted from 1702 until 1713.

21. *Atkin Report,* p.63.

22. *Nairne's Muskhogean Journals,* p.75.

23. Vernon James Knight, Jr., and Sheree L. Adams, "A Voyage to the Mobile and Tomeh in 1700, with Notes on the Interior of Alabama," *Ethnohistory* 28 (Spring 1981): 182.

24. *Nairne's Muskhogean Journals,* pp.47–48.

25. When William Bartram inquired about who originally owned certain lands in Flordia, Creeks told their story of conquest and slave raiding. "Travels in Georgia and Florida," p.171.

26. Report of John Stuart to the Lords Commissioners of Trade and Plantations on the Southern Indian Department, March 9, 1764, CO323/17, pp.8–9.

27. Corkran, *Creek Frontier,* p.57.

28. Richard L. Haan, "The 'Trade Do's Not Flourish as Formerly': The Ecological Origins of the Yamassee War of 1715," *Ethnohistory* 28 (Fall 1982): 341–58; Crane, *Southern Frontier,* pp.162–86; Hann, *Apalachee,* pp.295–301; Corkran, *Creek Frontier,* pp.60–63.

29. Corkran, *Creek Frontier,* pp.62–65. Captive Indians were still taken in by the Carolina traders and sold into slavery. By this time, most were purchased from the Cherokees. William L. McDowell, Jr., ed., *Journals of the Commissioners of the Indian Trade, September 20, 1710–August 29, 1718,* Colonial Records of South Carolina, Series 2 (Columbia: South Carolina Department of Archives and History, 1955), pp.viii–x, 189, 267; J. H. Easterby, ed., *The Journal of the Commons House of Assembly,* 12 vols., Colonial Records of South Carolina (Columbia: Historical Commission of South Carolina and South Carolina Department of Archives, 1951–83), 1:77.

30. Clowse, *Economic Beginnings in Colonial South Carolina,* pp.163–64.

31. Crane, *Southern Frontier,* pp.116–20; Wright, *Only Land They Knew,* pp.121–25; Jeanne A. Calhoun, Martha A. Zierden, and Elizabeth A. Paysinger, "The Geographic Spread of Charleston's Mercantile Community, 1732–1767," *South Carolina Historical Magazine* 86 (July 1985): 182–200; Clowse, *Economic Beginnings of Colonial South Carolina,* pp.162–64.

32. Gregory A. Waselkov, "Economics of a French Colonial Trade Enclave: Historical and Archaeological Perspectives," in *Culture Change on the Creek Indian Frontier,* Final Report to the National Science Foundation, Grant #BNS-8305437, Washington, D.C. (Auburn, Ala.: Auburn University Department of Sociology and Anthropology, 1985), p.115.

33. Corkran, *Creek Frontier,* p.68.

34. See ibid., pp.41–60, for an overview of early Creek trade contacts. Hudson, *Southeastern Indians,* pp.438–39; Patricia Wood Dillon, *French-Indian Relations on the Southern Frontier, 1699–1762* (Ann Arbor, Mich.: UMI Research Press, 1980), pp.51–53; Gregory A. Waselkov, "French Colonial Trade in the Upper Creek Country," in *Fleur-de-Lys and Calumet: French-Indian Interaction in the Midcontinent,* edited by Thomas Emerson and John Walthall (Smithsonian Institution Press, forthcoming); Daniel H. Usner, Jr., "The Deerskin Trade in French Louisiana," in *Proceedings of the Tenth Meeting of the French Colonial Historical Society, April 12–14, 1984,* edited by Philip Boucher (Lanham, Md.: University Press of America, 1985); Donald P. Heldman, "Fort Toulouse of the Alabamas and the Eighteenth-Century Indian Trade," *World Archaeology* 5 (October 1973): 163–69.

35. Patricia Kay Galloway, ed., *Mississippi Provincial Archives: French Dominion,* vols.4 and 5, originally collected, edited, and translated by Dunbar Rowland and A. G. Sanders (Baton Rouge: Louisiana State University Press, 1984), 4:208–9. See also, 4:221 and 5:129. Hereafter cited as Galloway, MPAFD.

36. *Atkin Report,* p.12; McDowell, *1754–1765,* pp.72–73, 295, 372; Waselkov, "French Colonial Trade in the Upper Creek Country"; Nancy Marie Surrey, *The Commerce of Louisiana during the French Regime, 1699–1763,* Studies in History, Economics, and Public Law, no.167 (New York: Columbia University Press, 1916), pp.319–20, 359–61; Crane, *Southern Frontier,* p.330. Joel W. Martin, "Cultural Hermeneutics on the Frontier: Colonialism and the Muscogulge Millenarian Revolt of 1813" (Ph.D. diss., Duke University, 1988), reckons that the French share of the Creek market was never more than 10% of the total. Usner, *Indians, Settlers, and Slaves,* pp.246–68, examines the French-Indian trade in the Lower Mississippi Valley.

37. Galloway, MPAFD 4:209.

38. Ibid. 4:223.

39. Daniel H. Thomas, *Fort Toulouse: The French Outpost at the Alabamas on the Coosa,* introduction by Gregory A. Waselleor (Tuscaloosa: University of Alabama Press, 1989), pp.xxvii, 32–38.

40. Lachlan McGilvray [sic] to William Pinckney, December 18, 1751, in

McDowell, *1750–1754,* p.216. During the Seven Years' War, Daniel Pepper, the agent for South Carolina to the Creeks, hired William Bonar to make a map of the Creek towns and provide intelligence on Fort Toulouse. Bonar, disguised as a packhorseman, got close enough to realize the fort was not heavily defended. The French saw through his ruse and captured him. A party of pro-British Creeks secured his release. See McDowell, *1754–1765,* pp.373, 378, 380.

41. Easterby, *Journal of the Commons House,* pp.77–85; Galloway, MPAFD 4:221.

42. Galloway, MPAFD 4:221.

43. Edward J. Cashin, Jr., "The Gentlemen of Augusta," in *Colonial Augusta "Key of the Indian Countrey,"* (Macon, Ga.: Mercer University Press, 1986), p.39; Report of John Stuart to the Lords Commissioners of Trade and Plantations on the Southern Indian Department, March 9, 1764, CO323/17, p.41.

44. Georgia Council Meeting, June 5, 1760, in CRG 8:323.

45. *Adair's History,* p.442. Chickasaw traders resided at the center of town most of the time.

46. Kathryn E. Holland [Braund], "The Path between the Wars: Creek Relations with the British Colonies, 1763–1774" (master's thesis, Auburn University, 1980), pp.104, 123–24, 194, 206, 222; Corkran, *Creek Frontier,* pp.48–60. See James W. Covington, "The Cuban Fishing *Ranchos:* A Spanish Enclave within British Florida," in *Anglo-Spanish Confrontation on the Gulf Coast during the American Revolution,* edited by William S. Coker and Robert R. Rea (Pensacola: Gulf Coast History and Humanities Conference, 1982), pp.17–24, for information on Creek contacts with Spanish fishermen. For information on the Spanish colonization in the Southeast and the Spanish mission system, see Thomas *Spanish Borderlands East,* Part 2 and Part 3. Amy Turner Bushnell, "Ruling 'the Republic of Indians' in Seventeenth-Century Florida, in *Powhatan's Mantle,* pp.134–50. Anglo-Creek cooperation against Spanish Florida is summarized in Phinizy Spalding, *Oglethorpe in America* (Chicago: University of Chicago Press, 1977; reprint, Athens: University of Georgia Press, 1984). As a result of frequent Anglo-Spanish conflict, St. Augustine became a garrison town and welcomed escaped slaves as potential defenders. Creeks, of course, were always on the lookout for such escapees. See also Jane Landers, "Gracia Real de Santa Teresa de Mose: A Free Black Town in Spanish Colonial Florida," *American Historical Review* 95 (February 1990): 9–30.

47. Nuñez, "Stiggins Narrative," 5:142.

48. The English traders could sell their goods for less than half the prices charged by the French. This was largely due to the fact that there was virtually no

market for the hides in France. See Vaudreuil and Salmon to Maurepas, July 21, 1743, in Galloway, MPAFD 4:209; see also 5:182–84, 189. Lucille Griffith, "South Carolina and Fort Alabama, 1714–1763," *Alabama Review* 12 (October 1959): 269; Surrey, *Commerce of Louisiana,* pp.319–20; John G. Clark, *New Orleans, 1718–1812: An Economic History* (Baton Rouge: Louisiana State University Press, 1970), pp.58–59.

49. *Nairne's Muskhogean Journals,* p.75.

CHAPTER 3: *Merchants to the Muscogulges*

1. Crane, *Southern Frontier,* pp.121–22.

2. Although the identity of her trader father is not known, Edward Griffin, a licensed trader from South Carolina, is certainly a good candidate. McDowell, *1710–1718,* p.63. This supposition is based on the fact that Mary's brother, who was killed in the Siege of St. Augustine in 1740, was named Griffin. Juricek, *Georgia Treaties,* p.142. Doris Behrman Fisher, "Mary Musgrove: Creek Englishwoman" (Ph.D. diss., Emory University, 1990), pp.51, 129.

3. Juricek, *Georgia Treaties,* pp.141–42.

4. Corkran, *Creek Frontier,* pp.63, 80.

5. Ibid., p.82. E. Merton Coulter, "Mary Musgrove, 'Queen of the Creeks': A Chapter of Early Georgia Troubles," *Georgia Historical Quarterly* 11 (March 1927): 3, says they handled twelve hundred pounds of deerskins annually.

6. Cashin, "Gentlemen of Augusta," p.30.

7. Corkran, *Creek Frontier,* p.84.

8. Bartram, *Travels,* p.259.

9. Benjamin Martyn, "An Impartial Inquiry into the State and Utility of the Province of Georgia, 1741," pp.153–54, in *The Clamorous Malcontents: Criticisms and Defenses of the Colony of Georgia, 1741–1743,* edited by Trevor R. Reese (Savannah: Beehive Press, 1973) (hereafter cited as *Malcontents*). This essay can also be found in the *Collections of the Georgia Historical Society,* vol. 1 (Savannah: Georgia Historical Society, 1840). "A State of the Province of Georgia, 1742," in *Malcontents,* pp.6–7.

10. *The Journal of William Stephens, 1741–1743,* edited by E. Merton Coulter, Wormsloe Foundation Publications, no.2 (Athens: University of Georgia Press, 1958), p.243. During the late seventeenth century, Savannah Town, roughly five miles above the falls, had been built on the Carolina side of the river. The town was abandoned during the Yamasee War, and Fort Moore was established near the same site in 1716. Daniel Elliott and Roy Doyon, *Archaeology and Historical Geography of the Savannah River Floodplain near Augusta, Georgia,* Uni-

versity of Georgia Laboratory of Archaeology Series, no.22 (Athens: South-eastern Wildlife Series, 1981), p.20; Surry, *Commerce of Louisiana*, p.356.

11. *Atkin Report*, p.34; CRG 5:558–59.

12. CRG 23:185.

13. "Deposition of Kennedy O'Brien," reprinted in Charles C. Jones, Jr., and Salem Dutcher, *Memorial History of Augusta, Georgia* (Syracuse, N.Y.: D. Mason & Co., 1890; reprint, Spartanburg, S.C.: Reprint Co., 1966), pp.28–29. For information on O'Brien, see Berry Fleming, ed., *Autobiography of a Colony: The First Half-Century of Augusta, Georgia* (Athens: University of Georgia Press, 1957), p.7 and appendixes A and B for landowners in the town and parish (here-after cited as *Augusta*). CRG 1:353, 2:292, 5:199, 22, pt. 2, 108–9; Albert Saye and E. Merton Coulter, *A List of the Early Settlers of Georgia* (Athens: University of Georgia Press, 1949), p.91.

14. CRG 4:203.

15. *The Journal of William Stephens, 1743–1745*, edited by E. Merton Coul-ter, Wormsloe Foundation Publications, no.3 (Athens: University of Georgia Press, 1959), p.230; Kenneth Coleman and Charles S. Gurr, eds., *Dictionary of Georgia Biography*, 2 vols. (Athens: University of Georgia Press, 1983), 1:56 (hereafter cited as DGB).

16. Cashin, "Gentlemen of Augusta," p.33.

17. Martyn, "An Impartial Inquiry," p.179.

18. CRG 5:463.

19. J. F. Smithcors, *Evolution of the Veterinary Art: A Narrative Account to 1850* (Kansas City, Mo.: Veterinary Medicine Publishing, 1957), p.299. The plague eventually led to the founding of the first school of veterinary medicine in 1762 at Lyons, France, under the direction of Claude Bourgelat.

20. Walter E. Minchinton, comp. *The Growth of English Overseas Trade in the Seventeenth and Eighteenth Centuries* (London: Methuen, 1969), p.8.

21. Harris and Habersham to Benjamin Martyn, February 13, 1748/9, CRG 25:361; CRG 5:462–63; John Pitts Corry, *Indian Affairs in Georgia, 1732–1756* (Philadelphia: G. S. Ferguson, 1936; reprint, New York: AMS Press, 1980), p.32; Calhoun, Zierden, and Paysinger, "Charleston's Mercantile Com-munity," p.185; Leila Sellers, *Charleston Business on the Eve of the Revolution, 1776–1778* (Chapel Hill: University of North Carolina Press, 1934), p.43.

22. See Coulter, "Mary Musgrove," for the details of her career. John Pitts Corry, "Some New Light on the Bosomworth Claims," *Georgia Historical Quar-terly* 25 (September 1941): 195–224.

23. Philip M. Hamer and George C. Rogers, eds. *The Papers of Henry Lau-*

rens, II vols. (Columbia: South Carolina Historical Society and University of South Carolina Press, 1968–81), 3:32n.

24. Patrick Brown and Alexander Wood had been partners before joining Archibald McGillivray's company. *South Carolina Gazette,* August 29–September 5, 1741, and September 26–October 3, 1741 (quotation). Edward J. Cashin, Jr., *Lachlan McGillivray, Indian Trader: The Shaping of the Southern Colonial Frontier* (Athens: University of Georgia Press, 1992), p.34, lists Daniel Clark as a partner. Clark is not listed as a partner in the *South Carolina Gazette* announcements of 1741. Both Knott and Sludders were harassed by the Georgia agent Patrick McKay during the Georgia–South Carolina licensing controversy. Knott began his career among the Creeks in 1728. Easterby, *Journal of the Commons House* 1:117, 123. Douglas S. Brown, *The Catawba Indians: The People of the River* (Columbia: University of South Carolina Press, 1966), p.115; Robert L. Meriwether, *The Expansion of South Carolina, 1729–1765* (Kingsport: Southern Publishers, 1940), pp.190–91; Crane, *Southern Frontier,* p.127.

25. Meriwether, *South Carolina,* pp.70, 190–91. *South Carolina Gazette,* August 28–September 4, 1755. Martin Campbell's departure from South Carolina was partly due to his difficulties with Captain Daniel Pepper, the commander of South Carolina's Fort Moore, at Savannah Town. Cashin, *Lachlan McGillivray,* pp.47–49.

26. CRG 26:152–53. Cashin, *Lachlan McGillivray,* p.49, states that seven companies joined to form Brown, Rae, and Company. But in a letter dated February 13, 1750, Brown, Rae, and Company informed the Georgia Trustees: "There are Seven of us in Company. . . . we were formerly three Separate Houses in this place." CRG 26:152–53.

27. Galphin has been linked to both Archibald McGillivray and Company and Brown, Rae, and Company, but it seems likely he also conducted business independently. Sludders is sometimes rendered as Struthers. Willard E. Wight, *Abstracts of Colonial Wills of the State of Georgia, 1733–1777* (Atlanta: Town Committee of the National Society of the Colonial Dames of America in the State of Georgia for the Department of Archive and History, 1962; reprint, Spartanburg, S.C.: Reprint Co., 1981), p.126; McDowell, *1750–1754,* pp.129, 261, 518; Easterby, *Journal of the Commons House* 3:341, 343, 442, 428, 4:500, 6:119, 127, 157, 7:141, 8:249, 258. Cashin, *Lachlan McGillivray,* p.102, lists Thomas Deval, in addition to Brown, Rae, McGillivray, Galphin, Sludders, and Clark, as one of the seven partners in Brown, Rae, and Company. Fritz Hamer, "Indian Traders, Land, and Power: A Comparative Study of George Galphin on the Southern Frontier and three Northern Traders" (master's thesis, University

of South Carolina, 1982), pp.43–44, lists Barksdale as a partner in the firm and omits Deval. Perhaps both men were partners at different times. However, existing references seem to point to Barksdale as a full partner in the firm from a very early date. A list of traders present at a meeting of Upper Creeks in 1751 lists Lachlan McGillivray as the interpreter, and Isaac Barksdale heads the list of witnesses. Others on the list include Sludders and Galphin. Thomas Deval is listed as the ninth (and last) witness, following several little-known traders, an unlikely position for the partner of a major firm. CRG 26:891. Perhaps in the future, more conclusive evidence will be found to fully document the firm's history.

28. Clark died in 1757. E.E.R. Green, "Queensborough Township: Scotch-Irish Emigration and the Expansion of Georgia, 1763–1776," *William and Mary Quarterly* 17 (April 1960): 184; CRG 1:561, 7:461, 6:333, 8:61; Wight, *Abstracts of Colonial Wills*, pp.10, 19, 110–11; McDowell, *1750–1754*, pp.128–29, 214. The partners continued to obtain licenses from South Carolina as well as Georgia.

29. Hamer and Rogers, *Papers of Henry Laurens* 1:285–86.

30. McDowell, *1750–1754*, p.326; Wight, *Abstracts of Colonial Wills*, pp.125–126; CRG 9:318; George Galphin Account Books, 1767–1772, Georgia Historical Society, Savannah, folder 1.

31. Wight, *Abstracts of Colonial Wills*, p.10; "Estimate of Annual Expense for Officers, Etc. in Southern Indian Department," in John Stuart to Shelburne, April 11, 1767, CO5/68, fo.125.

32. Wight, *Abstracts of Colonial Wills*, pp.110–11; McDowell, *1750–1754*, pp.38, 365, 458. Jeromy Courtonne was Pettigrew's partner. Courtonne was in partnership with John Brown, a Chickasaw trader, for a time. See McDowell, *1750–1754*, pp.10, 215, 509.

33. Mary Ann Oglesby Neeley, "Lachlan McGillivray: A Scot on the Alabama Frontier," *Alabama Historical Quarterly* 36 (Spring 1974): 7. McGillivray himself stated that he had resided in America "thirty seven years and upwards" before the beginning of the revolutionary war. Memorial of Lachlan McGillivray, Great Britain, Public Record Office, Audit Office, Records of the Loyalists Claims Commission, Class 13, volume 36, fo.560 (hereafter cited as AO).

34. Albert James Pickett, *History of Alabama and Incidentally of Georgia and Mississippi, from the Earliest Period* (Charleston: Walker and James, 1851; reprint, Birmingham: Birmingham Book and Magazine Co., 1962), p.343.

35. Fleming, *Augusta*, p.55; Saye and Coulter, *Early Settlers*, pp.83–84; McDowell, *1750–1754*, p.518; Neely, "Lachlan McGillivray," pp.7–8, dis-

putes that Sehoy was of mixed blood, but she was assuredly not of the Tuskegee tribe. This is evident from the power her son possessed at Little Tallassee. John W. Caughey, *McGillivray of the Creeks*, Civilization of the American Indian Series, no.18 (Norman: University of Oklahoma Press, 1938), pp.9–16. The best biography of a Creek deerskin trader to date is Cashin, *Lachlan McGillivray*. See pp.83–85 for information on the Choctaw affair.

36. DGB 1:335–37; Galphin's will provides much information on the man, his property, and his family, see Brent H. Holcomb, *Ninety Six District, South Carolina Journal of the Court of Ordinary, Inventory Book, Will Book, 1781–1786* (Easley, S.C.: Southern Historical Press, 1978), pp.37–49 (hereafter cited as Holcomb, *Will Book*). CRG 6:331. See also John McKay Sheftall, "George Galphin and Indian-White Relations in the Georgia Backcountry during the American Revolution," (master's thesis, University of Virginia, 1983). Volume 13 (1981) of *Richmond County History* is devoted to George Galphin. One of Galphin's contemporaries quipped that "of the five varieties of the human family; he raised children from three, and no doubt would have gone the whole hog, but the Malay and Mongol were out of his reach." Galphin made provisions for all his offspring, no matter their color, and his red and black descendants lived most of their lives in the Lower Creek Nation. The quote is from Thomas Simpson Woodward, *Woodward's Reminiscences of the Creek or Muscogee Indians* (Montgomery, Ala.: Barrett and Wimbish, 1859; reprint, Mobile, Ala.: Southern University Press, 1965), p.91.

37. McDowell, *1750–1754*, p.261.

38. Hamer and Rogers, *Papers of Henry Laurens* 1:284–85.

39. Ibid. 1:284–85.

40. It is quite likely that the company did own slaves. The firm of Clark and McGillivray owned forty-two slaves at one time, and Rae, Whitefield and Company applied for a land grant of five hundred acres because they owned twelve blacks. CRG 7:461, 10:827. Thomas Stephens, "A Brief Account of the Causes That Have Retarded the Progress of the Colony of Georgia, 1743," in *Malcontents*, p.331; McDowell, *1754–1765*, p.357; Holcomb, *Will Book*, pp.42–43.

41. "Thomas Bosomworth's Journal, 1752–1753," in McDowell, *1750–1754*, p.329.

42. CRG 6:333.

43. CRG 26:168–70.

44. CRG 26:169.

45. CRG 26:153–54.

46. CRG 1:561.

47. CRG 28, pt. 2, p.125; CRG 9:110, 13:78. For lists of traders, see McDowell, *1750–1754*, pp.128–29, and CRG 8:522–24.

48. The one remaining account book of Macartan and Campbell, "Augusta Store, Georgia Account Book, August 1762–June 1766," sheds much light on the firm's business. The account book is located at the Clemson University Library. A microfilm copy is available at the South Caroliniana Library, University of South Carolina, Columbia. W. O. Moore, Jr., "The Largest Exporters of Deerskins from Charles Town, 1735–1775," *South Carolina Historical Magazine* 74 (July 1973): 147–48. The anonymous writer of "A Gurnal of my Travling to the Indian Countrary," 1767, File No.10, Georgia Historical Society, Savannah, was an employee of Macartan and Campbell (hereafter cited as Anonymous Journal, Georgia Historical Society). Hamer and Rogers, *Papers of Henry Laurens* 3:165n. The relationship between Augusta firms is discussed in Hamer, "Indian Traders," pp.63–64.

49. Crooke also appears as Crook; Macintosh as McIntosh. CRG 8:522–24; Journal of the Superintendent's Proceedings, April 21, 1767–June 6, 1767, Gage Papers; Callahan, "Colonial Life in Augusta," p.98.

50. "Talks with the Trustees on Trade Regulation," in Juricek, *Georgia Treaties*, p.25.

51. Sirmans, *South Carolina*, p.188; Louis De Vorsey, Jr., "The Colonial Georgia Backcountry," in Cashin, *Colonial Augusta*, p.10.

52. Governor James Wright to the Board of Trade, November 10, 1764, CO323/20, fo.70.

53. Memorial of Lachlan McGillivray, AO13/36, fo.560.

54. For an explanation of Georgia's land policy, see Percy S. Flippin, "The Royal Government in Georgia, 1752–1776," *Georgia Historical Quarterly*, 10 (March 1926): 1–25. An initial grant of five hundred acres was possible for any settler who had six able-bodied menservants. Land grants for various Augusta traders are scattered throughout volumes of the published *Colonial Records of Georgia*.

55. Wright to Board of Trade, November 18, 1766, and November 29, 1766, in CRG 28, pt.2, pp.175, 176, 184–85; Henry Ellis to Board of Trade, January 28, 1759, in CRG 28, pt.1, p.176; Romans, *A Concise Natural History of East and West Florida*, pp.91–92; *Adair's History*, pp.138–39, 490; Sellers, *Charleston Business*, pp.31–43; Talk of Emistisiguo, September 3, 1768, in CRG 10:566–71; Fleming, *Augusta*, p.33.

56. Green, "Queensborough," pp.183–99.

57. AO12/5/1.

58. From the *Belfast News-Letter*, May 17, 1765, quoted in Green, "Queensborough," p.186.

59. See Edward J. Cashin, Jr., and Heard Robertson, *Augusta and the American Revolution: Events in the Georgia Backcountry, 1773–1783* (Darien, Ga.: Ashantilly Press, 1975), for an overview. Cashin's essay, "'But Brothers, It Is Our Land We are Talking About': Winners and Losers in the Georgia Backcountry," in *An Uncivil War: The Southern Backcountry during the American Revolution,* edited by Ronald Hoffman, Thad W. Tate, and Peter J. Albert (Charlottesville: United States Capitol Historical Society by the University Press of Virginia, 1985), pp.240–75 examines the effect of the Revolution on the Indians, their traders, and the Scotch-Irish.

60. *South Carolina Gazette*, February 2–9, 1765; DGB 1:367; CRG 8:426, 18:73, 7:134. See Callahan, "Colonial Life in Augusta," pp.96–119, for an engaging discussion of social life in Augusta.

61. Fleming, *Augusta,* p.75. Hamer, "Indian Traders," pp.54–56; Cashin, "Gentlemen of Augusta," pp.37–39; Cashin, *Lachlan McGillivray,* pp.195–98.

62. Fleming, *Augusta,* pp.48–49; CRG 26:303–6.

63. CRG 12:154–55.

64. Fleming, *Augusta,* p.83.

65. Lachlan McGillivray's mixed-blood son was educated at Charleston. See James H. O'Donnell, "Alexander McGillivray: Training for Leadership, 1777–1783," *Georgia Historical Quarterly* 49 (June 1965): 172–86; DGB 2:664–65. George Galphin left strict provisions in his will regarding the education of his children. Holcomb, *Will Book,* p.47. Creek mothers were often reluctant to let their children go away to school. James Germany's wife refused to let her children leave the Creek nation. Bartram, *Travels,* p.284.

66. Wight, *Georgia Wills,* p.25.

67. *Adair's History,* pp.xxxiii–xxxiv.

68. The full title of Bartram's book, originally published in Philadelphia by James & Johnson in 1790, was *Travels through North and South Carolina, Georgia, East and West Florida, the Cherokee Country, the Extensive Territories of the Muscogulges, or Creek Confederacy, and the Country of the Chactaws; Containing an Account of the Soil and Natural Productions of Those Regions, Together with Observations on the Manners of the Indians.* For instances of Bartram's debt to traders, see his *Travels,* pp.98–99, 258, 286, 348.

69. Malachy Postlethwayt, *The Universal Dictionary of Trade and Commerce,* 4th ed., Reprints of Economic Classics, reprint of 1774 edition, 2 vols. (New York: Augustus M. Kelly, 1971), Entry for Leather-Seller, vol.2.

70. Ibid. Unfortunately, no business records for these firms have been located as yet.

71. Copies of Three Suits by William Higginson of London Against George Galphin Estate and Galphin, Holmes & Co. To Recover Pre-Revolutionary Trading Debts Under Treaty of Paris, 1783, Suits Filed in U.S. Court, Charleston, October 1791, Settlement in U.S. Court, Columbia, June, 1792. Copy located in the South Caroliniana Library, University of South Carolina, Columbia, South Carolina.

72. Netherclift to Samuel Douglas, Savannah, February 24, 1781. See also John Gordon to Thomas Netherclift and Andrew Lord, Charleston, S.C., August 22, 1773. Both in the Papers of Panton, Leslie, and Company, microfilm edition, 26 reels (Woodbridge, Conn.: Research Publication, 1986), John C. Pace Library, University of West Florida, Pensacola. Reel 1.

73. Hamer and Rogers, *Papers of Henry Laurens* 8:214.

74. Corkran, *Creek Frontier,* p.281; Dartmouth to Wright, December 12, 1772, in Davies, DAR 5:243–45; Bartram, *Travels,* pp.22, 205–6; Kenneth Coleman, *The American Revolution in Georgia, 1763–1789* (Athens: University of Georgia Press, 1958), p.8; *Adair's History,* p.396.

75. The Memorial of James Gordon, AO12/5/38.

76. "The Galphin Claim," *Appendix to the Congressional Globe for the First Session, Thirty-First Congress* (Washington, D.C.: John C. Rivers, 1850), vol.22, pt.1:546–47. Scurry, Walter, and Hamer, *Silver Bluff,* pp.25–26. Cherokee traders burned their account books as a show of good faith when the Cherokees gave their consent to the cession. Though the record does not state that the Creek traders did the same, it seems logical to assume that many did. In any case, it seems a likely explanation for the dearth of trade accounts dating from the eighteenth century. See John Stuart to General Gage, July 5, 1773, Sir Frederick Haldimand Papers, 1758–1784, British Museum, London.

77. James Russell Snapp, "Exploitation and Control: The Southern Frontier in Anglo-American Politics in the Era of the American Revolution" (Ph.D. diss., Harvard University, 1988), pp.221–22.

78. Extract of a letter from George Galphin to Greenwood and Higginson, August 27, 1773, in William Greenwood and William Higginson vs. George Galphin, Thomas Galphin, and William Dunbar, Southern Circuit of the United States of America, October 25, 1791, copy located in the South Caroliniana Library, University of South Carolina, Columbia. John Parkinson was a Savannah merchant of the firm Pooler and Parkinson. Pooler and Galphin were related. John Shaw Billings, "Analysis of the Will of George Galphin." *Richmond County History* 13 (1981): 33. Galphin died in 1780.

79. George Galphin to Henry Laurens, July 20, 1777, in Hamer and Rogers, *Papers of Henry Laurens* 11:403.

80. "The Galphin Claim," pp.546–47. See Scurry, Walter, and Hamer, *Silver Bluff*, pp.25–26.

81. In Lachlan McGillivray's sworn statement to the Loyalist Claims Commission, he identifies John McGillivray as his nephew. AO13/36/560. A published version of Lachlan's 1767 will identifies John McGillivray as the cousin of Lachlan McGillivray. Edward Cashin, Lachlan McGillivray's biographer, also identifies John McGillivray as Lachlan's cousin. Lachlan had announced as early as 1763 that he intended to return to Scotland, and he did return for a visit in the early 1770s. Hamer and Rogers, *Papers of Henry Laurens* 8:349 and 14:119, and Cashin, *Lachlan McGillivray*, pp.267–70. In his claim before the Loyalist Claims Commission, Lachlan did not mention any provision he made for his Creek son, Alexander. He did make provisions for Alexander in his 1767 will. In any case, Georgia confiscated the land in question, and both Lachlan and John lost their source of income. AO13/36/560. I am grateful to Edward J. Cashin, Jr., for providing me with the published copy of Lachlan McGillivray's will and other papers.

82. Journal of the Superintendent's Proceedings, April 21, 1767–June 6, 1767, Gage Papers.

83. William S. Coker and Thomas D. Watson, *Indian Traders of the Southeastern Spanish Borderlands: Panton, Leslie, and Company and John Forbes and Company, 1783–1847* (Gainesville: University Presses of Florida, 1985), pp.15–16; Moore, "Largest Exporters of Deerskins," p.147.

84. Gordon's early partner was James McQueen, another leading Creek merchant. Kenneth E. Lewis, "The History and Archaeology of Spalding's Store (PU-23), Putnam County, Florida" (master's thesis, University of Florida, 1969), pp.25–28; Homer E. Wright, *Diplomacy of Trade on the Southern Frontier: A Case Study of the Influence of William Panton and John Forbes, 1784–1817* (Ann Arbor, Mich.: University Microfilms, 1972), pp.20–23; Wight, *Georgia Wills*, pp.84–85; E. Merton Coulter, *Thomas Spalding of Sapelo* (Baton Rouge: Louisiana State University Press, 1940), pp.2–9; John M. Goggin, "A Florida Indian Trading Post, ca. 1673–1784," *Southern Indian Studies* 1 (October 1949): 35–38; Snapp, "Exploitation and Control," pp.44–46; Bartram, *Travels*, p.100.

85. Coker and Watson, *Indian Traders*, pp.15–30.

86. Snapp, "Exploitation and Control," pp.29–33; Robin F. A. Fabel, "St. Mark's, Apalache, and the Creeks," *Gulf Coast Historical Review* (Spring 1986): 18.

87. The Memorial of John McGillivray, late Lieutenant Colonel Comman-

dant of a corps of Volunteers doing duty in West Florida, AO13/36. J. Leitch Wright, Jr., "The Queen's Redoubt Explosion in the Lives of William A. Bowles, John Miller, and William Panton," in *Anglo-Spanish Confrontation on the Gulf Coast during the American Revolution: Proceedings of the Gulf Coast History and Humanities Conference,* edited by William S. Coker and Robert R. Rea (Pensacola: Gulf Coast History and Humanities Conference, 1982), 9:178–79.

88. Ibid., p.177.

89. Robin F. A. Fabel, *The Economy of British West Florida, 1763–1783* (Tuscaloosa: University of Alabama Press, 1988), pp.46, 55–56; Pickett, *History of Alabama,* pp.338, 340.

90. See Margaret F. Dalrymple, ed., *The Merchant of Manchac: The Letterbooks of John Fitzpatrick, 1768–1790* (Baton Rouge: Louisiana State University Press, 1978), for information on the business activities of William Struthers and John McGillivray. Daniel Clark to Brig. General Tayler, July 18 and October 18, 1766, in Haldimand Papers, reel 5, BM21, 671, fo.19 and fo.96.

91. Mrs. Dunbar Rowland, ed., "Peter Chester: Third Governor of the Province of West Florida," in *Mississippi Historical Society Publications,* Centenary Series, vol. 5 (Jackson: Press of Mississippi Department of Archives and History, 1925), p.174.

92. Talk from Upper Creeks to John Stuart, 4 February 1774, CO5/75, fo.67.

93. Robert R. Rea, "British West Florida Trade and Commerce in the Customs Records," *Alabama Review* 37 (April 1984): 142–44; Fabel, *Economy of British West Florida,* pp.60, 198.

94. Haldimand to Gage, September 18, 1766, Haldimand Papers, reel 5, BM21,671, fo. 62; Clarence E. Carter, ed., *The Correspondence of General Thomas Gage with the Secretaries of State, and with the War Office and Treasury, 1763–1775,* 2 vols., Yale Historical Publications, Manuscripts and Edited Texts, vol. 12 (New Haven: Yale University Press, 1931–33), 1:122 (hereafter cited as *Gage Correspondence*); Bartram, *Travels,* p.348; Chester to Hillsborough, July 8, 1772, in Davies, DAR 5:139; "Survey of West Florida in 1768," in *Colonial Captivities, Marches, and Journeys,* edited by Isabel M. Calder, under the Auspices of the National Society of the Colonial Dames of America (New York: Macmillan, 1935; reprint, Port Washington, N.Y.: Kennikat Press, 1967), p.230; Paul C. Phillips, *The Fur Trade,* 2 vols. (Norman: University of Oklahoma Press, 1961), 1:573; Charles Stuart to Peter Chester, n.d., in Chester's letter to Hillsborough of April 15, 1771, in Rowland, "Peter Chester," p.49;

Charles Loch Mowat, *East Florida as a British Province, 1763–1784,* University of California Publications in History, vol.32 (Berkeley: University of California Press, 1943), p.25; Clark, *New Orleans,* p.163; Clinton N. Howard, *The Development of British West Florida, 1763–1769,* University of California Publications in History, vol.34 (Berkeley: University of California Press, 1947), p.17.

95. Rea, "British West Florida Trade," p.150.

96. Coker and Watson, *Indian Traders,* p.127; Jane Dysart, "Creek Indians and the Deerskin Trade, 1783–1803," paper delivered at the Forty-sixth International Congress of Americanists, Amsterdam, the Netherlands, July 1988, pp.7–8.

CHAPTER 4: *The Creeks as Producers for a Trade Economy*

1. Harold Hickerson, "Fur Trade Colonialism and the North American Indians," *Journal of Ethnic Studies* 1 (Summer 1973): 39. The sociologist Stephen Cornell has noted, "The first phase of Indian-White relations, dominated by the fur trade, was the only time in which the widespread incorporation of Native Americans into larger economic and political structures was based primarily on the need for Indian labor." See *The Return of the Native: American Indian Political Resurgence* (New York: Oxford University Press, 1988), p.28.

2. Rowland, MPAED, p.193.

3. Henry F. Dobyns, *Their Number Become Thinned: Native American Population Dynamics in Eastern North America,* Native American Historic Demography Series, Newberry Library Center for the History of the American Indians (Knoxville: University of Tennessee Press, 1983), pp.81–85.

4. *Nairne's Muskhogean Journals,* pp.52–55.

5. *Adair's History,* pp.140, 259; Bartram, "Observations," p.31; Bossu, *Travels in the Interior,* p.146.

6. Tim L. Ivey and M. Keith Causey, "Movements and Activity Patterns of Female White-Tailed Deer during Rut," *Proceedings of the Thirty-Fifth Annual Conference of Southeastern Association of Fish and Wildlife Agencies, October 18–21, 1981,* pp.149–66, and A. G. Hosey, Jr., "Activity Patterns and Notes on Behavior of Male White-Tailed Deer during Rut" (master's thesis, Auburn University, 1980), provide exact measurements and information on this topic.

7. John Weiss, *The Whitetail Deer Hunter's Handbook* (New York: Winchester Press, 1979), p.70.

8. Stuart to Hillsborough, June 12, 1772, in Davies, DAR 5:116. Bernard Romans made the same claim in *A Concise Natural History of East and West Florida,* p.93.

9. Dobyns, *Their Number Become Thinned*, p.84.

10. Nuñez, "Stiggins Narrative," p.32; *American State Papers, Indian Affairs*, p.79.

11. Abstract of letter from Taitt to Stuart, Sept. 21, 1772, CO5/74, fo.28; Alexander McGillivray to William Clark, April 24, 1785, Papers of Panton, Leslie, and Company, reel 2.

12. Nuñez, "Stiggins Narrative," pp.32–33; Bartram, "Observations," p.37; Romans, *A Concise Natural History of East and West Florida*, pp.91, 187, 280–81; Rowland, MPAED, p.204.

13. Taitt to Stuart, October 31, 1772, CO5/74, fo.30, and November 22, 1771, in Davies, DAR 5:224.

14. *Letters, Journals, and Writings of Benjamin Hawkins* 1:48–49.

15. Denys Rolle, *To the Right Honourable the Lords of His Majesty's Most Honourable Privy Council, the humble petition of Denys Rolle, esq, setting forth the hardships, inconveniencies, and grievances, which have attended him in his attempts to make a settlement in east Florida,* facsimile reproduction of the 1765 edition (Gainesville: University Presses of Florida, 1977), p.53.

16. Wright, *Creeks and Seminoles*, pp.63–64.

17. See Louis Capron, "Notes on the Hunting Dance of the Cow Creek Seminoles," *Florida Anthropologist* 9 (1956): 67–78, for a description of the dance in the twentieth century.

18. Gatschet, *Migration Legend of the Creek Indians*, pp.79–80.

19. Swanton, *Social Organization*, pp.444–45.

20. Bartram, *Travels*, p.59. The scientific name for the physic-nut is *Nestronia umbellula* Raf. This specimen is sometimes incorrectly identified as the Allegheny oil nut (*Pyrularia pubens* Michx.). Joseph Ewan, ed., *William Bartram: Botanical and Zoological Drawings, 1756–1788,* Memoirs of the American Philosophical Society, vol. 74 (Philadelphia: American Philosophical Society, 1968), p.65.

21. *Adair's History*, p.251.

22. Howard, *Southeastern Ceremonial Complex*, p.80; Hudson, *Southeastern Indians*, pp.168–69, 357.

23. William C. Sturtevant, "The Medicine Bundles and Busks of the Florida Seminole," *Florida Anthropologist* 7 (May 1954): 35–38, discusses these charms in some detail.

24. Bartram, *Travels*, p.184. Calvin Martin, in his study of Indian-animal relationships, rejects the notion that the Algonkian-speaking tribes of the Northeast participated in the "fur-to-trade-goods-exchange" because of simple eco-

nomic reasons. Instead, Martin examines these peoples' traditional belief system in which man and animals coexisted for mutual benefit. As long as the hunter obeyed certain rituals, the animal spirit surrendered to the hunter. If the hunter disobeyed the rules, the spirits retaliated by causing illness. Martin theorizes that with the introduction of European diseases, the old belief system was severely shaken; the Indians blamed their animal compatriots for their distress, and when traditional remedies could not halt the pandemics, the Indians attempted to destroy their tormentors. *Keepers of the Game: Indian-Animal Relationships and the Fur Trade* (Berkeley: University of California Press, 1978; reprint, 1982), 144–49. Creek scholars have dismissed Martin's theory as having no relevance for the Southeast. See Charles M. Hudson, "Why the Southeastern Indians Slaughtered Deer," in *Indians, Animals, and the Fur Trade: A Critique of Keepers of the Game,* edited by Shephard Krech III (Athens: University of Georgia Press, 1981), pp.157–76.

25. *Adair's History,* p.138; Holland, "Path between the Wars," p.53.

26. *Adair's History,* p.124.

27. Ibid., pp.123–24. See Hudson, *Southeastern Indians,* pp.340, 346, for discussion of these beliefs.

28. Bossu, *Travels in the Interior,* p.146. See De Bry engraving, from a Le Moyne drawing, reproduced in Emma Lila Fundaburk and Mary Douglass Foreman, *Sun Circles and Human Hands: The Southeastern Indians—Art and Industry* (Fairhope, Ala.: Southern Publications, 1957) p.206. Some modern hunters still use the same technique. Weiss, *Whitetail Deer Hunter's Handbook,* p.84.

29. Bossu, *Travels in the Interior,* p.146; Hvidt, *Von Reck's Voyage,* p.46. Male turkeys are also susceptible to this ruse.

30. Bartram, *Travels,* p.107.

31. William Cronon, *Changes in the Land: Indians, Colonists, and the Ecology of New England* (New York: Hill & Wang, 1983), p.51; Hudson, *Southeastern Indians,* pp.279–80.

32. *Letters, Journals, and Writings of Benjamin Hawkins* 1:42, 294.

33. Gregory A. Waselkov, "Evolution of Deer Hunting in the Eastern Woodlands," *Mid-Continental Journal of Archaeology* 3 (1978): 15–34; Hudson, *Southeastern Indians,* pp.275–77; Luther A. Anderson, *How to Hunt Whitetail Deer* (New York: Funk & Wagnalls, 1968), p.5.

34. The use of fire drives was common throughout the Southeast. Lawson, *New Voyage,* pp.215–16.

35. *Nairne's Muskhogean Journals,* pp.52–53.

36. John H. Logan, *A History of the Upper Country of South Carolina, from the Earliest Periods to the Close of the War of Independence,* vol. 1, South Carolina Heritage Series, no.5 (Charleston: S. G. Courtenay & Co., 1859; reprint, Spartanburg, S.C.: Reprint Co., 1966), p.29 (quotation). Indians were exempt from the South Carolina law banning night hunting. See ibid., pp.28–31; Antonio J. Waring, ed., *Laws of the Creek Nation,* University of Georgia Libraries Miscellaneous Publications, no.1. (Athens: University of Georgia Press, 1960), Law 16th and Law 17th, p.20.

37. Anderson, *How to Hunt Whitetail Deer.*

38. *Adair's History,* p.457.

39. Hvidt, *Von Reck's Voyage,* p.50. Von Reck left the only known sketch of a Creek hunting camp, pp.116–17. Benjamin Hawkins saw a number of hunting camps in his various sojourns through the Creek country. His descriptions are brief, as in *Letters, Journals, and Writings of Benjamin Hawkins* 1:51: "At this camp the Indians have left a very convenient camp standing. It had been used during the winter's hunt." Hawkins was one of the few white travelers to note camps.

40. *Letters, Journals, and Writings of Benjamin Hawkins* 1:303.

41. *Adair's History,* p.432.

42. D. W. Eakins, "Some Information Respecting the Creeks, or Muscogees," in *Historical and Statistical Information Respecting the History, Condition, and Prospects of the Indian Tribes of the United States,* 6 vols., edited by Henry Rowe Schoolcraft (Philadelphia: J. B. Lippincott, 1855), 1:278.

43. Fabel and Rea, "Lieutenant Thomas Campbell's Sojourn," pp.106, 109 (quotation); Bossu, *Travels in the Interior,* p.146; Bartram, *Travels,* pp.205–6; Hvidt, *Von Reck's Voyage,* pp.46–47. Bartram, "Observations," pp.31–32, says that women remained in the towns while the men were away. This was not the case, and numerous other sources are clear in stating that only the elderly or those unable to travel remained in the village.

44. Bartram, *Travels,* pp.205–6.

45. Lieut.-Governor John Moultrie to Earl of Dartmouth, February 21, 1774, in Davies, DAR 8:55.

46. Rowland, MPAED, p.204.

47. *Letters, Journals, and Writings of Benjamin Hawkins* 1:381.

48. Fabel and Rea, "Lieutenant Thomas Campbell's Sojourn," p.106. He was delivering messages from the governor of West Florida and the superintendent of Indian affairs.

49. *Letters, Journals, and Writings of Benjamin Hawkins* 1:50; John Lawson, *A*

New Voyage to Carolina, edited by Hugh T. Lefler (Chapel Hill: University of North Carolina Press, 1967), p.217. Though Lawson describes life among the Indians of North Carolina, many of his observations are true for the Creeks as well.

50. *Letters, Journals, and Writings of Benjamin Hawkins* 1:381; Hvidt, *Von Reck's Voyage,* pp.46–47; Fabel and Rea, "Lieutenant Thomas Campbell's Sojourn," p.108.

51. John Stuart to William Bull, December 2, 1769, CO5/71, fo.12. For information on how deerskins were processed, see Swanton, *Indians of the Southeastern United States,* pp.442–48; Hudson, *Southeastern Indians,* pp.266–67.

52. John Stuart to William Bull, December 2, 1769, CO5/71, pt.1, fo.12.

53. "Memorial of Traders to Creek and Cherokee Nations to Governor James Wright," June 1771, in Davies, DAR 3:125–26; Memorial to Stuart, September 10, 1771, in Davies, DAR 3:177–78; CRG 28, pt.2, p.375; John Stuart to William Bull, December 2, 1769, CO5/71, fo.12. The fact that the traders accepted the undressed hides had more to do with the demands of European buyers than those of Creek producers.

54. Swanton, *Social Organization,* p.405; Bossu, *Travels in the Interior,* p.146.

55. *De Brahm's Report of the General Survey in the Southern District of North America,* edited by Louis DeVorsey, Jr. (Columbia: University of South Carolina Press, 1971), pp.110–11.

56. Hvidt, *Von Reck's Voyage,* p.46.

57. Martyn, "An Impartial Inquiry," p.179. The same essay appears in *Malcontents,* p.154.

58. Bartram, *Travels,* p.329.

59. Carter, "Observations," p.818.

60. Ibid., pp.825–26. Stuart used a figure of 3,600 Creek gunmen (hunters), but 4,000 seems reasonable, especially in light of the fact that Creek population was on the rise when Stuart penned his report. Reid estimates the Cherokees took about 30 deer per year. *A Better Kind of Hatchet,* p.85. White, *Roots of Dependency,* pp.9–13, 26–29, 92–93, estimates the Choctaws took at least 20 to 25 deer each, and by the 1790s, three times that number. According to John Stuart, the Choctaws were notoriously poor hunters: "the Very limited Extent of their Hunting Ground, are become indolent and very bad Hunters." Carter, "Observations," p.820. That was not entirely true. Adair relates that once they acquired guns, the Choctaws became better at killing deer, and they excelled in killing bears, panthers, and wildcats found in the cane swamps, *Adair's History,* p.330. The main force in Choctaw life before 1763 was the inability of their

French allies to provide them with adequate supplies. Stuart to Earl of Egremont, June 1, 1763, CO5/65, fo.53. Guns were in short supply: "When the owners . . . [of guns] had hunted one moon, they lent them for hire to others, for the like space of time, which was the reason, that their deer-skins, by being chiefly killed out of season, were then much lighter than now." The shortage was due to the fact that the French awarded guns only to those who would fight the Chickasaws. *Adair's History*, p.305. It was only after the establishment of a trade with British West Florida in 1765 that the Choctaws were able to acquire large numbers of guns. As a result, Choctaw production levels increased, the system of using the chief's gun stopped, and their skins were worth more, since hunting occurred during the winter season when deer pelts were thicker. Given that the Choctaws were not very productive, it is likely that the Creeks were responsible for more than 200,000 skins per year. White, *Roots of Dependency*, pp.42–45, discusses the Choctaw system of sharing guns. For information on the drop in Cherokee production, see Hatley, "The Dividing Paths," pp.473–76, 445. Hatley believes that Stuart's figure for the Cherokees is high.

61. Leather breechcloths were about five feet long and one and one half feet wide. Hudson, *Southeastern Indians*, p.261.

62. The estimate was achieved by calculating approximately how many deerskins would be required for the following, designed with the needs of an adult male, adult female, and two children in mind: flaps (2), moccasins (4), leggings (4), sashes (1), shot pouches (1), deerskin shirts (4), bedding (6), bindings, straps, laces (1), and other uses (5).

63. This figure is achieved by multiplying the number of gunmen recorded by Stuart (13,941) by 50 pounds of deerskin each: 697,050. When added to Stuart's 800,000-pound upper limit for the number of deerskins exported, we reach 1,497,050. I have rounded for convenience.

64. Choctaw production averaged about 15,000 deerskins per year during the French regime. Usner, "The Deerskin Trade," p.79. This increased after 1763, with the influx of English guns and trade incentives.

65. Rowland, MPAED, p.204; Also see James W. Covington, ed., *The British Meet the Seminoles: Negotiations between the British Authorities in East Florida and the Indians, 1763–1768,* Contributions of the Florida State Museum, Social Sciences no.7 (Gainesville: University of Florida Press, 1961), p.27.

66. Daniel Lay, "Foods and Feeding Habits of White-Tailed Deer," in *White-Tailed Deer in the Southern Forest Habitat: Proceedings of a Symposium at Nacogdoches, Texas, March 25–26, 1969* (Nacogdoches, Tex.: Southern Forest Experiment Station, U.S. Forest Service, USDA, in cooperation with the Forest Game

Committee of the Southeastern Section of the Wildlife Society and the School of Forestry, Stephen F. Austin University, 1969), pp.1, 8–9; Timothy Silver, *A New Face on the Countryside: Indians, Colonists, and Slaves in South Atlantic Forests, 1500–1800,* Studies in Environment and History (Cambridge: Cambridge University Press, 1990), p.91. Virginia, North Carolina, Georgia, and South Carolina passed hunting regulations that did not apply to Indians but that were designed to preserve deer population in the colonies. Regulations were passed to protect other game animals as well. CRG 12:77, 15:349–50; Logan, *History of the Upper Country of South Carolina,* p.29; Phillips, *Fur Trade* 1:412n, 414; Silver, *New Face on the Countryside,* pp.94–101.

67. William Panton to Adam Gordon, July 24, 1799, Papers of Panton, Leslie, and Company. Panton does not specifically state the source of these deerskins.

68. The export figures for Panton, Leslie, and Company are scattered throughout the company's voluminous correspondence. The Creek factory records are found in United States Bureau of Indian Affairs, Records of the Office of the Indian Trade: Creek Factory Records, Correspondence, 1795–1814, Record Group 75, National Archives, Washington, D.C. Wright, *Creeks and Seminoles,* p.59, cites the export figures listed above.

69. The paucity of records and the limited nature of those that still exist leave room for much debate concerning the viability of the deerskin trade. However, it seems fair to conclude that in 1764, the Creeks produced at least one-half of Stuart's 400,000 deerskins, cited above. Of Panton's minimum 124,000 hides during the closing years of the century, perhaps as many as three-fourths were Creek. If so, then we obtain a figure of at least 93,000 hides per year for the Creeks. Add to that the 25,000 deerskins procured through the Creek factory, and the total amounts to 118,000 hides per year. Although these figures are incomplete, it does not seem likely that large numbers of Creek deerskins were finding other outlets. In any case, this is considerably less than the 200,000 estimate produced by the Creeks during the 1760s and 1770s. And finally, the Creek portion of the southeastern output in 1764 may well have been more than half. In other words, the Creeks most likely produced more than 200,000 skins in the 1760s and 1770s. Given the limited Choctaw harvest, the small number of Chickasaws and minor tribes, and the distressed state of the Cherokee trade, the Creek portion of Stuart's 800,000-pound figure may have been between one-half and three-fourths the total.

70. In 1785, a report by the five American commissioners to the Creeks estimated 2,000 Cherokee gunmen, 6,000 Choctaw gunmen, 5,400 Creek gun-

men, and 800 Chickasaw gunmen. *American State Papers, Indian Affairs,* p.39. Other estimates for the Choctaws were considerably smaller. One 1798 estimate placed the number of Choctaw gunmen at 3,000. *American State Papers, Indian Affairs,* p.79.

71. At the 1765 Congress of Picolata, John Bartram noted that two chiefs, each carrying a bundle of about twenty dressed deerskins, presented these to the governor of East Florida and the superintendent of Indian affairs, along with a rattle box and eagle feathers. John Bartram, "Diary," p.51.

72. Bartram, "Diary," p.51; McDowell, *1750–1754,* p.391; "Journal of Captain Tobias Fitch's Mission from Charleston to the Creeks, 1726," in *Travels in the American Colonies,* edited by Newton D. Mereness (New York: Macmillan Co., 1916), p.177; *Adair's History,* p.277.

73. Lieut.-Governor John Moultrie to Earl of Dartmouth, February 21, 1774, in Davies, DAR 8:54.

74. See Charles Stuart to Chester, n.d., incl. in Chester's letter of April 15, 1771, to Hillsborough, in Rowland, "Peter Chester," p.51; Robert L. Gold, *Borderland Empires in Transition: The Triple-Nation Transfer of Florida* (Carbondale: Southern Illinois University Press; Edwardsville, Ill.: Feffer & Simons, 1969), p.179.

75. The quote is from Dorothy V. Jones, *License for Empire: Colonialism by Treaty in Early America* (Chicago: University of Chicago Press, 1982), p.43.

76. Struthers to Johnstone, May 20, 1766, in Rowland, MPAED, p.521; Stuart to Pownall, August 24, 1765, CO5/66, fo.356. Prices, in pounds of deerskin, for the above goods in 1766 were: two kegs of rum, 50; gun, 16; blanket, 8; boots, 2; shirt, 3; flap, 1; 10 flints, 1; 40 bullets, 1; 1/2 pint gun powder, 1. McDowell, *1750–1754,* p.398; CRG 18, pt.2, p.121; Rowland, MPAED, p.215.

77. "General Oglethorpe to Trustees, Dec. 29, 1739," CRG 22, pt.2, p.287; Kathryn E. Holland, "The Anglo-Spanish Contest for the Gulf Coast as Viewed from the Townsquare," in *Anglo-Spanish Confrontation on the Gulf Coast during the American Revolution: Proceedings of the Gulf Coast History and Humanities Conference,* vol.9, pp.101, edited by William S. Coker and Robert R. Rea (Pensacola: Gulf Coast History and Humanities Conference, 1982).

78. Philimeon Kemp to Gov. of Georgia, June 6, 1771, in Davies, DAR 3:118; Martha C. Searcy, "The Introduction of African Slavery into the Creek Indian Nation," *Georgia Historical Quarterly* 66 (1982): 22–23; Braund, "Creek Indians, Blacks, and Slavery," pp.611–14.

79. Daniel H. Usner, Jr. "The Frontier Exchange Economy of the Lower Mississippi Valley in the Eighteenth Century," *William and Mary Quarterly* 44

(April 1987): 165–92. For a more detailed examination of the regional exchange of the Lower Mississippi Valley, see Usner, *Indians, Settlers, and Slaves.*

80. Pickett, *History of Alabama*, p.422; "Account by LaRochefoucauld-Liancourt," in Mills Lane, ed., *The Rambler in Georgia: Desultory Observations on the Situation, Extent, Climate, Population, Manners, Customs, Commerce, Constitution, Government, Etc., of the State from the Revolution to the Civil War Recorded by Thirteen Travelers* (Savannah: Beehive Press, 1973), p.13; Bartram, *Travels*, p.342.

81. Rowland, MPAFD 4:250.

82. Robert R. Rea and Milo B. Howard, Jr., eds. *The Minutes, Journals, and Acts of the General Assembly of British West Florida* (Tuscaloosa: University of Alabama Press, 1979), p.382.

83. *Letters, Journals, and Writings of Benjamin Hawkins* 1:312.

84. For instance, Benjamin Hawkins was told by the headman of Saugahatchee in 1797 that the women there needed a trader willing to "supply them with salt and thread for such articles of food as they can spare." Hawkins, *Sketch*, p.246.

85. *Adair's History*, p.444; see also Rowland, "Peter Chester," p.83.

86. Bartram, "Observations," p.48.

87. Swan, "Position and State of Manners," p.282; *Letters, Journals, and Writings of Benjamin Hawkins* 1:25.

88. Proceedings of a Congress with the Creeks, October 29–November 2, 1771, in Davies, DAR 3:224.

89. Hatley, "The Dividing Paths," pp.146, 448.

90. Headman of Upper Creek Nation to Governor Lyttelton, August 9, 1756, in McDowell, *1754–1765*, pp.153–54; Creek Traders to Governor Lyttelton, July 31, 1756, in McDowell, *1754–1756*, p.152; Mico Lucko to Stuart, April 19, 1772, CO5/73, fo.268. Cattle allowed free forage often turned feral, thus requiring cattle hunters to round them up. Saye and Coulter, *List of Early Settlers*, pp.74, 85; David R. Chesnutt, *South Carolina's Expansion into Colonial Georgia, 1720–1765* (Ann Arbor, Mich.: University Microfilms, 1976), pp.148–49; CRG 26:22 and vol.22, pt.2, pp.171, 245.

91. *Adair's History*, p.490; Romans, *Concise Natural History of East and West Florida*, pp.62–63; Lieut. Colonel Provost to Sec at War, September 7, 1763, in Rowland, MPAED, p.136; Gordon, "Journal," p.383. See also CRG (September 3, 1768) 10:574, (January 28, 1759) 28, pt.1, p.176.

92. Fabel and Rea, "Lieutenant Thomas Campbell's Sojourn," pp.108–9; Struthers to Governor Johnstone, May 20, 1766, in Rowland, MPAED, p.522; Bartram, *Travels*, pp.164–65; Wright, *The Only Land They Knew*, p.145.

93. "David Taitt's Journal to and through the Lower Creek Nation," in Davies, DAR 5:280; CRG 10:569–70; "Proceedings of 1774 Treaty with Creeks," GHSC 10:3–4; Taitt to Stuart, May 4, 1772, CO5/73, fo.263; Proceedings of a Congress with the Creeks, October 29–November 2, 1771, in Davies, DAR 3:224; Talk of Emisteseguo, September 3, 1768, in CRG 10:566–71, 574; Fabel and Rea, "Lieutenant Thomas Campbell's Sojourn," p.108; Taitt to Stuart, May 4, 1772, CO5/73, fo.263; Mico Lucko to Stuart, April 19, 1772, CO5/73, fo.268.

94. *Adair's History,* p.138. The disease was most likely mumps, an acute contagious viral disease marked by fever and by swelling of the parotid gland. Adult males who contract mumps are frequently rendered sterile. One could speculate endlessly about the impact of this happenstance on Creek bloodlines. Adair does not specifically state that the disease was mumps, but the description is better suited to mumps than undulant fever or brucellosis, which is caused by a bacteria that can be contracted by eating contaminated beef or drinking milk from infected cattle. The primary symptoms are fever and swelling at the joints. The Indians affected were certainly Creeks, since in 1767, the year Adair gives for the incident, traders were attempting to drive cattle from Georgia, through the Creek towns, to Pensacola. Hudson, *Southeastern Indians,* discusses other diseases that the Indians believed were caused by animals, along with the cures, on pp.340–42, 346.

95. *Adair's History,* pp.242 (quotation), 436.

96. Bartram, *Travels,* pp.185–86 (quotations are on p.185). Bartram called the horses among the Upper Creeks "Chactaw" horses. For information on these horses, see *Adair's History,* pp.340, 430n.

97. Mortar's Talk to John Stuart, May 20, 1769, CO5/70, fo.254; Gordon, "Journal," p.385; Headmen and Warriors of the Upper Creeks to Stuart, August 8, 1769, CO5/70, fo.307; CRG 10:246–49; Bartram, "Observations," pp.13–14; McDowell, *1710–1718,* p.311.

98. At a Council Meeting held April 14, 1769, in CRG 10:748–51.

99. Ibid.

100. Mortar's Talk to John Stuart, May 20, 1769, CO5/70, fo.254; Georgia Council Meeting, April 14, 1769, in CRG 10:748–51.

101. Congress of Pensacola, 1765, in Rowland, MPAED, pp.201, 207.

102. Bartram, *Travels,* pp.214–15.

103. Romans, *Concise Natural History of East and West Florida,* p.97.

104. Of interest is a speech recorded by an elderly conjurer who denounced, among other things, the "prostitutes" whom he blamed for a particularly rainy year. John Pope, *A Tour through the Southern and Western Territories of the*

United States of North-America, facsimile reproduction of the 1792 edition, Bicentennial Floridiana Facsimile Series (Gainesville: University Presses of Florida, 1979), p.61.

105. Richd. Heughes to Lieut. Outerbridge, Dec. 26, 1757, in McDowell, *1754–1765,* p.424; Creek Traders to Lieut. Outerbridge, in McDowell, *1754–1765,* p.423.

106. Romans, *Concise Natural History of East and West Florida,* pp.93–94; Rolle, *Humble Petition,* pp.20, 30, relates the efforts of Philoki of Latchoway on behalf of James Spaulding.

107. Rolle, *Humble Petition,* p.48.

108. The young man's marriage ceremony was recounted by William Bartram in his *Travels,* pp.353–57. While Bartram specifically states that the women were daughters of the headman, it is more likely they were his nieces. The headman at Muccolossus was the Wolf King, a Great Medal Chief of the Creeks. The licensed trader at the town was John Adam Tapley, whom David Taitt charged with "digging up the bodies of the Coweta Indians and likewise for several felonies." Governor Chester of West Florida refused to hear Taitt's charges. David Taitt to John Stuart, November 22, 1772, CO5/74, fo.64. Although there are various meanings for the term *mustee,* in the Creek experience it designated a person of mixed white and Indian blood. For a fuller discussion of the subject, see Jack D. Forbes, "Mustees, Half-Breeds, and Zambos in Anglo North America: Aspects of Black-Indian Relations," *American Indian Quarterly* 7 (Fall 1983): 57–83.

109. Bartram, "Observations," pp.37–39.

110. Ibid., pp.55–56. Bartram also provided a diagram of the habitations. Unfortunately, Bartram did not note the exact relationship of the fifteen other Indians who lived with Bosten. See Hudson, *Southeastern Indians,* pp.213–14, 218, for more information on the Creek households. Hudson suggests that the number of buildings increased as family size grew. Older married people with many children would need space that younger couples would not.

CHAPTER 5: *Traders and Trading*

1. Stuart Bruchey, ed., *The Colonial Merchant: Sources and Readings,* Forces in American Economic Growth Series (New York: Harcourt, Brace & World, 1966), p.120; Sellers, *Charleston Business,* pp.49ff.; Henry Laurens to James Cowles, July 4, 1755, in Hamer and Rogers, *Papers of Henry Laurens* 1:284–85.

2. For an examination of the use of black slaves by deerskin traders, see Braund, "Creek Indians, Blacks, and Slavery," pp.608–10.

3. When Patrick McKay, Georgia's first (and most zealous) Indian agent,

suggested to the traders that they form a partnership in 1735, they told him they had already attempted it the year before. Easterby, *Journal of the Commons House,* p.122.

4. Crane, *Southern Frontier,* p.127.

5. Walter E. Minchinton, "The Merchants in England in the Eighteenth Century," *Explorations in Entrepreneurial History* 10 (December 1957): 68, discusses these bonds. See Coker and Watson, *Indian Traders,* chapter one.

6. George Galphin to Henry Laurens, February 7, 1776, Sims Collection of Laurens Papers, South Caroliniana Library, University of South Carolina, Columbia. This letter is reproduced in Hamer and Rogers, *Papers of Henry Laurens* 11:94.

7. Stuart to Pownell, August 24, 1765, CO5/66, fo.356.

8. Meeting of Upper Creeks, April 10, 1764, Gage Papers; Romans, *Concise Natural History of East and West Florida,* p.97.

9. This of course was not true for Creek husbands.

10. Vaudreuil and Salmon to Maurepas, July 21, 1743, in Galloway, MPAFD 4:209.

11. *Nairne's Muskhogean Journals,* pp.60–61.

12. Bartram, *Travels,* p.170.

13. *Letters, Journals, and Writings of Benjamin Hawkins* 1:22.

14. Ibid. 1:21.

15. McDowell, *1750–1754,* p.407; Bartram, *Travels,* pp.110–11.

16. *Adair's History,* p.443.

17. Ibid.; *Letters, Journals, and Writings of Benjamin Hawkins* 1:28, 34, 38, 42.

18. *Adair's History,* pp.444–47, first quote on p.447, second on p.444.

19. Ibid., p.443.

20. *Letters, Journals, and Writings of Benjamin Hawkins* 1:25.

21. *Adair's History,* p.443.

22. Bartram, *Travels,* p.354.

23. Ibid., p.356; *Adair's History,* p.436.

24. *Letters, Journals, and Writings of Benjamin Hawkins* 1:33–34.

25. Ibid. 1:34.

26. Ibid. 1:63.

27. *Adair's History,* p.443.

28. Ibid., pp.465 (first quotation), 480 (second quotation).

29. Easterby, *Journal of the Commons House,* pp.139, 114.

30. Corkran, *Creek Frontier,* p.107.

31. Ralph Davis, *The Industrial Revolution and British Overseas Trade* (Leices-

ter, England: University Press, 1979), p.30; L. A. Clarkson, "The Organization of the English Leather Industry in the Late Sixteenth and Seventeenth Centuries," *Economic History Review*, n.s., 13, no.2 (1960): 245–56.

32. Postlethwayt, *Universal Dictionary of Trade and Commerce*, Entry for Leather, vol.2.

33. Ibid., Entry for Leather Breeches-Maker, vol.2.

34. See the advertisement in the *South Carolina Gazette*, August 17, 1738, for buckskin breeches. An example of gentleman's buckskin breeches is preserved in the London Museum. Zillah Halls, *Men's Costume, 1750–1800*, London Museum Publication (London: Her Majesty's Stationery Office, 1973), pp.6, 53; Postlethwayt, *Universal Dictionary of Trade and Commerce*, Entry for Leather Breeches-Maker, vol.2. Romans, *Concise Natural History of East and West Florida*, p.184, speculates on the American shoe market. Bennie C. Keel, "The Conservation and Preservation of Archaeological and Ethnological Specimens," *Southern Indian Studies* 15 (October 1963): 5–65; John W. Waterer, *Leather in Life, Art, and Industry* (London: Faber & Faber, 1946), p.159; M. T. Thompson, "Historic Role of the Rivers of Georgia: The Charles Town Traders," *Georgia Mineral Newsletter* 3, no.5 (September–October 1950): 173; Elizabeth B. Schumpeter, *English Overseas Trade Statistics, 1697–1808* (Oxford: Oxford University Press, 1960), tables 7 and 8; John R. Alden, *John Stuart and the Southern Colonial Frontier: A Study of Indian Relations, War, Trade, and Land Problems in the Southern Wilderness, 1754–1775*, University of Michigan Publications in History and Political Science, no.15 (Ann Arbor: University of Michigan Press, 1944; reprint, New York: Gordian, 1966), p.15n.

35. Postlethwayt, *Universal Dictionary of Trade and Commerce*, Entry for Leather Breeches-Maker, vol.2. A *drawback* is a portion of the import duty that is paid by the government to those who exported the product. See Entry for Drawbacks, vol.1.

36. See Clarkson, "English Leather Industry," pp.245–56, for a discussion of uses and processing of leather in Britain.

37. James Habersham to Mr. Joseph Tuckwell, May 18, 1765, James Habersham Papers, Folder 1: Letterbook, 1764–1766, Georgia Historical Society, Savannah. In the 1750s, Cherokee leather had been preferred by London markets because it was thicker. At least this is what the governor of South Carolina told Creek headmen in 1753 when the Creeks demanded an explanation for the better prices paid for Cherokee deerskins. McDowell, *1750–1754*, p.407.

38. "Regulations for the Better Carrying on the Trade with the Indian Tribes in the Southern District," CO5/68, fo.110, Regulation #19.

39. Bartram, *Travels*, p.186; McDowell, *1750–1754*, p.146; Hudson, *South-*

eastern Indians, pp.266–67. Sellers, *Charleston Business,* p.173, says the standard medium of exchange was a skin weighing one pound; however, only small skins weighed one pound. Crane, *Southern Frontier,* p.111, says two pounds when half-dressed; White, *Roots of Dependency,* p.67; *Atkin Report,* p.85; J. Anthony Paredes and Kenneth J. Plante, "Economics, Politics, and the Subjugation of the Creek Indians," Final Report for National Park Service Contract CX500041689, October 1975, copy located at Southeast Archaeological Center, National Park Service, Tallahassee, Florida, p.63.

40. *Atkin Report,* p.35; Meriwether, *South Carolina,* p.193; Henry Laurens to James Cowles, 7 February 1756, Hamer and Rogers, *Papers of Henry Laurens* 2:90; Surrey, *Commerce of Louisiana,* p.354; McDowell, *1750–1754,* pp.192, 262–63.

41. William Panton, Statement of June 2, 1787, Papers of Panton, Leslie, and Company, reel 3. Panton says a pound weighed 18 ounces.

42. Traders were allowed to use their own judgment in assigning value to furs or Indian slaves. McDowell, *1710–1718,* p.269.

43. William Panton, Statement of June 2, 1787, Papers of Panton, Leslie, and Company, reel 3. The average weight for dressed skins was derived from several sources by dividing pounds of deerskins by number reported. Dalrymple, *Merchant of Manchac,* p.94, also gives the weight of raw skins at three pounds.

44. For example, see McDowell, *1754–1765,* pp.401–8, and Rowland, MPAED, pp.188–215.

45. Postlethwayt, *Universal Dictionary of Trade and Commerce,* Entry for British America, vol. 1; Juricek, *Georgia Treaties,* p.87; McDowell, *1754–1765,* p.155.

46. McDowell, *1754–1765,* pp.155, 417, 213, 240, 255, 296, 352, also xvii. A steelyard was simply "a balance consisting of a lever with unequal arms, which moves on a fulcrum; the article to be weighed is suspended from the shorter arm, and a counterpoise is caused to slide upon the longer arm until equilibrium is produced, its place on this arm (which is notched or graduated) showing the weight." They were also known as Roman scales. *The Compact Edition of the Oxford English Dictionary,* 2 vols. (Oxford: Oxford University Press, 1982), 2:3037. "Regulations for the Better Carrying on the Trade with the Indian Tribes of the Southern District," in John Stuart to Shelburne, April 1, 1767, C05/68, fo.110. See Regulation #19, "An Act for the Better Regulation of the Indian Trade in the Province of West Florida, May 19, 1770," in Robert R. Rea and Milo B. Howard, Jr., eds., *The Minutes, Journals, and Acts of the General Assembly of British West Florida* (Tuscaloosa: University of Alabama Press, 1979),

p.381. Edmond Atkin recommended that small scales, able to measure from one-half to three pounds, and a copper yardstick be lodged with each trader. *Atkin Report,* pp.85–86.

47. McDowell, *1754–1765,* p.105.

48. *Adair's History,* p.297 (quotation); Talks from Upper Creek Meeting, April 10, 1764, Gage Papers; Hatley, "The Dividing Paths," p.118.

49. Talk from Headmen and Warriors of Upper Creek Nation, May 1, 1771, C05/72, fo.346.

50. John H. Goff, "The Path to Oakfuskee: Upper Trading Route in Georgia to the Creek Indians," *Georgia Historical Quarterly* 39 (March 1955): 2; see also John H. Goff, "The Path to Oakfuskee: Upper Trading Route in Alabama to the Creek Indians," *Georgia Historical Quarterly* 39 (June 1955): 157–71, and William E. Myer, "Indian Trails of the Southeast," *Bureau of American Ethnology, Forty-Second Annual Report,* pp.727–857 (Washington, D.C.: U.S. Government Printing Office, 1928).

51. McDowell, *1754–1765,* pp.255–56.

52. McIntosh to Stuart, November 16, 1767, in Stuart to Gage, December 26, 1767, Gage Papers; "David Taitt's Journal to and through the Lower Creek Nation," Appendix B, in Davies, DAR 5:279; Crane, *Southern Frontier,* p.135.

53. Pickett, *History of Alabama,* p.424.

54. Fabel and Rea, "Lieutenant Thomas Campbell's Sojourn," p.103. Campbell recorded 213 miles. David Taitt, who made virtually the same trip in 1772, calculated 225 miles.

55. "A State of the Province of Georgia in 1742," in Reese, *Malcontents,* p.6.

56. Bartram, *Travels,* pp.305, 363; Bartram, "Diary," footnote to entry for September 9, p.25.

57. Brown, "Early Indian Trade," p.127.

58. Pickett, *History of Alabama,* p.422. Pickett obtained his information from a number of retired traders, including Abram Mordecai, James Moore, and Lachlan Durant.

59. Bartram, *Travels,* pp.350–51. Bartram states in his book that he began his journey on November 27, 1777. This is almost certainly incorrect, since he was back in Philadelphia in that same year. There are several occasions on which Bartram's dates are questionable. See Francis Harper, "William Bartram and the American Revolution," *American Philosophical Society Proceedings* 97 (October 1957): 574.

60. Pickett, *History of Alabama,* p.341.

61. Bartram, *Travels*, p.354; "David Taitt's Journal to and through the Lower Creek Nation," in Davies, DAR 5:251.

62. *Nairne's Muskhogean Journals*, pp.55–56.

63. "Ranger's Report," p.219; "David Taitt's Journal to and through the Lower Creek Nation," in Davies, DAR 5:280. David George, a slave who worked with the packhorsemen employed by George Galphin, noted that when he traveled with the caravans from Augusta to the Creek country, they used "leather boats" to cross the rivers. John Rippon, ed., "An Account of the Life of Mr. David George, from Sierra Leone to Africa, given by himself in a Conversation with Brother Rippon of London, and Brother Pearce of Birmingham," *Baptist Annual Register for 1790, 1791, 1792, and Part of 1793, Including Sketches of the State of Religion among Different Denominations of Good Men at Home and Abroad* (London: Dilly, Butler, and Thomas, 1793), p.474.

64. *Adair's History*, p.291.

65. *Letters, Journals, and Writings of Benjamin Hawkins* 1:51.

66. Bartram, *Travels*, p.353.

67. Ibid. A *withe* is a flexible young branch suitable for use as a line or as binding. Pickett, *History of Alabama*, pp.423–24, says much the same thing, having also read Bartram in addition to his interviews. James Adair also described trading rafts. *Adair's History*, p.291.

68. Bartram, *Travels*, p.353.

69. Swan, "Position and State of Manners," pp.253–54.

70. Bartram, *Travels*, pp.312, 352–53, 363; Stuart to Conway, August 8, 1766, CO5/67, fo.102.

71. Pickett, *History of Alabama*, p.423; *Letters, Journals, and Writings of Benjamin Hawkins* 1:51–52.

72. Bartram, *Travels*, p.362. This figure can also be derived from figures given in the *South Carolina Gazette*, July 5–12, 1760. Wagons were used in the Cherokee trade. Sellers, *Charleston Business*, pp.174–75.

73. Hamer and Rogers, *Papers of Henry Laurens* 8:74.

74. See the *South Carolina Gazette*, September 8–15, 1739, advertising a slave for sale who knows how to dress skins. Sellers, *Charleston Business*, p.172.

75. Postlethwayt, *Universal Dictionary of Trade and Commerce*, Entry for Georgia; Martyn, "An Impartial Inquiry," p.153. The quote is from "A State of the Province of Georgia in 1742," in Reese, *Malcontents*, p.6.

76. Crane, *Southern Frontier*, p.128; Thompson, "Historic Role of Rivers in Georgia in Navigation Era," *Georgia Mineral Newsletter* 4, no.1, pp.18–19. Such a boat was sketched by Von Reck. Hvidt, *Von Reck's Voyage*, p.85.

77. Bartram, "Diary," p.28.

78. John Highrider was an associate of John Petticrew, an important figure in the Chickasaw trade. McDowell, *1750–1754*, p.40.

79. W. O. Moore, Jr., "Largest Exporters of Deerskins"; Sellers, *Charleston Business*, p.172; Thomas C. Barrow, *Trade and Empire: The British Customs Service in Colonial America, 1660–1775* (Cambridge: Harvard University Press, 1967), p.183; CRG 19:456.

80. Hamer and Rogers, *Papers of Henry Laurens* 2:207n, 8:74n; Habersham to Martyn, February 3, 1752 in CRG 26:343. See GHSC, no.8, endsheets.

81. Sellers, *Charleston Business*, p.172; Habersham to Benjamin Martyn, February 3, 1752, in CRG 26:336; *The Letterbook of Thomas Raspberry, 1758–1761,* edited by Lilla Mills Hawes, Georgia Historical Society Collections, vol.13 (Savannah: Georgia Historical Society, 1959), pp.55, 62, 131. See "Price Current" lists in the *South Carolina Gazette,* for instance May 11 to May 18, 1765. A barrel was equal to one-half a hogshead, a tierce to two-thirds a hogshead, a cask to one-fourth a hogshead. Converse D. Clowse, *Measuring Charleston's Overseas Commerce, 1717–1767: Statistics from the Port's Naval Lists* (Washington, D.C.: University Press of America, 1981), p.56.

82. Postlethwayt, *Universal Dictionary of Trade and Commerce,* Entry for Leather, vol.2; Fabel, *Economy of British West Florida,* p.199. Fabel prefers the larger average weight of 2.5 pounds and thus figures the total weight of these hogsheads at 11,590.

83. See "An Account of Deer Skins Indian Dressed Reported from Charles Town from Lady Day 1740 to Lad Day 1763 taken from the Custom House Books," in Report of John Stuart to the Lords Commissioners of Trade and Plantations on the Southern Indian Department, March 9, 1764, CO323/17, pp.34–36.

84. This was in 1759. *Letterbook of Thomas Raspberry,* p.55.

85. Hamer and Rogers, *Papers of Henry Laurens* 8:74.

86. Ibid. 8:22.

87. A French report in 1715 claimed that the English procured 100,000 deerskins a year, but this was an exaggeration. Rowland and Sanders, MPAFD 3:188.

88. Martyn, "An Impartial Inquiry," pp.153–54; Letter from Mr. Habersham to Mr. Benjamin Martyn, February 3, 1752, in CRG 26:337; Waselkov, "French Colonial Trade in the Upper Creek Country."

89. Determining export numbers is a tricky business. The figures in this paragraph are based on tables found in "An Account of Deer Skins Indian

Dressed," in Report of John Stuart to the Lords Commissioners of Trade and Plantations on the Southern Indian Department, March 9, 1764, CO323/17, pp.34–36. These figures have been published in De Vorsey, "Colonial Georgia Backcountry," p.11. (The table lists Stuart's report but incorrectly states the date as 1769, a typographical error. The report is cited correctly elsewhere in the article.) For published figures, see Crane, *Southern Frontier,* pp.327–30. More scientific presentation of the same data is found in Clowse, *Measuring Charleston's Overseas Commerce,* pp.54–56. Customs figures and tax records did not consistently record the same data; therefore, some figures must be deduced. For instance, determining the number of deerskins per barrel or hogshead shipped calls for educated guesswork. Moreover, for some customs data, the number of pounds of dressed deerskins recorded does not correspond to the numbers of deerskins recorded elsewhere. It is impossible to determine the meaning of these discrepancies given the available data. For a general discussion of the Custom Office and its procedures and West Florida export figures, see Rea, "British West Florida Trade," pp.124–59. In an attempt to correct the discrepancy between pounds of deerskins and numbers of deerskins, Rea speculated that each raw deerskin weighed 30 pounds. The records do suggest this, but other sources clearly indicate that the average weight of half-dressed skins was between one and three pounds, usually one and one-half to two pounds. Raw deerskins weighed three pounds. William Panton, Statement of June 2, 1787, Papers of Panton, Leslie, and Company, reel 3.

90. "An Aggregate and Valuation of Exports of Produce from the Province of Georgia, with the Number of Vessels employed therein, annually distinguished, from the Year 1754, to 1773, compiled by William Brown, Comptroller and Searcher of his Majesty's Customs in the Port of Savannah," in Romans, *Concise Natural History of East and West Florida,* chart following p.104.

91. Carter, "Observations," p.818.

92. Fabel, *Economy of British West Florida,* appendix 5, p.237.

93. William Panton to Adam Gordon, July 24, 1799, Papers of Panton, Leslie, and Company, microfilm edition. Panton had no reason to hedge on the numbers of deerskins he exported. In fact, in the letter cited, he was attempting to impress British policymakers with the amount of customs duties the deerskin trade had generated from 1783 to 1799. It is likely that he was stretching the figures as far as possible. Also, Panton does not specifically state where the deerskins are coming from. Although the majority of the trade was conducted with the Creeks, the company also traded with the other southeastern tribes.

94. Wright, *Creeks and Seminoles,* p.59.

95. Governor James Wright to the Board of Trade, November 10, 1764, CO323/20. Alden, *John Stuart,* pp.16–17, footnote 38, discusses this letter in some detail.

96. Pope, *Tour,* p.45.

97. John Percival, First Earl of Egmont, *The Journal of the Earl of Egmont,* edited by Robert McPherson (Athens: University of Georgia Press, 1962), pp.66–67.

98. William Panton, Statement of June 2, 1787, Papers of Panton, Leslie, and Company, reel 3. The statement includes a chart comparing the price that traders paid for goods at Pensacola, the number of skins each article sold for in the Creek towns, and the profit made on each item.

99. Hamer and Rogers, *Papers of Henry Laurens* 4:417.

100. Fabel, *Economy of British West Florida,* pp.56ff., discusses the problems of the trade.

101. Sellers, *Charleston Business,* p.173.

102. James A. Bernard, *An Analysis of British Mercantilism as It Related to Patterns of South Carolina Trade from 1717 to 1767* (Ann Arbor, Mich.: University Microfilms, 1976), pp.113–14; T. S. Ashton, *Economic Fluctuations in England, 1700–1800* (Oxford: Oxford University Press, 1959), p.39; See Arthur Harrison Cole, *Wholesale Commodity Prices in the United States, 1700–1861* (Cambridge: Harvard University Press, 1938; reprint, New York: Johnson Reprint Co., 1969), chapter 6.

103. See Alden, *John Stuart,* pp.240–42, 207–9, for a concise discussion of the Proclamation of October 7, 1763, with regard to trade.

104. *Adair's History,* pp.395–96.

105. To the Honourable John Stuart, Esq., His Majesty's Agent for and Superintendent of Indian Affairs for the Southern District in North America The Memoriall of the Merchants and Traders of the Province of Georgia Trading From Augusta to the Creek Nation, in Mr. Stuart's Letter of July 28, 1767, CO5/68, fo.142.

106. Ibid.

CHAPTER 6: *"Runagadoes" and the Regulation of the Trade*

1. Rowland, MPAED, p.206.

2. Nuñez, "Stiggins Narrative," p.142.

3. McDowell, *1750–1754,* p.263.

4. *Adair's History,* p.394.

5. John Stuart to Earl of Hillsborough, June 12, 1772, CO5/73, fo.162.

6. Wright to Board of Trade, August 27, 1764, in CRG, 28, pt.2, p.51.

7. Ibid., p.52.

8. Memorial to John Stuart from Merchants and Traders to Georgia, July 28, 1767, CO5/68, fo.142.

9. Romans, *Concise Natural History of East and West Florida*, p.60.

10. *Adair's History*, p.444.

11. Taitt to Stuart, March 16, 1772, CO5/73, fo.259. James McQueen deserted the Royal Navy after striking an officer, according to Thomas Woodward. Woodward, *Reminiscences*, p.10.

12. Swan, "Position and State of Manners," p.282.

13. John Stuart to Earl of Hillsborough, June 12, 1772, CO5/73, fo.162.

14. Percival, *Journal of the Earl of Egmont*, pp.66–67 (quotation); McDowell, *1750–1754*, p.441.

15. William Struthers to Gov. Johnstone, April 10, 1766, in Rowland, MPAED, pp.516–17, and Speech of the Mortar, May 16, 1766, in Rowland, MPAED, p.529; "David Taitt's Journal to and through the Upper Creek Nation," in Davies, DAR 5:259.

16. McDowell, *1754–1765*, p.354.

17. Charles Stuart to John Stuart, August 26, 1770, CO5/72, fo.89.

18. John Stuart to Germaine, October 26, 1776, CO5/78, fo.15.

19. Answer to Gov. Johnson's Talk to the Upper Creeks, May 16, 1766, CO5/67, fo.15.

20. Creek attitudes and reactions toward the introduction of alcohol will be discussed in chapter 7.

21. *Adair's History*, p.445.

22. James Beamer to Governor Glen, February 21, 1756, in McDowell, *1754–1765*, p.105.

23. David Taitt to John Stuart, March 16, 1772, CO5/73, fo.259.

24. "David Taitt's Journal to and through the Upper Creek Nation," in Davies, DAR 5:255, see also p.259.

25. David Taitt to John Stuart, March 16, 1772, CO5/73, fo.259.

26. McDowell, *1750–1754*, p.283.

27. Juricek, *Georgia Treaties*, p.40.

28. McDowell, *1754–1765*, p.297. For Ross's version of the incident, see pp.211–12.

29. Percival, *Journal of the Earl of Egmont*, p.66.

30. David Taitt to John Stuart, November 22, 1772, CO5/74 fo.64.

31. *Adair's History*, p.151; At a Meeting of the Head Men at Little Talsey, April 10, 1764, Gage Papers; McDowell, *1750–1754*, p.407.

32. Stuart to Bull, December 2, 1769, CO5/71, pt.1, fo.12; "Journal of the Augusta Congress, 1763," in Saunders, CRNC 11:183, 185; CRG 9:75; "David Taitt's Journal to and through the Upper Creek Nation," in Davies, DAR 5:255, 258–59, 266; Stuart to Gage, July 2, 1768, Gage Papers; McDowell, *1754–1765*, p.355.

33. David Taitt to John Stuart, March 16, 1772, CO5/73, fo.259.

34. McDowell, *1754–1765*, p.354–55.

35. Stuart to Shelburne, April 1, 1767, CO5/68, fo.110, comment on Article 3.

36. Ibid., comment on Article 1.

37. Wight, *Abstracts of Colonial Wills*, p.120. The name of this village is spelled a variety of ways in eighteenth-century documents, including Tchoulouchpouque (French), Soogaspooga, Suckapogas, and Soguspogus. Rowland, MPAED, p.95; CRG 8:523, 28, pt.2, p.89; Swan, "Position and State of Manners," p.262; Swanton, *Early History*, p.245, renders this village as Lutcapoga.

38. *South Carolina Gazette*, June 14–21, 1760. David Corkran believes that the murders were politically motivated. See Corkran, *Creek Frontier*, pp.216–19.

39. Journal of the Superintendent's Proceedings, April 21, 1767–June 6, 1767, Gage Papers.

40. For instance, see Bartram, "Travels in Georgia and Florida," p.157.

41. "David Taitt's Journal to and through the Upper Creek Nation," in Davies, DAR 5:266.

42. Crane, *Southern Frontier*, pp.190–205; Corkran, *Creek Frontier*, pp.65–70.

43. Fitch, "Journal," p.208.

44. Oglethorpe was in search of allies for his campaigns against the Spanish, but matters of trade concerned the Creeks. "A Ranger's Report," p.221; Corkran, *Creek Frontier*, p.101.

45. Alden, *John Stuart*, pp.17–18.

46. See Corry, *Indian Affairs*, for a look at regulation by Georgia. Phinizy Spalding, *Georgia and South Carolina during the Oglethorpe Period, 1732–1743* (Ann Arbor, Mich.: University Microfilms International, 1976), chapters 2 and 3.

47. See *Atkin Report*, pp.xviii–xix, xxxv, for information on Atkin and his plan. His report to the Board of Trade and his plan for Indian management are reprinted in the book. For more information on the creation of the Indian Department, see John R. Alden, "The Albany Congress and the Creation of the Indian Superintendencies," *Mississippi Valley Historical Review* 27 (September 1940): 193–210.

48. See Alden, *John Stuart,* pp.156–75, for biographical information on Stuart. Clarence W. Alvord's study, *The Mississippi Valley in British Politics: A Study of the Trade, Land Speculation, and Experiments in Imperialism Culminating in the American Revolution,* 2 vols. (1916; reprint, New York: Russell & Russell, 1959), is required reading for an understanding of the policy goals behind the organization of the Indian Department and the Proclamation of 1763.

49. Report of John Stuart to the Lords Commissioners of Trade and Plantations on the Southern Indian Department, March 9, 1764, CO323/17, p.53.

50. Carter, "Observations," p.817.

51. "Southern Governors and Stuart to Egremont, November 10, 1763," in Saunders, CRNC 11:205.

52. Alden, *John Stuart,* p.209. A printed copy of the plan can be found in E. B. O'Callaghan, *Documents Relative to the Colonial History of the State of New York; Procured in Holland, England, and France,* 15 vols. (Albany: Weed, Parsons, & Co., 1856–57), 7:637–41.

53. Alden, *John Stuart,* pp.240–48.

54. O'Callaghan, *Documents* 7:637–41.

55. Governor Johnstone's Observations on the Trade, January 2, 1765, CO323/20, fo.84.

56. Carter, "Observations," pp.817–25.

57. Stuart to Hillsborough, July 14, 1768, CO5/69, fo.214.

58. Carter, "Observations," p.821.

59. Regulations Settled as Necessary for the Better Carrying the Trade with the Indian Nations Surrounding West Florida, 10 April 1765, CO5/66, fo.35. These regulations are reprinted in Alden, *John Stuart,* pp.341–43. Stuart and Johnstone had followed the same procedure at the Choctaw and Chickasaw congress held at Mobile the previous month. Rowland, MPAED, pp.252–54.

60. *Adair's History,* pp.395–96.

61. Shelburne to Stuart, September 13, 1766, copy located in Haldimand Papers, reel 5, fo.57; John Stuart to Shelburne, April 1, 1767, CO5/68, fo.108; Shelburne to Stuart, December 11, 1766, CO5/225, fo.15; Stuart to Shelburne, April 11, 1767, CO5/68, fo.125.

62. Stuart to Shelburne, July 28, 1767, CO5/68, fo.142.

63. Stuart to Shelburne, April 11, 1767, CO5/68, fo.125.

64. Stuart to Shelburne, July 28,1767, CO5/68, fo.136.

65. Journal of the Superintendent's Proceedings, April 21, 1767–June 6, 1767, Gage Papers.

66. The Memoriall of the Merchants and Traders of the Province of Georgia

Trading From Augusta to the Creek Nation, in Stuart's letter of July 28, 1767. CO5/68, fo.142. See also William Struthers to Johnstone, in Rowland, MPAED, p.517.

67. Journal of the Superintendent's Proceedings, April 21, 1767–June 6, 1767, Gage Papers.

68. Report of John Stuart to the Lords Commissioners of Trade and Plantations on the Southern Indian Department, March 9, 1764, CO323/17, p.52.

69. *Georgia Gazette,* August 5, 1767, carried Stuart's announcement. Stuart to Shelburne, July 28, 1767, CO5/68, fo.136.

70. Stuart to Shelburne, October 3, 1767, CO5/68, fo.162.

71. Report of the Lords of Trade to George III, March 7, 1768, CO5/69, fo.60.

72. Ibid.

73. Hillsborough to Stuart and Johnson, April 15, 1768, CO5/69, fo.118. For the reorganization of the Indian Department, see John Stuart to Governors of the Southern District, September 15, 1768, CO5/69, fo.300, and Stuart to Hillsborough, September 15, 1768, CO5/69, fo.260.

74. Alden, *John Stuart,* p.256.

75. Circular Letter to Colonial Governors from Hillsborough, April 15, 1768, CO5/69, fo.115.

76. Stuart to Wright, ? November 1768, CO5/73, fo.180.

77. Stuart to William Bull, December 2, 1769, CO5/71, pt.1, fo.12.

78. Stuart to Hillsborough, July 25, 1769, CO5/70, fo.243.

79. John Stuart to William Bull, December 2, 1769, CO5/71, pt.1, fo.12.

80. "An Act for the Better Regulation of the Indian Trade in the Province of West Florida, 19 May 1770," in Rea and Howard, *Minutes, Journals, and Acts* pp.379–83.

81. Ibid. Trade with the Cussados, an Alabama tribe that had been allowed to settle near Pensacola, was exempted from certain regulations.

82. Address of the Council of West Florida to Hillsborough, July 4, 1770, in Davies, DAR 2:142.

83. Stuart to Hillsborough, July 16, 1770, CO5/71, pt.2, fo.23; Rowland, "Peter Chester," p.10.

84. Alden, *John Stuart,* p.296.

85. Charles Stuart was stationed in Mobile. Abstract of a letter from Charles Stuart to John Stuart, August 26, 1770, CO5/72, fo.89. See also Charles Stuart to Peter Chester, n.d., enclosed in Chester's letter to Hillsborough of April 15, 1771, in Rowland, "Peter Chester," p.48.

86. Georgia Council Meeting, September 5, 1768, in CRG 10:584.

87. Charles Stuart to John Stuart, December 26, 1770, CO5/72, fo.179. Gage did not know "whether the means have been wanting to carry on the Prosecutions or that it has been feared the verdict of jurys would render them ineffectual." Gage to Shelburne, August 20, 1767, in Carter, *Correspondence of General Thomas Gage* 2:144.

88. Peter Chester to Hillsborough, March 9, 1771, in Davies, DAR 3:644–67.

89. *Adair's History,* p.443.

CHAPTER 7: *Consumerism and its Consequences*

1. Bartram, *Travels,* p.184.

2. For example, see CRG 10:571 (September 5, 1768); Answer to Governor Johnstone's Talk by the Upper Creek Headmen, May 16, 1766, CO5/67, fo. 15; Council of Fourteen Towns of Tallipooses, October 11, 1766, CO5/68, fo.89.

3. "Regulations for the Better Carrying on the Trade with the Indian Tribes of the Southern District," in John Stuart to Shelburne, April 1, 1767, CO5/68, fo.110. See Regulation #7.

4. McDowell, *1754–1765,* p.296 (quotation); Rolle, *Humble Petition,* p.56.

5. Lewis, "Spalding's Store," pp.115–28.

6. M. L. Brown, *Firearms in Colonial America: The Impact on History and Technology, 1492–1792* (Washington, D.C.: Smithsonian Institution Press, 1980), p.79.

7. McDowell, *1710–1718,* pp.82, 89, 127, 137, 142, 154, 174, 176; McDowell, *1750–1754,* pp.238, 520; Thomas Norton, *The Fur Trade in Colonial New York, 1686–1776* (Madison: University of Wisconsin Press, 1974), p.31; Alfred Plummer and Richard E. Early, *The Blanket Makers, 1669–1969: A History of Charles Early and Marriott (Witney) Ltd.* (London: Routledge & Kegan Paul, 1969), pp.39, 196.

8. "William Bartram, On Certain Plants and their use by the Indians," Indian Materials, Benjamin Smith Barton Papers, American Philosophical Society Library, Philadelphia, Pennsylvania. Barton noted further that the Indians also used the juice of the *Galium boreale* to dye quills. There are no native species of *Rubia* in North America (*peregrina* denotes "foreign"). *Rubia peregrina* was most likely *Rubia tinctorum,* which was used as a dye in Europe and was commonly called Dyer's Cleavers. Conversation with Dr. John Freeman, Auburn University, April 3, 1991.

9. Norton, *Fur Trade in Colonial New York,* p.31; Carolyn Gilman, *Where Two*

Worlds Meet: The Great Lakes Fur Trade, Publications of the Minnesota Historical Society, Museum Exhibit Series, no.2 (St. Paul: Minnesota Historical Society, 1982), pp.33–34. See Habersham to Martyn, February 3, 1752, in CRG 26:337.

10. "Tariff arranged for the commerce of the Creek and Talapoosa Nation in the General Congress celebrated in Pensacola the days of 31 May and 1 June 1784," in Coker and Watson, *Indian Traders,* p.60; "Prices of goods in the Indian trade under Georgia licenses . . ." in CRG 28, pt.2, pp.121–22.

11. *Adair's History,* p.178.

12. Stuart to Hillsborough, February 6, 1772, CO5/73, fo.46. Miller and Hamell, "Indian-White Contact," pp.324–27.

13. John Stuart to Pownall, August 24, 1765, CO5/66, fo.356; Hudson, *Southeastern Indians,* pp.261–64; Bethune to Cameron, August 27, 1780, CO5/82, fo.92; Wright, *The Only Land They Knew,* pp.218–19; Corkran, *Creek Frontier,* pp.10–11; Harold E. Driver, *Indians of North America,* 2d rev. ed. (Chicago: University of Chicago Press, 1969), pp.509–11.

14. Bartram, *Travels,* p.394. See Cashin, *Lachlan McGillivray,* p.16.

15. "Letter from a Gentleman at Pensacola, October 30, 1764," *British Magazine* 6 (February 1765) 97.

16. Bartram, *Travels,* p.395.

17. Galloway, MPAFD 4:208.

18. Swan, "Position and State of Manners," p.275; Gordon, "Journal," p.385.

19. John Stuart to Pownall, August 24, 1765, CO5/66, fo.356.

20. See Dorothy Downs, "British Influences on Creek and Seminole Men's Clothing, 1733–1858," *Florida Anthropologist* 33 (1980): 46–65, for Scottish influence on clothing and the best overall discussion of this subject.

21. Bartram, *Travels,* p.401.

22. Ibid.; "Letter from a Gentleman," p.97.

23. Romans, *Concise Natural History of East and West Florida,* p.95.

24. Rolle, *Humble Petition,* p.11 (quotation). See Bartram, *Travels,* pp.214–15, for a description of a Creek orgy. For a good sample of what sort of behavior a visitor to Creek towns could observe, see David Taitt's journals to the Upper and Lower Creek towns, in Davies, DAR 5:251–81. Rolle, *Humble Petition,* catalogues the frequency of alcohol abuse among East Florida Seminoles; for instance see pp.48, 52.

25. Frank G. Speck, *Ceremonial Songs of the Creek and Yuchi Indians,* Music transcribed by Jacob D. Sapir, University of Pennsylvania Museum Anthropo-

logical Publications, vol.1, no.2 (Philadelphia: University Museum, 1911), p.197.

26. Nuñez, "Stiggins Narrative," p.35.

27. *De Brahm's Report,* p.108.

28. *Adair's History,* p.394.

29. Anthropologists and psychologists have presented various reasons for excessive consumption of alcoholic beverages among Native Americans. Very few seem to think that the Indians simply enjoyed it—most look for deeper meaning. None of their theories seem appropriate from an eighteenth-century Creek perspective. For those interested, the following works provide an entry into this troubled field: Michael W. Everett, Jack O. Waddell, and Dwight B. Heath, eds., *Cross-Cultural Approaches to the Study of Alcohol: An Interdisciplinary Perspective* (The Hague, Netherlands: Mouton, 1976); Joan Weibel-Orlando, "Indians, Ethnicity, and Alcohol: Contrasting Perceptions of the Ethnic Self and Alcohol Use," in *The American Experience with Alcohol: Contrasting Cultural Perspectives,* edited by Linda A. Bennett and Genevieve M. Ames, pp.201–26 (New York: Plenum Press, 1985); Nancy Oestreich Lurie, "The World's Oldest On-Going Protest Demonstration: North American Indian Drinking Patterns," *Pacific Historical Review* 40 (August 1971): 311–32.

30. One of the earliest published price schedules is found in "Oglethorpe's Treaty with the Lower Creek Indians," *Georgia Historical Quarterly* 4 (March 1920): 14–15.

31. Carter, "Observations," p.829.

32. According to *Adair's History,* p.457, Indians constructed their own saddles from wood and buffalo and bear hides. Mortar was willing to pay only one pound of leather for rum. Answer to Governor Johnstone's Talk to the Upper Creeks, May 16, 1766, CO5/67, fo.15. Price schedules can be found in Rowland, MPAED, p.215, and CRG 28, pt.2, pp.121–22.

33. Bartram, "Observations," p.42.

34. Hudson, *Southeastern Indians,* pp.312–13; Holland, "Path between the Wars," pp.223–45; Report of John Stuart to the Lords Commissioners of Trade and Plantations on the Southern Indian Department, March 9, 1764, CO323/17, p.48.

35. George Fenwick Jones, ed. and trans., "Commissary Von Reck's Report on Georgia," *Georgia Historical Quarterly* 47 (March 1963): 105; Emisteseguo's speech, Meeting of Upper Creeks, April 10, 1764, Gage Papers; McDowell, *1754–1765,* p.67; *Adair's History,* p.277.

36. Meeting of Upper Creeks, April 10, 1764, Gage Papers.

37. Bartram, *Travels,* p.399. Whether Creeks also destroyed items that were

still usable, as opposed to "worn-out," is unclear. Some accounts of the Busk relate that households and utensils were cleaned rather than destroyed. Nuñez, "Stiggins Narrative," pp.40–41, 131–33.

38. *Adair's History*, 186–87.

39. Fabel and Rea, "Lieutenant Thomas Campbell's Sojourn," pp.308–9. Campbell also reported that a man's horses and dogs were shot at his death. William S. Willis, Jr., "Patrilineal Institutions in Southeastern North America," *Ethnohistory* 10 (Winter 1963): 254; Swan, "Position and State of Manners," p.270, relates that a warrior's pipes, ornaments, and "warlike appendages" still followed him to the grave in 1791.

40. Romans, *Concise Natural History of East and West Florida*, pp.98–99. This is confirmed by archaeological evidence. Peter A. Brannon, *The Southern Indian Trade, Being Particularly a Study of Material from the Tallapoosa River Valley of Alabama* (Montgomery, Ala.: Paragon Press, 1938), p.41.

41. David Taitt to John Stuart, November 22, 1772, CO5/74, fo.64.

42. McGillivray to McLatchy, December 25, 1784, in Caughey, *McGillivray,* p.85.

43. Galphin Account Books, folder 1, entry for January 18, 1767. Kettles as well as gourds appear in "An Indian Camp as They Make Them When They Are Hunting," in Hvidt, *Von Reck's Voyage,* p.117. See also "Indians going a-hunting," p.126, in the same work. One anthropologist has asserted that the women's persistence in manufacturing their own utensils points to the stability of the female role, whereas that of the male was in a state of flux. This study needs to be updated and new archaeological evidence examined. Carol T. Mason, "Eighteenth Century Culture Change among the Lower Creeks" *Florida Anthropologist* 16 (September 1963): 68–73. Brass and copper kettles are listed on both the following tariff lists: Congress of Pensacola, 1765, in Rowland, MPAED, p.215, and Journal of the Superintendent's Proceedings, April 21, 1767–June 6, 1767, Gage Papers. Arthur J. Ray explores the adoption of certain trade goods by nomadic tribes in "Indians as Consumers in the Eighteenth Century," in *Old Trails and New Directions: Papers of the Third North American Fur Trade Conference,* edited by Carol M. Judd and Arthur J. Ray (Toronto: University of Toronto Press, 1980), p.251.

44. W[illiam] B[artram], "Some Hints & Observations concerning the Civilization of the Indians, or Aborigines of America," 1792, in Henry Knox Papers, Massachusetts Historical Society, Boston; Mason, "Eighteenth Century Culture Change," pp.67–68; Bartram, *Travels,* p.401; Fundaburk and Douglass, *Sun Circles and Human Hands,* p.15; Bartram, "Observations," p.291.

45. Corkran, *Creek Frontier,* pp.25–26, discusses "Creek Young Men." The

records of the British Indian Department are filled with references to the problems of unruly youth, or "restless young men."

46. Roderick MackIntosh to John Stuart, November 16, 1767, in Stuart to Gage, December 26, 1767, Gage Papers.

47. William G. McLoughlin, "Cherokee Anomie, 1794–1810," in *The Cherokee Ghost Dance: Essays on the Southeastern Indians, 1789–1861* (Macon, Ga.: Mercer University Press, 1984), pp.30ff.

48. Mason, "Eighteenth Century Culture Change," pp.68–69.

49. For instance, see Swan's account in "Position and State of Manners," p.273.

50. Logan, *History of the Upper Country of South Carolina,* 1:288.

51. Bartram, *Travels,* 357; *Letters, Journals, and Writings of Benjamin Hawkins* 1:47–48; J. N. B. Hewitt, *Notes on the Creek Indians,* edited by John R. Swanton, Bureau of American Ethnology Bulletin no.123 (Washington, D.C.: Government Printing Office, 1939), p.128; Nuñez, "Stiggins Narrative," p.132.

52. Bartram, *Travels,* pp.382–83.

53. *Adair's History,* p.275, see also 297–99.

54. Corkran, *Creek Frontier,* pp.113–14, 123, 128–30, 146–48, 150, 153, 163; David H. Corkran, *The Cherokee Frontier: Conflict and Survival, 1740–1762* (Norman: University of Oklahoma Press, 1962), pp.22–25, 33–35; Hatley, "The Dividing Paths," pp.269–73, for information on the Creek-Cherokee wars.

55. Bartram, *Travels,* p.216.

56. For more information on the Choctaws, see Patricia K. Galloway, "Choctaw Factionalism and Civil War, 1746–1750," in *The Choctaw before Removal,* edited by Carolyn Keller Reeves, pp.120–56 (Jackson: University Press of Mississippi, 1985), and White, *Roots of Dependency.*

57. Bartram, *Travels,* p.348.

58. Holland, "Path between the Wars," pp.120–22, 126–27, 141–45, 222. The most important Upper Creek micos—including the Mortar, Emisteseguo, and the Young Lieutenant—were involved in both fighting the Choctaws and attempting to negotiate with them.

59. *Letters, Journals, and Writings of Benjamin Hawkins* 1:320.

60. Bartram, "Travels in Georgia and Florida," p.171.

61. Talleachey's Talk to John Stuart, April 26, 1772, CO5/73, fo.274; Bartram, *Travels,* pp.182, 306–7; William C. Sturtevant, "Creek into Seminole," in *North American Indians in Historical Perspective,* edited by Eleanor Leacock and Nancy Oestreich Lurie (New York: Random House, 1971), pp.92–128;

James W. Covington, "Migration of the Seminoles into Florida, 1700–1820," *Florida Historical Quarterly* 46 (1968): 340–57. Benjamin Hawkins states that the Seminoles were composed of people who had left "the towns of Oconee, Sauwoogelo, Eufaula, Tummaultlau, Palachocola and Hitchiti." *Letters, Journals, and Writings of Benjamin Hawkins* 1:289. He listed seven Seminole towns in 1799.

62. Bartram, *Travels,* p.367, lists nine towns; Swanton, *Early History,* pp.399–401; John Stuart to Hillsborough, February 7, 1772, in Davies, DAR 5:36. Brent Richards Weisman, *Like Beads on a String: A Culture History of the Seminole Indians in Northern Peninsular Florida* (Tuscaloosa: University of Alabama Press, 1989), p.59, states that the British "regulation" of limiting villages to one trader placed a "premium" on the founding of new Indian villages in Florida. This observation ignores the fact that regulation of the trade was almost entirely lacking during this period. British trade regulation had no impact, one way or the other, on the establishment of new Seminole sites.

63. Bartram, *Travels,* p.214.

64. John Stuart to Hillsborough, January 27, 1770, CO5/71, pt.1, fo.69.

65. Charles Stuart to John Stuart, December 2, 1772, in Davies, DAR 5:228–29; Corkran, *Creek Frontier,* pp.280–81.

66. Talk of Topoye, alias the Fighter, to Deputy Superintendent, June 23, 1766, CO5/67, fo.236; Stuart to Board of Trade, December 2, 1766, CO5/67, fo.199, *Pennsylvania Gazette,* December 11, 1766; Gage to Shelburne, April 29, 1767, in Carter, *Correspondence of General Thomas Gage* 1:138; Taitt to Stuart, October 31, 1772, CO5/74, fo.30.

67. Stuart to Gage, July 2, 1768, Gage Papers.

68. *Adair's History,* p.271.

69. One village along the Oconee River caused repeated problems. See Corkran, *Creek Frontier,* pp.262, 275. John Stuart to William Bull, December 2, 1769, CO5/71, pt.1, fo.12.

70. See Affidavit of William Frazier, March 16, 1768, in Stuart to Gage, July 2, 1768, Gage Papers.

71. In all probability, this village was established after Houmahta's detached Oconee River village was burned by whites in 1767 and again in 1770. Corkran, *Creek Frontier,* pp.262, 275; CRG 10:272–78; Grant to Gage, August 27, 1767, Gage Papers. The settlement had sprang up as a convenient location for a tippling house and trading post. John Stuart to Haldimand, February 3, 1774, in Davies, DAR 8:35; David Taitt to John Stuart, January 22, 1774, CO5/75, fo.49. Pucknawheatly should not be confused with the Upper Creek Town of

Puckantallahassee. The term *E-puc-cun-nau* denotes a peach in Muskogean. Stuart is very precise in saying the village was located on the Ocmulgee in 1774, but by 1818, the Standing Peach Tree had shifted to the Chattahoochee. This was due to the repeated advance of the Georgia boundary. The Standing Peach Tree is famous to this day as the Chattahoochee site that eventually grew into Atlanta, Georgia. Swanton, *Early History,* pp.272–74, and plate 9: "Towns of the Creek Confederacy as shown on the Early Map of Georgia, 1818." Franklin M. Garrett, *Atlanta and Environs: A Chronicle of Its People and Events,* 2 vols., facsimile reprint of the 1954 edition by Lewis Historical Publishing Co. (Athens: University of Georgia Press, 1969), 1:8–19.

72. Galphin Account Books, folder 2, entry for March 10, 1772; Conference between Sir James Wright and Upper Creek Indians, April 14, 1774, in Davies, DAR 8:93. Complaints had been lodged against the White Boy by headmen: Complaints of Sundry Headmen in the Creek Nation for nonperformance of some articles of the last treaty of Augusta, January 3, 1774, CO5/75, fo.46.

73. Report of John Stuart to the Lords Commissioners of Trade and Plantations on the Southern Indian Department, March 9, 1764, CO323/17, p.48.

74. *Nairne's Muskhogean Journals,* pp.34–35. Nairne says that a dead man's debts would be paid before any other and that if the family could not easily take care of the debts, the entire town would contribute toward paying off the debt.

75. "Regulations for the Better Carrying on the Trade with the Indian Tribes of the Southern District," in John Stuart to Shelburne, April 1, 1767, CO5/68, fo.110, Regulation #9. The West Florida regulations of 1770 carried the same restrictions. "An Act for the Better Regulation of the Indian Trade in the Province of West Florida, May 19, 1770," in Rea and Howard, *Minutes, Journals, and Acts,* p.38.

76. For their explanation, see Memorial of Traders to Creek and Cherokee Nations to Governor James Wright, June 1771, in Davies, DAR 3:125–27. *Atkin Report,* p.35.

77. Bartram, *Travels,* pp.216, 217.

78. Journal of the Superintendent's Proceedings, April 21, 1767–June 6, 1767, Gage Papers; Report of John Stuart to the Lords Commissioners of Trade and Plantations on the Southern Indian Department, March 9, 1764, CO323/17, p.48. There is no indication that the Creeks were charged interest on their debts during the colonial period.

79. John Stuart to Germain, October 26, 1776, CO5/78, fo.15.

80. Ibid; Alexander Hewatt, *An Historical Account of the Rise and Progress of the Colonies of South Carolina and Georgia,* 2 vols. (1779; reprint, Spartanburg,

S.C.: Reprint Co., 1962), p.300; Galphin, MacKay, and Jackson and McLean to John Stuart, November 13, 1771, CO5/73, fo.99. See Minchinton, *Growth of English Overseas Trade*, pp.17ff., for a general discussion of the credit situation worldwide. Samuel Douglas to John Wallace, June 7, 1787, Colonial Dames of America, File No. 965, folder 66, John Wallace Papers, Georgia Historical Society, Savannah; Bartram, *Travels*, pp.215–17; McDowell, *1754–1765*, pp.44–45.

81. *Adair's History*, p.443.

CHAPTER 8: *Politics and the Trade Alliance*

1. Corkran, *Creek Frontier*, pp.15, 61.

2. For example, Council of Fourteen Towns of Tallipooses, October 11, 1766, CO5/68, fo.89; Juricek, *Georgia Treaties*, p.53.

3. CRG 8:432.

4. Emisteseguo for Upper Chiefs, April 20, 1767, in Journal of the Superintendent's Proceedings, April 21, 1767–June 6, 1767, Gage Papers.

5. Swanton, *Social Organization*, p.321.

6. For instance, in 1755, after holding talks with leading Cherokees, the Gun Merchant of Okchai called a general meeting of all the headmen of the Upper Towns to inform them of the state of affairs with that nation and the British. McDowell, *1754–1765*, p.62; Fitch, "Journal," p.178. Headmen from all the Upper Towns assembled at Tuckabatchee in 1759 to hear what Edmund Atkin, the first Superintendent of Indian Affairs, had to say. Corkran, *Creek Frontier*, p.206. In 1768, representatives from both the Upper and the Lower towns assembled and appointed Emisteseguo of Little Tallassee to visit Georgia and discuss their mutual concerns CRG (September 3, 1768) 10:568. Louis Milfort, *Memoirs; or, A Quick Glance at My Various Travels and My Sojourn in the Creek Nation*, edited and translated by Ben C. McCary (1802; reprint, Kennesaw, Ga.: Continental Book Co., 1959), p.129, reports that the yearly assembly of all the headmen of the nation was in May.

7. David Taitt to John Stuart, March 16, 1772, CO5/73, fo.259; "David Taitt's Journal to and through the Upper Creek Nation," in Davies, DAR 5:268.

8. Unfortunately, we do not know the precise details of the arrangements. Swanton, *Social Organization*, pp.310–11. "Talks" from meetings held at Cheehaw Square can be found in CRG 12:148ff., 316ff., CO5/69, fo.131, CO5/70, fo.60. One Talk from Apalachicola can be found in CRG 9:74. No meetings listed in the CO5/65–75 were held at Coweta. Among the Upper Towns, three meetings were held at Little Tallassee: Meeting of Head Men at Little Talsey,

April 10, 1764, Gage Papers; Meeting of Head Men at Little Talsey, July 15, 1764, Gage Papers; and CO5/574. One meeting is listing as Great Tallassees, CO5/72, fo.101. Six were held at Okchai: CO5/67, fo.15; CO5/72, fo.19; CO5/73, fo.259; CO5/75, fo.19; CO5/72, fo.346; and CRG 9:70ff. One was held at Tuckabatchee: CO5/73, fo.259. In addition, two meetings of Upper chiefs did not indicate which town: CO5/75, fo.69, and CO5/68, fo.89.

9. Corkran, *Creek Frontier,* p.x.

10. Nuñez, "Stiggins Narrative," p.31. Though he was more properly referring to the National Council instituted by Hawkins, his observation holds true for the earlier period.

11. Juricek, *Creek Treaties,* p.309.

12. The most pointed case of British favor helping a Creek headman is Stuart's friendship with Emisteseguo. However, it should be pointed out that Emisteseguo was a renowned warrior and an influential member of the Tyger clan who first gained prominence after his appointment as spokesman for the Upper Creek Towns at the 1763 Congress of Augusta. The British, though they tried, could not displace the Mortar. And to their dismay, they found they could not buy him with a Great Medal either.

13. For instance, as early as 1718, Theophilus Hastings, the South Carolina agent to the Creeks, was told that he should deliver commissions "only to such of the Head Men as shall be voluntarily chosen and recommended by the Indians themselves." McDowell, *1710–1718,* p.311; Holland, "Path between the Wars," pp.32–33.

14. Congress at Pensacola, 1765, in Rowland, MPAED, p.199.

15. Journal of the Picolata Congress, in Covington, *British Meet the Seminoles,* p.28. Also Congress of Augusta, November 12, 1768, CO5/70, fo.386.

16. Swanton, *Social Organization,* pp.194, 269; Rowland, MPAED, p.209.

17. Georgia Council Meeting, September 3, 1768, in CRG 10:568.

18. McDowell, *1750–1754,* p.403.

19. Ibid., pp.407–8 (quotation on p.407).

20. McDowell, *1754–1765,* pp.62–71 (quotation on p.63). The Gun Merchant's attempts to lower trade prices are detailed in Corkran, *Creek Frontier,* pp.160–73.

21. Mortar's Talk, Congress of Pensacola, 1765, in Rowland, MPAED, pp.204–5.

22. The effect of the Proclamation of 1763 is discussed in chapter 6. Journal of the Superintendent's Proceedings, April 21, 1767–June 6, 1767, Gage Papers.

23. Report of the Lords of Trade to George III, March 7, 1768, CO5/69, fo.60; Stuart to Hillsborough, September 15, 1768, CO5/69, fo.260.

24. Proceedings of Congress with Upper Creeks, October 29–November 2, 1771, in Davies, DAR 3:222–23.

25. Mad Dog's Speech, Congress of Augusta, 1767, in Journal of the Superintendent's Proceedings, April 21, 1767–June 6, 1767, Gage Papers.

26. The raid, which caused quite a stir, was undertaken with the knowledge of the commissary Roderick McIntosh. Affidavit of William Frazier, March 16, 1768, in Stuart to Gage, July 2, 1768, Gage Papers; Proceedings of Congress with Upper Creeks, October 29–November 2, 1771, in Davies, DAR 3:221.

27. At a Congress Held at Mobile in the Province of West Florida, December 31, 1771–January 6, 1772, CO5/73, fo.67; Regulations for the Better Carrying on the Trade with the Indian Tribes in the Southern District, in John Stuart to Lord Shelburne, April 1, 1767, CO5/68, fo.110, Regulations #15 & #16.

28. David Taitt to John Stuart, May 4, 1772, CO5/73, fo.263; Anonymous, "A Gurnal of my Travling to the Indinas Countrary [1767]," Georgia Historical Society, Savannah, File No. 10.

29. Bartram, *Travels*, p.387.

30. The situation was the same among the Chickasaws and Choctaws. At a Congress Held at Mobile in the Province of West Florida, December 31, 1771–January 6, 1772, CO5/73, fo.67.

31. John Stuart to Dartmouth, May 6, 1774, CO5/75, fo.117.

32. See John Stuart to Dartmouth, May 6, 1774, CO5/75, fo.117; John Stuart to William Bull, December 2, 1769, CO5/71, fo.12.

33. John Stuart to Lord George Germaine, August 23, 1776, CO5/77, fo.247.

34. McDowell, *1754–1765*, p.64.

35. Proceedings of Congress with Upper Creeks, October 29–November 2, 1771, in Davies, DAR 3:217.

36. Corkran, *Creek Frontier*, pp.152, 171; Bartram, "Observations," p.37.

37. Juricek, *Georgia Treaties*, p.15. See also "Oglethorpe's Treaty," pp.3–16; Louis De Vorsey, Jr., "Indian Boundaries in Colonial Georgia," *Georgia Historical Quarterly* 54 (Spring 1970): 65; De Vorsey's map in *The Indian Boundary in the Southern Colonies, 1763–1775* (Chapel Hill: University of North Carolina Press, 1966), fig. 17, delineates the boundary.

38. A quick summary of Creek cessions in colonial Georgia is De Vorsey, "Indian Boundaries in Colonial Georgia," pp.63–78. Georgia's early history

was enlivened by the actions of Mary Musgrove Bosomworth. Mary, the niece of Brims, married a succession of fortune hunters who laid claim to the sea islands excluded in the 1733 treaty. The affair is put into the context of Creek diplomatic history by Corkran, *Creek Frontier,* pp.131ff. CRG 28, pt.1, pp.266–67. See also Fisher, "Mary Musgrove," pp.412–61.

39. Holland, "Path between the Wars," pp.1–47; Jones, *License for Empire,* pp.36–57.

40. For white attitudes toward Indians, see Robert F. Berkhofer, Jr., *The White Man's Indian: Images of the American Indian from Columbus to the Present* (New York: Alfred A. Knopf, 1978), pp.129–31; Wilbur R. Jacobs, "British Colonial Attitudes and Policies toward the Indian in the American Colonies," in *Attitudes of Colonial Powers toward the American Indian,* edited by Howard Peckham and Charles Gibson (Salt Lake City: University of Utah Press, 1969), pp.98–99; Holland, "Path between the Wars," pp.239–48.

41. Georgia Council Meeting, September 3, 1768, in CRG 10:567.

42. Stuart to Gage, December 26, 1767, Gage Papers.

43. Journal of the Superintendent's Proceedings, Congress of Augusta, November 12, 1768, CO5/70, fo.386; Philemon Kemp to Governor of Georgia, including Talks from Emisteseguo and Gun Merchant, June 6, 1771, in Davies, DAR 3:118–19; Bartram, "Travels in Georgia and Florida," pp.138–40; Proceedings of Congress with Upper Creeks, October 29–November 2, 1771, in Davies, DAR 3:221–23.

44. Stuart to Hillsborough, July 14, 1768, CO5/69, fo.216. See Georgia Council Meeting, September 5, 1768, in CRG 10:575–80.

45. Thomas Gage to John Stuart, October 16, 1770, CO5/72, fo.41.

46. John Stuart to Dartmouth, January 4, 1773, CO5/74, fo.22.

47. Romans, *Concise Natural History of East and West Florida,* p.91.

48. This idea—the active encouragement of debt in order to secure land cessions—was an American innovation and is discussed in detail in chapter 9.

49. Stuart to Hillsborough, February 9, 1772, CO5/73, fo.95.

50. "David Taitt's Journal to and through the Upper Creek Nation," in Davies, DAR 5:271.

51. Ibid., 5:274.

52. Percy S. Flippin, "The Royal Government in Georgia, 1752–1776," *Georgia Historical Quarterly* 10 (March 1926): 15.

53. Affidavit of Joseph Dawes, August 4, 1772, in Davies, DAR 5:161–62. One could argue that the New Purchase of 1773 did disrupt Creek life, but outlawry contributed more to Creek actions of December 1773 than distress over loss of territory.

54. The proceedings of the conference are found in CO5/662, fo.53–58. De Vorsey, *Indian Boundary*, pp.161–72. For information on how land was to be sold and how the money was to be distributed, see Dartmouth to Wright, December 12, 1772, in Davies, DAR 5:243–45. Settlers began taking up the land immediately. Cashin, "Winners and Losers," pp.240–42; Cashin, *Lachlan McGillivray*, pp.271–80.

55. Bartram, *Travels*, p.382.

56. The situation in the Creek country is described in detail in David Taitt's journals to the Upper and Lower Creek towns, in Davies, DAR 5:251–82.

57. Bartram, "Travels in Georgia and Florida," p.138.

58. Bartram, *Travels*, p.55.

59. Abstract of a Letter from David Taitt, January 3, 1774, CO5/75, fo.45; Complaints of Sundry Headmen in the Creek nation for nonperformance of some articles of the last Treaty of Augusta, January 3, 1774, CO5/75, fo.46.

60. John Stuart to Frederick Haldimand, February 3, 1774, in Davies, DAR 8:36.

61. M. Thomas Hatley, "The Eighteenth-Century Tallapoosa Landscape Re-Visited," in Gregory A. Waselkov, John W. Cottier, and Craig T. Sheldon, Jr., "Archaeological Excavations at the Early Historic Creek Indian Town of Fusi-hatchee (Phase 1, 1988–1989)," a report to the National Science Foundation, May 1990, Grant No. BNS-8718934, p.92.

62. For instance, see Hamer and Rogers, *Papers of Henry Laurens* 8:186, 9:210, 249.

63. Paredes and Plante, "Creek Indian Population Trends," pp.3–28; Cameron to John Stuart, June 3, 1774, CO5/75, fo.174.

64. At a meeting held at Oakchoys, April 19, 1772, Mico Lucko to John Stuart, from Taitt, CO5/73, fo.268.

65. The best study available on Creek land cessions is De Vorsey, *Indian Boundary*. Regarding the colonial land cessions, one should keep in mind the vast extent of the Creek land claims and the small number of Creeks, most of whom were concentrated in towns along interior river valleys.

66. Talk from Stuart to Ruling Chiefs of Creek Nation, September 15, 1774, CO5/76, fo.6.

67. Report of John Stuart to the Lords Commissioners of Trade and Planta-tions on the Southern Indian Department, March 9, 1764, CO323/17, p.30.

68. Johnstone to Conway, June 23, 1766, in Rowland, MPAED, p.511.

69. Report of John Stuart to the Lords Commissioners of Trade and Planta-tions on the Southern Indian Department, March 9, 1764, CO323/17, p.30; CRG 12:316–17. In 1774, Alexander Cameron, Stuart's Cherokee deputy, re-

ported that when one murderer escaped before his family could put him to death, his family persuaded the victim's family to take goods valued at seven hundred pounds of leather in compensation. Cameron to Stuart, March 1, 1774, in Davies, DAR 8:57–58.

70. McDowell, *1750–1754*, pp.316–17; John Stuart to Lords Commissioners of Trade, March 23, 1764, CO323/17, fo.527, photocopy from the Library of Congress, Washington, D.C.

71. Stuart to Lords Commissioners of Trade, March 23, 1764, CO323/17, fo.527.

72. McDowell, *1750–1754*, p.279.

73. For example, Emisteseguo's speech, in Davies, DAR 8:93–94.

74. CRG 9:115, 171, 150.

75. Corkran, *Creek Frontier*, pp.155–56.

76. McDowell, *1750–1754*, p.279.

77. Ibid., pp.279–80ff.

78. Council of Chiefs of 14 Towns of the Tallapooses and Two of the Chiefs of the Lower Creeks, October 11, 1766, CO5/68, fo.89; Taitt to Stuart, March 16, 1772, CO5/73, fo.259; Georgia Council Meeting, April 1772, in CRG 12:317.

79. Corkran, *Creek Frontier*, p.259.

80. Nuñez, "Stiggins Narrative," p.139. In 1715, Creeks massacred their traders as their opening volley in the Yamasee War. The Cherokees, who decided to stay out of the conflict, killed the Creek diplomats in their towns. Corkran, *Creek Frontier*, p.59.

81. Journal of the Congress of Augusta, 1763, in Saunders, CRNC 11:199–200; Congress at Pensacola, 1765, in Rowland, MPAED, p.192.

82. Journal of the Superintendent's Proceedings, April 21, 1767–June 6, 1767, Gage Papers.

83. Corkran, *Creek Frontier*, pp.110–11.

84. McDowell, *1750–1754*, p.316.

85. "David Taitt's Journal to and through the Lower Creek Nation," in Davies, DAR 5:275–78; Talk to Chiefs and Leaders of Lower Creek Nation from John Stuart, January 20, 1772, CO5/73, fo.53; Tomatchichi's Talk of April 18, 1772, CO5/73, fo.270.

86. For examples, see Corkran, *Creek Frontier*, pp.177, 195, 226–27, 234; Answer to Governor from Upper Creek Headmen, May 16, 1766, in Rowland, MPAED, pp.526–31 (murder of John Kemp); CRG 10:272–73 (Oconee burned, July 26, 1767); Tallechea's Talk in Covington, *British Meet the Seminoles*, p.57; Grant's Talk of June 1, 1768, in ibid., p.58; Stuart to Shelburne, October 3, 1767, CO5/68; Chester to Hillsborough, April 13, 1771, in Rowland,

"Peter Chester," p.44; Gage to Hillsborough, June 4, 1771, in Carter, *Correspondence of General Thomas Gage* 1:151, 300; George Galphin to John Stuart, February 19, 1771, CO5/72, fo.175; James Grant to Thomas Gage, August 27, 1767, Gage Papers; CRG 10:272–78.

87. Gordon, "Journal," p.384. Creek hospitality was well-known: "Ranger's Report," pp.218–22; Bartram, "Observations," p.41; Nuñez, "Stiggins Narrative," p.34.

88. Abstract of letter from David Taitt to John Stuart, September 24, 1773, CO5/75, fo.15; Fitch, "Journal," pp.178–80; *Letters, Journals, and Writings of Benjamin Hawkins* 1:18. Choctaw traders were frequently assaulted. See Abstract of David Taitt to John Stuart, November 12, 1773, CO5/75, fo.18.

89. Abstract of a letter from David Taitt to John Stuart, November 12, 1773, CO5/75, fo.18.

90. Charles Stuart to Peter Chester, n.d., enclosed in Chester's letter of April 15, 1771, to Hillsborough, in Rowland, "Peter Chester," p.49.

91. Ellis to Board of Trade, October 25, 1758, CRG 28, pt.1, p.166.

92. Wolf's Answer to a Joint Talk received from James Wright and John Stuart, April 29, 1766, CO5/67, fo.41.

93. John Stuart to Upper Creeks, December 17, 1766, CO5/68, fo.95; CRG 9:115.

94. Corkran, *Creek Frontier*, p.280; To the Great Chiefs of the Upper Creek Nation from John Stuart, January 20, 1772, CO5/73, fo.55.

95. Journal of the 1768 Augusta Congress, CO5/70, fo.386.

96. Corkran, *Creek Frontier*, pp.229–30; CRG 9:111–17.

97. Rolle, *Humble Petition*, p.15.

98. Answer of Headmen of the Lower Creek Nation to Stuart's Talk, September 19, 1767, CO5/68, fo.135.

99. Stuart to Dartmouth, February 13, 1774, CO5/75; *South Carolina Gazette*, January 31, 1774; Governor Sir James Wright to Earl of Dartmouth, January 31, 1774, in Davies, DAR 8:30–32; Proceedings of the congress at Savannah, October 20, 1774, CO5/664, fo.13.

100. John Stuart to Earl of Dartmouth, February 13, 1774, in Davies, DAR 8:48–49; David Taitt to John Stuart, January 22, 1774, CO5/75, fo.49; *South Carolina Gazette*, February 14, 1774. At first it was believed that White and Sherrill had been pursuing horse thieves and killed the Indian, which was the story that Ogulki gave out. Conference between Sir James Wright and the Creek Indians, April 14, 1774, in Davies, DAR 5:94; David Taitt to John Stuart, January 22, 1774, CO5/75, fo.49.

101. David Taitt to John Stuart, January 22, 1774, CO5/75, fo.49.

102. Report of Sir James Wright on the condition of the province of Georgia, on 20th September 1773, in *Letters from Governor Sir James Wright*, p.167; Paredes and Plante, "Creek Indian Population Trends," p.14.

103. James Wright to Earl of Dartmouth, January 31, 1774, in Davies, DAR 8:31.

104. "An Aggregate and Valuation of Exports of Produce from the Province of Georgia, with the Number of Vessels and Tonnage employed therein, annually distinguished, from the Year 1754 to 1773, Compiled by William Brown, Comptroller and Searcher of his Majesty's Customs in the Port of Savannah," in Romans, *Concise Natural History of East and West Florida*, p.104; Coleman, *American Revolution in Georgia*, pp.66–67; Cashin, "Winner and Losers," pp.240–75; Alden, *John Stuart*, p.306.

105. At a Meeting of the Abeikas, Tallipooses, and Alibamas at the Little Tallassies, February 4, 1774, Talk by Emisteseguo, CO5/75, fo.23.

106. Abstract of a letter from David Taitt, January 3, 1774, CO5/75, fo.45; Abstract of letter from John McIntosh, March 12, 1774, CO5/75, fo.131.

107. At a Meeting held at Sugar town the 24th Day of February, 1774, of the Warriors, Headmen, and Beloved Men of the Middle and Lower Cherokee Settlements, CO5/75, fo.85; John Stuart to the Earl of Dartmouth, May 6, 1774, CO5/75, fo.117.

108. Conference between Governor Sir James Wright and Upper Creek Indians, April 14, 1774, in Davies, DAR 8:91.

109. John Stuart to Dartmouth, May 6, 1774, CO5/75, fo.117.

110. Emisteseguo to John Stuart, April 19, 1772, CO5/73, fo.272; A Talk from the Upper Creeks to John Stuart, February 4, 1774, CO5/75, fo.67.

111. David Taitt to John Stuart, December 17, 1774, CO5/76, fo.37; Georgia Council Meeting, August 30, 1774, CRG 12:405–9.

112. Charles Stuart to John Stuart, December 12, 1774, CO5/76, fo.35.

113. The Bryan lease lacked the "signatures" of the leading Creek headmen from both the Upper and Lower towns, and it did not have the backing of the leading Lower Town of Coweta, which was critical. See "Lease of Land from the Creek Indians to Jonathan Bryan, October 28, 1774," Jonathan Bryan Papers, file 98, item 1, Georgia Historical Society, Savannah. John Stuart to Dartmouth, January 3, 1775, CO5/76, fo.30. Bryan's activities are recounted in Alan Gallay, *The Formation of a Planter Elite: Jonathan Bryan and the Southern Colonial Frontier* (Athens: University of Georgia Press, 1989), pp.127–52; Corkran, *Creek Frontier*, pp.286–87.

114. Conference Between Governor Sir James Wright and Upper Creek Indians, April 14, 1774, in Davies, DAR 8:90–91.

115. Corkran, *Creek Frontier,* p.285–86; John Stuart to Dartmouth, October 6, 1774, C05/75, fo.230; Proceedings of the congress at Savannah, October 20, 1774, C05/664, fo.13.

116. Alden, *John Stuart,* pp.312–13.

117. Stuart to Dartmouth, December 15, 1774, in Davies, DAR 8:245.

CHAPTER 9: *Old Needs and New Partners*

1. *South Carolina Gazette,* October 3, 1774.

2. C. Ashley Ellefson, "James Habersham and Georgia Loyalism, 1764–1775," *Georgia Historical Quarterly* 44 (December 1960): 361–62; Sellers, *Charleston Business,* pp.178–91; James Habersham, *The Letters of the Honorable James Habersham, 1756–1775,* Georgia Historical Society Collections, vol. 6 (Savannah: Georgia Historical Society, 1904), p.67.

3. Sellers, *Charleston Merchants,* p.209.

4. Circular letter to All the Governors on the Continent from Lord Dartmouth, October 19, 1774, C05/75, fo.198.

5. John Stuart to Dartmouth, May 20, 1775, C05/76, fo.120.

6. Stuart to Dartmouth, September 17, 1775, C05/76, fo.172; Stuart to Dartmouth, July 21, 1775, C05/76, fo.150; Stuart to Germaine, October 26, 1776, C05/76, fo.15.

7. Habersham, *Letters,* p.235.

8. Stuart was forced to flee South Carolina because it was widely believed he had encouraged the Cherokees to attack the backcountry. The best account of the role of the southeastern Indians during the Revolution is James H. O'Donnell III, *Southern Indians in the American Revolution* (Knoxville: University of Tennessee Press, 1973).

9. Cameron to John Stuart, June 3, 1774, C05/75, fo.174.

10. John Stuart to the Cowetas, August 15, 1775, C05/76, fo.181.

11. A Talk to the Honble. John Stewart Esquire Sole Agent and Superintendent of Indian Affairs for the Southern District in Answer to his of 15th August 1775 to the Upper Creeks, dated September 20, 1775, Papers of Sir Henry Clinton, 1750–1812, William L. Clements Library, Ann Arbor, Michigan. Stuart's talk is "To the Great and Small Medal Chiefs and Rulers of the Cowetas, Tallapusses, Abechkas, and Alibamons, from John Stuart, August 15, 1775, C05/76, fo.181.

12. "Talk to the Honble. John Stewart Esquire." Stuart was awarded the honorific title of Alabama Micco at the 1771 Congress of Pensacola. According to the Creeks, "As the Alibamas are great in war and in peace and solicitous for the good of all the tribes, and as you are the father of all the Southern Indians

and constantly employed in taking care of their interests, we call you Alibamo Micco." See Proceedings of a Congress with the Upper Creeks October 29–November 2, 1771, in Davies, *DAR* 3:213.

13. To the Great and Small Medal Chiefs and Rulers of the Cowetas, Tallapusses, Abechkas, and Alibamons, from John Stuart, August 15, 1775, CO5/76, fo.181; A Talk from the Headmen and Warriors of the Lower Creeks Nation in Answer to a Message from the Honorable John Stuart, at the Cussitias, March 23, 1776, CO5/77, fo.255.

14. John Stuart to Germain, October 26, 1776, CO5/78, fo.15.

15. In July 1775, Galphin, along with David Zulby and Leroy Hammond, was named to the Creek Committee of Inquiry for Indian Affairs by the South Carolina Provisional Congress. Later that year, Galphin and Rae were appointed as two of the five Indian commissioners for the Southern District under the direction of the Continental Congress.

16. Corkran, *Creek Frontier*, pp.303–8; Stuart to Dartmouth, May 20, 1775, CO5/76, fo.120; Stuart to Dartmouth, July 21, 1775, CO5/76, fo.150.

17. George Galphin to Henry Laurens, February 7, 1776, in Hamer and Rogers, *Papers of Henry Laurens* 11:94.

18. George Galphin to Henry Laurens, March 13, 1776, in Hamer and Rogers, *Papers of Henry Laurens* 11:157–58. See also George Galphin to Henry Laurens (Council of Safety), February 7, 1776, Sims Collection of Laurens Papers, South Caroliniana Library, University of South Carolina, Columbia.

19. George Galphin to Henry Laurens, October 13, 1777, in Hamer and Rogers, *Papers of Henry Laurens* 11:552–53.

20. John Stuart to Germain, October 26, 1776, CO5/78, fo.15. See Corkran, *Creek Frontier*, pp.288–94.

21. John Stuart to Germain, October 26, 1776, CO5/78, fo.15. The Creeks, as well as Stuart, had attempted to arrange a peace for a number of years. George Galphin to John Stuart, June 2, 1768, in Stuart to Gage, July 2, 1768, Gage Papers. Negotiations fell through on numerous occasions because individuals refused to end the conflict before they had avenged the deaths of relatives. See Charles Stuart to John Stuart, September 27, 1770, CO5/72, fo.93. Many colonials did not wish to see the conflict end, since they feared that if the Creeks were not occupied with the Choctaws, the Indians would be more likely to descend on white settlements. For instance, see Charles Stuart to Peter Chester, n.d., enclosed in Chester's letter of April 15, 1771, to Hillsborough, in Rowland, "Peter Chester," p.50.

22. O'Donnell, *Southern Indians in the American Revolution*, pp.42–49.

23. Lilla M. Hawes, ed., *The Papers of Lachlan McIntosh, 1774–1779*, Collections of the Georgia Historical Society, vol. 12 (Savannah: Georgia Historical Society, 1957), p. 59.

24. The best account of war along the Georgia frontier is Martha Condray Searcy, *The Georgia-Florida Contest in the American Revolution, 1776–1778* (Tuscaloosa: University of Alabama Press, 1985). For action in West Florida, see Helen Hornbeck Tanner, "Pipesmoke and Muskets: Florida Indian Intrigues of the Revolutionary Era," in *Eighteenth-Century Florida and Its Borderlands,* edited by Samuel C. Proctor pp. 13–39 (Gainesville: University Presses of Florida, 1975). O'Donnell, *Southern Indians in the American Revolution,* puts Creek participation in larger context.

25. McGillivray's mother was from Otciapofa, better known as the Hickory Ground, an offshoot of Little Tallassee. Swanton, *Early History,* p. 242, asserts that Otciapofa was a descendant of ancient Coosa, one of the founding towns of the confederacy, thus McGillivray is frequently listed as a Koasiti.

26. Holland, "Anglo-Spanish Contest," pp. 97–100; Michael D. Green, "The Creek Confederacy in the American Revolution: Cautious Participants," In *Anglo-Spanish Confrontation on the Gulf Coast during the American Revolution: Proceedings of the Gulf Coast History and Humanities Conference,* vol. 9, edited by William S. Coker and Robert R. Rea (Pensacola: Gulf Coast History and Humanities Conference, 1982), pp. 66–72.

27. "Official Letters of Governor John Martin, 1782–1783," *Georgia Historical Quarterly* 1 (December 1917): 313.

28. Cashin, "Gentlemen of Augusta," p. 54.

29. CRG 19, pt. 2, pp. 163–64.

30. Searcy, *Georgia-Florida Contest* p. 19; DGB 1:335–37; Joseph Johnson, *Traditions and Reminiscences, Chiefly of the American Revolution in the South* (Charleston: Joseph Johnson, 1851), p. 356.

31. For information of Galphin during the Revolution, see Sheftall, "George Galphin and Indian-White Relations." Also see Robert Scott Davis, "George Galphin and the Creek Congress of 1777," in *Proceedings and Papers of the Georgia Association of Historians, 1982,* pp. 13–29 (Marietta: Georgia Association of Historians, 1983).

32. CRG 20:131–40; Joseph Clay to General Green, March 15, 1783, File No. 152, item no. 8, Joseph Clay Papers, 1765–1802, Georgia Historical Society, Savannah; File No. 121, Sarah Campbell Paper, 1782, Georgia Historical Society, Savannah.

33. Basil Cowper vs. Edmund Telfair, Verdict, April 24, 1800, File No. 179,

item no.1, Basil Cowper Papers, 1770–1779, Georgia Historical Society, Savannah; William Harden, "Basil Cowper's Remarkable Career in Georgia," *Georgia Historical Quarterly* 1 (March 1917): 24–35; Coker and Watson, *Indian Traders,* pp.26–32; Coleman, *American Revolution in Georgia* p.212; Bernard Bailyn, *Voyagers to the West: A Passage in the Peopling of America on the Eve of the Revolution* (New York: Alfred A. Knopf, 1986), p.20.

34. Quote is from Cashin, "Winners and Losers," p.241. Florette Henri, *The Southern Indians and Benjamin Hawkins, 1796–1816* (Norman: University of Oklahoma Press, 1986), p.130; *Letters, Journals, and Writings of Benjamin Hawkins* 1:31; Coleman, *American Revolution in Georgia,* pp.211–12.

35. Brown to Guy Carleton, January 8, 1884, C05/82; Substance of a Talk from the Chiefs of the Upper Creeks to Lieut. Colonel Thomas Brown, December 30, 1783, C05/82.

36. William C. Sturtevant, "Commentary," in *Eighteenth Century Florida and Its Borderlands,* edited by Samuel Proctor (Gainesville: University Presses of Florida, 1975), p.44.

37. The best summary of McGillivray's life is by Michael D. Green, "Alexander McGillivray," in *American Indian Leaders: Studies in Diversity,* edited by R. David Edmunds (Lincoln: University of Nebraska Press, 1980), pp.41–63; McGillivray to Miró, May 1, 1786, in Caughey, *McGillivray,* pp.107–8.

38. Green, "Alexander McGillivray," pp.52–55; *Letters, Journals, and Writings of Benjamin Hawkins* 1:768.

39. Corkran, *Creek Frontier,* pp.322–25.

40. Timothy Barnard to Major Patrick Carr, October 21, 1784, in Louise F. Hays, comp., "Unpublished Letters of Timothy Barnard, 1784–1820," Georgia Department of Archives and History, Atlanta, p.36.

41. R. S. Cotterill, *The Southern Indians: The Story of the Civilized Tribes before Removal,* Civilization of the American Indian Series, no.38 (Norman: University of Oklahoma Press, 1954), pp.65–70.

42. McGillivray to O'Neill, March 28, 1786, in Caughey, *McGillivray,* p.104.

43. Ibid.

44. McGillivray to Miró, May 1, 1786, in ibid., pp.106–10 (quotation on p.109).

45. McGillivray to O'Neill, June 20, 1787, in ibid., p.153. For information on Creek-Chickamauga cooperation, see James P. Pate, "The Chickamauga: A Forgotten Segment of Indian Resistance on the Southern Frontier" (Ph.D. diss., Mississippi State University, 1969), pp.168, 172, 180, 189, 229.

46. McGillivray to O'Neill, July 10, 1787, in Caughey, *McGillivray,* p.155.

47. Coker and Watson, *Indian Traders,* is the starting place for any study of the Florida Indian trade after the American Revolution.

48. Caughey, *McGillivray,* p.65.

49. Coker and Watson, *Indian Traders,* pp.81–82.

50. Ibid., pp.56–61.

51. McMurphy to O'Neill, July 11, 1786, in Caughey, *McGillivray,* pp.118–19.

52. Ibid., pp.118–20; Green, "Alexander McGillivray," p.51.

53. McGillivray was instrumental in securing Spanish permission for a West Florida trade by former British traders. They had already consented to an East Florida route. As other Creeks had done during the war, McGillivray pointed out that St. Augustine was a long way from the Upper Towns and that there was already a path from Pensacola. Caughey, *McGillivray,* p.65.

54. *American State Papers, Indian Affairs,* p.31.

55. *Letters, Journals, and Writings of Benjamin Hawkins* 1:63.

56. Caughey, *McGillivray,* pp.117–18; Coker and Watson, *Indian Traders,* pp.81–82.

57. *American State Papers, Indian Affairs,* p.36; Wright, *Creeks and Seminoles,* pp.136–37; Caughey, *McGillivray,* p.119.

58. For the remarkable career of Bowles, see J. Leitch Wright, Jr., *William Augustus Bowles: Director General of the Creek Nation* (Athens: University of Georgia Press, 1967). Bowles's backer was John Miller, a former West Florida merchant who had been an associate of John McGillivray's.

59. Swan, "Position and State of Manners," pp.260–61.

60. *Letters, Journals, and Writings of Benjamin Hawkins* 1:288.

61. *American State Papers, Indian Affairs,* p.19.

62. Ibid., p.23.

63. Wright, *Bowles,* pp.28–32; Henri, *Southern Indians,* p.75.

64. *American State Papers, Indian Affairs,* p.77. See also Caughey, *McGillivray,* pp.119–20.

65. Gov. Geo. Mathews to Timothy Barnard, August 7, 1878, in Hays, "Letters of Timothy Barnard," p.80.

66. James D. Richardson, ed., *A Compilation of the Messages and Papers of the Presidents,* 10 vols. (Washington: Bureau of National Literature and Art, 1910), 1:68.

67. The federal government claimed sole authority to negotiate with the Indian tribes, by virtue of the treaty-making power conferred by the Constitution. This, in effect, abrogated the three Georgia-Creek treaties of the 1780s.

68. *American State Papers, Indian Affairs*, p.65.

69. The treaty is printed in Charles J. Kappler, Jr., *Indian Affairs: Laws and Treaties*, 5 vols. (Washington: Government Printing Office, 1904–41), 2:25–28. For the whole story of the 1790 negotiations, see Green, "Alexander Mc-Gillivray," pp.54–57; *American State Papers, Indian Affairs*, p.15–16; J. Leitch Wright, Jr., "Creek-American Treaty of 1790: Alexander McGillivray and the Diplomacy of the Old Southwest," *Georgia Historical Quarterly* 51 (December 1967): 379–400.

70. Kappler, *Indian Affairs* 2:28. For a discussion of the civilization policy, see Bernard W. Sheehan, *Seeds of Extinction: Jeffersonian Philanthropy and the American Indian* (Chapel Hill: University of North Carolina Press, 1973), pp.119–23. McGillivray died in February 1793. The Mad Dog of the Tucka-batchee assumed the role as leading Upper chief.

71. Francis Paul Prucha, *American Indian Policy in the Formative Years: The Indian Trade and Intercourse Acts, 1790–1834* (Cambridge: Harvard University Press, 1962), p.86; Richardson, *Messages and Papers of the Presidents* 1:141, 167.

72. The factory did carry the standard goods common to the Indian trade. "List of Goods wanted for the factory in the trade with the Creek Indians," January 19, 1797, in United States Bureau of Indian Affairs, Records of the Office of the Indian Trade: Creek Factory Records, Correspondence, 1795–1814, Record Group 75, microfilm reproductions of original correspondence, reel one, National Archives, Washington, D.C.

73. *Letters, Journals, and Writings of Benjamin Hawkins* 1:280, 284, 2:503; Nella J. Chambers, "The Creek Indian Factory at Fort Mitchell," *Alabama Historical Quarterly* 21 (1959): 15–53. See Ora Brooks Peake, *A History of the United States Indian Factory System, 1795–1822* (Denver: Sage Books, 1954), for an examination of the factory system. Other studies include Royal B. Way, "The United States Factory System for Trading with the Indians, 1796–1822," *Mississippi Valley Historical Review* 6 (September 1919): 220–35; George D. Harmon, "Benjamin Hawkins and the Federal Factory System," *North Carolina Historical Review* 9 (April 1932): 138–52.

74. The provisions for establishing a trading post were included in the 1796 Treaty of Coleraine. *American State Papers, Indian Affairs*, pp.586–87. Ray H. Mattison, "The Creek Trading House," *Georgia Historical Quarterly* 30 (September 1946): 169–84; Cotterill, *Southern Indians*, pp.113–15; Henri, *Southern Indians and Benjamin Hawkins*, pp.130–34. On pp.118–20, Henri discusses the chalk system, which is not described in any records of the colonial period. Henri states that the chalk was equal to one deerskin, worth twenty-five cents. During

the colonial period, the British pound-shillings-pence currency was in use, making references to dollars and cents meaningless. Colonial references consistently omit the word *chalk* and use pounds of deerskin as the standard unit of exchange.

75. James Seagrove to Edward Price, 1795, Instruction to the Factor for establishing a trading house on the River St. Marys, in Creek Factory Records, reel one.

76. *Letters, Journals, and Writings of Benjamin Hawkins* 1:243.

77. *American State Papers, Indian Affairs*, p.79.

78. Coker and Watson, *Indian Traders*, pp.227–28.

79. See Coker and Watson, *Indian Traders*, pp.228–31.

80. *Letters, Journals, and Writings of Benjamin Hawkins* 1:233–34.

81. Ibid. 1:240.

82. Michael D. Green, *The Politics of Indian Removal: Creek Government and Society in Crisis* (Lincoln: University of Nebraska Press, 1982), pp.34–36, 46–47. As early as 1799, Hawkins believed that another cession would be necessary; see letter to William Panton, January 2, 1799, in *Letters, Journals, and Writings of Benjamin Hawkins* 1:233–34.

83. Andrew A. Lipscomb and Albert E. Bergh, eds. *The Writings of Thomas Jefferson*, 20 vols. (Washington, D.C.: Thomas Jefferson Memorial Association, 1903–4), 17:373.

84. Ibid. 10:362.

85. Ibid. 17:374.

86. Sheehan, *Seeds of Extinction*, p.167.

87. *Letters, Journals, and Writings of Benjamin Hawkins* 1:50.

88. Ibid. 1:241.

89. Ibid. 1:242.

90. Ibid. 1:294.

91. Pope, *Tour*, p.44; *Letters, Journals, and Writings of Benjamin Hawkins* 1:280.

92. *Letters, Journals, and Writings of Benjamin Hawkins* 2:411.

93. Ibid. 2:446.

94. Henri, *Southern Indians and Benjamin Hawkins*, pp.228–33; Kappler, *Indian Affairs* 2:58–59; *Letters, Journals, and Writings of Benjamin Hawkins* 2:446–48. Cotterill, *Southern Indians*, p.137, says the perpetual annuity was worth three hundred dollars. Coker and Watson, *Indian Traders*, p.240.

95. *Letters, Journals, and Writings of Benjamin Hawkins* 1:329; See Coker and Watson, *Indian Traders*, p.243, including the charts on pp.265, 271.

96. Coker and Watson, *Indian Traders*, p.243; *Letters, Journals, and Writings*

of Benjamin Hawkins 1:493. See "A Journal of John Forbes, May, 1803: The Seizure of William Augustus Bowles," *Florida Historical Quarterly* 9 (April 1931): 279–89. The only white man to oppose these cessions and to encourage Creek resistance to the idea was William Augustus Bowles. Panton saw him as a rival; Hawkins as a threat. The two conspired and captured him in 1803.

97. Quotation is from *American State Papers, Indian Affairs*, p.691, speech of Hopie Micco. See also *Letters, Journals, and Writings of Benjamin Hawkins* 1:225, 241, 2:537.

98. For the complicated proceedings surrounding these transactions, see Coker and Watson, *Indian Traders*, pp.243–72; Henri, *Southern Indians and Benjamin Hawkins*, pp.249–50; Kappler, *Indian Affairs* 2:85–86; *American State Papers, Indian Affairs*, p.690–92.

99. *American State Papers, Indian Affairs*, p.691.

100. Henry DeLeon Southerland, Jr., and Jerry Elijah Brown, *The Federal Road through Georgia, the Creek Nation, and Alabama, 1806–1846* (Tuscaloosa: University of Alabama Press, 1989), 36; Green, *Politics of Indian Removal*, p.39.

101. Henri, *Southern Indians and Benjamin Hawkins*, p.134.

102. Coker and Watson, *Indian Traders*, pp.247, 251, 252. The debt amounted to 66,533.5 reales.

103. "The Creek Nation, Debtor to John Forbes & Co., Successors to Panton, Leslie & Co., A Journal of John Innerarity, 1812," *Florida Historical Quarterly* 9 (October 1930): 83. It is no wonder the Creeks were alarmed by the interest of the debt. Of $40,000 claimed by the company, only $21,916 was principal.

104. Coker and Watson, *Indian Traders*, pp.270–71; Thomas C. Kennedy, "Sibling Stewards of a Commercial Empire: The Innerarity Brothers in the Floridas," *Florida Historical Quarterly* 67 (January 1989): 265–66.

105. John Stuart to Lord Germain, August 23, 1776, CO5/77, fo.200, and October 6, 1777, CO5/79, fo.29; Swan, "Position and State of Manners," p.263.

106. *Letters, Journals, and Writings of Benjamin Hawkins* 1:21, 22, 28.

107. Ibid. 1:353, 2:558, 563.

108. Ibid. 1:301, 309–10, 316, 353, 2:553. Daniel F. Littlefield, Jr., *Africans and Creeks: From the Colonial Period to the Civil War*, Contributions in Afro-American and African Studies, no.47 (Westport, Conn.: Greenwood Press, 1979), pp.41, 44. For a more detailed discussion on this topic, see Braund, "Creek Indians, Blacks, and Slavery."

109. Rippon, "Mr. David George," p.474.

110. Searcy, "Introduction of African Slavery," pp.21–32. *Letters, Journals, and Writings of Benjamin Hawkins* 1:316.

111. Swan, "Position and State of Manners," p.261.

112. Eugene Current-Garcia and Dorothy B. Hatfield, eds. *Shem, Ham, and Japeth: The Papers of W. O. Tuggle* (Athens: University of Georgia Press, 1973), p.80, also pages 34, 37 (hereafter cited as Current-Garcia, *Tuggle Papers*). *Letters, Journals, and Writings of Benjamin Hawkins* 1:340–41.

113. Current-Garcia, *Tuggle Papers*, pp.18–24; Wright, *Only Land They Knew*, pp.248–78, especially pp.266–67.

114. *The Proceedings and Minutes of the Governor and Council of Georgia, October 4, 1774, through November 7, 1775, and September 6, 1779, through September 20, 1780*, Collections of the Georgia Historical Society, vol.10 (Savannah: Georgia Historical Society, 1952), pp.13–14; Cashin and Robertson, *Augusta and the American Revolution*, pp.9, 59; DGB 1:367–68.

115. *Letters, Journals, and Writings of Benjamin Hawkins* 1:301, 2:658; Littlefield, *Africans and Creeks*, pp.36–37.

116. Wright, *Creeks and Seminoles*, p.79.

117. Wright, *Only Land They Knew*, p.253; Edwin C. McReynolds, *The Seminoles*, Civilization of the American Indian Series, no.47 (Norman: University of Oklahoma Press, 1957), pp.73–74.

118. Davies, DAR 5:260; *Letters, Journals, and Writings of Benjamin Hawkins* 1:290; Woodward, *Reminiscences*, p.10.

119. Osceola's mother was McQueen's daughter. She married another trader, named Powell. McReynolds, *The Seminoles*, pp.146–47. Osceola's wife has been a matter of some controversy. The entire issue of volume 33, numbers 3 and 4, of the *Florida Historical Quarterly* are devoted to Osceola. Charles H. Coe, "The Parentage of Osceola," *Florida Historical Quarterly* 33 (January–April 1955): 202–5, denies Osceola had any white blood. Boyd, "Asi-yahola," pp.252–55 accepts the notion that Osceola was a descendent of McQueen's but rejects the idea that his wife was black (p.264). Wright, *Only Land They Knew*, p.260, holds that at least one of Osceola's wives was black. See also Wright, *Creeks and Seminoles*, pp.80, 290, 316.

120. Nash, *Red, White, and Black*, pp.236–46; Eggan, *American Indian*, pp.29–33; Paredes and Plante, "Subjugation of the Creek Indians," pp.150–57.

121. *Letters, Journals, and Writings of Benjamin Hawkins* 2:411.

122. Ibid. 1:293, 187, 312.

123. Ibid. 1:293. Information on the Bailey family can be found on pp.21, 22, 28, 186–88.

124. Ibid. 1:209.

125. R. David Edmunds, *The Shawnee Prophet* (Lincoln: University of Nebraska Press, 1983), pp.36–37.

126. Tecumseh's visit and the subsequent hostilities are covered in Frank L. Owsley, Jr., *Struggle for the Gulf Borderlands: The Creek War and the Battle of New Orleans, 1812–1815* (Gainesville: University Presses of Florida, 1981). See Nuñez, "Stiggins Narrative" pp.1–17, for a discussion of the concepts of "nativism" and "revitalization."

127. Nuñez, "Stiggins Narrative," p.150.

128. Political power struggles within the Creek Nation were of paramount importance in actually bringing on the fighting. Town autonomy suffered as the Creek National Council, directed by Hawkins, gained strength. Competition for political power accentuated old divisions in the Creek alliance. Yet the source of these political divisions lay in economic and cultural issues over land and trade.

129. *Letters, Journals, and Writings of Benjamin Hawkins* 1:294. Nuñez, "Stiggins Narrative," p.150.

130. Hatley, "Dividing Paths," p.471, notes that Cherokee attacks against cattle and hogs "represented a denial of the manner in which their colonial neighbors made a living—and their human identity itself." See also Hatley, "Tallapoosa Landscape," pp.90–92. Joel W. Martin, *Sacred Revolt: The Muskogees' Struggle for a New World* (Boston: Beacon Press, 1981), p.143, believes that the destruction of livestock by the Creek rebels was "homologous with those sometimes performed before the Busk. . . . By renouncing their dependence on Anglo-American civilization, the people readied themselves for the assumption of a new collective identity."

131. *Letters, Journals, and Writings of Benjamin Hawkins* 2:652. See *American State Papers, Indian Affairs,* p.858.

132. Nuñez, "Stiggins Narrative," p.160, also p.165.

133. The most recent study of the Creek War is Martin, *Sacred Revolt*. Martin stresses the religious aspects of the revolt and ignores other scholarship on intertribal ethnic conflicts and foreign agitation. The book provides a brief and inadequate summary of the actual fighting. For coverage of the war itself, see Henry Sale Halbert and T. H. Ball, *The Creek War of 1813 and 1814* (1895; reprint, Tuscaloosa: University of Alabama Press, 1969). Owsley, *Struggle for the Gulf Borderlands,* pp.178–95.

134. The Battle of Horseshoe Bend took place on March 27, 1814. Robert V. Remini, *Andrew Jackson and the Course of American Empire, 1767–1821* (New York: Harper & Row, 1977), pp.214–17, gives a good account of the battle.

Owsley, *Struggle for the Gulf Borderlands,* pp.78–83; Halbert and Ball, *Creek War,* pp.275–78.

135. Halbert and Ball, *Creek War,* pp.276–77.

136. The Answer of Major Genl. Jackson to the reply of the Big Warrior to his first address in Andrew Jackson's address to Cherokee and Creek Chiefs and Warriors, August 5, 1814, in *The Papers of Andrew Jackson, 1770–1845,* edited by Harold D. Moser et al. (Wilmington, Del.: Scholarly Resources, 1986), microfilm edition, vol.3, frame 1222.

137. Remini, *Andrew Jackson,* pp.224–33, discusses the treaty negotiations. Henri, *Southern Indians and Benjamin Hawkins,* pp.295–307.

138. "The Treaty of Fort Jackson, Fort Jackson, August 9, 1814," in *The American Indian and the United States: A Documentary History,* edited by Wilcomb E. Washburn, 4 vols. (Westport, Conn.: Greenwood Press, 1973; reprint, 1979), 4:2348–50.

139. The Prophet was captured by Jackson and executed soon after his return. Frank L. Owsley, Jr., "Prophet of War: Josiah Francis and the Creek War," *American Indian Quarterly* 9 (Summer 1985): 285–88.

Bibliography

MANUSCRIPTS

American Philosophical Society Library. Philadelphia, Pennsylvania.

Benjamin Smith Barton Papers.

British Museum. London, England.

Haldimand, Sir Frederick. Unpublished Papers and Correspondence, 1758–1784. Microfilm copies of manuscripts by Microfilm World Publications.

Georgia Department of Archives and History. Atlanta, Georgia.

"Unpublished Letters of Timothy Barnard, 1784–1820." Typescript. Compiled by Louise F. Hays.

Georgia Historical Society. Savannah, Georgia.

Anonymous. "A Gurnal of my Travling to the Indian Countrary [1767]." File no. 10.

Bryan, Jonathan. Papers, 1774–1792. File no.98.

Campbell, Sarah. Paper, 1782. File no.121.

Clay, Joseph. Papers, 1765–1802. File no.152.

Cowper, Basil. Papers, 1770–1779. File no.179.

Galphin, George. Account Books, 1767–1772. 3 folders. File no.269.

Habersham, James. Papers, 1752–1776. File no.337.

Wallace, John. Paper, 1787. File no.965.

Great Britain. Public Record Office.

Audit Office. Records of the Loyalist Claims Commission. Class 12 and class 13, Georgia Claims.

Colonial Office. American and West Indies. Class 5, vols.65–82, 225, 588, 664.

Colonial Office. Colonies General. Class 323, vol.17. Report of John Stuart to the Lords Commissioners of Trade and Plantations on the Southern Indian Department, March 9, 1764.

John C. Pace Library, University of West Florida. Pensacola, Florida.

The Papers of Panton, Leslie, and Company. Microfilm edition. Woodbridge, Conn.: Research Publications, 1986. 26 reels.

Massachusetts Historical Society. Boston, Massachusetts.

Knox, Henry. Papers. Microfilm edition. Cambridge, Mass.: MIT Micro-reproduction Laboratory, 1960. 55 reels.

National Archives and Records Service. Washington, D.C.

United States Bureau of Indian Affairs. Records of the Office of the Indian Trade: Creek Factory Records. Correspondence, 1795–1814. Record Group 75. Microfilm reproductions of original correspondence.

Royal Library of Denmark. Copenhagen, Denmark.

Sketches by Philip Georg Friedrich Von Reck. Ny kgl. Saml. 565, 4°.

South Caroliniana Library, University of South Carolina. Columbia, South Carolina.

Copies of Three Suits by William Higginson of London Against George Galphin Estate and Galphin, Holmes & Co. To Recover Pre-Revolutionary Trading Debts Under Treaty of Paris, 1783. Suits Filed in U.S. Court, Charleston, October 1791. Settlement in U.S. Court, Columbia, June, 1792.

Macartan and Campbell. Augusta Store, Georgia Account Book. Augusta 1762–June, 1766. Microfilm copy of original located at Clemson University Library.

Sims Collection of Laurens Papers.

William L. Clements Library. Ann Arbor, Michigan.

Clinton, Sir Henry. Papers, 1750–1812.

Gage, Thomas. Papers of General Thomas Gage Relating to His Command in North America, 1762–1776.

NEWSPAPERS

Pennsylvania Gazette, 1766, 1774.
South Carolina Gazette, 1739–41, 1760–65.

PUBLISHED PRIMARY SOURCES

Adair, James. *Adair's History of the American Indians.* Edited by Samuel Cole Williams. Johnson City, Tenn.: Watauga Press, 1930. Reprint. New York: Argonaut Press, 1966.

American State Papers: Documents, Legislative and Executive, of the Congress of the United States, from the First Session of the First to the Third Session of the Thirteenth Congress, Inclusive: Commencing March 3, 1789, and Ending March 3, 1815. Vol. 1, Class II, Indian Affairs. Edited by Walter Lowrie and Matthew St. Clair Clarke. Washington, D.C.: Gales & Seaton, 1832.

Atkin, Edmund. *The Appalachian Indian Frontier: The Edmund Atkin Report and Plan of 1755.* Reprint edition of *Indians of the Southern Colonial Frontier.* Edited by Wilbur R. Jacobs. Columbia: University of South Carolina Press, 1954. Reprint. Lincoln: University of Nebraska Press, 1967.

Bartram, John. "Diary of a Journey through the Carolinas, Georgia, and Florida from July 1, 1765, to April 10, 1766." Edited by Francis Harper. *Transactions of the American Philosophical Society,* n.s., 33, part 1. Philadelphia: American Philosophical Society, 1942.

Bartram, William. "Observations on the Creek and Cherokee Indians, 1789, with Prefatory and Supplementary Notes by E. G. Squier." *Transactions of the American Ethnological Society,* vol. 3, part 1. New York: American Ethnological Society, 1853.

———. "Travels in Georgia and Florida, 1773–1774: A Report to Dr. John Fothergill." Annotated by Francis Harper. *Transactions of the American Philosophical Society,* n.s., 33, part 2. Philadelphia: American Philosophical Society, 1942.

———. *Travels of William Bartram.* Edited by Mark Van Doren. New York: Dover Publications, 1955.

Bossu, Jean Bernard. *Jean Bernard Bossu's Travels in the Interior of North America, 1751–1762.* Edited and translated by Seymour Feiler. Norman: University of Oklahoma Press, 1962.

Calendar of State Papers, Colonial Series, America and West Indies Preserved in the Public Record Office. Vol. 31, *January, 1719, to February, 1720.* Edited by Cecil Headlam. London: HM Stationery Office, 1933. Reprint. Vaduz: Kraus Reprint, 1964.

Candler, Allen D.; Coleman, Kenneth; and Ready, Milton; eds. *The Colonial Records of the State of Georgia.* 28 vols. Atlanta: C. P. Byrd, 1904–16; Athens: University of Georgia Press, 1974–76.

Carter, Clarence E., ed. *The Correspondence of General Thomas Gage with the Secretaries of State, and with the War Office and Treasury, 1763–1775.* 2 vols. Yale Historical Publications, Manuscripts and Edited Texts, vol. 12. New Haven: Yale University Press, 1931–33.

———. "Observations of Superintendent John Stuart and Governor James

Grant of East Florida on the Proposed Plan of 1764 for the Future Management of Indian Affairs." *American Historical Review* 20 (July 1915): 815–31.

Caughey, John W. *McGillivray of the Creeks*. Civilization of the American Indian Series, no.18. Norman: University of Oklahoma Press, 1938.

Corbitt, D. C., trans. "Papers Relating to the Georgia-Florida Frontier, 1784–1800, II." *Georgia Historical Quarterly* 21 (March 1937): 73–83.

Covington, James W., ed. *The British Meet the Seminoles: Negotiations between the British Authorities in East Florida and the Indians, 1763–1768*. Contributions of the Florida State Museum, Social Sciences, no.7. Gainesville: University of Florida Press, 1961.

Current-Garcia, Eugene, and Hatfield, Dorothy B., eds. *Shem, Ham, and Japeth: The Papers of W. O. Tuggle*. Athens: University of Georgia Press, 1973.

Dalrymple, Margaret F., ed. *The Merchant of Manchac: The Letterbooks of John Fitzpatrick, 1768–1790*. Baton Rouge: Louisiana State University Press, 1978.

Davies, Kenneth G., ed. *Documents of the American Revolution, 1770–1783*. 20 vols. Dublin, Ireland: Irish University Press, 1972–79.

De Brahm's Report of the General Survey in the Southern District of North America. Edited by Louis De Vorsey, Jr. Columbia: University of South Carolina Press, 1971.

Eakins, D. W. "Some Information Respecting the Creeks, or Muscogees." In *Historical and Statistical Information Respecting the History, Condition, and Prospects of the Indian Tribes of the United States*. 6 vols. Edited by Henry Rowe Schoolcraft, 1:265–83. Philadelphia: J. B. Lippincott, 1855.

Easterby, J. H., ed. *The Journal of the Commons House of Assembly*. 12 vols. Colonial Records of South Carolina. Columbia: Historical Commission of South Carolina and South Carolina Department of Archives, 1951–83.

Fitch, Tobias. "Journal of Captain Tobias Fitch's Mission from Charleston to the Creeks, 1726." In *Travels in the American Colonies*, edited by Newton D. Mereness, pp.175–212. New York: Macmillan Co., 1916.

Forbes, John. "A Journal of John Forbes, May, 1803: The Seizure of William Augustus Bowles." *Florida Historical Quarterly* 9 (April 1931): 279–89.

Galloway, Patricia Kay, ed. *Mississippi Provincial Archives: French Dominion*. Vols. 4 and 5. Originally collected, edited, and translated by Dunbar Rowland and A. G. Sanders. Baton Rouge: Louisiana State University Press, 1984.

Gordon, Lord Adam. "Journal of an Officer's Travels in America and the West Indies, 1764–1765." In *Travels in the American Colonies*, edited by Newton D. Mereness, pp.367–456. New York: Macmillan Co., 1916.

Habersham, James. *The Letters of the Honorable James Habersham, 1756–1775*. Georgia Historical Society Collections, vol.6. Savannah: Georgia Historical Society, 1904.

Hamer, Philip M., and Rogers, George C., eds. *The Papers of Henry Laurens*. 11 vols. Columbia: South Carolina Historical Society and University of South Carolina Press, 1968–81.

Hawes, Lilla M., ed. *The Papers of Lachlan McIntosh, 1774–1779*. Collections of the Georgia Historical Society, vol.12. Savannah: Georgia Historical Society, 1957.

Hawkins, Benjamin. *Letters, Journals, and Writings of Benjamin Hawkins*, edited by C. L. Grant. 2 vols. Savannah: Beehive Press, 1980.

————. *A Sketch of the Creek Country in the Years 1798 and 1799 and Letters of Benjamin Hawkins, 1796–1806*. A one-volume reproduction of vol.3, part 1, and vol.9 of *Collections of the Georgia Historical Society*. Spartanburg, s.c.: Reprint Co., 1982.

Holcomb, Brent H. *Ninety Six District, South Carolina Journal of the Court of Ordinary, Inventory Book, Will Book, 1781–1786*. Easley, s.c.: Southern Historical Press, 1978.

Hvidt, Kristian, ed. *Von Reck's Voyage: Drawings and Journal of Philip Georg Friedrich Von Reck*. Savannah: Beehive Press, 1980.

Innerarity, John. "The Creek Nation, Debtor to John Forbes & Co., Successors to Panton, Leslie & Co.: A Journal of John Innerarity, 1812." *Florida Historical Quarterly* 9 (October 1930): 67–89.

Jackson, Andrew. *The Papers of Andrew Jackson, 1770–1845*. Edited by Harold D. Moser et al. Microfilm edition, 39 reels. Wilmington, Del.: Scholarly Resources, 1986.

Johnson, Joseph. *Traditions and Reminiscences, Chiefly of the American Revolution in the South: Including Biographical Sketches, Incidents and Anecdotes, Few of Which Have Been Published, Particularly of Residents in the Upper Country*. Charleston: Joseph Johnson, 1851.

Jones, George Fenwick, ed. and trans. "Commissary Von Reck's Report on Georgia." *Georgia Historical Quarterly* 47 (March 1963): 95–110.

Juricek, John T., ed. *Georgia Treaties, 1733–1763*. Volume 11 of *Early American Indian Documents: Treaties and Laws, 1607–1789*, edited by Alden T. Vaughan. Frederick, Md.: University Publications of America, 1989.

Kappler, Charles J., Jr. *Indian Affairs: Laws and Treaties*. 5 vols. Washington, D.C.: Government Printing Office, 1904–41.

Kimball, Gertrude Selwyn, ed. *Correspondence of William Pitt When Secretary of*

State with Colonial Governors and Military and Naval Commissioners in America. 2 vols. New York: Macmillan, 1906. Reprint. New York: Kraus, 1969.

Lane, Mills, ed. *The Rambler in Georgia: Desultory Observations on the Situation, Extent, Climate, Population, Manners, Customs, Commerce, Constitution, Government, Etc., of the State from the Revolution to the Civil War Recorded by Thirteen Travelers.* Savannah: Beehive Press, 1973.

Lawson, John. *A New Voyage to Carolina.* Edited by Hugh T. Lefler. Chapel Hill: University of North Carolina Press, 1967.

"Letter from a Gentleman at Pensacola, October 30, 1764." *British Magazine* 6 (February 1765): 97.

Lipscomb, Andrew A., and Bergh, Albert E., eds. *The Writings of Thomas Jefferson.* 20 vols. Washington, D.C.: Thomas Jefferson Memorial Association, 1903–4.

McDowell, William L., Jr., ed. *Documents Relating to Indian Affairs, May 21, 1750–August 7, 1754.* Colonial Records of South Carolina, Series 2. Columbia: South Carolina Department of Archives and History, 1958.

———. *Documents Relating to Indian Affairs, 1754–1765.* Colonial Records of South Carolina, Series 2. Columbia: South Carolina Department of Archives and History, 1970.

———. *Journals of the Commissioners of the Indian Trade, September 20, 1710–August 29, 1718.* Colonial Records of South Carolina, Series 2. Columbia: South Carolina Department of Archives and History, 1955.

Martin, John. "Official Letters of Governor John Martin, 1782–1783." *Georgia Historical Quarterly* 1 (December 1917): 281–335.

Martyn, Benjamin. "An Impartial Inquiry into the State and Utility of the Province of Georgia, 1741." *Collections of the Georgia Historical Society,* vol. 1 Savannah: Georgia Historical Society, 1840.

Milfort, Louis. *Memoirs; or, A Quick Glance at My Various Travels and My Sojourn in the Creek Nation.* Edited and translated by Ben C. McCary. 1802. Reprint. Kennesaw, Ga.: Continental Book Co., 1959.

Nairne, Thomas. *Nairne's Muskhogean Journals: The 1708 Expedition to the Mississippi River.* Edited by Alexander Moore. Jackson: University Press of Mississippi, 1988.

Nuñez, Theron A., Jr. "Creek Nativism and the Creek War of 1813–1814 (George Stiggins Manuscript)." *Ethnohistory* 5 (Winter 1958): 1–47, 131–75, 292–301.

O'Callaghan, E. B., ed. *Documents Relative to the Colonial History of the State of New York: Procured in Holland, England, and France.* 15 vols. Albany, N.Y.:

Weed, Parsons, & Co., 1856–87. Microfilm Edition: Published American Colonial Records, vol.7. New York: Research Publications.

"Oglethorpe's Treaty with the Lower Creek Indians." *Georgia Historical Quarterly* 4 (March 1920): 3–16.

Payne, John Howard. "The Green Corn Dance." Edited by John R. Swanton. *Chronicles of Oklahoma* 10 (1932): 170–95.

Percival, John, First Earl of Egmont. *The Journal of the Earl of Egmont.* Edited by Robert McPherson. Athens: University of Georgia Press, 1962.

Pope, John. *A Tour through the Southern and Western Territories of the United States of North-America.* Facsimile reproduction of the 1792 edition, Bicentennial Floridiana Facsimile Series. Gainesville: University Presses of Florida, 1979.

Postlethwayt, Malachy. *The Universal Dictionary of Trade and Commerce.* 4th ed. Reprints of Economic Classics. A reprint of the 1774 edition. 2 vols. New York: Augustus M. Kelly, 1971.

Potter, Elam. "An Account of Several Nations of Southern Indians, in a Letter from Reverend Elam Potter to Reverend Dr. Stiles, A.D. 1768." *Massachusetts Historical Society Collections,* 1st ser. 10 (1908): 119–21.

The Proceedings and Minutes of the Governor and Council of Georgia, October 4, 1774, through November 7, 1775, and September 6, 1779, through September 20, 1780. Collections of the Georgia Historical Society, vol.10. Savannah: Georgia Historical Society, 1952.

"A Ranger's Report of Travels with General Oglethorpe, 1730–1742." In *Travels in the American Colonies,* edited by Newton D. Mereness, pp.213–36. New York: Macmillan, 1916.

Raspberry, Thomas. *The Letterbook of Thomas Raspberry, 1758–1761.* Edited by Lilla Mills Hawes. Georgia Historical Society Collections, vol.13. Savannah: Georgia Historical Society, 1959.

Rea, Robert R., and Howard, Milo B., Jr., eds. *The Minutes, Journals, and Acts of the General Assembly of British West Florida.* Tuscaloosa: University of Alabama Press, 1979.

Reese, Trevor R., ed. *The Clamorous Malcontents: Criticisms and Defenses of the Colony of Georgia, 1741–1743.* Savannah: Beehive Press, 1973.

Richardson, James D., ed. *A Compilation of the Messages and Papers of the Presidents.* 10 vols. Washington, D.C.: Bureau of National Literature and Art, 1910.

Rippon, John, ed. "An Account of the Life of Mr. David George, from Sierra Leone to Africa, given by himself in a conversation with Brother Rippon of

London, and Brother Pearce of Birmingham." *Baptist Annual Register for 1790, 1791, 1792, and Part of 1793, Including Sketches of the State of Religion among Different Denominations of Good Men at Home and Abroad.* London: Dilly, Butler, and Thomas, 1793.

Rolle, Denys. *To the Right Honourable the Lords of His Majesty's Most Honourable Privy Council, the humble petition of Denys Rolle, esq, setting forth the hardships, inconveniencies, and grievances, which have attended him in his attempts to make a settlement in east Florida.* Facsimile reproduction of the 1765 edition. Gainesville: University Presses of Florida, 1977.

Romans, Bernard. *A Concise Natural History of East and West Florida.* Facsimile reproduction of the 1775 edition. Florida Facsimile and Reprint Series. Gainesville: University of Florida Press, 1962.

Rowland, Dunbar, ed. *Mississippi Provincial Archives, English Dominion, 1763–1766: Letters and Enclosures to the Secretary of State from Major Robert Farmar and Governor George Johnstone.* Vol. 1. Nashville: Brandon Printing Co., 1911.

Rowland, Dunbar, and A. G. Sanders, eds. and trans. *Mississippi Provincial Archives: French Dominion.* 3 vols. Jackson, Miss.: Mississippi Department of Archives and History, 1927–1932.

Rowland, Mrs. Dunbar, ed. "Peter Chester: Third Governor of the Province of West Florida." In *Mississippi Historical Society Publications,* Centenary Series, vol. 5. Jackson: Press of Mississippi Department of Archives and History, 1925.

Saunders, William, ed. *The Colonial Records of North Carolina; Published Under the Supervision of the Trustees of the Public Libraries, by Order of the General Assembly.* 16 vols. Raleigh: Josephus Daniels, 1886–90.

Saye, Albert, and Coulter, E. Merton, eds. *A List of Early Settlers of Georgia.* Athens: University of Georgia Press, 1949.

State of the British and French Colonies in North America with Respect to Number of People, Forts, Indians, Trade, and Other Advantages. 1755. Reprint. New York: Johnson Reprint Co., 1967.

Stephens, Thomas. "A Brief Account of the Causes That Have Retarded the Progress of the Colony of Georgia, 1743." In *The Clamorous Malcontents: Criticisms and Defenses of the Colony of Georgia, 1741–1743,* pp. 274–347. Edited by Trevor R. Reese. Savannah: Beehive Press, 1973.

———. *The Journal of William Stephens, 1741–1743.* Edited by E. Merton Coulter, Wormsloe Foundation Publications, no. 2. Athens: University of Georgia Press, 1958.

————. *The Journal of William Stephens, 1743–1745.* Edited by E. Merton Coulter, Wormsloe Foundation Publications, no.3. Athens: University of Georgia Press, 1959.

"Survey of West Florida, 1768." In *Colonial Captivities, Marches, and Journeys,* edited by Isabel M. Calder, under the auspices of the National Society of the Colonial Dames of America. New York: Macmillan, 1935. Reprint. Port Washington, N.Y.: Kennikat Press, 1967.

Swan, Caleb. "Position and State of Manners and Arts in the Creek or Muscogee Nation, 1791." In *Information Respecting the History, Condition, and Prospects of the Indian Tribes of the United States,* edited by Henry Rowe Schoolcraft, 6 vols. Philadelphia: J. B. Lippincott Co., 1852–57. 5:251–83.

Waring, Antonio J., ed. *Laws of the Creek Nation.* University of Georgia Libraries Miscellaneous Publications, no.1. Athens: University of Georgia Press, 1960.

Washburn, Wilcomb E., ed. *The American Indian and the United States: A Documentary History.* 4 vols. Westport, Conn.: Greenwood Press, 1973. Reprint, 1979.

Wight, Willard E. *Abstracts of Colonial Wills of the State of Georgia, 1733–1777.* Atlanta: Town Committee of the National Society of the Colonial Dames of America in the State of Georgia for the Department of Archive and History, 1962. Reprint. Spartanburg, S.C.: Reprint Co., 1981.

Woodward, Thomas Simpson. *Woodward's Reminiscences of the Creek or Muscogee Indians.* Montgomery, Ala.: Barrett and Wimbish, 1859. Reprint. Mobile, Ala.: Southern University Press, 1965.

Wright, James. *Letters from Governor Sir James Wright to the Secretaries of State for America, August 24, 1774, to February 16, 1782.* Collections of the Georgia Historical Society, vol.3. Savannah: Georgia Historical Society, 1873.

SECONDARY SOURCES

Abernethy, Thomas P. *The South in the New Nation, 1789–1819.* Volume 4 of *A History of the South,* edited by Wendell Holmes Stephenson and E. Merton Coulter. Baton Rouge: Louisiana State University, 1961.

Alden, John R. "The Albany Congress and the Creation of the Indian Superintendencies." *Mississippi Valley Historical Review* 27 (September 1940): 193–210.

————. *John Stuart and the Southern Colonial Frontier: A Study of Indian Relations, War, Trade, and Land Problems in the Southern Wilderness, 1754–1775.* University of Michigan Publications in History and Political Science, no.15.

Ann Arbor: University of Michigan Press, 1944. Reprint. New York: Gordian, 1966.

Alvord, Clarence W. *The Mississippi Valley in British Politics: A Study of the Trade, Land Speculation, and Experiments in Imperialism Culminating in the American Revolution.* 2 vols. 1916. Reprint. New York: Russell & Russell, 1959.

Anderson, Luther A. *How to Hunt Whitetail Deer.* New York: Funk & Wagnalls, 1968.

Ashton, T. S. *Economic Fluctuations in England, 1700–1800.* Oxford: Oxford University Press, 1959.

Bailyn, Bernard. *Voyagers to the West: A Passage in the Peopling of America on the Eve of the Revolution.* New York: Alfred A. Knopf, 1986.

Baker, Steven G. *Cofitachique, Fair Province of Carolina: History and Archaeology of the Carolina Indians.* Ann Arbor, Mich.: University Microfilms, 1983.

Barrow, Thomas C. *Trade and Empire: The British Customs Service in Colonial America, 1660–1775.* Cambridge: Harvard University Press, 1967.

Bell, Amelia R. "Separate People: Speaking of Creek Men and Women." *American Anthropologist* 92 (June 1990): 332–45.

Berkhofer, Robert F., Jr. *The White Man's Indian: Images of the American Indian from Columbus to the Present.* New York: Alfred A. Knopf, 1978.

Bernard, James A. *An Analysis of British Mercantilism as It Related to Patterns of South Carolina Trade from 1717 to 1767.* Ann Arbor, Mich.: University Microfilms, 1976.

Bieder, Robert E. *Science Encounters the Indian, 1820–1880: The Early Years of American Ethnology.* Norman: University of Oklahoma Press, 1986. Reprint, 1989.

Billings, John Shaw. "Analysis of the Will of George Galphin." *Richmond County History* 13 (1981): 29–37.

Bolton, Herbert E. "Spanish Resistance to the Carolina Traders in Western Georgia (1680–1704)." *Georgia Historical Quarterly* 9 (June 1925): 115–30.

Boyd, Mark F. "Asi-Yahola or Osceola." *Florida Historical Quarterly* 33 (January–April 1955): 249–305.

Boyd, Mark F.; Smith, Hale G.; and Griffin, John W. *Here They Once Stood: The Tragic End of the Apalachee Missions.* Gainesville: University of Florida Press, 1951.

Brannon, Peter A. "The Pensacola Indian Trade." *Florida Historical Quarterly* 31 (July 1952): 1–15.

———. *The Southern Indian Trade, Being Particularly a Study of Material from the Tallapoosa River Valley of Alabama.* Montgomery, Ala.: Paragon Press, 1938.

Braund, Kathryn E. Holland. "The Creek Indians, Blacks, and Slavery." *Journal of Southern History* 57 (November 1991): 601–36.

———. "Guardians of Tradition and Handmaidens to Change: Women's Roles in Creek Economic and Social Life during the Eighteenth Century." *American Indian Quarterly* 14 (Summer 1990): 239–58.

Brown, Douglas S. *The Catawba Indians: The People of the River.* Columbia: University of South Carolina Press, 1966.

Brown, M. L. *Firearms in Colonial America: The Impact on History and Technology, 1492–1792.* Washington, D.C.: Smithsonian Institution Press, 1980.

Brown, Philip M. "Early Indian Trade in the Development of South Carolina: Politics, Economics, and Social Mobility during the Proprietary Period, 1670–1719." *South Carolina Historical Magazine* 76 (July 1975): 118–28.

Bruchey, Stuart, ed. *The Colonial Merchant: Sources and Readings.* Forces in American Economic Growth Series. New York: Harcourt, Brace & World, 1966.

Bushnell, Amy Turner. "Ruling 'the Republic of Indians' in Seventeenth-Century Florida." In *Powhatan's Mantle: Indians in the Colonial Southeast,* edited by Peter H. Wood, Gregory A. Waselkov, and M. Thomas Hatley, pp.134–50. Lincoln: University of Nebraska Press, 1989.

Calhoun, Jeanne A.; Zierden, Martha A.; and Paysinger, Elizabeth A. "The Geographic Spread of Charleston's Mercantile Community, 1732–1767." *South Carolina Historical Magazine* 86 (July 1985): 182–220.

Callahan, Helen. "Colonial Life in Augusta." In *Colonial Augusta "Key of the Indian Countrey,"* edited by Edward J. Cashin, Jr., pp.96–119. Macon, Ga.: Mercer University Press, 1986.

Capron, Louis. "Notes on the Hunting Dance of the Cow Creek Seminoles." *Florida Anthropologist* 9 (1956): 67–78.

Carter, Clarence. "British Policy towards the American Indian in the South, 1763–1768." *English Historical Review* 33 (January 1918): 37–56.

Cashin, Edward J., Jr. "'But Brothers, It Is Our Land We Are Talking About': Winners and Losers in the Georgia Backcountry." In *An Uncivil War: The Southern Backcountry during the American Revolution,* edited by Ronald Hoffman, Thad W. Tate, and Peter J. Albert, pp.240–75. Charlottesville: United States Capitol Historical Society by the University Press of Virginia, 1985.

———. *The King's Ranger: Thomas Brown and the American Revolution on the Southern Frontier.* Athens: University of Georgia Press, 1989.

———. *Lachlan McGillivray, Indian Trader: The Shaping of the Southern Colonial Frontier.* Athens: University of Georgia Press, 1992.

————, ed. *Colonial Augusta "Key of the Indian Countrey."* Macon, Ga.: Mercer University Press, 1986.

Cashin, Edward J., Jr., and Robertson, Heard. *Augusta and the American Revolution: Events in the Georgia Backcountry, 1773–1783.* Darien, Ga.: Ashantilly Press, 1975.

Chambers, Nella J. "The Creek Indian Factory at Fort Mitchell." *Alabama Historical Quarterly* 21 (1959): 15–53.

Chesnutt, David R. *South Carolina's Expansion into Colonial Georgia, 1720–1765.* Ann Arbor, Mich.: University Microfilms, 1976.

Clark, John G. *New Orleans, 1718–1812: An Economic History.* Baton Rouge: Louisiana State University Press, 1970.

Clarkson, L. A. "The Organization of the English Leather Industry in the Late Sixteenth and Seventeenth Centuries." *Economic History Review,* n.s., 13, no.2 (1960): 245–56.

Clowse, Converse D. "Charles Town Export Trade, 1717–1737." Ph.D. diss., Northwestern University, 1963.

————. *Economic Beginnings of Colonial South Carolina, 1670–1730.* South Carolina Tricentennial Commission Studies, no.3. Columbia: University of South Carolina Press, 1971.

————. *Measuring Charleston's Overseas Commerce, 1717–1767: Statistics from the Port's Naval Lists.* Washington, D.C.: University Press of America, 1981.

Coe, Charles H. "The Parentage of Osceola." *Florida Historical Quarterly* 33 (January–April 1955): 202–5.

Coker, William S., and Watson, Thomas D. *Indian Traders of the Southeastern Spanish Borderlands: Panton, Leslie, and Company and John Forbes and Company, 1783–1847.* Gainesville: University Presses of Florida, 1985.

Cole, Arthur Harrison. *Wholesale Commodity Prices in the United States, 1700–1861.* Cambridge: Harvard University Press, 1938. Reprint. New York: Johnson Reprint, 1969.

Coleman, Kenneth. *The American Revolution in Georgia, 1763–1789.* Athens: University of Georgia Press, 1958.

Coleman, Kenneth, and Gurr, Charles Stephen, eds., *Dictionary of Georgia Biography.* 2 vols. Athens: University of Georgia Press, 1983.

Corkran, David H. *The Cherokee Frontier: Conflict and Survival, 1740–1762.* Norman: University of Oklahoma Press, 1962.

————. *The Creek Frontier, 1540–1783.* Civilization of the American Indian Series, no.86. Norman: University of Oklahoma Press, 1967.

Cornell, Stephen. *The Return of the Native: American Indian Political Resurgence.* New York: Oxford University Press, 1988.

Corry, John Pitts. *Indian Affairs in Georgia, 1732–1756.* Philadelphia: G. S. Ferguson, 1936. Reprint. New York: AMS Press, 1980.

———. "Some New Light on the Bosomworth Claims." *Georgia Historical Quarterly* 25 (September 1941): 195–224.

Cotterill, R. S. *The Southern Indians: The Story of the Civilized Tribes before Removal.* Civilization of the American Indian Series, no.38. Norman: University of Oklahoma Press, 1954.

Coulter, E. Merton. "Mary Musgrove, 'Queen of the Creeks': A Chapter of Early Georgia Troubles." *Georgia Historical Quarterly* 11 (March 1927): 1–30.

———. *Thomas Spalding of Sapelo.* Baton Rouge: Louisiana State University Press, 1940.

Covington, James W. "Apalachee Indians, 1704–1763." *Florida Historical Quarterly* 50 (April 1972): 366–84.

———. "The Cuban Fishing *Ranchos:* A Spanish Enclave within British Florida." In *Anglo-Spanish Confrontation on the Gulf Coast during the American Revolution,* edited by William S. Coker and Robert R. Rea, pp.17–24. Pensacola: Gulf Coast History and Humanities Conference, 1982.

———. "Migration of the Seminoles into Florida, 1700–1820." *Florida Historical Quarterly* 46 (April 1968): 340–57.

———. "Trade Relations between Southwestern Florida and Cuba, 1600–1840." *Florida Historical Quarterly* 38 (October 1959): 114–28.

Crane, Verner W. "The Origin of the Name of the Creek Indians." *Mississippi Valley Historical Review* 5 (December 1918): 339–42.

———. *The Southern Frontier, 1670–1732.* Ann Arbor: University of Michigan Press, 1929. Reprint. New York: W. W. Norton, 1981.

Crawford, James M. *The Mobilian Trade Language.* Knoxville: University of Tennessee Press, 1978.

Cronon, William. *Changes in the Land: Indians, Colonists, and the Ecology of New England.* New York: Hill & Wang, 1983.

Davis, Ralph. *The Industrial Revolution and British Overseas Trade.* Leicester, England: Leicester University Press, 1979.

Davis, Robert Scott. "George Galphin and the Creek Congress of 1777." In *Proceedings and Papers of the Georgia Association of Historians, 1982,* pp.13–29. Marietta: Georgia Association of Historians, 1983.

De Vorsey, Louis, Jr. "Indian Boundaries in Colonial Georgia." *Georgia Historical Quarterly* 54 (Spring 1970): 63–78.

———. *The Indian Boundary in the Southern Colonies, 1763–1775.* Chapel Hill: University of North Carolina Press, 1966.

Dillon, Patricia Wood. *French-Indian Relations on the Southern Frontier, 1699–1762.* Ann Arbor, Mich.: UMI Research Press, 1980.

Dobyns, Henry F. *Their Number Become Thinned: Native American Population Dynamics in Eastern North America.* Native American Historic Demography Series, Newberry Library Center for the History of the American Indians. Knoxville: University of Tennessee Press, 1983.

Doster, James F. *The Creek Indians and Their Florida Lands, 1740–1805.* 2 vols. Garland American Indian Ethnohistory Series: Southern and Southeast Indians. New York: Garland Publishing, 1974.

Downs, Dorothy. "British Influences on Creek and Seminole Men's Clothing, 1733–1858." *Florida Anthropologist* 33 (1980): 46–65.

Downs, Randolph C. "Creek-American Relations, 1790–1795." *Journal of Southern History* 8 (August 1942): 350–73.

Driver, Harold E. *Indians of North America.* 2d rev. ed. Chicago: University of Chicago Press, 1969.

Dysart, Jane. "Creek Indians and the Deerskin Trade, 1783–1803." Paper delivered at the Forty-sixth International Congress of Americanists, Amsterdam, the Netherlands, July 1988.

Edmunds, R. David. *The Shawnee Prophet.* Lincoln: University of Nebraska Press, 1983.

———. *Tecumseh and the Quest for Indian Leadership.* Library of American Biography. Boston: Little, Brown & Company, 1984.

Eggan, Frederick R. *The American Indian: Perspectives for the Study of Social Change.* Chicago: Aldine, 1966.

Ellefson, C. Ashley. "James Habersham and Georgia Loyalism, 1764–1775." *Georgia Historical Quarterly* 44 (December 1960): 359–80.

Elliott, Daniel, and Doyon, Roy. *Archaeology and Historical Geography of the Savannah River Floodplain near Augusta, Georgia.* University of Georgia Laboratory of Archaeology Series, no.22. Athens: Southeastern Wildlife Services, 1981.

Everett, Michael W., Waddell, Jack O., and Heath, Dwight B., eds. *Cross-Cultural Approaches to the Study of Alcohol: An Interdisciplinary Perspective.* Papers Presented at the Ninth International Congress of Anthropological and Ethnological Sciences. The Hague, Netherlands: Mouton, 1976.

Ewan, Joseph, ed. *William Bartram: Botanical and Zoological Drawings, 1756–1788.* Memoirs of the American Philosophical Society, vol.74. Philadelphia: American Philosophical Society, 1968.

Fabel, Robin F. A. *The Economy of British West Florida, 1763–1783.* Tuscaloosa: University of Alabama Press, 1988.

———. "St. Mark's, Apalache, and the Creeks." *Gulf Coast Historical Review* 1 (Spring 1986): 4–22.

Fabel, Robin F. A., and Rea, Robert R. "Lieutenant Thomas Campbell's Sojourn among the Creeks, November, 1764–May, 1765." *Alabama Historical Quarterly* 36 (Summer 1974): 97–111.

Fant, H. B. "The Indian Trade Policy of the Trustees for Establishing the Colony of Georgia in America." *Georgia Historical Quarterly* 15 (September 1931): 207–22.

Fisher, Doris Behrman. "Mary Musgrove: Creek Englishwoman." Ph.D. diss., Emory University, 1990.

Fleming, Berry, ed. *Autobiography of a Colony: The First Half-Century of Augusta, Georgia.* Athens: University of Georgia Press, 1957.

Flippin, Percy S. "The Royal Government in Georgia, 1752–1776." *Georgia Historical Quarterly* 10 (March 1926): 1–25.

Forbes, Jack D. "Mustees, Half-Breeds, and Zambos in Anglo North America: Aspects of Black-Indian Relations." *American Indian Quarterly* 7 (Fall 1983): 57–83.

Foreman, Carolyn Thomas. "The White Lieutenant and Some of His Contemporaries." *Chronicles of Oklahoma* 38 (Winter 1960): 425–40.

Friedlander, Amy Ellen. "Indian Slavery in Proprietary South Carolina." Master's thesis, Emory University, 1975.

Fundaburk, Emma Lila, and Foreman, Mary Douglass. *Sun Circles and Human Hands: The Southeastern Indians—Art and Industry.* Fairhope, Ala.: Southern Publications, 1957.

Gallay, Alan. *The Formation of a Planter Elite: Jonathan Bryan and the Southern Colonial Frontier.* Athens: University of Georgia Press, 1989.

Galloway, Patricia K. "Choctaw Factionalism and Civil War, 1746–1750." In *The Choctaw before Removal,* edited by Carolyn Keller Reeves, pp.120–56. Jackson: University Press of Mississippi, 1985.

"The Galphin Claim." *Appendix to the Congressional Globe for the First Session, Thirty-First Congress.* 22, pt.1: 546–56. Washington, D.C.: John C. Rivers, 1850.

Garrett, Franklin M. *Atlanta and Environs: A Chronicle of Its People and Events.* 2 vols. Facsimile reprint of the 1954 edition by Lewis Historical Publishing Co. Athens: University of Georgia Press, 1969.

Gatschet, Albert S. *A Migration Legend of the Creek Indians, with a Linguistic, Historic, and Ethnographic Introduction,* vol.1. Brinton's Library of Aboriginal American Literature, no.4. Philadelphia: N.p., 1884. Reprint. New York: AMS Press, 1969.

Gilman, Carolyn. *Where Two Worlds Meet: The Great Lakes Fur Trade*. Publications of the Minnesota Historical Society. Museum Exhibit Series, no.2. St. Paul: Minnesota Historical Society, 1982.

Goad, Sharon. "Exchange Networks in the Prehistoric Southeastern United States." Ph.D. diss., University of Georgia, 1978.

Goff, John H. "The Path to Oakfuskee: Upper Trading Route in Alabama to the Creek Indians." *Georgia Historical Quarterly* 39 (June 1955): 152–71.

———. "The Path to Oakfuskee: Upper Trading Route in Georgia to the Creek Indians." *Georgia Historical Quarterly* 39 (March 1955): 1–36.

Goggin, John M. "A Florida Indian Trading Post, ca. 1673–1784." *Southern Indian Studies* 1 (October 1949): 35–38.

Gold, Robert L. *Borderland Empires in Transition: The Triple-Nation Transfer of Florida*. Carbondale: Southern Illinois Press; Edwardsville, Ill.: Feffer & Simmons, 1969.

Green, E. E. R. "Queensborough Township: Scotch-Irish Emigration and the Expansion of Georgia, 1763–1776." *William and Mary Quarterly* 17 (April 1960): 183–99.

Green, Michael D. "Alexander McGillivray." In *American Indian Leaders: Studies in Diversity*, edited by R. David Edmunds, pp.41–63. Lincoln: University of Nebraska Press, 1980.

———. "The Creek Confederacy in the American Revolution: Cautious Participants." In *Anglo-Spanish Confrontation on the Gulf Coast during the American Revolution*, edited by William S. Coker and Robert R. Rea, pp.54–75. Pensacola: Gulf Coast History and Humanities Conference, 1982.

———. *The Politics of Indian Removal: Creek Government and Society in Crisis*. Lincoln: University of Nebraska Press, 1982.

Griffith, Lucille. "South Carolina and Fort Alabama, 1714–1763." *Alabama Review* 12 (October 1959): 258–71.

Haan, Richard L. "The 'Trade Do's Not Flourish as Formerly': The Ecological Origins of the Yamassee War of 1715." *Ethnohistory* 28 (Fall 1982): 341–58.

Haas, Mary R. "Creek Inter-town Relations." *American Anthropologist* 42 (1940): 479–89.

———. "What is Mobilian?" In *Studies in Southeastern Indian Languages*, edited by James M. Crawford, pp.257–61. Athens: University of Georgia Press, 1975.

Halbert, Henry Sale. "Creek War Incidents." *Transactions of the Alabama Historical Society, 1897–1898*, vol.2. Montgomery: Alabama Historical Society, 1898.

Halbert, Henry Sale, and Ball, T. H. *The Creek War of 1813 and 1814.* 1895. Reprint. Tuscaloosa: University of Alabama Press, 1969.

Halls, Zillah. *Men's Costume, 1750–1800.* London Museum Publication. London: Her Majesty's Stationery Office, 1973.

Hamer, Fritz. "Indian Traders, Land, and Power: A Comparative Study of George Galphin on the Southern Frontier and Three Northern Traders." Master's thesis, University of South Carolina, 1982.

Hann, John H. *Apalachee: The Land between the Rivers.* Ripley P. Bullen Monographs in Anthropology and History, no.7. Gainesville: University Presses of Florida, 1988.

Harden, William. "Basil Cowper's Remarkable Career in Georgia." *Georgia Historical Quarterly* 1 (March 1917): 24–35.

Harmon, George D. "Benjamin Hawkins and the Federal Factory System." *North Carolina Historical Review* 9 (April 1932): 138–52.

Harper, Francis. "William Bartram and the American Revolution." *American Philosophical Society Proceedings* 97 (October 1957): 571–77.

Harris, Walter A. *Here the Creeks Sat Down.* Macon, Ga.: J. W. Burke Co., 1958.

Hatley, M. Thomas. "The Dividing Paths: The Encounters of the Cherokees and the South Carolinians in the Southern Mountains, 1670–1785." Ph.D. diss., Duke University, 1989.

———. "The Eighteenth-Century Tallapoosa Landscape Re-Visited." In Gregory A. Waselkov, John W. Cottier, and Craig T. Sheldon, Jr., "Archaeological Excavations at the Early Historic Creek Indian Town of Fusihatchee (Phase 1, 1988–1989)." A report to the National Science Foundation, May 1990, Grant no. BNS-8718934.

Heldman, Donald P. "Fort Toulouse of the Alabamas and the Eighteenth-Century Indian Trade." *World Archaeology* 5 (October 1973): 163–69.

Helms, Mary W. "Native Cosmology and European Trade." Paper delivered at Forty-sixth International Congress of Americanists, Amsterdam, the Netherlands, July 1988.

———. *Ulysses' Sail: An Ethnographic Odyssey of Power, Knowledge, and Geographical Distance.* Princeton: Princeton University Press, 1988.

Henri, Florette. *The Southern Indians and Benjamin Hawkins, 1796–1816.* Norman: University of Oklahoma Press, 1986.

Herndon, G. Melvin. "Indian Agriculture in the Southern Colonies." *North Carolina Historical Review* 44 (Summer 1967): 283–97.

Hewatt, Alexander. *An Historical Account of the Rise and Progress of the Colonies of*

South Carolina and Georgia. 2 vols. 1779. Reprint. Spartanburg, s.c.: Reprint Co., 1962.

Hewitt, J. N. B. *Notes on the Creek Indians.* Edited by John R. Swanton. Bureau of American Ethnology Bulletin no.123. Washington, D.C.: Government Printing Office, 1939.

Hickerson, Harold. "Fur Trade Colonialism and the North American Indians." *Journal of Ethnic Studies* 1 (Summer 1973): 15–44.

Holland [Braund], Kathryn E. "The Anglo-Spanish Contest for the Gulf Coast as Viewed from the Townsquare." In *Anglo-Spanish Confrontation on the Gulf Coast during the American Revolution,* edited by William S. Coker and Robert R. Rea, pp.90–105. Pensacola: Gulf Coast History and Humanities Conference, 1982.

———. "The Path between the Wars: Creek Relations with the British Colonies, 1763–1774." Master's thesis, Auburn University, 1980.

Holmes, Jack D. L. "Benjamin Hawkins and United States Attempts to Teach Farming to Southeastern Indians." *Agricultural History* 60 (Spring 1986): 216–32.

———. "A Mystery Map of West Florida: A Cartographical Puzzle." In *Threads of Traditional Culture along the Gulf Coast,* edited by Ronald V. Evans, pp.216–29. Pensacola: Gulf Coast History and Humanities Conference, 1986.

Hosey, A. G., Jr. "Activity Patterns and Notes on Behavior of Male White-Tailed Deer during Rut." Master's thesis, Auburn University, 1980.

Howard, Clinton N. *The Development of British West Florida, 1763–1769.* University of California Publications in History, vol.34. Berkeley: University of California Press, 1947.

Howard, James H. *The Southeastern Ceremonial Complex and Its Interpretation.* Memoir no.6. Columbus: Missouri Archaeological Society, 1968.

Hudson, Charles M., ed. *Black Drink: A Native American Tea.* Athens: University of Georgia Press, 1979.

———. *The Southeastern Indians.* Knoxville: University of Tennessee Press, 1976.

Hurt, Douglas R. *Indian Agriculture in America: Prehistory to the Present.* Lawrence: University of Kansas Press, 1987.

Hyde, W. Lewis. *The Gift: Imagination and the Erotic Life of Property.* New York: Random House, 1983.

Ivey, Tim L., and Causey, M. Keith. "Movements and Activity Patterns of Female White-Tailed Deer during Rut." In *Proceedings of the Thirty-Fifth An-*

nual Conference of Southeastern Association of Fish and Wildlife Agencies, October 18–21, 1981, pp.149–66. N.p., n.d.

Jacobs, Wilbur R. "British Colonial Attitudes and Policies toward the Indian in the American Colonies." In *Attitudes of Colonial Powers toward the American Indian,* edited by Howard Peckham and Charles Gibson, pp.81–106. Salt Lake City: University of Utah Press, 1969.

Jones, B. Calvin. "Colonel James Moore and the Destruction of the Apalachee Missions in 1704." In *Bureau of Historic Sites and Properties Bulletin no.2,* pp.25–33. Tallahassee: Florida Department of State, 1972.

Jones, Charles C., Jr., and Dutcher, Salem. *Memorial History of Augusta, Georgia.* Syracuse, N.Y.: D. Mason & Co., 1890. Reprint. Spartanburg, S.C.: Reprint Co., 1966.

Jones, Dorothy V. *License for Empire: Colonialism by Treaty in Early America.* Chicago: University of Chicago Press, 1982.

Keel, Bennie C. "The Conservation and Preservation of Archaeological and Ethnological Specimens." *Southern Indian Studies* 15 (October 1963): 5–65.

Kennedy, Thomas C. "Sibling Stewards of a Commercial Empire: The Innerarity Brothers in the Floridas." *Florida Historical Quarterly* 67 (January 1989): 259–89.

Kinnaird, Lawrence. "The Significance of William Augustus Bowles' Seizure of Panton's Apalachee Store in 1792." *Florida Historical Quarterly* 9 (January 1931): 156–92.

Knight, Vernon James, Jr. "Social Organization and the Evolution of Hierarchy in Southeastern Chiefdoms." *Journal of Anthropological Research* 46 (Spring 1990): 1–23.

———. "Tukabatchee: Archaeological Investigations at an Historic Creek Town, Elmore County, Alabama, 1984." Report of Investigations 45, Office of Archaeological Research, Alabama State Museum of Natural History, University of Alabama, Tuscaloosa, 1985. Mimeographed report.

Knight, Vernon James, Jr., and Adams, Sherée L. "A Voyage to the Mobile and Tomeh in 1700, with Notes on the Interior of Alabama." *Ethnohistory* 28 (Spring 1981): 179–94.

Krech, Shephard, III, ed. *Indians, Animals, and the Fur Trade: A Critique of Keepers of the Game.* Athens: University of Georgia Press, 1981.

Landers, Jane. "Gracia Real de Santa Teresa de Mose: A Free Black Town in Spanish Colonial Florida." *American Historical Review* 95 (February 1990): 9–30.

Lewis, Kenneth E. "The History and Archaeology of Spalding's Store (PU-23), Putnam County, Florida." Master's thesis, University of Florida, 1969.

Littlefield, Daniel F., Jr. *Africans and Creeks: From the Colonial Period to the Civil War*. Contributions in Afro-American and African Studies, no.47. Westport, Conn.: Greenwood Press, 1979.

Logan, John H. *A History of the Upper Country of South Carolina, from the Earliest Periods to the Close of the War of Independence*, vol.1. South Carolina Heritage Series, no.5. Charleston: S. G. Courtenay & Co., 1859. Reprint. Spartanburg, S.C.: Reprint Co., 1966.

Lurie, Nancy Oestreich. "The World's Oldest On-Going Protest Demonstration: North American Indian Drinking Patterns." *Pacific Historical Review* 40 (August 1971): 311–32.

McLoughlin, William G. *The Cherokee Ghost Dance: Essays on the Southeastern Indians, 1789–1861*. Macon, Ga.: Mercer University Press, 1984.

McReynolds, Edwin C. *The Seminoles*. Civilization of the American Indian Series, no.47. Norman: University of Oklahoma Press, 1957.

Martin, Calvin. *Keepers of the Game: Indian-Animal Relationships and the Fur Trade*. Berkeley: University of California Press, 1978. Reprint, 1982.

Martin, Joel W. "Cultural Hermeneutics on the Frontier: Colonialism and the Muscogulge Millenarian Revolt of 1813." Ph.D. diss., Duke University, 1988.

———. *Sacred Revolt: The Muskogees' Struggle for a New World*. Boston: Beacon Press, 1991.

Mason, Carol R. "Eighteenth Century Culture Change among the Lower Creeks." *Florida Anthropologist* 16 (September 1963): 65–80.

Mattison, Ray H. "The Creek Trading House." *Georgia Historical Quarterly* 30 (September 1946): 169–84.

Meriwether, Robert L. *The Expansion of South Carolina, 1729–1765*. Kingsport: Southern Publishers, 1940.

Milanich, Jerald T. "The European Entrada into La Florida: An Overview." In *Archaeological and Historical Perspectives on the Spanish Borderlands East*, pp.3–29, vol.2 of *Columbian Consequences*, edited by David Hurst Thomas (Washington, D.C.: Smithsonian Institution Press, 1990).

Miller, Christopher L., and Hamell, George R. "A New Perspective on Indian-White Contact: Cultural Symbols and Colonial Trade." *Journal of American History* 73 (September 1986): 311–28.

Milner, George R. "Epidemic Disease in the Postcontact Southeast: A Reappraisal." *Mid-Continental Journal of Archaeology* 5 (1980): 39–56.

Minchinton, Walter E., comp. *The Growth of English Overseas Trade in the Seventeenth and Eighteenth Centuries*. London: Methuen, 1969.

———. "The Merchants in England in the Eighteenth Century." *Explorations in Entrepreneurial History* 10 (December 1957): 62–71.

Moore, Alexander. "Thomas Nairne's 1708 Western Expedition: An Episode in the Anglo-French Competition for Empire." In *Proceedings of the Tenth Meeting of the French Colonial Historical Society, April 12–14, 1984,* edited by Philip P. Boucher, pp.47–58. Lanham, Md.: University Press of America, 1985.

Moore, W. O., Jr. "The Largest Exporters of Deerskins from Charles Town, 1735–1775." *South Carolina Historical Magazine* 74 (July 1973): 144–50.

Mowat, Charles Loch. *East Florida as a British Province, 1763–1784.* University of California Publications in History, vol.32. Berkeley: University of California Press, 1943.

Myer, William E. "Indian Trails of the Southeast." In *Bureau of American Ethnology, Forty-Second Annual Report,* pp.727–857. Washington, D.C.: Government Printing Office, 1928.

Nash, Gary B. *Red, White, and Black: The Peoples of Early America.* Englewood Cliffs, N.J.: Prentice-Hall, 1974.

Neely, Mary Ann Oglesby. "Lachlan McGillivray: A Scot on the Alabama Frontier." *Alabama Historical Quarterly* 36 (Spring 1974): 5–14.

Norton, Thomas. *The Fur Trade in Colonial New York, 1686–1776.* Madison: University of Wisconsin Press, 1974.

O'Donnell, James H., III. "Alexander McGillivray: Training for Leadership, 1777–1783." *Georgia Historical Quarterly* 49 (June 1965): 172–86.

———. *Southern Indians in the American Revolution.* Knoxville: University of Tennessee Press, 1973.

Owsley, Frank L., Jr. "Prophet of War: Josiah Francis and the Creek War." *American Indian Quarterly* 9 (Summer 1985): 273–93.

———. *Struggle for the Gulf Borderlands: The Creek War and the Battle of New Orleans, 1812–1815.* Gainesville: University Presses of Florida, 1981.

Paredes, J. Anthony. "Kinship and Descent in the Ethnic Reassertion of the Eastern Creek Indians." In *The Versatility of Kinship: Essays Presented to Harry W. Basehart,* edited by Linda S. Cordell and Stephen Beckerman, pp.165–94. New York: Academic Press, 1980.

———. "Some Creeks Stayed: Comments on Amelia Rector Bell's 'Separate People: Speaking of Creek Men and Women.'" *American Anthropologist* 93 (September 1991): 697–99.

Paredes, J. Anthony, and Plante, Kenneth J. "Economics, Politics, and the Subjugation of the Creek Indians." Final Report for National Park Service Contract CX500041689, October 1975. Copy located at Southeast Archaeological Center, National Park Service, Tallahassee, Florida.

————. "A Reexamination of Creek Indian Population Trends, 1738–1832." *American Indian Culture and Research Journal* 6 (1983): 3–28.

Pate, James P. "The Chickamauga: A Forgotten Segment of Indian Resistance on the Southern Frontier." Ph.D. diss., Mississippi State University, 1969.

Peake, Ora Brooks. *A History of the United States Indian Factory System, 1795–1822.* Denver: Sage Books, 1954.

Perdue, Theda. "Southern Indians and the Cult of True Womanhood." In *The Web of Southern Social Relations: Women, Family, and Education,* edited by Walter J. Fraser, Jr., Frank Saunders, Jr., and Jon L. Wakelyn, pp.35–51. Athens: University of Georgia Press, 1985.

Phillips, Paul C. *The Fur Trade.* 2 vols. Norman: University of Oklahoma Press, 1961.

Pickett, Albert James. *History of Alabama and Incidentally of Georgia and Mississippi, from the Earliest Period.* Charleston: Walker and James, 1851. Reprint. Birmingham: Birmingham Book and Magazine Co., 1962.

Plummer, Alfred, and Early, Richard E. *The Blanket Makers, 1669–1969: A History of Charles Early and Marriott (Witney) Ltd.* London: Routledge & Kegan Paul, 1969.

Prucha, Francis Paul. *American Indian Policy in the Formative Years: The Indian Trade and Intercourse Acts, 1790–1834.* Cambridge: Harvard University Press, 1962.

Ray, Arthur J. "Indians as Consumers in the Eighteenth Century." In *Old Trails and New Directions: Papers of the Third North American Fur Trade Conference,* edited by Carol M. Judd and Arthur J. Ray, pp.255–71. Toronto: University of Toronto Press, 1980.

Rea, Robert R. "British West Florida Trade and Commerce in the Customs Records." *Alabama Review* 37 (April 1984): 124–59.

Reese, Trevor R. *Colonial Georgia: A Study in British Imperial Policy in the Eighteenth Century.* Athens: University of Georgia Press, 1963.

Reid, John Phillips. *A Better Kind of Hatchet: Law, Trade, and Diplomacy in the Cherokee Nation during the Early Years of European Contact.* University Park: Pennsylvania State University Press, 1976.

Remini, Robert V. *Andrew Jackson and the Course of American Empire, 1767–1821.* New York: Harper & Row, 1977.

Royce, Charles C., comp. "Indian Land Cessions in the United States." In *Eighteenth Annual Report of Bureau of American Ethnology,* part 2, pp.521–997. Washington, D.C.: Government Printing Office, 1899.

Schumpeter, Elizabeth B. *English Overseas Trade Statistics, 1697–1808*. Oxford: Oxford University Press, 1960.

Scurry, James D.; Joseph, J. Walter; and Hamer, Fritz. *Initial Archeological Investigations at Silver Bluff Plantation, Aiken County, South Carolina*. Research Manuscript Series 168. Institute of Archeology and Anthropology. Columbia: University of South Carolina, 1980.

Searcy, Martha Condray. *The Georgia-Florida Contest in the American Revolution, 1776–1778*. Tuscaloosa: University of Alabama Press, 1985.

———. "The Introduction of African Slavery into the Creek Indian Nation." *Georgia Historical Quarterly* 66 (1982): 21–33.

Sellers, Leila. *Charleston Business on the Eve of the American Revolution, 1776–1778*. Chapel Hill: University of North Carolina Press, 1934.

Sheehan, Bernard W. *Seeds of Extinction: Jeffersonian Philanthropy and the American Indian*. Chapel Hill: University of North Carolina Press, 1973.

Sheftall, John McKay. "George Galphin and Indian-White Relations in the Georgia Backcountry during the American Revolution." Master's thesis, University of Virginia, 1983.

Silver, Timothy. *A New Face on the Countryside: Indians, Colonists, and Slaves in South Atlantic Forests, 1500–1800*. Studies in Environment and History. Cambridge: Cambridge University Press, 1990.

Sirmans, Marion Eugene. *Colonial South Carolina: A Political History*. Chapel Hill: University of North Carolina Press, 1966.

Smith, Daniel M. "James Seagrove and the Mission to Tuckaubatchee, 1793." *Georgia Historical Quarterly* 44 (March 1960): 41–55.

Smith, Louis R., Jr. "British-Indian Trade in Alabama, 1670–1756." *Alabama Review* 27 (January 1974): 65–75.

Smith, Marvin T. *Archaeology and Aboriginal Culture Change in the Interior Southeast: Depopulation during the Early Historic Period*. Ripley P. Bullen Monographs in Anthropology and History, no.6. Gainesville: University Presses of Florida/Florida State Museum, 1987.

Smithcors, J. F. *Evolution of the Veterinary Art: A Narrative Account to 1850*. Kansas City, Mo.: Veterinary Medicine Publishing, 1957.

Snapp, James Russell. "Exploitation and Control: The Southern Frontier in Anglo-American Politics in the Era of the American Revolution." Ph.D. diss., Harvard University, 1988.

Snell, William R. *Indian Slavery in Colonial South Carolina, 1671–1795*. Ann Arbor: University Microfilms, 1973.

Sosin, Jack. *Whitehall and the Wilderness: The Middle West in British Colonial Policy, 1760–1775*. Lincoln: University of Nebraska Press, 1961.

Southerland, Henry DeLeon, Jr., and Brown, Jerry Elijah. *The Federal Road through Georgia, the Creek Nation, and Alabama, 1806–1846.* Tuscaloosa: University of Alabama Press, 1989.

Spalding, Phinizy. *Georgia and South Carolina during the Oglethorpe Period, 1732–1743.* Ann Arbor, Mich.: University Microfilms International, 1976.

———. *Oglethorpe in America.* Chicago: University of Chicago Press, 1977. Reprint. Athens: University of Georgia Press, 1984.

"Special George Galphin Issue." *Richmond County History* 13, nos. 1 & 2 (1981).

Speck, Frank G. *Ceremonial Songs of the Creek and Yuchi Indians.* Music transcribed by Jacob D. Sapir. University of Pennsylvania Museum Anthropological Publications, vol. 1, no. 2. Philadelphia: University Museum, 1911.

Spencer, Robert F., et al. *The Native Americans: Ethnology and Backgrounds of the North American Indians.* 2d ed. New York: Harper & Row, 1977.

Spoehr, Alexander. "Changing Kinship Systems: A Study in the Acculturation of the Creeks, Cherokee, and Choctaw." *Publications of the Field Museum of Natural History, Anthropological Series* 33, no. 4 (January 1947): 153–235.

Sturtevant, William C. "Commentary." In *Eighteenth-Century Florida and Its Borderlands,* edited by Samuel Proctor, pp. 40–47. Gainesville: University Presses of Florida, 1975.

———. "Creek into Seminole." In *North American Indians in Historical Perspective,* edited by Eleanor Leacock and Nancy Oestreich Lurie, pp. 91–128. New York: Random House, 1971.

———. "The Medicine Bundles and Busks of the Florida Seminole." *Florida Anthropologist* 7 (May 1954): 30–71.

Surrey, Nancy Marie. *The Commerce of Louisiana during the French Regime, 1699–1763.* Studies in History, Economics, and Public Law, no. 167. New York: Columbia University Press, 1916.

Swanton, John R. *Early History of the Creek Indians and Their Neighbors.* Bureau of American Ethnology Bulletin no. 73. Washington, D.C.: Government Printing Office, 1922. Reprint. New York: Johnson Reprint Co., 1970.

———. *The Indians of the Southeastern United States.* Bureau of American Ethnology Bulletin no. 137. Washington, D.C.: Government Printing Office, 1946. Reprint. New York: Greenwood Press, 1969.

———. "Religious Beliefs and Medical Practices of the Creek Indians." In *Forty-Second Annual Report of the Bureau of American Ethnology,* pp. 473–672. Washington, D.C.: Government Printing Office, 1928.

———. *Social Organization and Social Usages of the Indians of the Creek Confederacy.* Bureau of American Ethnology Bulletin no. 42. Washington, D.C.:

Government Printing Office, 1928. Reprint. New York: Johnson Reprint Co., 1970.

Tanner, Helen Hornbeck. "Pipesmoke and Muskets: Florida Indian Intrigues of the Revolutionary Era." In *Eighteenth-Century Florida and Its Borderlands,* edited by Samuel Proctor, pp.13–39. Gainesville: University Presses of Florida, 1975.

TePaske, John J. "French, Spanish, and English Indian Policy on the Gulf Coast, 1513–1763: A Comparison." In *Spain and Her Rivals on the Gulf Coast: Proceedings of the Gulf Coast History and Humanities Conference,* edited by Ernest F. Dibble and Earle W. Newton, pp.9–39. Pensacola: Pensacola Preservation Board, 1971.

Thomas, Daniel H. *Fort Toulouse: The French Outpost at the Alabamas on the Coosa.* Tuscaloosa: University of Alabama Press, 1989.

Thomas, David Hurst. *Archaeological and Historical Perspectives on the Spanish Borderlands East.* Vol.2 of *Columbian Consequences.* 3 vols. Washington, D.C.: Smithsonian Institution Press, 1990.

Thompson, M. T. "Historic Role of the Rivers of Georgia: The Charles Town Traders." *Georgia Mineral Newsletter* 3, no.5 (September–October 1950): 167–79.

Trigger, Bruce G. "Early Native American Responses to European Contact: Romantic versus Rationalistic Interpretations." *Journal of American History* 77 (March 1991): 1195–1215.

Usner, Daniel H., Jr. "The Deerskin Trade in French Louisiana." In *Proceedings of the Tenth Meeting of the French Colonial Historical Society, April 12–14, 1984,* edited by Philip Boucher, pp.75–93. Lanham, Md.: University Press of America, 1985.

———. "The Frontier Exchange Economy of the Lower Mississippi Valley in the Eighteenth Century." *William and Mary Quarterly* 44 (April 1987): 165–92.

———. *Indians, Settlers, and Slaves in a Frontier Exchange Economy.* Chapel Hill: University of North Carolina Press, for the Institute of Early American History and Culture, Williamsburg, 1992.

Walthall, John A. *Galena and Aboriginal Trade in Eastern North America.* Illinois State Museum Scientific Papers, no.17. Springfield: Illinois State Museum, 1981.

Waselkov, Gregory A. "Economics of a French Colonial Trade Enclave: Historical and Archaeological Perspectives." In *Culture Change on the Creek Indian Frontier.* Final Report to the National Science Foundation, Grant

#BNS-8305437, Washington, D.C. (Auburn, Ala.: Auburn University Department of Sociology and Anthropology, 1985).

———. "Evolution of Deer Hunting in the Eastern Woodlands." *Mid-Continental Journal of Archaeology* 3 (1978): 15–34.

———. "French Colonial Trade in the Upper Creek Country." In *Fleur-de-Lys and Calumet: French-Indian Interaction in the Midcontinent,* edited by Thomas Emerson and John Walthall. Smithsonian Institution Press, forthcoming.

———. "Seventeenth-Century Trade in the Colonial Southeast." *Southeastern Archaeology* 8 (1989): 117–33.

———, ed. *Fort Toulouse Studies.* Auburn University Archaeological Monograph, no.9. Auburn, Ala.: Auburn University Department of Sociology and Anthropology, 1984.

Waselkov, Gregory A., and Cottier, John W. "European Perceptions of Eastern Muskogean Ethnicity." In *Proceedings of the Tenth Meeting of the French Colonial Historical Society, April 12–14, 1984,* edited by Philip Boucher, pp.23–45. Lanham, Md.: University Press of America, 1985.

Waterer, John W. *Leather in Life, Art, and Industry.* London: Faber & Faber, 1946.

Watson, Thomas D. "Continuity in Commerce: Development of the Panton, Leslie and Company Trade Monopoly in West Florida." *Florida Historical Quarterly* 54 (April 1976): 548–64.

Way, Royal B. "The United States Factory System for Trading with the Indians, 1796–1822." *Mississippi Valley Historical Review* 6 (September 1919): 220–35.

Weibel-Orlando, Joan. "Indians, Ethnicity, and Alcohol: Contrasting Perceptions of the Ethnic Self and Alcohol Use." In *The American Experience with Alcohol: Contrasting Cultural Perspectives,* edited by Linda A. Bennett and Genevieve M. Ames, pp.201–26. New York: Plenum Press, 1985.

Weisman, Brent Richards. *Like Beads on a String: A Culture History of the Seminole Indians in Northern Peninsular Florida.* Tuscaloosa: University of Alabama Press, 1989.

Weiss, John. *The Whitetail Deer Hunter's Handbook.* New York: Winchester Press, 1979.

White, Richard. *The Roots of Dependency: Subsistence, Environment, and Social Change among the Choctaws, Pawnees, and Navajos.* Lincoln: University of Nebraska Press, 1983.

White-Tailed Deer in the Southern Forest Habitat: Proceedings of a Symposium at Nacogdoches, Texas, March 25–26, 1969. Southern Forest Experiment Station, U.S. Forest Service, USDA, in cooperation with the Forest Game Committee of the Southeastern Section of the Wildlife Society and the School of Forestry, Stephen F. Austin University, Nacogdoches, Texas, 1969.

Willis, William S., Jr. "Patrilineal Institutions in Southeastern North America." *Ethnohistory* 10 (Winter 1963): 250–69.

Woods, Patricia Dillon. *French-Indian Relations on the Southern Frontier, 1699–1762.* Ann Arbor, Mich.: UMI Research Press, 1980.

Wood, Peter H. "The Changing Population of the Colonial South: An Overview by Race and Region, 1685–1790." In *Powhatan's Mantle: Indians in the Colonial Southeast,* edited by Peter H. Wood, Gregory A. Waselkov, and M. Thomas Hatley, pp.35–103. Lincoln: University of Nebraska Press, 1989.

Wright, Homer E. *Diplomacy of Trade on the Southern Frontier: A Case Study of the Influence of William Panton and John Forbes, 1784–1817.* Ann Arbor, Mich.: University Microfilms, 1972.

Wright, J. Leitch, Jr. *Anglo-Spanish Rivalry in North America.* Athens: University of Georgia Press, 1971.

———. *Britain and the American Frontier, 1783–1815.* Athens: University of Georgia Press, 1975.

———. "Creek-American Treaty of 1790: Alexander McGillivray and the Diplomacy of the Old Southwest." *Georgia Historical Quarterly* 51 (December 1967): 379–400.

———. *Creeks and Seminoles: The Destruction and Regeneration of the Muscogulge People.* Lincoln: University of Nebraska Press, 1986.

———. *Florida in the American Revolution.* Gainesville: University Presses of Florida, 1975.

———. *The Only Land They Knew: The Tragic Story of the American Indians in the Old South.* New York: Free Press, 1981.

———. "The Queen's Redoubt Explosion in the Lives of William A. Bowles, John Miller, and William Panton." In *Anglo-Spanish Confrontation on the Gulf Coast during the American Revolution,* edited by William S. Coker and Robert R. Rea, pp.177–93. Pensacola: Gulf Coast History and Humanities Conference, 1982.

———. *William Augustus Bowles: Director General of the Creek Nation.* Athens: University of Georgia Press, 1967.

Index

leather sellers, 53
Lewis, Francis, 106
Limbourg, 123
Little Tallassee, 141
Logan, Guerin, and Vanderhorst, 54
London, England, 87, 96
Lower Creek Towns, 6, 140–41

Macartan, Francis, 49
Macartan and Campbell Company, 49
McGillivray, Alexander, 21, 168,
  170–71, 173
McGillivray, Archibald, 43
McGillivray, John, 55, 56–57
McGillivray, Lachlan, 45–46, 51, 52,
  55, 169
McIntosh, James, 57
McKay, Donald, 56
Mackintosh, Alexander, 49
McLatchy, Charles, 56, 137
McQueen, James, 183
McQueen, Peter, 183–84, 186
Mad Turkey, 162
Malatchi of Coweta, 21, 129, 203
  n.80
Manchac, 57
manufactures, imported: 121–25;
  impact on Creek society, 130
manufactures, native: as trade goods,
  74; impact of trade on, 130–32
Matthews, Jacob, 43
merchants, 47, 82, 96, 114
Metawney, 46
mico (Creek headman): role of, 19–
  20; relations with deerskin traders,
  83–84; role in foreign relations,
  141; selection of, 11–12, 20
Miller, Bonnany, and Company, 175
Miller, John, 42, 57
mixed-blood Creeks: adoption of
  white culture by, 184; as leaders,

170–71; as traders, 78–79, 147,
  182; economic impact of, on Creek
  society, 184–85
Mobile, 57–58
Mobilian language, 27
Molton, John, 108
Moore, James, 32
Mortar of Ockai, 71, 135, 142, 149–
  50, 161, 170
Moultrie, John, 73
Muscogulges. See Creek Indians
Musgrove, Johnny, 35, 41
Musgrove, Mary, 35, 41

Netherclift, Thomas, 54
New Purchase, 54, 150–51, 159

O'Brien, Kennedy, 42
Oconee Indians, 135
Oglethorpe, James, 41, 109
Ogulki of Coweta, 159, 162
Okchai, 141
Okfuskee, 18
ornaments: obtained through trade,
  122–23, 124, 125; traditional,
  124
Osceola, 184
Osnaburg (ozenbrig), 123
Otassee, 181

packhorsemen, 82, 95–96, 103; regulations regarding, 189–92
packhorses. See horses
Panton, Leslie, and Company, 56, 72,
  98, 173, 177–78, 179–80
Panton, William, 169
Patrick Brown and Company, 44
Pensacola, 57, 166, 168, 173
Pettigrew, John, 45
"physic-nut," 63
plains, 123

Printed in the United States
33607LVS00005B/154-186